TRAGEDY OF THE SALMON

HILLFIELD BOOKS BY DAVID SHAW

In Search of Salmon

More Searching for Salmon

TRAGEDY OF THE SALMON: THE SCOTTISH FISHERY AND THE 1986 SALMON ACT

DAVID SHAW

THE HILLFIELD PRESS
1995

Published by The Hillfield Press
P.O. Box 3
East Grinstead
West Sussex RH19 4YN

Front cover illustration by Colin Gibson

ISBN 1-870388-02-X

British Library Cataloguing-in-Publication Data.
A catalogue record for this book
is available from the British Library

Typeset in New Century 11/13pt by Scriptmate Editions
Manufacture coordinated in UK by Booksprint
20 Shepherds Hill, London N6 5AH

Printed in Great Britain by The Cromwell Press
Broughton Gifford, Wiltshire

For my wife Pat—known otherwise
as the redoubtable Kate—whose
contribution has been great and
forbearance remarkable

"If the history of England be ever written by one who has the knowledge and courage—and both qualities are equally requisite for the undertaking—the world would be astonished... Generally speaking, all the great events have been distorted, most of the important causes concealed, some of the principal characters never appear, and all who figure are so mis-understood and mis-represented, that the result is a complete mystification!"

Benjamin Disraeli, *Sybil*, 1845

FOREWORD
By Anthony Netboy*

David Shaw is one of the best informed students of the wild salmon in the United Kingdom. As a journalist, he has kept the nation well-informed on the status and plight of *Salmo salar*. He has now put his knowledge to good use in a carefully researched and revealing book.

The plight of *Salmo salar* in the British Isles has been the same as in other European countries. We don't know how many rivers in the United Kingdom in earlier times were accustomed to accommodate the hordes of salmon returning every year from the sea to spawn. We do know, however, that in the past century or two many rivers were deserted, or their stocks reduced to only token populations. By the 1980s no more than two score salmon streams in England and Wales were still productive. Scotland, whose salmon rivers were not as badly maltreated, was among the few countries in Europe that still had considerable stocks. The great majority of these rivers were owned by landlords who fished them almost without restraint.

In 1861, Charles Dickens, in his sprightly weekly, *All The Year Round,* alarmed the nation with the cry "Salmon in danger". It resounded across the land. Parliament responded to this alarm and in the next four years passed Acts which, though weak, helped somewhat to arrest the decline of salmon fisheries in England and Wales, and to a lesser extent in Scotland. Salmon became an expensive food and a highly desirable game-fish.

Between 1865 and 1985 little was done to alter the Salmon Acts to meet growing conservation needs. There was almost uncontrolled exploitation by the netting interests. I once asked the late W.J.M. Menzies, a leading authority on the Scottish salmon, if the proprietors and the shareholders of the netting companies made any contribution to conservation. He replied: "Not a damn thing"!

In the century before the 1986 Act appeared, several thorough studies and recommendations for saving the salmon in the United

* A leading authority on the salmon, Anthony Netboy is the author of *The Atlantic Salmon: A Vanishing Species?* (London: Faber, 1968); *The Salmon: Their Fight for Survival* (Boston: Houghton Mifflin, 1974); *Salmon: The World's Most Harassed Fish* (London: Andre Deutsch, 1980); *The Columbia River Salmon: Their Fight for Survival* (Seattle: University of Washington Press, 1980); and *Salmon of the Pacific North-West: Fish vs. Dams* (Portland: Binfords & Mort, 1958), amongst other publications.

Kingdom were produced. These included the monumental *Elgin Report* of 1902, the *Hunter Report* (1963 and 1965), the writings and recommendations of many leading authorities from Frank Buckland and Archibald Young in the 1870s to W.L. Calderwood and Menzies in the 1930s. Only minor pieces of legislation however were passed. More efficient methods of garnering the fish in the sea were developed, such as drift-netting, better bag nets and haaf-nets, and others. In estuaries and rivers netsmen reaped the benefits of light-weight nylon nets, power winches, motorised boats and night lights. The nets worked night and day except for the 36 hours—42 from 1951—weekly close-time. The net-fishing season usually began in February and lasted till the end of August. Nets often took up to 97 per cent of the peak-period (net and rod) total catch.

Over the years, the sport of angling for salmon greatly increased, as did the value of the dependent Scottish rod-tourism economy. By 1983 it was estimated to be worth over £140m annually and possessed enormous growth potential mainly in rural areas of low employment. It dwarfed the contribution by nets.

1986 was a kind of watershed year for *Salmo salar* in the United Kingdom. Some of the supporters of the 1986 Salmon Bill, including the barons and netting companies that controlled the industry, were determined not to give up any privileges. Anglers, conservationists and tourism interests strove to halt the decline and to break the legal stranglehold exercised by the nets over the salmon resource.

David Shaw sat through the debates on the Salmon Bill, first in the House of Lords, and later in the House of Commons. With a keen eye he recreates for us the daily drama as Members of the various Committees, selected according to the proportion of their party—Conservative, Labour and Liberal—in both Houses, debated with much wit and frequent sarcasm, hardly ever persuading the Tory ministers and lordly proprietors to yield to demands for modern conservation and economic reforms.

This book masterfully reveals the thrust and tactics of what the author calls "salmon politics". Among the actors in the drama were Lord Thurso, Lord Ross, Lord Moran, the Earl of Onslow, Lord Denning, Lord Trenchard, the Marquess of Lansdowne, the Earl of Home, Lady Saltoun, Lord Burton, Lord Gray, and many others in the Lords, and commoners in the lower House. Many of their remarks are indeed remarkable, like Lord Onslow's: "The idea seems to me extraordinarily dangerous, that this House from its position of privilege and from its wide experience of owning and fishing salmon rivers, should pass a law which will look like very heavy sectional class interest, and that is something we should not in any circumstance tolerate". This is exactly what happened. The 1986 Salmon Act came out looking like it was tailored to class interest, and ignored almost completely the public interest.

When the debates ended and the fury died, the salmon Lords went home, well satisfied, while reforming Peers and MPs who did their best, hardly gained anything for salmon conservation. The Salmon Conservancy summed it all up: "The [Salmon] Bill was seen as the greatest opportunity for many years to ensure that effective conservation measures are embodied in legislation, that control is not left in the hands of the commercial netting interests, and for the United Kingdom to develop a coherent National Salmon Policy. ...Unfortunately the Bill fails to address these issues".

Eight years have passed since the Bill was enacted. Sir David Nickson, Chairman of the Atlantic Salmon Trust, told the International Salmon Symposium at St. Andrews, New Brunswick (Canada), in June 1992, that the wild Atlantic salmon are in serious trouble. The combined world catch has declined by 60 per cent in the last 20 years. In Scotland, catches have fallen by nearly 80 per cent in the same period, "and the decline is most marked since 1986". Commenting on the Scottish situation, Lord Marnoch, Chairman of the Salmon and Trout Association's Scottish Council, said, "It is a scandal that interceptory netting by drift and fixed nets should be allowed to continue around our coasts when catches are falling at such a rate. Reports of catches in 1992 are no better and I am very gloomy about the future". David Shaw's book helps us to understand the reasons for decline, and suggests how seemingly imminent collapse may yet be averted.

This book fills a yawning gap in the field of informed writing on the plight of the Scottish and United Kingdom salmon. It is important and timely, with a compelling message which not only salmon interests and environmentalists will find valuable. Students of the history, politics and economics of resource management, of pressure groups and vested interests, of the role and operation of parliament and Government in relation to conservation of a valuable and threatened resource; all will find here rich and deep veins of fact, theory and hypothesis to be mined to advantage. If awareness is the precursor of change, David Shaw's book must finally bring reform close.

Anthony Netboy died, 17 March 1993, at Portland, Oregon, USA.

PREFACE

I had been a salmon fisher a long time before it occured to me it might be useful to discover why great *Salmo salar* is, and over the past quarter century or so has been, in increasing trouble here in its native United Kingdom and particularly Scottish home waters.

It turned out to be a lengthy journey of discovery. What follows is the fruit of my quest.

I might add it is not a quest that has made me popular in any salmon fishery quarter. But perhaps the fact that my writings are regarded with equal reserve by many leading rod as well as commercial (net) fishery elements is the best recommendation that these offerings can have.

The long and short of it is that there was an important, revealing and quite astonishing story to be told. Quickly, however, it became apparent there were many influential persons and powerful vested interests who were determined I should not tell it. Certainly this truculent resistance added a little spice to the challenge.

The 1986 Salmon Bill, the background preceding it, the proceedings of the Bill itself and what has followed from it, provide the chronological and thematic frame within which the book has been written.

My hope is that it will provide a useful "text" and reference work for the informed; that it may serve as informative and revealing to those closely and practically, perhaps academically, concerned with the central issues of resource management, conservation, environmental politics and economics; and finally for the general reader, that he or she may gain an expanded awareness of the gravity of the situation that *Salmo* faces, together with an appreciation of the avenues of escape still available.

While I am tempted to write something of the often dramatic events and circumstances which marked my experiences in gathering the great variety of information from which this book has been written, extraordinary experiences in themselves—influential persons and interests do not always appreciate questions asked of them!—I shall resist. The book is about *Salmo,* what has happened, and is happening to *him*, not me.

Without assistance from a very large number of persons

throughout the world community of the Atlantic salmon, this book could never have been written, let alone published. To all of these, and they will know who they are, I say thank you. I would express particular thanks to Lord Hunter and his justly famed (Scottish Office Departmental Committee) *Hunter Report* (1963 and 1965). The *Hunter Report* sought to penetrate to the roots of the modern salmon fishery malaise, and for its efforts received—and in some quarters still receives—a response marked by a contempt and hostility with which I am not entirely unfamiliar.

Mainly, however, my gratitude is extended not to the living, but to certain persons no longer with us—some long dead, some more recently. These include W.L. Calderwood, probably Scotland's greatest servant of the salmon; the 9th Earl of Elgin; the writer and salmon fisher, Augustus Grimble; Walter Archer and Archibald Young, eminent late-19th century Inspectors of Scottish Salmon Fisheries; Frank Buckland, an Inspector of English/Welsh Salmon Fisheries of the same era; and more recently Jock Menzies; and more recently still, "Blair of Kincardine" (aka Bill Blair, of Kincardine O'Neil, Deeside), Lord (Willie) Ross of Marnock, Esmond Drury, Adam McMurray of Dumfries and the Nith, and Anthony Netboy. It was not just the information these persons conveyed to me, nor the intellectual stimulation they provided through their works or living contact; it was their spirit. Each possessed an enlightened awareness of, and firm grip on salmon realities. All were determined and committed "improvers". It is my hope that this book may provide some salve for their restive spirits; that they may be reassured that their message is not forgotten.

I would remind the reader that this book (with the exception of the final chapter) is concerned with events leading up to and including the year 1986. Consequently all names, titles, designations of persons, places and agencies; all descriptions of events and activities whether in the text or in relation to illustrations (maps, photographs, figures) are those which were applicable in 1986, unless otherwise specified.

Finally, for providing information used in constructing maps produced for this book, I should like to acknowledge the contributions of: ICES (International Council for Exploration of the Sea), NASCO (North Atlantic Salmon Conservation Organisation), NASF (North Atlantic Salmon Fund), RASA (Restoration of Atlantic Salmon In America), MAFF (Ministry of Agriculture, Fisheries and Food), DAFS (Department of Agriculture and Fisheries for Scotland), Northumbrian Water Authority/NRA (Water Authority/National Rivers Authority) and Anthony Netboy.

DS

CONTENTS

LIST OF ILLUSTRATIONS

MAPS

DIAGRAM

FIGURES

TABLES

PHOTOGRAPHS

LIST OF ABBREVIATIONS
Used in this book

ACT	Annual Close Time
AGAINST	Action Group Against Interceptory Netting for Salmon and Sea-Trout
ASA	Atlantic Salmon Association
ASDFB	Association of Scottish District (Salmon) Fishery Boards
ASF	Atlantic Salmon Federation
AST	Atlantic Salmon Trust
BFSS	British Field Sports Society
CEC	Crown Estate Commissioners
EC	European Community
FMC	Fishmongers' Company
MFC	Migratory Fish Committee
NASCO	North Atlantic Salmon Conservation Organisation
NFU	National Farmers' Union
NSP	National Salmon Policy
RASA	Restoration of Atlantic Salmon in America
SLF	Scottish Landowners' Federation
S&TA	Salmon and Trout Association
S&TA (FM Hall)	S&TA (Fishmongers' Hall) Central Office
S&TA (Scot)	S&TA (Scotland)
UDN	Ulcerative Dermal Necrosis
WSTAA	Welsh Salmon and Trout Angling Association

Introduction

OF MAN AND SALMON

> "The salmon is in trouble. Man, as usual, is the culprit. Until we started to take serious interest in 'exploiting' his ancestral kin some 200 years ago, the salmon, from all recorded reports, was doing very nicely. Now look what we've done! Nor with all our modern cleverness have our 'salmon scientists' done more than compound the problem. If *salmo* is to escape his seeming demise, it is commonsense and determined effort by informed laymen that will save him".
>
> *'Blair of Kincardine'* [1]

In keeping with our increasingly materialistic and commercial age, concern for the much-threatened and immensely valuable Scottish wild Atlantic salmon has little to do with species conservation. Principally it has to do with "exploitation potential", "maximum harvest" and "optimum benefit"; or put in plain language, unabated greed and unbridled acquisitiveness.

This magnificent and mysterious fish is hunted relentlessly by exploiting interests from its feeding grounds in far Arctic seas to the rippling pools of its home rivers. Arctic and sub-Arctic netsmen operating in the salmon's feeding grounds, open-seas long-liners, coastal drift netsmen in North-east England and off Irish shores, coastal and estuary netsmen within UK domestic waters, illegal sea-fishers and poachers, anglers fishing UK rivers; all, with the assistance of lethal modern fishing gear and methods, exert immense pressure on remnant populations.

Now it is clear that two principal requirements are essential if in the 21st century the salmon is not to become merely a memory of a once-proud heritage and source of wealth, of wondrous sport and food. First, a profound *change in attitude* is vital. Indeed, already there is growing public awareness that the salmon, like all other creatures on this overcrowded planet, has a right to survival. Second, moving from principle to practice, *more salmon must be allowed to ascend their home rivers.* In most instances this means merely that some restraints must be placed on netsmen and anglers. Time and again, given even small opportunity to restore and gradually to enhance native stocks, the salmon has proven its ability to rally, to grow

WINDOW ON THE SALMON FISHER'S WORLD ...
Blair's "works" at Kincardine O'Neil, Deeside.

in strength of numbers and seasonal races; to confirm once again that many millions of years of evolution and adaptation generate a force and instinct for survival which is a lesson to us all.

To achieve these twin objectives cannot, however, be easy. Such paramount attainments involve use of those most rare of human capacities: common sense, and consideration which may extend to embrace other interests and beings beyond the immediate centre of self.

The North American Initiative

In the Atlantic salmon world, a start at least has been made. Indeed from North America a fresh "clearing wind" is blowing. But the tragic and terrible historical experience which is perhaps principally responsible for generating this wind should not be forgotten. In the name of liberty and economic development the immense and rich natural resources of North America have in the past 150 years been systematically savaged; and still man's devastating assault on this vast and once bounteous environment continues. The wild Atlantic salmon was one of the first victims.

My early years were spent close to the upper reaches of the Credit River, 50 miles north of Lake Ontario. It was then, and may well remain, a fine trout river. Its waters were so clear and pure that "Canada Dry" once abstracted these for its Ginger Ale. Imagine my surprise on learning not so many years ago that in the early 1800s the Credit was a great Upper Canada salmon river! It was Anthony Netboy's book, *The Atlantic Salmon: A Vanishing Species?,* which brought this to my attention. And what had happened to what Wilfred Carter termed these "hordes of sleek salmon" which filled such rivers?[2] They had been subjected to "murder on the fishing grounds".[3] The last recorded indigenous Lake Ontario salmon was a 7-pounder netted near Scarborough beach, Toronto, in 1896. Similar terminal blows had been earlier dealt to salmon stocks of the myriad rivers and feeder streams entering Lake Ontario on both the American and Canadian sides along the full extent of the lake's 500-mile shore-line perimeter.[4]

These are facts to be borne in mind when considering the current most promising growth of conservation awareness amongst North American salmon interests. Having squandered much of their rich Atlantic salmon heritage over a century ago, and now with remnant stocks in no-longer-remote East coast fisheries under serious threat, they have at last decided to take those steps which may serve to maintain and hopefully enhance remnant stocks, and hence make amends for past comprehensive abuse. The path is not easy.

Hence in American and Canadian Atlantic salmon fisheries strong controls are being placed on exploitation. Net and rod licensing have long been in operation. More recently quotas have been placed on both nets and rods. In many Canadian East coast fisheries anglers must return all adult salmon to the river; a limited number of grilse only may be kept. Catch-and-Release schemes are widely operative. Tagging of salmon retained by fishermen has ensured much-improved catch controls and equally vital catch statistics. Such controls on exploitation, backed by strong legal sanctions and tough penalties for offenders, have, along with the availability of more reliable salmon data, enabled rational fishery management geared to modern requirements to become a reality in many fishery areas.

This rising westerly "wind of change" and conservation promise has also infused international salmon fishery forums. Salmon harvesting and producing nations over the past 20 years have begun to recognise that all depends on the presence of a shared stock. As a result, NASCO (North Atlantic Salmon Conservation Organisation) was brought into existence in the early 1980s. NASCO offers the promise of an effective body with powers adequate to safeguard salmon stocks in their Arctic feeding grounds, on migration routes and in the open seas. Indeed the "1986 multi-national agreement" on

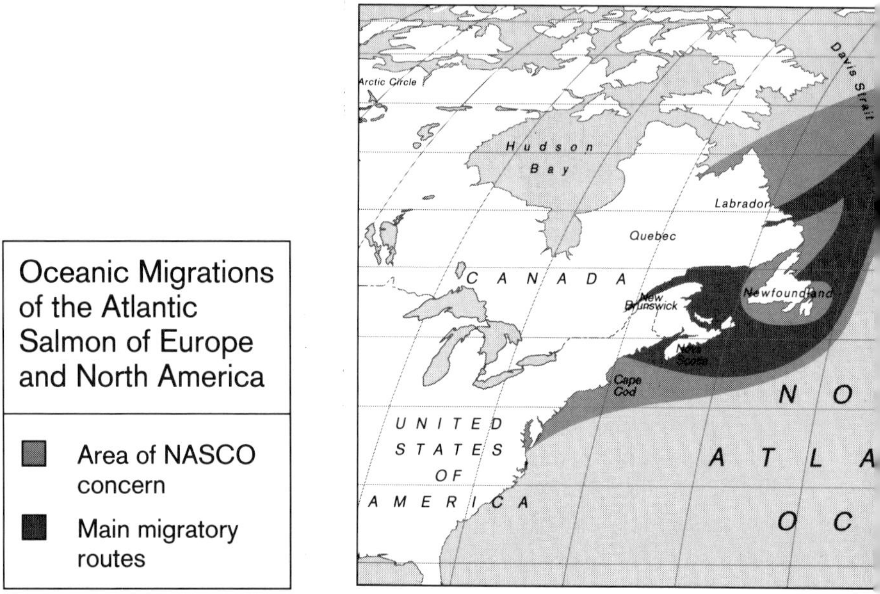

basic domestic conservation imperatives provided the break-through to those principles—restraint, equity and rational management—upon which an integrated and ordered international salmon fishery could be constructed.[5]

In domestic fishery contexts outside North America international pressure and persuasion by the mid-1980s had produced positive results. Speaking at the 1986 Biarritz International Salmon Symposium, Richard Buck, Chairman of Restoration of Atlantic Salmon in America (RASA) noted that since the NASCO treaty had come into effect in 1983 there had been several encouraging developments.

> "Denmark has accepted two reductions in the Greenland fishery quota. The Faroes Islands has come to two separate cut-back agreements within the EEC. Iceland continues its exemplary example: neither drift-netting nor in-river netting, with the exception of several small traditional stations, is permitted. In Norway the government has announced that as of January 1989, drift-netting for salmon will no longer be permitted; as of January 1988 inshore netting seasons are to be reduced. In France, a number of conservation and restoration projects were underway, [and tagging of all salmon caught is now to be implemented nationally]. Spain has dedicated its salmon fishery entirely to angling. Russia, a new NASCO signatory, has never permitted fishing for salmon in the ocean [net fishing being restricted to estuaries only] and permits the taking of salmon in rivers only by rod and line".[6]

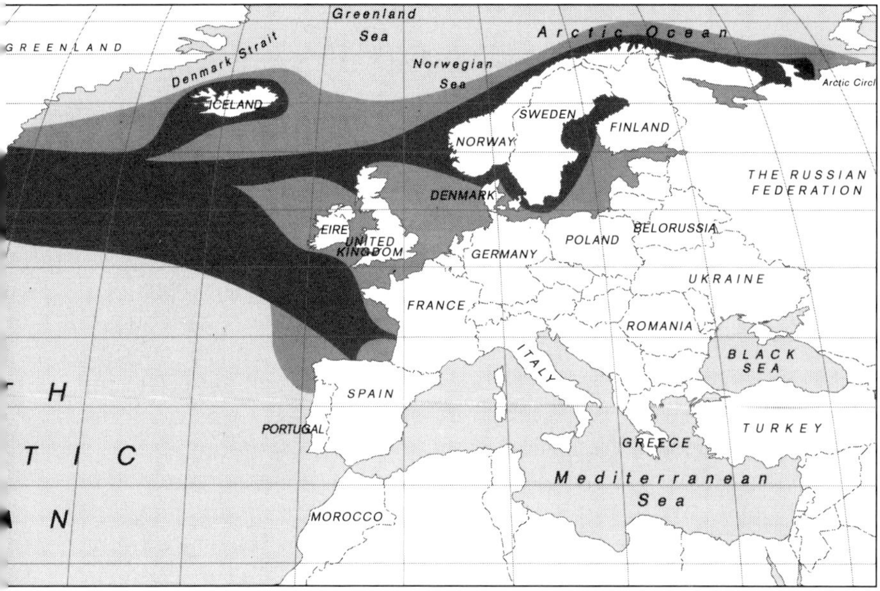

By the mid-1980s, growth of conservation awareness and recognition of regulatory requirements was manifest in the activities and prospects within a widening international salmon fishery arena. But what of the UK contribution? How did it measure up to attainments achieved by other nations?

The UK Record: Reluctant Conservationists

In the international field the UK had been active through voluntary bodies like the Atlantic Salmon Trust (AST), and through its input to formal European Economic Community (EEC) reform undertakings. In the attainment of restraints on Greenland and Faroes fisheries the UK played an important part. Furthermore studies and reports on these sub-Arctic fisheries in which the AST had been prominent added much to their knowledge and understanding.

Positive United Kingdom attainments, however, stopped here. The record on domestic fishery conservation remained a sorry one. In his Closing Address to the 1986 Biarritz Symposium, Richard Buck observed: "Sad to say, in both [the United Kingdom and the Republic of Ireland] which produce around one-half of the world [wild Atlantic salmon] supply, there has not been a major forward movement".[7]

Buck went on: "Is it possible that the fisheries bureaucracies in the EEC-UK-Irish complex do not fully comprehend that the other NASCO members have already begun the long and arduous task of reversing the trend towards over-exploitation? [Do] they realise their obligations to other signatories of the salmon treaty?"

And if the question were asked whether the "recalcitrance of this triumvirate" had any serious effect on further progress under NASCO, the answer he declared must be a very definite "yes". Denmark was unlikely to make further catch concessions unless there was "fair-sharing of the burden of conservation".

There was, said Buck, "no question as to the direction in which Denmark points the finger. So what might be the response of these states of origin, such as the UK, for instance, to the question 'What are you going to do about all this'? ...Are we to believe that these salmon-producing nations can so easily walk away from problems and responsibilities, hiding forever behind the cloak of Community representation"?[8]

What was needed, concluded Buck, was for the UK and Ireland to embark "on a long-term plan for the future enhancement of salmon stocks throughout the whole of their area of competence, including strict interim regulatory measures on an emergency basis wherever necessary".

Exploitation and Management

The basic attitude of UK salmon fishers related almost exclusively to maximum exploitation. This attitude was manifest in the behaviour of netsmen and, all too often, anglers. Netsmen had always fought hard—and successfully—to maintain their antiquated legal rights which gave them in their separate fishery districts virtual "local monopolistic control" of the salmon resource.*

The record of UK angling beat owners and rodsmen was little better. In view of salmon scarcity, most anglers seldom have the opportunity to indulge in a bonanza. Nevertheless the traditional angler's maxim retained only slightly diminished vitality and relevance: and this was, "the more--and with a little luck the bigger—the better"![9] Amongst a minority of anglers there was growing interest in and support for Catch-and-Release.[10] But this concept was little favoured by most rod fishery owners.[11] Even where netting restraints had been purchased, proprietors still endorsed the principle of maximum exploitation.

On the premier river Spey, for instance, much money in the early 1980s had been expended to reduce early season netting, and hence to allow more scarce Spring salmon to enter up-stream waters, and in time, it was hoped, to multiply. So had these fortunate proprietors put in place catch quotas or at least rod-number limits to ensure reasonable conservation? Not at all! [12] Nor did most take kindly to

* See Appendix A, pp. 304-307

MAXIMUM EXPLOITATION ... *By nets*

... *and by rods.*

suggestions that only by such exercises in voluntary restraint could the conservation pay-off envisaged—and for which they had paid dearly—be realised.

But what of stock management? Modern management of the Scottish, and to a great extent remnant English and Welsh salmon, with a few exceptions, had been by what might be called the "by guess and by God" system. There was no reliable data on how many fish enter rivers, at what times of the year and in what numbers. Up-stream stocking capacities were unknown. Optimum densities of spawning and juvenile fish nursery areas were based on guesstimates. Management to maintain, enhance or restore varying racial stocks which comprise river salmon populations had traditionally been virtually ignored. Catch statistics, due to the absence of even rudimentary monitoring and control, could at best be regarded only as "guides" to actual exploitation.

On a few small rivers nets had been totally removed. The Canada-based time-share company, *Salar Properties,* had pioneered this approach—with very favourable results by the mid-1980s—on the few small rivers it had purchased in the North and West of Scotland. On a few other Scottish rivers Spring netting bans long had been operative. But why had proper management of so valuable a resource never been implemented? And why only now is a start being made?

The reason was that those who dominated these fisheries were interested only in catching the maximum number of salmon. They were not interested in "managing" the resource. Until recently the "by guess and by God" method had proved adequate to maintain fat profits for the commercial interests. And, of course, this method costs very little.

Netsmen, who continued to take up to 97 per cent of the summer catch while accounting for less than 5 per cent of the benefits generated by the Scottish salmon economy, preferred, understandably, to operate with minimum restraints.[13] Nor were dominant rod proprietors prepared seriously to challenge this staggering imbalance. Most were reluctant to support reform initiatives while still they found themselves in possession of fisheries which, despite heavily diminished catches, continued to command high fees and showed steady increases in capital values. Furthermore, if rod fishery owners pushed too hard for statutory restraints on downstream netsmen, what might be the reciprocal restraints they would have to accept? "Conservation" was acceptable only so long as it might result in larger catches, as interpreted by net or rod interest. In any other sense "conservation" was at best regarded as distasteful, at worst an extremely suspect, even dangerous concept.

Nor was this resistance to reform without some popular support. More than one Scottish angling association which *leased* water was reluctant fully to support reform initiatives which would put more fish into rivers. How long, they asked, would they then be able to afford their leases once their catches started to show marked increases? Indeed, they might find their leases were terminated, and those waters they had so long and lovingly—and often at considerable cost—husbanded sold off to the highest bidder; one who might be a foreigner. This already had happened on many waters where time-share syndicates had moved in.

So it was not that the techniques, methods and facilities to set efficient modern systems of fishery management into operation were not known. Rather the dominant interests regarded rational management as a profound threat to their profits and control. Particularly they knew that this inevitably would entail such issues as equity between net and rod interests; in-river fishing restraints; systematic monitoring of catches and stocks; and certain requisite conservation measures which could include catch quotas, salmon tagging, rigourous systems of net and rod licencing along with much-improved inspection and tough sanctions to back them up. Furthermore, if such systems were to be introduced this could only be done with substantial state funding support. In Scotland this would mean a reduction in the near-total control proprietors exercised over the fisheries they owned.

The Salmon Bill and Reform Prospects

Whether viewed from abroad or closer to home, there was no mistaking the basic concern about Scotland's wild salmon resource. The dominant ethic of Scottish operators remained "maximum exploitation" and profits. So it was that the introduction into Parliament of comprehensive salmon legislation for Scotland in December 1985 provided an unique and great opportunity to put right what had been going wrong for well over a century. The question was: what advantage would Government and legislators take of this opportunity?

Would Government and the concerned Fisheries Departments, Department of Agriculture and Fisheries, for Scotland (DAFS) and the Ministry of Agriculture, Food and Fisheries for England and Wales (MAFF) construct a Bill to meet the challenge of urgently needed reforms? Would this Bill reflect the imperatives of "conservation, equity and economy"? Would its provisions make due allowance for the soaring dominance of farmed salmon, which by 1985 was 15:1 over wild salmon in the commercial market?[14]

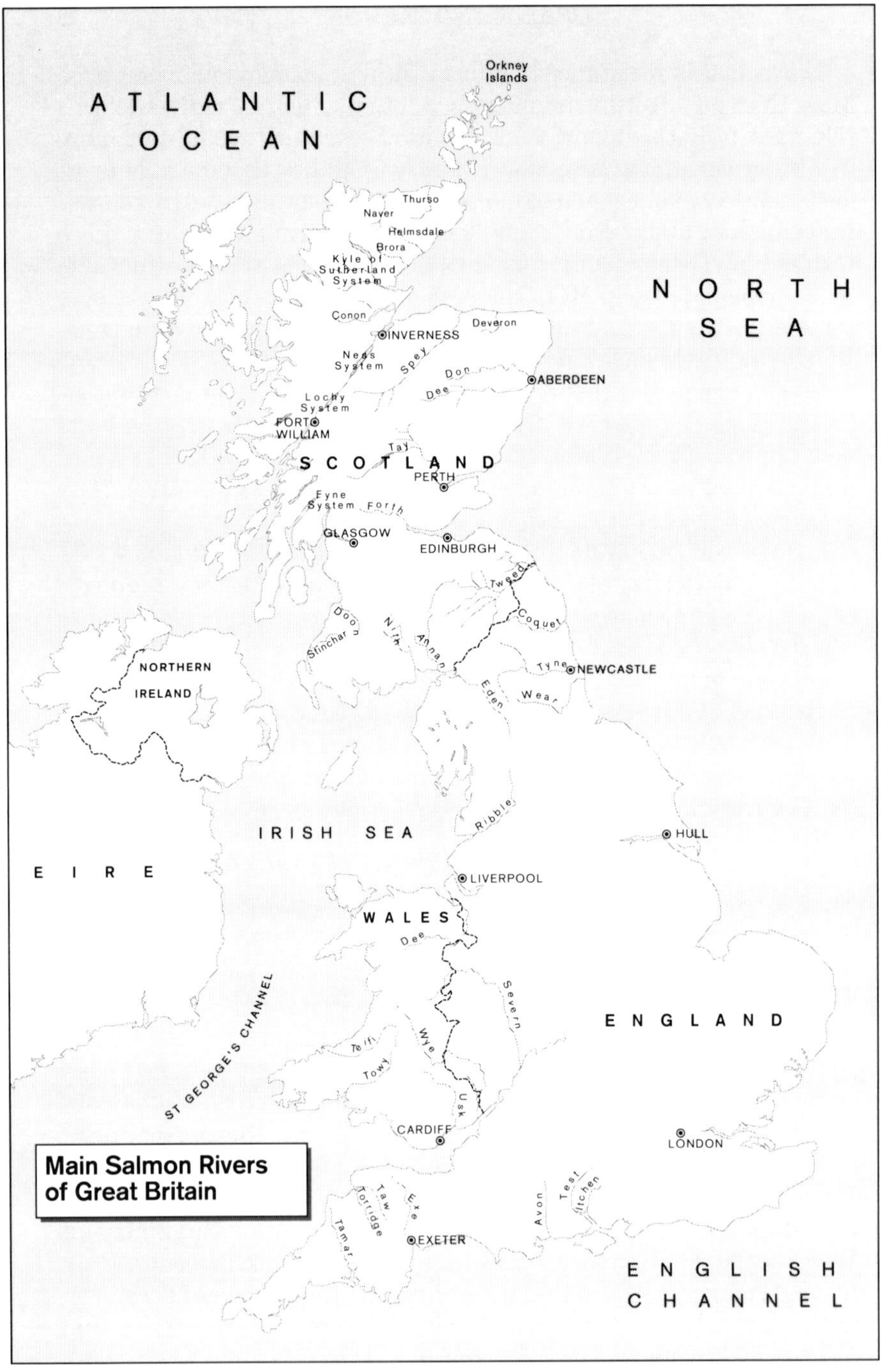

Main Salmon Rivers of Great Britain

Would the "nettle" of rod-tourism, which generated more than 95 per cent of the Scottish salmon industry's revenue while taking as little as three per cent of the peak-season catch, be grasped? Would the needed provisions to swing the balance of power from nets to rods, be built into the Bill?[15]

And what of the need for new and effective conservation measures to ensure enhancement of fish numbers returning from their ocean and coastal journeys? What of measures for increasing the production and survival—indeed perhaps for triggering the very restoration—of in-season, pan-racial, up-stream spawning stocks? Scottish reported catches, it was to be noted, had declined by 50 per cent since the mid-1960s, with a sharper 25 per cent drop in the five year (1977 to 1981) period.[16] Altogether, the situation was grave.[17] Might not a National Salmon Policy (NSP), urged by nearly all UK salmon fishery interests, be introduced?

Finally, there was the important issue of "protection and enforcement". If basic conservation of stocks, both within the rivers and at sea, was to be achieved, new and much-strengthened regulatory provisions were vital. Since the mid-1970s there had been much talk of salmon-tagging and Dealer-Licensing. Many persons considered these to be the "twin foundation stones" for achieving this objective. Could this be secured in the Bill? Would the relevant provisions be included?

These were the key questions which informed and responsible fishery interests were asking. The Salmon Bill of 1985-86 offered the first major opportunity for over a century to put things right. But there were also the equally vital legislative realities to be confronted. Could sufficient support of parliamentarians be generated? And what of needed provisions? If these were included in the Bill, could they be carefully guided through their parliamentary stages? If not, would legislators take those actions needed to ensure they were included?

Salmon fishery reformers and conservationists had realistic apprehensions. But also they were hopeful. It was now up to Government, legislators, conservationists, reformers and other interested bodies to see what might be made of this opportunity.

Before turning to the Salmon Bill itself, it may be useful to consider a few of the main historical issues and influences which were to cause the Bill to take the form it did. Indeed, to understand these issues and influences is to recognise why reformers, though hoping for the best, had their fears!

What few persons realise is that the UK salmon fishery, at the turn of this century, did come within tantalising reach of "common sense" conservation. The principles laid down at that time still provide the guidelines upon which effective and equitable management and conservation must one day proceed. It is to these principles that attention now may usefully be directed.

References

1. Interview with William (Bill) Blair (*aka* "Blair of Kincardine") at his Kincardine O'Neil "works"; March 1982. Celebrated Dee-side sage, Blair was known by all, and respected by most, within the local salmon establishment and much further afield, for his encyclopedic knowledge, his forthright views, and his commonsense grasp of all matters relating to *salmo salar.* A tackle-maker by occupation, he was inventor of the renowned "Blair Spoon". Blair had an important influence on the writer during the early years of his interest in the politics of salmon. Blair died in 1986.

2. Anthony Netboy, *Salmon: The World's Most Harassed Fish,* (London: Andre Deutsch, 1980), p.188.

3. Anthony Netboy, *The Atlantic Salmon: A Vanishing Species?,* (London: Faber, 1968), p.334.

4. There have been recent efforts to restore Atlantic salmon to Lake Ontario rivers on both American and Canadian sides. See David Shaw, "Salar Restored?: Ontario Saga", *Trout and Salmon,* (November, 1991), p.62; also Gerry Wolfram, "Won't You Come Back Home?", *Atlantic Salmon Journal,* (Winter, 1991), pp.18-19.

5. See David Shaw, "Biarritz Breakthrough", *Trout and Salmon,* (December, 1986), p.71.

6. Richard A. Buck, "Stewards of the Salmon: Closing Address", *Third International Salmon Symposium,* Biarritz, France, 21-23 October, 1986, p.2.

7. Ibid., pp.2-3, (Italics added).

8. Ibid., p.3.

9. A photograph of two anglers displaying their weekend catch of 31 salmon taken on shrimp from the Cumbrian Eden in September 1986, was published with an accompanying critical letter in *Trout and Salmon* magazine, (December 1986), p.45. The response was interesting. First the unusual size of reader response gave a clear indication of interest in the issue. Second, while the majority of respondents strongly backed the anglers who took this bonanza catch, a number deplored the act. It is perhaps significant that in defense of his action one angler criticised referred to much larger catches taken on various Scottish rivers which the angling press publishes without comment.

10. See Laurence Catlow, "A Question of Sport", *Trout and Salmon,* (December, 1986), pp.58-59. For response to this article see "Letters: A Question of Sport", *Trout and Salmon,* (February, 1987), pp.49-50.

11. A novel and encouraging exception is to be found on the Spey. The late Gerald Panchaud, owner of the premier Tulchan Estate water, put into operation

during the 1987 season a variation on catch-and-release. Anglers had the choice of killing and keeping fish caught, or depositing them in riverside "keeps" for later transportation to the estate's broodstock tanks—the estate compensating the angler for fish deposited at the current market rate. It is hoped that if the scheme proves a success, that by "keeping" precious Spring fish in particular, stocks of these early-running fish may gradually increase. See, Sandy Leventon, "Comment", *Trout and Salmon* (March, 1987), p.2.

12. For an encouraging and exceptional variation on the angler-conservation theme, see n.9 above.

13. See Anthony Netboy, "The Plight of the Scottish Salmon", *Atlantic Salmon Journal,* (Spring, 1986), p.18; and David Shaw and Colleagues, *A Survey of Salmon Angling and the Scottish Tourism Economy: Revenue Input and Employment Support,* (mimeo.), March 1983, pp.5-16. The above *Survey* showed that: "In terms of their contribution to the Scottish economy, salmon anglers, while taking 15 per cent of the annual catch [and less than 3 per cent of the summer peak-period catch], generate 97 per cent [up to £210m.] of the salmon industry's earnings. Commercial netsmen, while taking 85 per cent of the catch [and up to 97 per cent during the peak summer months] generate the remaining three per cent (£5m.) annually". (See *Survey*'s introductory "Summary"). The *Survey* also showed that salmon angling provided employment support for over 30,000 Scottish jobs (96 per cent), while netting supported another 1200 (4 per cent).

14. "Fish Farming Statistics, 1985", *Progress Report* (Atlantic Salmon Trust), May 1986, p.25.

15. See n.12 above.

16. See, "Landings of Salmon, Grilse and Sea Trout in Scotland", *The Salmon Net, No.XV,* (1982), p.21; and David Shaw, *The Disappearing Scottish Salmon: Economic Effects and Conservation Requirements,* (A Brief for Scottish MPs and other interested parties), (mimeo.), October 1982, p.2.

17. See, *Association of Scottish District Fishery Boards,* circular, dated 23 July, 1982, p.1: "The average netsman in 1982 is securing, in real terms, only 35 per cent of the catch value he earned in 1976". Also see, Editorial, *The Salmon Net,* No.XV, (1982), p.11. It was claimed that Scottish netsmen were facing a crisis of "crippling proportions, ...a tragedy for salmon fishers all over Scotland, and for the wild salmon which will disappear with our industry".

Chapter 1

THE GOLDEN AGE OF COMMON SENSE

> "The broad lines of salmon fishery improvement have been of late [that is, 1900-1909] pretty generally recognised. The services rendered to the country by the Elgin Commission on Salmon Fisheries is far greater than most people suppose. Never was there so enlightened and so complete a review of the whole situation, so definite and so thorough a grasp of what is most needed for the conservation and improvement of the salmon interests".
>
> *W.L. Calderwood*[1]

It could be said that the preliminaries to the 1986 UK Salmon Act started seriously in 1902. In that year a Royal Commission under the chairmanship of Lord Elgin submitted to Parliament its Report on the salmon fisheries of England, Wales and Scotland (*The Elgin Report*). It was a monumental work which contained a number of basic, commonsense recommendations. Had these been adopted and implemented by Government, most of the primary causes of decline in the dominant Scottish salmon fishery would have been corrected. Also the principal requirements of equity between competing net and rod interests would have been largely satisfied.

Conservation Promise: The Elgin Report

The eminent W.L. Calderwood, Chief Inspector of Salmon Fisheries for Scotland at that time, was clearly heartened and greatly reassured by the recommendations in *The Elgin Report*:

> "The reduction of netting in narrow waters where fish congregate before ascending to their natural spawning grounds; the opening up of man-made barriers to ascent; the wider control of the supervising Central Authority; and a considerable number of lesser points de-

pendent therefrom are all necessities which the experience of half a century of our present [1862-'68] Salmon Acts and the changed conditions of our salmon fisheries have clearly enough demonstrated".[2]

But long experience in the hard school of Scottish fisheries had also taught him to temper hope with caution. He went on to observe that:

> "Unhappily, as yet, no practical result has been attained therefrom, but I venture to think it is very certain that when legislation does come about it is bound to follow the general lines laid out by the Royal Commission Report referred to".

"Unhappily as yet, no practical result has been attained therefrom..."! It was quite incredible that these words echoing down the years should have been as applicable in the mid-1980s as they were in 1909. No legislation in the interim had met these vital and long recognised requirements. As a result local netting proprietors continued to enjoy "home rule", and as Calderwood put it, a virtual monopoly over the salmon resource.

Estuary and River Netting Controls

Pointing to this key "true conservation" issue, *The Elgin Report* made clear that there could be no alternative: much strengthened *statutory control* on *estuary and river netting* was essential. Recognising that it would be "impossible to leave the matter entirely to voluntary associations"—like the River Dee Fishing Improvement Association, founded in 1872—*The Elgin Report* declared that at the point "where netting [in narrow estuary/river waters] becomes injurious [to other up-stream fishery interests] local fishery boards should be empowered to acquire nets above that point compulsorily". *Compulsion,* it was pointed out, *was necessary "because to omit even one net might ruin the whole scheme;* it being demonstrable that any restrictions lower down the river would simply transfer a large number of fish to the station higher up which was allowed to remain".[3]

Nor was it merely with securing more fair and equitable treatment of rod fishery interests that the Commissioners were concerned. There was the vital matter of conservation. While the Commissioners recognised that each river must be treated on its own merits, one consideration was basic and essential. Calderwood put it this way: "In every case, the netting should be so limited as *to allow a proportion of every run of fish to pass into the comparatively safe haven of the upper river*". Only in this way, he stated, "could a river be supplied with stock from both early and late-running fish and have its full extent of available spawning ground occupied".[4] In addressing this principal concern, Calderwood and the Commissioners touched directly on the issue which to the present day has elicited the most fierce, determined and successful resistance of the netting interests.

Interestingly, coastal nets (fixed nets set in the sea), which today are targets for extensive voluntary net-reduction initiatives; these were adjudged to be far less damaging to stocks than estuary nets. Since these nets harvested fish from a "mixed stock" of salmon heading for various rivers up and down the coast, it was evident, the Commissioners declared, that such nets exacted a tolerable toll, as against estuary nets which cropped the native stocks of those rivers in which they operated.[5]

LORD ELGIN (The Ninth Earl) c. 1900...former Viceroy of India and Chairman of the Royal Commission.

Indeed, putting the case for strengthening coastal net fisheries, and reducing estuary and river net fisheries, one witness before the Elgin Commission pointed out that: "Where a proportion of every run of salmon has been protected, it has been followed, firstly, by the fisheries yielding more fish; secondly, by the employment of a greater number of persons; thirdly, an increase in the value of the existing fisheries, both of the upper and the lower waters; and fourthly, by the places in which fishing can be exercised becoming more numerous. ...All these results have been recorded as resulting from a change in the mode of fishing from river netting to sea netting".[6]

On the basis of such evidence, together with that supplied by the estuary netsmen which failed to demonstrate any damage either to their interests or to the stock of fish in rivers, the Commissioners concluded that continued "use of fixed nets on the sea coast and their introduction where they do not exist and can be used—provided such nets are placed at a sufficient distance from the mouths of rivers—[is] justified" and warranted.

Calderwood was aware that views expressed by himself and the Commissioners could be regarded as reflecting an angling bias. He declared, however, "that it is this very improvement of salmon angling and the increase in the desire for this form of sport which is the safeguard of the best economic interests of our salmon fisheries". Referring to voluntary river net reduction schemes undertaken on Dee, Spey and Deveron, he pointed to the increases in catches, capital and tenancy values achieved. It was merely common sense and sound management to obtain an increase in the numbers of salmon in rivers, "since it secures as an inevitable accompaniment an adequate stock of breeding fish".[7]

Management for Stock Improvement

The Elgin Report considered virtually every matter relevant to the maintenance and improvement of salmon stocks and dependent rod and net fisheries. Noting that evidence from widely separated areas indicated no significant difference in the sexual development of salmon as they prepared for spawning, the Commissioners called for a uniform Annual Close Time(ACT), to extend from 27 August to 10 February, (168 days) for all of the UK.

The Weekly Close Time (WCT), they held, should be increased from 36 hours in Scotland to 48 hours nationally. And they went further. A 48 hour WCT, the Commissioners held, was in itself not enough on many rivers to ensure safe passage of a proportion of fish past the netting areas and into the relative safety of up-stream waters. They therefore called for the creation of a "small Commission armed with executive powers" to visit each river, and to decide "after an inquiry on the spot", the point above which netting should compulsorily—though with compensation—be terminated. On such premier rivers, including Tay, Tweed, North Esk, Spey and Findhorn they had received compelling evidence of inequity and damage to potential spawning stocks. The combination of an increased WCT, and the termination of netting above the point decided would, they maintained, provide an adequate and workable remedy. [8]

Much strengthened powers for the Central Authority under an independent head were seen as essential to attainment of the above and various other objectives. It was envisaged that collection of "reliable statistics as to salmon fishings" would thereby be facilitated. And while the Commissioners acknowledged the strenuous resistance, particularly of netsmen, to such statutory provision, they felt that in this instance the interests of the fishery as a whole should take precedence. "We think this is a case where the public advantage should outweigh the private objection, and that powers should be given to the Central Authority to obtain statistics by methods already adopted for other purposes of Government".[9] They further noted that the creation of "one Central Authority for Great Britain, or even the United Kingdom ... which would have charge of all questions relating to fishing in the sea and in the rivers" was a vital provision, of which it was "impossible to over-estimate the advantages". Not only would this allow transaction of fishery business on a common unified base, as in other countries, but with "a recognised position in the official hierarchy" such an office would be vested with "a status and influence which can scarcely be secured in any other way".[10]

The Elgin Report also drew attention to many basic issues and problems relating to local management, maintenance and development of fisheries which were as central then as they are now. It recognised that amalgamation of neighbouring small boards—or amalgamated boards for certain districts without created boards, particularly in the West of Scotland—could afford great advantage. By joining forces, so to speak, adequate finance could be made available to fund the needed administration and fishery management which one board or fishery district on its own could not meet.

What most concerned the Commissioners about local fishery management was the underlying ill feeling between rod and net interests on all premier fishery District Boards. Good management and effective conservation of common stocks could not be achieved where such feelings persisted. The root of the problem, as they saw it, lay in the system of election to local District Boards.* "The mode of election of members" to the Boards; one which divided upper (angling) and lower (netting) representatives "into two distinct, and it may be, hos-

* The typical Scottish District Salmon Fishery Board comprised: three upper (normally angling), and three lower (normally netting) proprietors, together with a Chairman who was the proprietor with the highest ratable value. As the Chairman was usually a netsman, this meant that on most Boards the netting interests retained in perpetuity a 4:3 majority.

Due to the line dividing lower from upper proprietors often being in the lowest reaches of the river, and the fact that each group (upper and lower) elected its own representatives; this meant that a very small number of netsmen—perhaps less than six persons—could elect their three members, while an often very large number (on Tay, more than 170) still could elect only three members.

tile camps [could] scarcely fail to accentuate" differences, and indeed merely increased the difficulty of "taking any step to improve the condition of the river [due to] the suspicion with which one side regards proposals emanating from the other".[11] Remedy, however, could, they felt, be easily attained. There were two alternatives. The Commissioners preferred the first which called for "the system of distinctions and preferences" to be abolished, and for *all* proprietors to meet and together elect a *common list* of members; the Chairman to be chosen by the elected members. If, however, this reform could not be secured, and it was considered desirable to retain the system of "separate elections of [upper and lower] members", it would be imperative that at least the Board Chairman be elected "from amongst their own number at a meeting of [*all* eligible] owners within the District".

Beyond these core issues, *The Elgin Report* demonstrated full awareness of the remaining principal modern fishery concerns. The Central Authority, or failing this, the local authorities could assist greatly in fishery protection through direct funding and/or personnel support. Such support would be of particular value in areas like Tweedside and certain West coast locales where damaging illegal assaults on river and coastal stocks, often accompanied by gang violence, were known to be endemic. Bailiffs too, they felt, should be given strengthened powers.

While in Scotland pollution was not on a scale of other parts of Britain, there was need for protection. Particular mention was made of the Spey and the scandal of distillery effluent discharge. Pollution control, *The Elgin Report* stated, could best be provided by proposed Watershed Boards—predecessors of today's Scottish River Purification Boards. The threat posed by water abstraction already was well-recognised, the Commissioners noting that "the promotion of Water Bills does not adequately provide for the defence of fishery interests". [12] Needed controls again best might be achieved by assigning the role of defender of fishery interests to the proposed Watershed Boards.

Regarding water-course obstructions, the Commissioners recommended that "the removal of obstructions should be facilitated: in the first place by improving the financial resources of the Boards, and in the second place by so amending the law that in the case of all artificial obstructions the formation of an approved fish-pass should be compulsory, and that in the case of natural obstructions Local Fishery Boards should have power to take action if the owners decline to do so. ...No Fishing should be allowed within a reasonable distance of any obstruction".[13]

The Elgin Report had reservations about "artificial cultivation". The Commissioners preferred that the matter be more closely studied before making programme and Government funding commitments. But concerning "Experiment and Research", they strongly recommended that the Central Authority institute and fund schemes which might considerably advance "investigation of the natural history of the salmon and the problems connected therewith".

W .L. CALDERWOOD (c. 1900).

Elgin Proposals: Failure of Enlightenment

The Elgin Report was based on a two year exhaustive consideration of evidence from all concerned fishery, scientific and other informed interests. The path to restoration, maintenance and enhancement of the Scottish fishery was clearly marked. The Commissioners concluded that there were three principal requirements which must be fulfilled.

First, it was vital that UK fisheries as a whole be placed under the protective umbrella of a Central Authority or a separate department with ministerial status at Whitehall. While appreciative of the great efforts made by the then-operative Fishery Board for Scotland, it was recognised that a body with more than "powers to advise and consult" was essential. A separate fisheries ministry was suggested, with overall authority, and both wider and more specific decision-making powers, a ministry with access to Whitehall and Westminster; an inner cog in the governmental wheel which could ensure that fisheries received their full share of backing from the public purse. Such a ministry or Central Authority acting forcefully under its independent head could "do", rather than merely "talk". Furthermore it would afford the best possible opportunities for securing the funding and statutory powers to carry out what the Commissioners regarded as priority needs.

Second, it was recognised that in the interest of equity, or "fair treatment" of *all* salmon fishery owners, and to ensure adequate conservation of river spawning stocks, clear provision must be made to enable suffi-

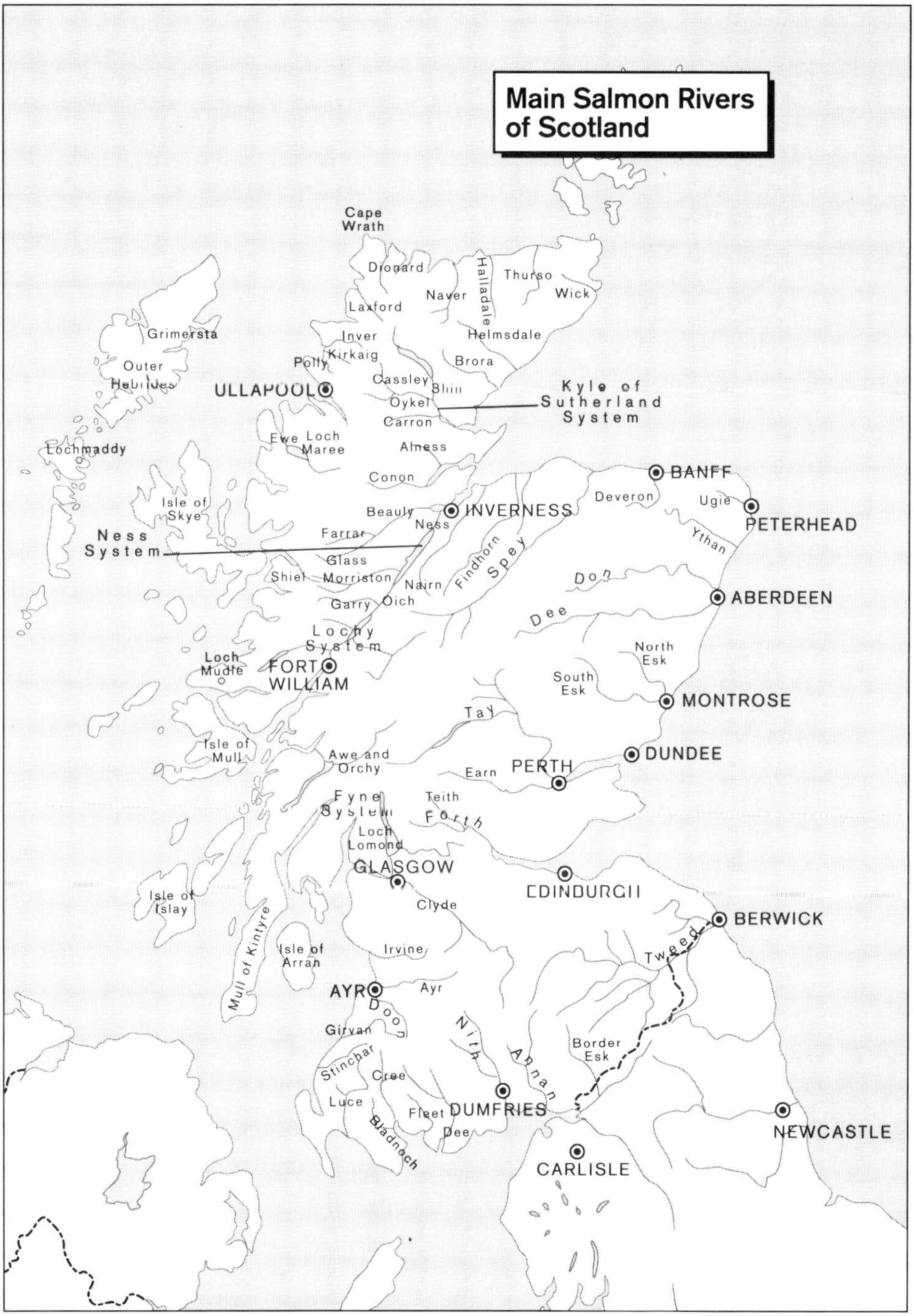
Main Salmon Rivers of Scotland
Cape Wrath
Dionard
Halladale
Thurso
Wick
Naver
Laxford
Grimersta
Inver
Helmsdale
Kirkaig
Polly
Brora
Outer Hebrides
Cassley
Shin
ULLAPOOL
Kyle of Sutherland System
Oykel
Carron
Ewe
Loch Maree
Alness
Lochmaddy
Conon
BANFF
Deveron
Ugie
PETERHEAD
Isle of Skye
Beauly
INVERNESS
Ness
Ness System
Farrar
Ythan
Glass
Findhorn
Spey
Shiel
Morriston
Nairn
Don
Garry
Oich
ABERDEEN
Dee
Lochy System
North Esk
Loch Moidart
FORT WILLIAM
South Esk
MONTROSE
Tay
Isle of Mull
Awe and Orchy
DUNDEE
Earn
PERTH
Fyne System
Teith
Forth
Loch Lomond
GLASGOW
EDINBURGH
Isle of Islay
Clyde
BERWICK
Tweed
Isle of Arran
Irvine
Mull of Kintyre
AYR
Ayr
Doon
Nith
Girvan
Annan
Border Esk
Stinchar
Cree
Luce
DUMFRIES
Fleet
Bladnoch
Dee
NEWCASTLE
CARLISLE

cient salmon to ascend their home rivers. The Commissioners agreed this could only be assured by placing appropriate and direct restraints on estuary and river nets. The 48-hour WCT, and compulsory removal—with compensation—of river nets above an established point would substantially meet this requirement.

Third, the Commissioners agreed that effective management of Scottish fisheries could only be achieved by statutory re-construction of local District Boards. The proposed changes would ensure the growth of unity and common interest amongst all fishery owners. It was only through such re-constructed bodies that the interests of the fishery, rather than those of rival net and rod factions, could become paramount.

Given fulfilment of these three fundamental requirements, a firm base would be established from which stable and productive fishery development could proceed. With goodwill and benefits envisaged for all concerned interests, gradual fulfilment of other requirements relating to protection, pollution, water abstraction and "experiment and research" would follow.

Not one of these three basic requirements was met. Indeed, since 1902 the issue of these requirements has rarely been officially raised. The Government in 1907 produced a small Bill calling for implementation of certain Elgin Commission recommendations.[14] It received the wholehearted approval of the Salmon and Trout Association (S&TA), which had been founded in 1903, the year after the Elgin Commission had completed its work. Amongst its founder-members were leading Scottish and Irish fishery owners with valuable commercial interests. The Salmon Net Fishing Association of Scotland (SNFAS), with many of the same elements represented in its founding membership, was established in 1906. The Bill was duly passed and became law in August 1907. There was, however, one rather serious failing in the new legislation. *It did not apply either to Ireland or to Scotland*!

Subsequently, in England and Wales further reform was secured by the Salmon Act of 1923, which was extended in 1948 and 1972. In Ireland the Government of the new Republic passed the separate Acts of 1924 and 1925. Northern Ireland passed a Fishery Act in 1928—here too there has since been added legislative provision. While in each Act commercial and food-producing interests retained priority consideration, some progress was made towards modern regulation and management requirements.[15]

But what of Scotland? In 1930, Calderwood, after more than 40 years' service to the salmon and the Scottish fishery, was a deeply disappointed man. "In Scotland", he stated, "we have seen no salmon legislation for fifty years. I speak feelingly after one or two moves in that direction. There is a very good salmon fishery Bill getting dusty in the Scottish Office—at least it is, or was, a very good Bill in my opinion".[16] Minor alterations which affected the Scottish fishery were made in the 1951 and 1976 Acts.

It may be said that the greatest achievement of the dominant Scottish commercial interests is that for over 70 years they successfully contrived to ensure that the Elgin Commission's basic recommendations were virtually erased from the public consciousness. At the same time, until recent years, the silence of rod fishery owners in parliamentary, ministerial and various related voluntary bodies did little to remedy the situation.

References

1. W.L. Calderwood, *The Salmon Rivers and Lochs of Scotland,* Second Edition (revised), (London: Edward Arnold, 1921), p.4.
2. Ibid.
3. *Report of the Royal Commission Appointed to Inquire into the Salmon Fisheries of England, Wales and Scotland,* Cmnd. 1188, (London: HMSO, 1902), p.36. (Hereafter, this document is referred to as *The Elgin Report*).
4. *Fishery Board for Scotland Report for 1906,* (Edinburgh: 1907), p.4.
5. See W.L. Calderwood, *Salmon and Sea-Trout,* (London: Edward Arnold, 1930), p.119.
6. *The Elgin Report,* op.cit., p.37.
7. Ibid., p.5.
8. See, *The Elgin Report,* op.cit., p.35.
9. Ibid., p.16
10. Ibid., p.17.
11. *The Elgin Report,* op.cit., p.13.
12. Ibid., p.63.
13. Ibid.
14. See *Parliamentary Debates,* Vol.173, 29 April, 1907,cols. 472-79.
15. In the early 1960s strong demands were made for adjustments in the English and Welsh fisheries to effect much more equitable treatment of rod fishery owners and anglers, and needed improvements in fishery management and regulation. See *Report of the Committee on Salmon and Freshwater Fisheries,* Cmnd. 1350, (London: HMSO, 1961)—popularly known as the *Bledisloe Report.* The Committee's recommendations were virtually ignored. See *Taking Stock,* (Association of River Authorities, March 1974), Chapter I, for critical comment and suggestions for legislation.
16. Calderwood, *Salmon and Sea-Trout,* op.cit., pp.2-3.

Chapter 2

TRIUMPH OF COMMERCIALISM

> "The salmon occupies a pinnacle of importance, especially in Scotland... Scottish salmon fisheries employ many people, often in remote rural areas where other work is hard to find. They earn substantial amounts of foreign currency. This considerable contribution to Scotland's economy is being made at a time when the salmon fisheries of other countries have been in decline. This feat must be regarded as an outstanding success story".
>
> *Viscount Thurso*[*]

> "In summary, viewed over this lengthy period [1950s to 1980s], it is clear that Scottish netsmen secured extensive statutory support for increased protection of their fishings. ...Although incessant outcries and complaints from netsmen suggested just the opposite, it was a period of considerable triumph for the interests of commercialism".[**]

Having successfully averted what they clearly regarded as the threat posed by the Elgin Commission recommendations, Scottish commercial interests were more or less able to relax for the next 20 years. Insofar as there might be need to lobby at Westminster or Whitehall, the new Salmon and Trout Association comfortably sited just down the Thames at Fishmongers' Hall—with its leadership drawn almost totally from the House of Lords—could see to such chores. It is perhaps interesting to note that it was not until after World War II that membership of this national organisation exceeded a few hundred persons.[***]

* See "Foreword" to *Salmon Fisheries of Scotland*, published by the Association of Scottish District Salmon Fishery Boards (ASDFB), (Farnham: Fishing News Books, 1977).

** See p.39 below.

***For details of S&TA's formation, aims, structure and activities, see below Chapter 4.

Fishery Board for Scotland and 'Salmon Science'

During this period legal and administrative responsibility remained with the Fishery Board for Scotland, a body which retained considerable independence. Much of the research which set the foundations for modern scientific studies of salmon and sea-trout was undertaken at this time. The energetic Calderwood pushed on with an enormously prolific output of life history, migration routes, disease, scale reading, kelt and smolt marking investigations. His assistant, research collaborator and future successor was W.J.M. Menzies. Their work was supplemented and much enriched by the sea-trout studies of Herbert Nall.

What is perhaps most commendable about the vast amount of basic research conducted by these largely unsung fisheries champions is that it was produced in a virtual vacuum of practical concern. Those who were in a position to implement the many and varied recommendations arising from this research showed little interest. As a frustrated Calderwood, at one point, put it: "To deal in a really useful way with the particular features of each salmon river, it is necessary to notice features which I consider to be adverse to the best interests of the rivers, many of which have already ... been dealt with by me in a series of reports bound in blue paper covers, and therefore only to be regarded, I presume, as ordinary waste paper".[1]

At the same time, the very zeal and extensive operations of Calderwood and his colleagues set the basis for the relationship of salmon researchers with commercial netting, or food-producing interests, which is the very core of the problem concerning achievement of common-sense salmon fishery reform today. Migration, smolt release and scale reading studies, for example, were readily arranged with those interests who could provide the access and quantitative sampling sought. These interests were the estuary and coastal netsmen.

Also, as primary concern was with productivity and maintenance of salmon fisheries for the requirements of the *commercial* market, official attention tended to be focused mainly on topics bearing most directly on these requirements. Though the writings of Calderwood and Menzies make clear that they were alert to the need for much greater up-stream fishery knowledge, nevertheless it was to downstream activity that nearly all their official research energies were directed. Considering what Calderwood and Menzies thought about the majority of Scottish netsmen,[2] this at times must have been a bitter pill to swallow.

In this way a "mutually reinforcing" relationship between Government scientists and Scottish netting interests was established. The Board's salmon scientists secured the access necessary to conduct their studies. In addition, extensive voluntary assistance was often supplied by netsmen in those districts where they were working. This meant that Government was spared the considerable costs it would have had to bear if scientists were required to supply their own boats, nets, fish houses and other facilities. It also meant they often acquired at no cost the labour and experience of those netsmen familiar with the salmon of their respective districts.[3] In return, the netsmen gained the practical information which these studies produced. This information could then be used to devise methods best designed to maintain and if possible increase

SCIENTIST AND NETSMAN CONFER. DAFS' North Esk Station chief scientist, Willie Shearer (left), and Joseph Johnston's Jonathan Stansfeld, on site.

catches, and to ensure that fish of the highest quality and condition reached the market.[4]

Given the extent of common interest between Government salmon scientists and netsmen, and that the principal concern of each has traditionally been with meeting the requirements of the commercial market, it is hardly surprising that succeeding fisheries administrations, to the present day, have been reluctant to adopt policies which might reduce the control exercised by netting interests over the Scottish salmon fishery as a whole. The enduring vitality of this relationship was clearly demonstrated at the 1983 *Deveron Inquiry*. (*See below*, pp.35-36).

Rod Fishery: Failure of Reform Demands

While there was growing emphasis on the importance of commercial food-production during the post-Elgin Commission era, this is not to say that the voices of bitter and aggrieved Scottish rod fishery owners were not heard. Many eminent persons pressed strongly for change. Challengers to the legislative *status quo* included such well-informed persons as Sir Herbert Maxwell and the Duke of Roxburghe (Tweed); Lord Knollys and the Balmoral Factor John Michie for HM King George V (Dee); the Earl of Dalhousie (North Esk); the Earl of Moray (Findhorn); Sir John Ramsden (Upper Spey); Col. Stewart-Mackenzie (Conon); Lord Breadalbane (Loch Tay); C.A. Murray, tenant of Lord Mansfield (Tay); Lord Esher (Teith); Lord Galloway (Cree); Lord Dalrymple (Stinchar/Luce).[5] Most of them gave strong support to the Elgin Commission's recommendations calling for reductions in estuary and river netting. Concern also was expressed principally about sea-netting, land-drainage, pollution and poaching.

Commenting on the North Esk, which even then had an established reputation as a nets-ravaged river, the angling journalist W. Earl Hodgson noted that a remedy was at hand. Lord Dalhousie had advanced a proposal in 1905 to remove the North Esk nets entirely. Hodgson predicted they would be off "before these words are published".[6]

Lord Dalhousie's proposal, however, failed. Indeed, with estimated net catches in 1982 of more than 20,000 native North Esk salmon and grilse, and more than 60,000 fish (principally by stake and bag nets on North Esk district foreshores) from stocks returning to other East coast rivers—the reported annual rod catch seldom exceeds 250!—this little river had even improved on its 1905 reputation.[7] For its size, it was probably the world's most productive Atlantic salmon commercial fishery. Nor should the significance of this early triumph of commercialism be overlooked. What happened to this initiative of even so powerful a land and riparian owner as Lord Dalhousie, was an omen. Similar initiatives on other Scottish rivers, particularly where all fishings have not been held by a sole proprietor, regularly suffered similar fates.

Bills to meet demands made by Lord Dalhousie and other prominent rod fishery owners were, with the assistance of the Fishery Board for Scotland, regularly prepared for submission to Parliament. Up to 1930 none had reached the statute book. Even a Bill "for the better regulation of the trout fisheries of Scotland"[8] was knocked on the head. In 1931, however, there were intimations that a new Salmon Bill which would deal with many Elgin Commission requirements was likely to fare better. It seemed auspicious that in the same year concerned Scottish fishery interests brought formally into existence a body entitled the Association of Scottish District Salmon Fishery Boards (ASDFB). The ASDFB was seen as "a means of mutual assistance to the Boards belonging to it".[9] It also was envisaged that it would be "in a position to advise the [Fishery] Board [for Scotland] as to the general consensus of opinion on any particular points connected with the salmon fisheries of Scotland".[10]

The ASDFB, as it turned out, was indeed keen to advise the Fishery Board for Scotland. However, due to the dominance of netting interests on most local District Boards, and the fact that it was the commercial interests which were principally represented in its membership and ruling Council, it was hardly surprising that the general pro-netting consensus it then expressed was little different from that which it still remained in the mid-1980s. [11] Needless to say, the envisaged Bill did not become law. For the next 20 years (until 1951) there was no notable challenge to the Scottish salmon fishery *status quo*.[12]

Dominant Interests and Structural Control

Looked at from the vantage point of the mid-1980s it could be seen that by the 1960s the following structure of representation, promotion and protection of the salmon fisheries was well settled into place.

First, there was the Department of Agriculture and Fisheries for Scotland (DAFS) which had replaced the old Fishery Board for Scotland. The functions of the Board, following a series of shifts in administrative accountability—which at one stage (1939) brought fisheries under the control of the then new Scottish Home Department!—came finally to rest by 1950 in the Scottish Agriculture Department. By 1960, the Department's formal title had become the Department of Agriculture and Fisheries for Scotland (DAFS). So far as seeking still to press for legislative reforms which might bring improved regulation of netting and greater equity between rods and nets, the new developments were retrograde

Gone was the autonomy and direct Whitehall access—normally via the President of the Board of Trade—enjoyed by the Fishery Board for Scotland during its early years. DAFS was merely one of the Scottish Secretary's many and onerous Cabinet responsibilities; and as agriculture was (and is) of far greater relative economic importance, fisheries were relegated to subordinate status. Furthermore, within the overall sector of DAFS' fisheries responsibilities, salmon fisheries were but a minor concern.

NORTH ESK NET FISHERY. Coastal Stake Nets; 106 interceptory nets on Montrose foreshore. Scotland's leading interceptory fishery — with possible exception of the Solway (See "Solway Stake Nets" photos below, p. 58).

WELL-GROOMED ESTUARY NETTING POOLS at Kinnaber. ▼

Gone too was the earlier autonomy of "successive [salmon fishery] Officers in Charge over a long period, [dating] from the days of Calderwood". [13] Inspectors of Salmon and Freshwater Fisheries, as they have since been called, were now Civil Service appointees operating under the bureaucratic direction of DAFS and "within the apparently truncated limits as now imposed".[14] Public information about Scotland's salmon fisheries, which before had been treated in a hush-hush manner, was now virtually non-existent. When compared with the Annual Reports of the old Fishery Board for Scotland, the new DAFS Reports were but "shadowy productions ... compressed into a few pages".[15] As of 1981, Annual Reports on the Fisheries of Scotland ceased.[16] Today, official information on Scottish salmon fisheries is restricted to reported catch figures published annually in a brief "Statistical Bulletin".

Second, there was the *Salmon Net Fishing Association of Scotland* (SNFAS). Given the close common interest in food production and scientific endeavour, the links of this body with DAFS were further strengthened during the 1950s as a result of the growth in salmon-orientated research by the Department's *Salmon and Freshwater Fisheries Laboratory* at Faskally, near Pitlochry on the River Tay. Research out-stations were subsequently developed at Almondbank (opposite Lord Mansfield's Scone Water) on the lower Tay; on the North Esk (with the co-operation of the *Joseph Johnston's* net-fishing company in Montrose); and on the Girnock Burn of the Aberdeenshire Dee at Ballater.

Third, there was the ASDFB which, due to its membership and Council composition, was a vital extension of SNFAS. Acknowledged by Government and DAFS as the authoritative voice of salmon fishery owners in Scotland, the ASDFB was ideally placed to ensure full protection and promotion of dominant netting interests.

Fourth, there was the Salmon and Trout Association (S&TA) with prominent members in both SNFAS and the ASDFB. With its Central Office at Fishmongers' Hall in London, the Association was in an advantageous position from which to monitor, guide, defend and promote Scotland's salmon fishery dominant interests at Westminster and Whitehall.

Finally, there was the *Atlantic Salmon (Research) Trust.* It was the "research arm" progeny of the S&TA. Founded in 1967, and re-christened in 1979 as the *Atlantic Salmon Trust* (AST), it was modelled on the *Salmon Research Trust of Ireland.* Its founding members comprised seven persons; four with prominent fishmongering links.[17] By 1986 the three surviving founding members were the Duke of Devon-

NORTH ESK NET FISHERY (cont'd) ... And sweep-nets below Morphie Dyke.

shire, Lord Lansdowne and Lord Cairns. They were the sole *members*. A limited company, the Trust secured Charitable status, and was committed solely to scientific research.[18] In practice, about 80 per cent of the Trust's annual expenditure between 1981 and 1986—its capital fund having derived mainly from an early 1980s "Save the Salmon" Campaign Appeal, and continued voluntary contributions—was absorbed by administrative costs.[19] Much of the rest was spent on supporting studies of the Greenland and Faroese salmon fisheries. Gravely concerned about declining Scottish catches—particularly of the premier quality Spring salmon—the dominant interests were keen to reverse this trend. Restraints on North Atlantic fisheries were seen as important in securing the return of increased runs to foreshore and estuary netting stations and to up-stream fisheries.

Given the commercial orientation of DAFS, and the collective structure and composition of these principal voluntary salmon organisations, the course of UK legislative initiatives from the 1960s onwards had followed a predictable path. Put briefly: *much had been done to safeguard stocks in open seas, in coastal and estuary waters.* On the other hand, *nothing had been done to increase the numbers of salmon enabled to get into and up their home rivers.* Laws which afforded "local monopolistic control" of the Scottish salmon resource by the commercial netting interests had survived virtually intact. Conservation and increasing angling requirements had been ignored. The result was that 80-85 per cent of recorded annual Scottish catches—and up to 97 per cent during the summer months—continued to be taken by coastal, estuary and river nets.

Commercial Interests And Legislation Initiatives

While the commercial interests had retained their dominance, this was not achieved without considerable and determined efforts. The complaints of tenant anglers and riparian owners were the least of their worries. Although there were periodic "uprisings" of concerned rod interests—expressed notably since the early 1970s in the gamefishing press and within the councils of S&TA—they failed to achieve support for remedial legislation.[20]

A 1971 Government *White Paper*[21] briefly presented a more imposing threat. A number of "radical" reforms were set out in the *Hunter Report* (Second Report, 1965)[22] such as phasing out and eventual removal of coastal fixed nets; concentration of estuary/river netting at a single point; use of a single trap for taking the commercial catch, counting fish and controlling up-stream escapement; improved methods for collection and production of catch statistics; creation of larger Area Fishery Boards; introduction of net and rod licensing; and statutory creation of a largely self-supporting and self-governing *Scottish Anglers' Trust.* While not all were supported by the Government, a vital opportunity for constructive parliamentary consideration seemed at last to have arrived. However, no formal discussion followed, and no Bill appeared.

Protecting Open Seas and Coastal Waters

Unrelenting efforts were made to safeguard returning salmon in the open seas and around the Scottish coast. In the early 1960s Scottish salmon interests, and netsmen in particular, were greatly alarmed by three recent developments: rapid growth of drift-netting on the East coast, use of highly efficient monofilament nets, and growth of a high seas salmon fishery off West Greenland. To combat these threats certain steps were taken.

"The use of drift nets to enmesh salmon was banned in Scottish coastal waters on the recommendation of the Committee on Scottish Salmon and Trout Fisheries [the *Hunter Report*] in their First Report of July 1963".[23] At the same time a concerted effort was made by Scottish interests to extend the drift-netting prohibition to the English North-East fishery. Due mainly to vigourous resistance by Northumbrian and

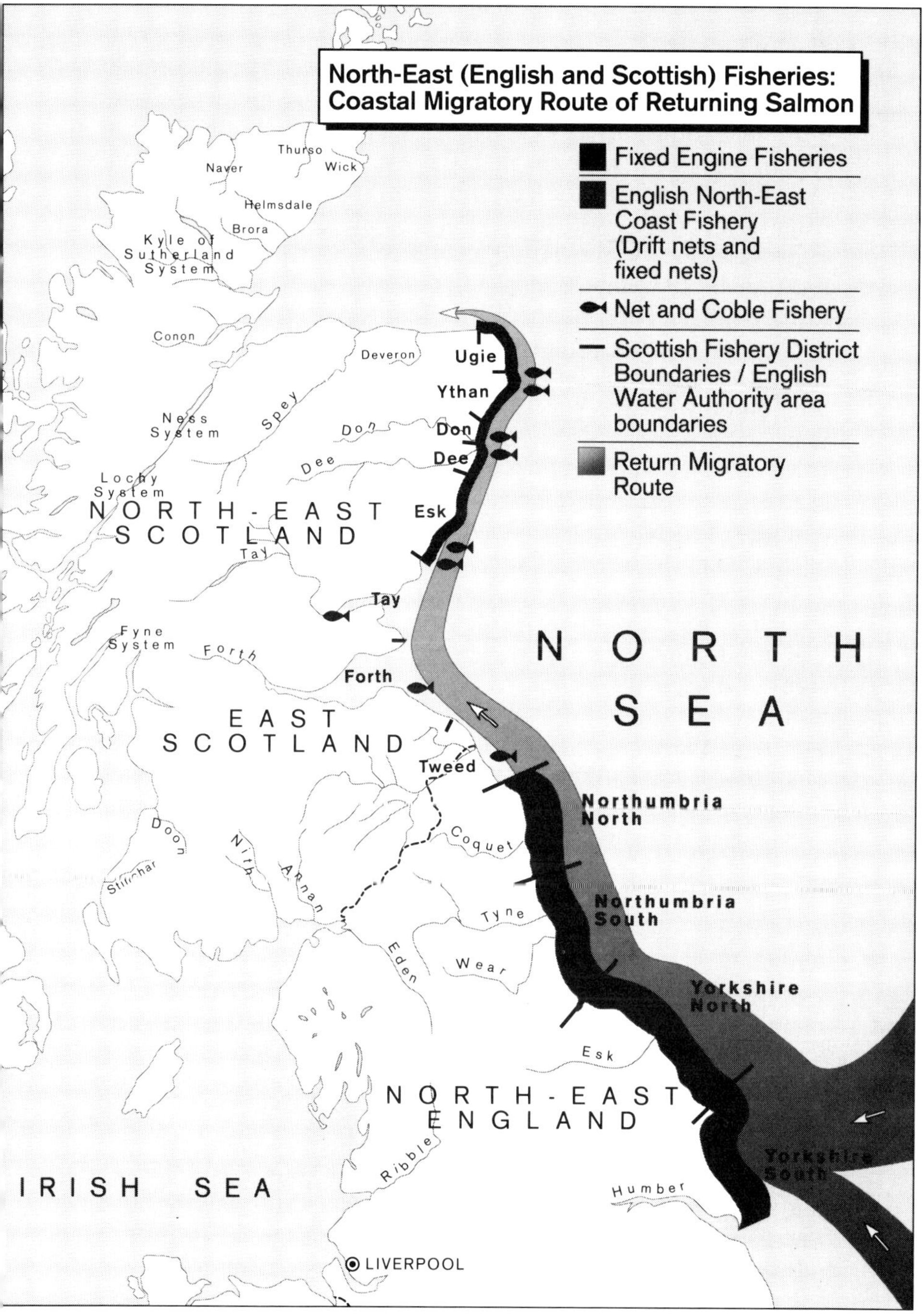
North-East (English and Scottish) Fisheries: Coastal Migratory Route of Returning Salmon
Fixed Engine Fisheries
English North-East Coast Fishery (Drift nets and fixed nets)
Net and Coble Fishery
Scottish Fishery District Boundaries / English Water Authority area boundaries
Return Migratory Route
Thurso
Naver
Wick
Helmsdale
Brora
Kyle of Sutherland System
Conon
Deveron
Ugie
Ythan
Ness System
Spey
Don
Dee
Lochy System
NORTH-EAST SCOTLAND
Esk
Tay
Fyne System
Forth
NORTH SEA
EAST SCOTLAND
Tweed
Northumbria North
Doon
Nith
Annan
Coquet
Stinchar
Northumbria South
Tyne
Eden
Wear
Yorkshire North
Esk
NORTH-EAST ENGLAND
Ribble
Yorkshire South
IRISH SEA
Humber
LIVERPOOL

Yorkshire netsmen, who argued that no conservation gain would be secured, these efforts failed. In the early 1970s further legislative provisions (Statutory Instruments) under the UK *Sea Fish (Conservation) Act of 1967* were enacted. These extended the ban on sea fishing for salmon from the 12-mile limit to the whole of the North Atlantic and outlawed a number of sea fishing methods.[24]

Suppression of the lethal monofilament nets was not easily secured. In 1977 the (English) South-West and North-West Water Authorities, and in 1982 the Welsh Water Authority passed bye-laws banning such nets for taking salmon. It was not, however, until 1986 that an effective prohibition in Scottish waters was secured. And this prohibition was achieved, so to speak, by the back-door. Using enabling powers under Section 2 of the *Inshore Fisheries Act (Scotland) 1984,* the Scottish Secretary, Malcolm Rifkind, in January 1986, instituted two (Statutory Instruments) Orders: (SI 60) "banning the carriage of monofilament nets in Scottish Inshore waters"; and (SI 59), banning the use of gill nets therein.

It should be noted that while the Scottish monofilament ban took a long time to achieve, there were interim attainments. These included the 1963 ban on drift-netting, cumulative restraint provisions secured during the 1970s (as noted above), and indeed important prohibitions secured through provisions in the 1984 *Inshore Fisheries Act.*[25] All these together with increased enforcement efforts—particularly by the DAFS Sea Fishery Protection Service—went far towards reducing the predations of illegal sea fishing.

Securing measures of control over open seas salmon fishing, and particularly the Greenland fisheries, also took time to achieve. By the mid-1970s, however, the Greenland off-shore fishery had been phased out, and the inshore catch reduced from over 2000 to 1190 tonnes. This quota was then gradually reduced. By 1986 it was 850 tonnes. Improved regulation and catch reductions were the result mainly of efforts by newly-created International organisations,[26] linked with initiatives by individual salmon-producing and harvesting countries, including the UK. This dual approach continued to ensure that agreed—if fragile—restraints were maintained on the Greenland, and the more recently developed Faroes fisheries. [27]

While these and other committed efforts from the 1960s to the mid-1980s eventually produced gratifying results for the leading Scottish netsmen, success was by no means total. Other initiatives advanced did not, it seemed, turn out so well.

Legislation Efforts: Failed

A 1979 DAFS *Discussion Document* [28] which was to set the basis for new salmon legislation, raised hopes of anglers and conservationists. However, closer investigation revealed that:

> "The sole beneficiary of any new/altered legislation will be the anglers' old rival, and the salmon's most deadly enemy, the estuary and coastal netting interests. While a 'permanent ban' on drift-netting at sea; the reduction or elimination of coastal netting beyond the "headlands"; the implementation of a system of Area [Fishery] Boards which will permit a strengthening of in-shore and off-shore protective measures; while these core proposals, if legislated, will ensure that a greater number of migratory fish reach the mouths of their home rivers, that largely is where their increased protection (or 'conservation') will end. ...There is not a whisper about legislation which would place equally urgently required controls ... on domestic [legal] netting interests".[29]

This initiative died with the departure of Lord Mansfield as DAFS Minister at the end of the Conservative Government's first term in June 1983.

The 1982, Private Member's (Lords) *Strathcona Bill* was aimed at extending controls over In-shore fishing by prohibiting the use of gill-nets for taking salmon.[30] Its intention was to secure a ban on monofilament netting for Scottish salmon.[31] After being passed by the Lords, it was killed in the House of Commons. "The not unreasonable position of objectors was that the major Scottish netting interests, who once again were behind the Bill, have quite enough legal control already, without this control being further extended".[32]

The greatest challenge Scottish netsmen had ever faced was at the *Deveron Inquiry* of June/July, 1983. In order to increase their catch, the Deveron netsmen, *J. and D.R. Sellar,* quietly set into motion in early 1982 an application to the Scottish Secretary, George Younger, to alter the opening and closing dates of the Deveron District netting season. The Deveron netsmen were prepared not to fish during the first two weeks of the season, if they were granted permission to net for an additional two weeks at the end. Their reasoning was simple: in the early Spring there were very few salmon about; while in the Autumn there were many salmon about and they wanted to catch them. When rod and conservation interests from the Deveron and further afield strongly objected, an Inquiry was held at Banff, the Moray Firth coastal County town in the Deveron District.

The Deveron application was generally regarded as a test-case. The late John Ashley-Cooper put it bluntly: "If the Deveron netsmen have their way, all other Scottish netsmen will want the same—or more"![33] It was an extra-ordinary, yet illuminating proceeding.[34] The close and mutually supportive relationship between netsmen and DAFS, particularly its leading research officers, seemed clearly to be demonstrated. Equally clearly demonstrated was the near-total absence of reliable scientific evidence to support virtually any specific net, rod, or general conservation argument.

Despite the seeming inadequacy of supporting evidence, many believed the Deveron netsmen would succeed. In fact, they did not.

TWILIGHT ON THE DEVERON ... *Searching for sea-trout*

While the Chairman of the Inquiry, the DAFS Inspector of Salmon and Freshwater Fisheries, Robert B. Williamson, in his December 1984 *Inquiry Report* recommended that the application be granted,[35] the Scottish Secretary, Mr. Younger, rejected it. He ruled that the netting season should not be extended.[36] For once the netsmen had lost. Yet while there were signs of new appreciation of rods/conservation issues in high places, it was observed that anglers and conservationists "would be wise not to drop their guard. ...The DAFS' Faskally people and the netsmen may be down at the moment, but they are not by any means out".[37]

In November, 1984, Lord Thurso introduced in Parliament what he called his "Anglers' Charter". This Private Member's Bill, entitled *District Salmon Fishery Boards (Scotland),* was a curious Anglers' Charter.

"Not one provision was directed towards reducing domestic netting and getting more salmon and sea-trout into Scottish rivers, the essential provision if spawning stocks are to be increased and anglers somewhat appeased".[38] As for Government and the dominant elements amongst netsmen, it was apparent that the *Thurso Bill* met favour with neither. Basically, the proposed reforms sought Government support for re-structuring the administration of Scottish district salmon fisheries. The structures, financial support requirements and powers envisaged for proposed new Boards called for much-increased involvement of the Central Authority—that is, DAFS and Government. Clearly, this was not acceptable to leading netsmen.

Lord Lansdowne, Chairman of Tay Salmon Fisheries Ltd., Scotland's leading and most profitable netting company, and Chairman also of the Tay District Salmon Fishery Board responsible for an inland and coastal area exceeding 2000 square miles, made his views quite clear. He was not prepared to accept any "Boards Amalgamation Scheme" which was not clearly spelled out. Nor would he accept that "the Scottish Secretary should play any (determining) role in the selection of *non*-proprietorial representatives to local District Fishery Boards".[39] He argued that "the local Boards, not the Scottish Secretary should have exclusive powers for altering the separate net and rod Annual Close-Times; and indeed that local Boards should also have power to apply to the Scottish Secretary for variations of local (as well as National) Weekly Close-Times".[40]

As for the DAFS Minister, Lord Gray, "the debate merely served to underline what we already know by rote: Scottish Office politicians and Government want as little as possible to do with this increasingly sensitive salmon issue. They would be much relieved to hand over most of their remaining powers to the largely nets-dominated local District Boards".[41] The *Thurso Bill* survived two Readings in the House of Lords only to die at Lords Committee Stage in July 1985.

Framework for the Future

This then completed the preliminaries to what was anticipated to be the most important salmon legislation of the twentieth century, the (1985-'86) *UK Salmon Bill.* Legislative achievements over the past 22 years, particularly since the mid-1970s, had secured for leading Scottish salmon interests most of the important goals they sought. Much tighter controls on inshore and coastal fishing had been secured, backed by stronger sanctions and greatly improved "external" enforcement—that is, enforcement by agencies of the Central Authority (DAFS). In Inland waters, controls and sanctions had been to some degree strengthened. Penalties for poaching (as well as illegal fishing) were up-dated mainly by provisions in the 1976

Freshwater and Salmon Fisheries (Scotland) Act. Equally important, this Act made available—through "River Protection Order" enabling provisions—powers which local Fishery Boards could duly use to improve control over access, numbers and fishing methods of trout anglers, and hence reduce fishing pressure on salmon. (*Free* fishing for trout in the rivers and lochs in Scotland—with the exception of the Solway—traditionally has been regarded as a Common Law right).

Legislative "failures" too had served valuable purposes. The demise of thoroughgoing reform provisions in the *1971 White Paper* demonstrated that Scottish netting interests in particular need not, for the foreseeable future, fear any major statutory encroachments on their century-old rights.

The demise of the *1971 White Paper* provided a graphic demonstration of what was not acceptable to the dominant salmon interests, while the *1979 DAFS Discussion Document* was a comprehensive means of discovering what was, or might be acceptable in new general salmon legislation to a much broader range of salmon and other concerned fishery interests. Equally important, the *Discussion Document* enabled DAFS to discover what omissions—including increased Weekly and Annual Close Time provisions—would be acceptable, or at least tolerated. Although dominant Scottish interests were much distressed that *Discussion Document* findings failed to produce envisaged legislation by the end of the Conservative Government's first term in June 1983, nevertheless there were benefits. Indeed there are few who would say this "failure" did not firmly establish the basic structure and principal contents of what became the *Salmon Bill,* and is now the 1986 *Salmon Act.*[42]

As for the *Strathcona Bill,* it in its small way, constituted not merely an exploratory effort to extend controls on illegal fishing in coastal waters; it sought also to secure an initial, albeit limited, statutory ban on the use of monofilament nets. While this initiative failed, it may be noted that Government then moved swiftly to legislate its *1984 Inshore Fishing (Scotland) Act.* This Act was used to ban virtually all other forms of commercial fishing—by means of "Static Net Reserve" and "Fish Nursery Area" Prohibition Orders—from those coastal reaches where the major salmon netting interests operated. It also provided the powers whereby Scottish Secretary Rifkind, was enabled to ban carriage of monofilament nets and the use of gill nets in Scottish waters.

Perhaps the greatest value of the failed "Anglers' Charter" (*Thurso Bill*), was that it demonstrated what was *not* acceptable either to the dominant netsmen, or to DAFS/Government. Clearly both were adamant in their resolve to ensure *status quo* maintenance of maximum local autonomy, minimum state involvement, and unaltered dominance by the principal commercial interests over exploitation and management of the salmon resource.

In summary, viewed over this lengthy "preliminary" period, it is clear that Scottish netsmen secured extensive statutory support for increased protection of their fishings. It is equally clear their failures served both to clarify the relevant positions and responses of Government and Parliament, and to sound out the views and reactions of varied fishery interests and representative bodies. These failures, would seem to have provided the grounds for inducing Government to take varied public legislative initiatives where Private Bill efforts had failed. In other words, "failed", or "successful", all these initiatives from 1962 to 1985 were directed towards, and did achieve, a large number of specific goals. Although incessant complaints and outcries from netsmen suggested the opposite, it was indeed a period of considerable triumph for the interests of commercialism.

Given these primary considerations, it could be said that the form, structure and contents of a general Government Salmon Bill which would be acceptable to the majority of netsmen, and to a broad range of non-dominant fishery and other interests, had been evolved. Trial and error, and judicious sampling had been important preliminary procedures. The legislative proposal duly produced was, of course, the *1985 / '86 Salmon Bill.*

References

1. Calderwood, *The Salmon Rivers and Lochs of Scotland,* op.cit., p.4.
2. When asked by Anthony Netboy, what was the netsmen's contribution to "salmon conservation", Menzies replied, "Not a damn thing!" (Private communication with Netboy).
3. In January 1987, Lady Saltoun of Abernethy tabled a Parliamentary Question. She asked the cost to the taxpayer if Government were to supply "the facilities which DAFS Freshwater Fisheries Laboratory, Faskally, at present received from certain private netting interests". She received an interesting Written Reply. Lord Glenarthur, Minister of State at the Scottish Office, stated that while detailed information on costs was not available, they "would be likely to involve additional finance and manpower". In conclusion, he added that "The present arrangements are felt to operate satisfactorily". (See, *Parliamentary Debates: House of Lords,* [hereafter *Lords Debates*], 9 February, 1987, col.505)
4. For an interesting modern DAFS research study which demonstrates these points, see A.D. Hawkins, C.G. Urquart and W.M. Shearer, *The Coastal Movements of Returning Atlantic Salmon,* Department of Agriculture and

Fisheries for Scotland, Scottish Fisheries Research Report Number 15, (1979), pp.14. While this early experiment in sonar tagging provided scientists with useful information "on the movements of salmon on their return to coastal waters off the east of Scotland", it was also valuable to commercial netsmen—particularly to Joseph Johnston and Sons of Montrose, where the experiment was conducted. Not only was information on tidal movements of salmon approaching Johnston's barrage of foreshore stake and bag nets revealing; but also the fact that 50% (three of the six grilse tagged) were found repeatedly to have escaped the coastal nets by passing between loose leader nets and stakes, and by negotiating round widely extended cleeks (entry mouths to net traps) provided important information. This is said to have caused Johnston's henceforth to ensure that leaders are very tight, and cleek openings of minimum requisite spread.

5. See W. Earl Hodgson, *Salmon Fishing,* (London: A&C Black, 1927), 2nd reprint, Chapter VII.

6. Ibid., p.172. The first edition of Hodgson's book was published in 1906.

7. See, David Shaw, "Behind the Scenes", *Trout and Salmon,* (May 1986), p.49.

8. *Annual Report of the Fishery Board for Scotland,* (Edinburgh: HMSO, 1932), p.69

9. Ibid.

10. Ibid.

11. See *Report of the Proceedings of the First Annual General Meeting of the ASDFB,* 2 December, 1931, pp.6-12. Expressing a minority sentiment which has been oft-repeated, Mr. Robb, ASDFB member for the Forth District, speaking in support of legislative proposals advanced by Chief Inspector Menzies, "stated that there should be no hush-hush policy regarding matters vitally affecting the salmon interests, and he thought the proposals ... would be found to work out to the general advantage". (p.ll) For recent ASDFB posture on the vital Weekly Slap conservation measure (Government's 1987 proposal for an 18-hour increase in the Weekly Slap was rejected outright by the ASDFB Council), see separately circulated "Amendment to Item 5(a)" of the "Minutes of a Meeting of Council, held on 23 January, 1987", *Association of Scottish District Salmon Fishery Boards,* Edinburgh. Despite the resistance of the ASDFB and netsmen, the Weekly Slap in 1988 was extended to 60 hours (or the equivalent of five tides).

12. In fact, the *Salmon and Freshwater Fisheries (Protection) (Scotland) Act, 1951,* contained only one provision which challenged the dominant commercial interests. Under Section 13(3) of the 1951 Act the Weekly Close Time was increased from 36 to 42 hours. This negligible increase (one half of a tide) was strongly resisted by the netsmen. A provision for a Statutory Review of the Weekly Slap in 1958 was written into the Act. When the Review was duly conducted netsmen again expressed their opposition to the 1951 increase and called for the 36 hours Weekly Slap to be re-introduced. The 42 hour Slap, however, remained in force.

13. D.W. Lawrence, *The Solway: Memorandum to Lord Hunter's Committee,* (Supplement to the Memorandum from the Nith Fishings Improvement Association, dated 24 October,1962.)

14. Ibid.

15. Ibid.
16. See *Fisheries Bill (1980),* Part V (Miscellaneous) Clause 32. This Clause, provides that Section 5(3) of the *Fishery Board (Scotland) Act of 1882,* (duty of the Secretary of State to make an Annual Report regarding fisheries) shall cease to have effect.
17. The seven persons were: the Duke of Devonshire, owner of important net and rod fishings on the Irish Cork Blackwater; Marquess of Lansdowne, prominent shareholder and Chairman of the Tay Salmon Fisheries Company, and a Tay rod fishery owner; Sir Edward Randal Chadwyck-Healey (deceased), then President of S&TA; Sir Richard Levinge (deceased), then Chairman of S&TA; Peter Liddell (deceased), a leading English salmon conservationist whose principal written contribution was to be his immensely informative 1971 *Report to Bord Failte Eirann on the Salmon Rivers of Eire;* Rear-Admiral The Earl Cairns, prominent shareholder in Tay Salmon Fisheries; and G.C.W. Radcliffe, solicitor to the Fishmongers' Company, and one of five Fishmongers nominees on the S&TA Council. See *Memorandum of Association of the Atlantic Salmon Research Trust Limited,* 10 April, 1967, p.5.
18. See *ibid.*, pp.l-2. All seven "Objects" specified relate exclusively to matters of scientific research.
19. See separate annual "Accounts" of the *Atlantic Salmon Trust Limited,* "Income and Expenditure Accounts", from the year ending 30 June, 1982, to the year ending 30 June, 1986.
20. See *The Field,* letters to the editor, in issues from 27 September, to 19 December, 1973; and leaders, articles and letters in issues from 9 January to 3 April, 1975. See also, David Shaw, "Net Realities" Series, *Trout and Salmon,* (January-May 1980), and accompanying letters columns.
21. See *Salmon and Freshwater Fisheries in Scotland: Proposals for Action Arising from the Hunter Report,* Cmnd. 4821, (Edinburgh: HMSO, November 1971).
22. See *Scottish Salmon and Trout Fisheries: Second Report By the Committee Appointed by the Secretary of State for Scotland,* Cmnd. 2691, (Edinburgh: HMSO, August 1965).
23. Association of Scottish District Salmon Fishery Boards (ASDFB), *Salmon Fisheries of Scotland,* (Farnham: Fishing News Books, 1977), p.34. See also, *Scottish Salmon and Trout Fisheries: First Report by the Committee Appointed by the Secretary of State for Scotland,* Cmnd. 2096, (Edinburgh: HMSO, July 1963). An initial ban on drift-netting for salmon in Scottish waters was secured on 15 September, 1962, by a Statutory Order made under the UK *Sea Fish Industry Acts, 1959 and 1962.* Under the terms of the same Order, "The landing of salmon taken by drift-net was also prohibited , subject to a proviso in favour of those taken off England and Wales under licence issued by River Board [now Water Authority] or the Minister of Agriculture, Fisheries and Food". (*Hunter Report: First Report,* p.26, para. 75).
24. See ibid.
25. Key provisions in the 1984 *Inshore Fisheries Act* gave the Scottish Secretary exclusive—and virtually arbitrary—powers to declare certain areas extend-

ing six miles from the coast, as "static net reserves" and "fish nursery areas". The stated object of the Act was to afford improved protection for *marine* fish stocks, by specific statutory restrictions and prohibitions. When in 1985, the Scottish Secretary (then Mr. Younger) exercised his powers under the Act, it was interesting to note where "full-year closure" prohibitions in coastal areas were to come into operation. These areas were in the vicinity of the Thurso, Tay, Tweed, in the Moray Firth basin, on the Angus (North and South) Esks foreshore. They coincided almost exactly with coastal sections where important salmon fishings (which were not included in the ban) were operating. (See "Proposals for Static Gear Reserves", *Scottish Office News Release,* 5 February, 1985, with appended Annex A, and Map showing areas of proposed prohibitions).

26. The international treaty organisations which during the 1960s and 1970s were concerned most closely with control and catch-monitoring of UK (principally Scottish) produced salmon, were the North-West Atlantic Fisheries Commission, the *North-East Atlantic Fisheries Commission,* and the *International Council for Northwest Atlantic Fisheries.*

27. The *International Council for North Atlantic Fisheries* (ICNAF) was in 1984 succeeded by the *North Atlantic Salmon Conservation Organisation* (NASCO). While it is difficult to assess the direct effect of NASCO initiatives in securing catch quota agreements in the Greenland fishery; it is clear that NASCO provides an "informed climate of opinion" within which bi-lateral negotiations have been annually conducted.

28. See *Salmon and Freshwater Fisheries: Review of the present Law and Administration,* mimeo., DAFS, 28 December, 1979.

29. David Shaw, "Forthcoming Salmon Legislation: But What About the Angler and Salmo Salar?", (mimeo.), February, 1980.

30. *Salmon Fisheries (Protection) (Scotland) Bill, 1982.*

31. This specific intention was designed "to ban the use of monofilament gill-nets as *leaders* to bag-nets" and provided for a fine not exceeding £1500 for offenders. (See, "Scots Ban on Gill-Nets?", *Trout and Salmon,* (April, 1982), p.19.

32. See David Shaw, "More Protection for the Netsmen?", (unpublished article), January, 1985.

33. "Deveron's Day of Judgement", *Trout and Salmon,* (June 1983), p.13.

34. See "The Nets on the Deveron: Trout and Salmon's Observer [David Shaw] Reports on the Banff Hearing", *Trout and Salmon,* (August, 1983), pp.41-2.

35. See *Report of An Inquiry into Representations on the Petition of The Deveron Salmon Fishery Board for a Change in the Annual Close Time in the District,* mimeo., File No. FRC/1/38/2, (Edinburgh: DAFS, Chesser House, December 1984), pp.68.

36. See "No Change in Deveron Salmon Arrangements", *Scottish Office News Release,* No.1487/84, 27 December, 1984.

37. See David Shaw, "Netsmen Are Down, But Not Out", *Trout and Salmon,* (May 1985), pp.52-3.

38. See David Shaw, "Behind the Scenes", *Trout and Salmon,* (September, 1985), p.46.

39. Ibid.
40. Ibid.
41. Ibid.
42. Some put it more strongly. Lord Thurso referred to the Bill as the product of 25 years' work and deliberations by DAFS. (See *Lords Debates,* 14 January, 1986, col. 1003.) On the other hand, DAFS Assistant Secretary, Ian Whitelaw, viewed the Bill as simply incorporating "the main salmon issues of the day". (See *Record of Meeting Organised by the British Field Sports Society (BFSS) to Discuss the Salmon Bill Now Before the House of Lords,* mimeo., Edinburgh, 17 January, 1986, p.4.)

Chapter 3

THE LEGISLATIVE BATTLE COMMENCES

"[The Bill is] a very wee tim'rous beastie".

Lord Lansdowne (col.1030)*

"We are hammering away at problems and a management structure that is out of date. [There is need for] a complete change of attitude in relation to those with interests [in wild salmon]. Everyone has to appreciate that changed importance from the point of view of the economy, from the point of view of justice, and above all from the point of view of the salmon itself".

Lord Ross of Marnock (col. 1048)

"...A disappointing 'half loaf of bread'".

Lord Tryon (col.1007)

"[The Bill is merely] a defence and entrenchment of the rights of proprietors ... with little to say about meaningful long-term conservation".

Lord Carmichael of Kelvingrove (col. 996)

The Salmon Bill Emerges

The intention of Government to introduce a principal Salmon Bill was announced in the Queen's Speech of 6 November, 1985. The stated aims of the Bill were "to modify and extend the management structure of [Scottish] salmon fisheries, including further measures to combat illegal fishing throughout Great Britain".[1] Elaborating on these modest aims, a Scottish Office briefing document emphasised that:

"There has been general acceptance of the need not only to revise Scot-

* This and following introductory citations are taken from *House of Lords: Parliamentary Debates,* Vol.469, No.26, 14 January, 1986.

tish salmon laws to take account of changing circumstances, but on a Great Britain basis to meet concerns about the general state of salmon stocks and the extent of illegal fishing.

"The legislation would provide for a more democratic and flexible aproach to the composition and operation of District Salmon Fishery Boards. ...There will also be modernisation of the procedure for regulating aspects of salmon fisheries such as close times, essentially by shifting the prescription of detailed arrangements from primary to subordinate legislation.

"To strengthen anti-poaching measures, the legislation will introduce for Scotland, England and Wales new offences and related provisions dealing with illegally taken salmon to block loopholes in the existing legislation. For Scotland, there would in addition be provision for the introduction of a scheme of licensing salmon dealers."[2]

If the Bill followed the lines indicated in these initial statements, few surprises could be expected. When on 12 December the Bill was introduced into the House of Lords, (First Reading involves only "reading of the title of the Bill", followed by brief comment) perusal of its main provisions made clear that it was indeed a modest measure. *The Bill was empty of provision for fundamental change.*

The main objectives of the Bill were to consolidate Scottish salmon legislation stretching back 300 years; to make provision for improved operation of the archaic District Fishery Boards; and to tighten controls on illegal fishing and poaching. Absent were any specific provisions to meet "conservation, equity and economy" requirements,regarded as basic in new legislation. Insofar as there was any promise for attaining these, it was to be found in provisions which called for: new powers for the Scottish Secretary; the possibility of strengthened representation of riparian interests through election of Board Chairmen within the Scottish District Salmon Fishery Boards; and improved controls on illegal fishing (in the sea) and poaching (in estuaries and rivers).

The question was: how would their Lordships respond to the Bill at Second Reading? Would they reject it outright? On the other hand, might they seek merely to defer consideration and send it back to the departmental civil servants for further consultations, fundamental re-drafting and re-introduction at a later stage, perhaps a year or two in the future? At the other extreme, was it possible they might accept the Bill *in toto* as presented to the House? Might they agree to accept the Bill but seek varying amendments to "improve" it?

Seldom was legislation which would have a direct effect on the jobs of thousands of people, along with a bearing on possibly the very survival of the resource upon which all were dependent, to be decided by so few. At no stage in the long parliamentary consideration of the Bill did the number of legislators in attendance exceed sixty. The usual number was about fifteen. Actual participants in the Debates never exceeded twenty. At Third Reading, when the final Lords vote was taken 15 Peers were in attendance; in the Commons 13. Yet the fact that the number of legislative participants was so few, and the Bill relatively non-political, meant that there was a rare if not unprecedented opportunity for this small body of legislators to take decisive and independent action.

Second Reading following introduction of any Bill is normally its most vulnerable stage. If the Bill requires substantial amendment, or is to be rejected outright, this—the temper of the House—will be known by the end of Second Reading. It is at this point that Government, its departmental civil servants and the interests which have promoted the Bill, are on tenterhooks. The question foremost in their minds is: "Will Parliament buy it?"

From Government's viewpoint, the Bill seemed safe. It represented a consensus of minimum demands by dominant salmon interests, a logical culmination of measures which had preceded it. Of course, it was always possible that unforeseen opposition might surface. Still, there was hardly time for Peers to acquire an informed and critical understanding of the Bill—Second Reading was set for 14 January, the very day of their return from Christmas Recess—let alone take soundings and receive advice from various interested bodies and individuals. It was unlikely, therefore, that any registered opposition would be sufficiently organised, coherent and intense to challenge the basic objects of the Bill and hence threaten its life. Yet certainty was far from assured. Briefly, if participant Peers * did not like the Bill it was possible it might not survive Second Reading.

'Lairds' Bill' Preliminaries

And so the great day, 14 January, arrived. Taking my place in the near-vacant House of Lords Press Gallery at 5:20 p.m. I discovered that debate on the Salmon Bill already was underway. I took a quick look down and round the Chamber. There were a few familiar faces. Lord Thurso, his striking matinee-idol features in sharp profile, was

* For listing of principal Lords participating in the Salmon Bill Debates, and their salmon interests, see *Table 1,* below, pp.49-50. See also, *Table 1(a)* and *Table 1(b),* p.50-51, for breakdowns of "Group Salmon Interests" and political affiliations of principal participant Lords.

in his customary place at the far (Liberal) end of the Opposition front bench. A good distance from Lord Thurso, at the centre of the Opposition front bench, was Willie (Lord) Ross. Sandy-haired with bristling moustache, be-spectacled gaze intent on the speaker—who happened to be the only other participant Labour Baron, Lord Carmichael—it was apparent that this no-nonsense former Ayr schoolmaster and Scottish Secretary was once again preparing for "salmon battle" at the normal odds of about 10:1. Sprinkled around the rest of the Opposition and Cross-benches (occupied by Independent or politically unaffiliated Lords) were a few more solitary Lords. I recognised none.

On the Government front bench was the small, neat, domed figure of the DAFS Minister, Lord Gray. Beside him, was the much larger and more ample figure of Kenneth (Lord) Cameron of Lochbroom, Lord Advocate for Scotland, and others. I had not seen Cameron since his rivetting performance as Counsel for rods/conservation objectors at the July 1983 Deveron Inquiry. That fine head of wavy black hair, though now salted with a little more grey, was still intact, as was the composed and dignified bearing I well remembered. Yet how different the venue. These genteel surroundings were in sharp contrast to the dour, gray, down-at-the-heels Banff County Hall building on the wild Moray coast of Northern Scotland where I had last seen him perform. Only a few months after the Deveron Inquiry he had been appointed Lord Advocate (Government's senior Scottish law officer). Had the Scottish (salmon) Establishment decided it would be better to have him as ally than opponent? It was sad to see him on the "other side": a most useful "weapon" for the established interests.

Amongst other persons on the slightly less vacant Government benches I recognised the tiny, skeletal figure of the 83 year-old Lord Home, former Prime Minister. Two benches above was Lord Lansdowne, his gleaming hearing trumpet tuned to the debate. High up, at the far end of the Government benches was Marcus (Lord) Kimball. The sleek, ruddy former British Field Sports Society (BFSS) Chairman was engaged in animated conversation with the BFSS President, Lord Margadale. Amongst the other 12 or so Lords present there were no faces I knew. By the end of October it would be different.

LORD GRAY OF CONTIN ... Government Leader on the Salmon Bill.

LORD ROSS OF MARNOCK ... Opposition Leader on the Salmon Bill.

TABLE 1

LORDS DEBATES ON THE SALMON BILL:
CAST OF CHARACTERS

1. *Lord Gray of Contin.* Conservative; Life Peer, 1983; Minister of State for Agriculture and Fisheries at the Scottish Office (DAFS); July 1983-September, 1986; no private salmon interests.
2. *Lord Carmichael of Kelvingrove.* Labour; Life Peer, 1983; no private salmon interests.
3. *Lord Ross of Marnock.* Labour; Life Peer, 1979; former Secretary of State for Scotland who in May 1965 received *The Second Report of the Committee on Scottish Salmon and Trout Fisheries* (the *Hunter Report*); no private salmon interests.
4. *The Viscount Thurso.* Liberal; owner of the River Thurso, Caithness, Northern Scotland; rod and net proprietor; long-time President of the Association of Scottish District Salmon Fishery Boards (ASDFB).
5. *Lord Biddulph.* Conservative; rod proprietor, Makerstoun Water, Tweed; Atlantic Salmon Trust, Council member.
6. *Lord Home of the Hirsel.* Conservative; owner of Birgham Water and with interests in other Tweed fishings; President of the Salmon and Trout Association, Fishmongers' Hall, London.
7. *Lord Tryon.* Independent; salmon angler; no salmon proprietorial interests.
8. *Lord Margadale.* Family name Morrison; Conservative; hereditary title created 1965; owner of salmon fishings on the Isle of Islay, Inner Hebrides; President of the British Field Sports Society (BFSS). Listed as No.143 of UK's 200 richest citizens, with estimated wealth of £45m. Father of Charles Morrison, MP for Devizes, who is a former Prime Warden, The Fishmongers' Company, London, current President of the National Anglers' Council and Fishmongers' appointee to the Council of Salmon and Trout Association. Father also of Hon. Peter Morrison, MP for the City of Chester.
9. *Lord Kimball.* Conservative; Life Peer, 1985; owner of net and rod salmon fishings on the River Naver, Sutherland, Northern Scotland; former Chairman, BFSS.
10. *Lady Saltoun of Abernethy.* Independent; owner of net and rod fishings, Cairnbulg, near Fraserburgh, North-east Aberdeenshire. Wife of Upper Dee (rod) proprietor, Captain Ramsay of Mar.
11. *The Viscount Trenchard.* No stated political affiliation; salmon angler; fished over 50 UK rivers in 50 years; particular knowledge of the River Tamar, South Devon/Cornwall.
12. *Lord Gibson-Watt.* Conservative; Life Peer, 1979; Upper Wye rod fishery owner.
13. *Lord Moran.* Independent; Upper Wye rod fishery owner; Atlantic Salmon Trust, Management Committee member; spokesman for UK salmon interests at various international salmon fishery conferences.
14. *The Earl Haig.* Conservative; owner of Bemersyde rod fishery, Tweed; also "derives benefit from salmon nets on Tweed".

15. *The Viscount Ridley.* Conservative; owner of small rod-fishing beat on Upper Tay.
16. *The Marquess of Lansdowne.* Conservative; Chairman and shareholder in the Tay Salmon Fisheries Co. Ltd.; former Prime Warden of the Fishmongers' Company; Chairman (during the period of the Salmon Bill) of the Tay District Salmon Fishery Board; owner of Meikleour rod-fishery, and long-term lessee (from TSF) of Islamouth Pool, once reputed to be the single most prolific angling pool in the Atlantic salmon world.
17. *Lord Burton.* Conservative; owner of Dochfour rod fishery, River Ness, Inverness; director and shareholder in Moray Firth Salmon (Net) Fishing Company.
18. *Lord Clinton.* Conservative; riparian owner, with substantial holdings on the North Devon, River Torridge.
19. *The Viscount Massereene and Ferrard.* Conservative; owner of net and rod fishings, Isle of Mull, Inner Hebrides; "landlord of a very large [Mull] salmon farm".

Other Participants (Most being anglers or with rod fishery interests)

Duke of Atholl (Cons)
Lord Balfour of Inchrye (Cons)
Lord Campbell of Croy (Cons)
Lord Chelwood (Cons)
Lord Gisborough (Cons)
Lord John-Mackie (Lab)
Lord Mackie of Benshie (Lib)
Earl of Onslow (Cons)
Earl of Perth (Ind)
Lord Denning (Ind)

Government Officers

Lord Belstead, MAFF Minister for Environment, Countryside and Water.
Lord Cameron of Lochbroom, Lord Advocate for Scotland.

TABLE 1 (a)

PRINCIPAL PARTICIPANT LORDS:
POLITICAL AFFILIATION

National Area of Salmon Interest	**Cons**	**Lab**	**Lib**	**Ind**	**NPA**	**Totals**
Scotland	10	2	1	1	-	14
England	-	-	-	1	2	3
Wales	1	-	-	1	-	2
TOTALS	11	2	1	3	2	19

* *Political party affiliation:* Cons = Conservative; Lab = Labour; Lib = Liberal; Ind = Independent; NPA = No stated political affiliation.

TABLE 1 (b)

PRINCIPAL PARTICIPANT LORDS:
SALMON INTERESTS AND POLITICAL AFFILIATION

Group	**Scotland**	**England**	**Wales**	**Total**
Nets Only	-	-	-	-
Rods Only	*3 (Cons)	*1 (Ind)	1 (Ind)	
		*1 (NPA)	1 (Cons)	7
Nets and Rods	6 (Cons)	-	-	
	*1 (Lib)			
	1 (Ind)			8
No Private Salmon Interests	1 (Cons)	1 (NPA)	-	
	*2 (Lab)			4
TOTALS	14	3	2	19

A journalist from one of the Scottish papers leaned across to exchange greetings. He gestured towards the Floor of the Chamber: "Lairds' Bill"!

"Pardon?" I was still tallying a head count.

"A wee Lairds' Bill", he repeated. "One or two of these every Session. Deer, forestry, salmon. Always the same. And usually the same faces—though I see a few new ones here tonight".

"Let's hope this one's a bit more than that!" I replied.

A wry smile creased his face. "This time it's a Government Bill. Not Private. Nice work! New *public* statutory force, *state* authority to bolster and perhaps enhance *private* interests of these very few and very privileged Lairds and their colleagues. And by the by, very few of the really big boys are present"!* He noted my reserve. "To this lot—on these matters—it's as though the 1832 (electoral) reforms never

* For listing of *Absent Lords with Substantial Scottish Salmon Interests: Ranking by Estimated Wealth,* see *Table 2,* below, pp.52-3. See *Tables 2(a)* and *2(b)*, p.54, for "Unlisted Wealthy Proprietors", and "Listed Wealthy Proprietors" of Scottish salmon fishings.

existed! Feudal business-as-usual in the name of 20th century democracy! ABCs of political reality to us Highland Scots!"

In a few jolting, pithy phrases this Scottish journalist had summed up my own fears. Still, it was early days. I shrugged. "Time will tell".

I now returned my attention to the Floor of the House. Lord Gray was at the Dispatch Box. He started to set out the main objectives of the Bill. Serious debate was about to begin.

TABLE 2

ABSENT SALMON LORDS WITH SUBSTANTIAL SCOTTISH SALMON INTERESTS: RANKING BY ESTIMATED WEALTH AMONGST THE 200 MOST WEALTHY UK CITIZENS*

Rank	Salmon Interests	Estimated Wealth
1. Her Majesty the Queen	Balmoral Estates; Aberdeenshire Dee rod fishings	£5200m.
7. Lord Vestey (Cons)	Sutherland rod and net fishings; including Rivers Kirkaig and Inver	£1200m.
20. Duke of Buccleuch and Queensberry (Cons)	Drumlanrig and Buccleuch Estates; including River Nith and Border Esk fishings.	£300m.
79. Duke of Argyll (Cons)	Argyllshire rod and net fishings; including River Aray and Loch Fyne	£87m.
92. Duke of Roxburghe (Cons)	Roxburghe Estates; Tweed rod and net interests	£70m.
- Duke of Norfolk (Cons)	River Nith; haaf netting interests	£70m.
100. Earl Cawdor (Cons)	Moray Firth and River Nairn interests	£57m.

* *Sources:* Richard Savill, "League of Rich Dominated by Self-Made Men", *Daily Telegraph,* 24 February, 1988; and Philip Beresford and Patrick Masters, "Britain's Rich: The Top 200", *Sunday Times Magazine,* 30 July, 1989.

110. Lord Lovat (Cons)	Beauly, Cromarty and Moray Firth rod and net fishing interests; director and shareholder in Moray Firth Salmon (Net) Fishing Co.; shareholder in Scotsal (wholesale salmon marketing company)	£55m.
143. Earl of Stair (NPA)	Solway net and rod interests; including rivers Luce & Bladnoch	£54m
158. Duke of Wellington (Cons)	River Stinchar, Ayrshire; net and rod fishings; including holding retained in the name of his son Lord Richard Wellesley	£40m.
178. Earl of Seafield (Cons)	Spey and Moray Firth; rod and net fishings	£35m.
188. Countess of Sutherland (Cons)	Sutherland Estates; rod and net fishings; including River Fleet and far North-East £30m.Scotland coastal areas.	£30m.

TABLE 2 (a)

ABSENT SALMON LORDS: UNLISTED WEALTHY PROPRIETORS OF SCOTTISH SALMON FISHINGS

	Salmon Fishery Interests
Lord Granville (Cons)	North Uist, Outer Hebrides rod and commercial fishings
Lord Leven and Melville	Moray Firth, and River Findhorn (NPA)fishings; director and shareholder in Findhorn Salmon (Net) Fisheries Ltd; shareholder in Scotsal
Lord Mansfield (Cons)	River Tay; rod and net fishings; including holdings retained by Trustees of Viscount Stormont (son of Lord Mansfield)
Lord Moray (NPA)	Rivers Findhorn and Forth/Teith fishings

TABLE 2 (b)

PARTICIPANT SALMON LORDS: LISTED WEALTHY PROPRIETORS OF SCOTTISH SALMON FISHINGS *

	Salmon Fishery Interests	Estimated Wealth
47. Duke of Atholl (Cons)	Upper Tay; rod fishings	£143m.
143. Lord Margadale (Cons)	Isle of Islay; rod & net estate fishings	£45m.
- Marquess of Lansdowne (Cons)	River Tay; rod and net fishing interests	£18m.

* *Sources:* See Sources reference for *Table 2* above.

Lords Second Reading: Main Objectives Examined

Administrative "Modernisation"

The first objective of the Bill, declared Lord Gray, was "to modernise and improve administrative arrangements". He stated that

> "At present the management of salmon stocks is the responsibility of District Boards which are comprised of an equal number of Upper (i.e. rod) proprietors, and Lower (i.e. netting) proprietors, with the person owning the fishery with the highest rateable value as Chairman. There is provision in the Statutes for 108 Salmon Fishery Districts, but Boards are currently in existence in only about half of them including all the main rivers. We are proposing to modernise, and in a sense democratise, the arrangments for administration by providing for the *Chairman to be elected* and for the *co-option of representatives of anglers and tenant netsmen,* who have a significant interest in the proper management of the fisheries. Because of their substantial financial investment, we felt it necessary to provide for a constitution which gives proprietors a majority of the votes and in some matters sole voting rights. The existing arrangements for the election of proprietors by weighted voting have been retained and updated. The Bill also provides for the *Amalgamation of Districts,* where the proprietors consider this necessary to create a more viable management unit".[3]

1. Elected Board Chairmen Participant Lords expressed particular interest in the Bill's provision for *elected* District Board chairmen. Lord Thurso, while welcoming "the elective principle", strongly questioned why the Board Chairman should be elected by a vote of *all* District proprietors. "Would it not be better to do this *after* the representatives of qualified proprietors had been chosen?" (col. 1001) The choice would then be from one of the six (3 Upper river; 3 Lower river) Board members elected. In many Districts the Lower, or netting interests, control one or more Upper seats on the local Board through ownership of rod fishings.

Lord Ridley, owner of an Upper Tay angling beat, was delighted with the prospect of an elected Board chairman. This would be "a real step forward" (col.1029), he said, "because the boards must be seen to be acting in the interests of the whole river, and not just a minority of its users".[4] Lord Lansdowne, Chairman of TSF and the Tay Board agreed. "I do not think that the way I became a chairman is the best way. The right way is by election". (col. 1032) Lord Burton, owner of the Dochfour rod fishery on the River Ness and a director and shareholder in the dominant Moray netting concern, the Moray Firth

Salmon Fishery Districts and Boards* in Scotland

1. Add *
2. Ailort
3. Aline
4. Alness *
5. Annan *
6. Applecross
7. Arnisdale
8. Awe *
9. Ayr *
10. Baa and Coladoir
11. Badachro and Kerry
12. Beauly
13. Berriedale
14. Bervie *
15. Bladnoch
16. Broom *
17. Brora *
18. Carradale
19. Carron (Wester Ross)
20. Clayburn (Harris) *
21. Clyde and Leven
22. Conon *
23. Cree *
24. Creed (Lewis)
25. Creran
26. Croe and Shiel (Wester Ross)
27. Dee (Aberdeenshire) *
28. Dee (Solway) *
29. Deveron *
30. Don *
31. Doon *
32. Drummachloy or Glenmore
33. Dunbeath *
34. Eachaig
35. North Esk *
36. South Esk *
37. Ewe *
38. Fincastle (Harris) *
39. Findhorn *
40. Fleet (Solway)
41. Fleet (Sutherland)
42. Forss *
43. Forth and Teith *
44. Fyne, Shira and Aray
45. Girvan *
46. Glenelg
47. Gour
48. Greiss, Laxdale and Tong
49. Grudie or Dionard
50. Gruinard and Little Gruinard
51. Halladale *
52. Helmsdale *
53. Hope and Polla *
54. Howmore
55. Inchard
56. Inner
57. Inver
58. Iorsa
59. Irvine and Garnock
60. Kannaird
61. Kilchoan or Inverie
62. Kinloch (Kyle of Tongue) *
63. Kirkaig and Polly
64. Kishorn
65. Kyle of Sutherland (including Carron, Cassley, Oykel and Shin) *
66. Laggan and Sorn (Islay)
67. Laxford
68. Leven
69. Little Loch Broom
70. Loch Long
71. Loch Roag (Lewis) *
72. Lochy *
73. Lossie
74. Luce *
75. Lussa
76. Moidart
77. Morar
78. Mullanageren, Horasary and Lochnaciste (North Uist)
79. Nairn *
80. Naver and Borgie *
81. Nell, Feochan and Euchar
82. Ness (including Moriston, Garry and Oich) *
83. Nith *
84. Ormsary, Loch Head and Stornoway (Mull of Kintyre)
85. Part of Lochy
86. Pennygowan or Glenforsa and Aros
87. Resort
88. Ruel
89. Sanda
90. Scaddle
91. Shiel (Argyll)
92. Sligachan, Broadford and Portree (Skye)
93. Snizort, Otley, Oze and Drynoch (Skye)
94. Spey *
95. Stinchar *
96. Strathy
97. Sunart
98. Tay *
99. Thurso *
100. Torridon, Balgay and Shieldaig
101. Tweed * (Special Area: administered by Tweed Commissioners)
102. Ugie *
103. Ullapool *
104. Urr
105. Wick *
106. Ythan *

* Denotes Salmon Fishery Districts with constituted *District Salmon Fishery Boards*—48 (including Tweed Special Area).

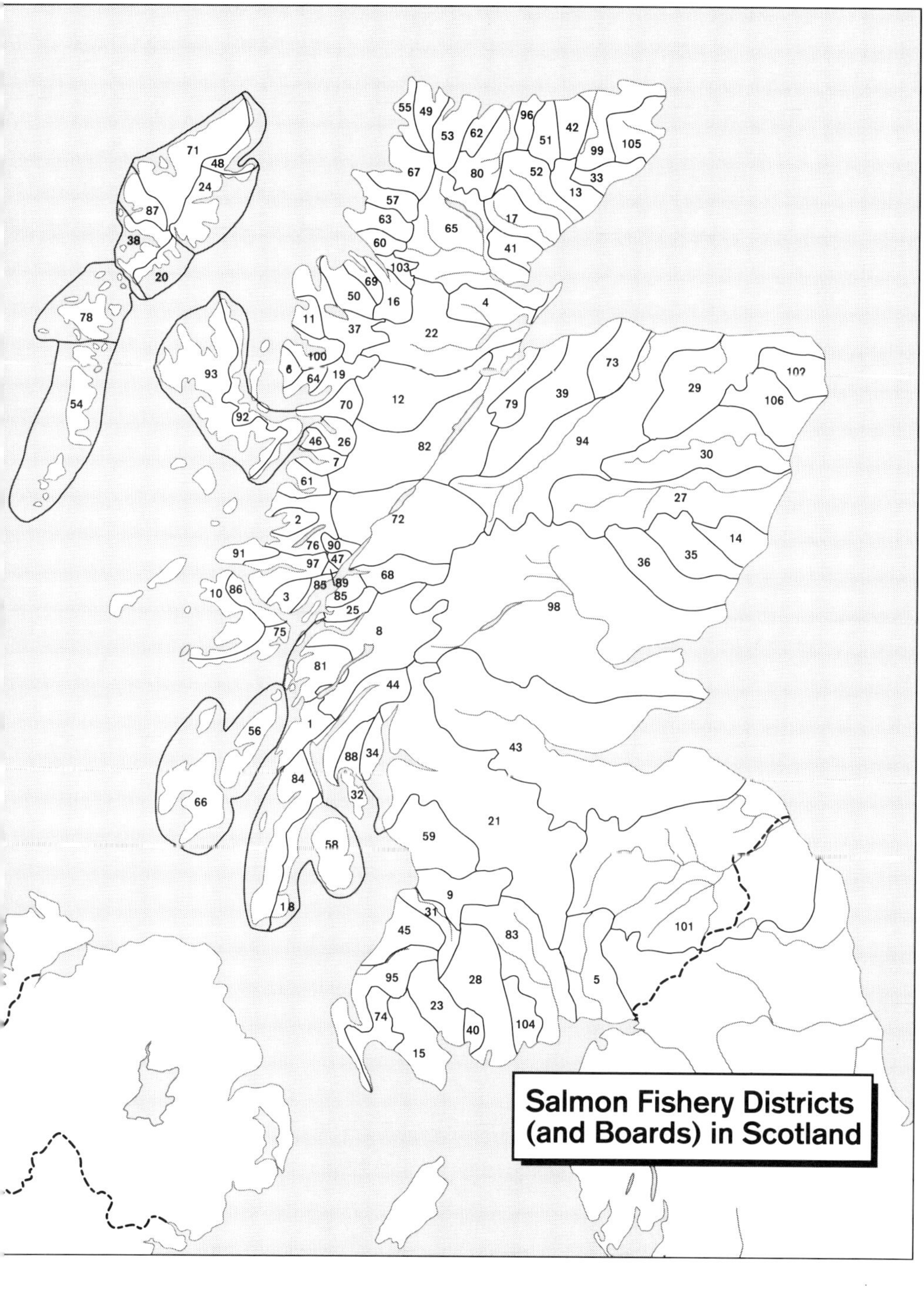

Salmon Fishery Districts (and Boards) in Scotland

Salmon Fishing Co., stated that one of the few points in the Bill which met with general approval was that which provided for an elected Board chairman.

2. Tenant Co-Option The co-option of tenant anglers and netsmen onto District Boards was regarded by many as a sensitive issue. In fact, there was a good deal of support for the concept. Some Lords felt Government should have gone much further. Lord Thurso maintained that tenant anglers and netsmen should be elected, not co-opted. He volunteered to "run an experiment on the [River] Thurso ... to demonstrate that this is a method which is feasible to use". (col. 1001) This offer was a little puzzling. Most Lords were aware that the Thurso is a rather special case. As owner of the river he is the sole qualified proprietor and member of the Thurso Board. Lord Lansdowne also expressed disquiet. While happy to see co-optees coming onto the Boards, he was satisfied neither with "the way they are to come on [by co-option]" (col. 1032); nor once they were on the Boards, why they should not have "full voting rights ... the same as every other member". Lord Carmichael, one of two Labour Peers to speak on the Bill, stated that he thought the co-option provision very limited. The persons co-opted would be from a "very limited group, and on the decision of the District Fishery Board". (col. 997-998).

Lord Burton was the only participant to express serious reservations about the wisdom of Government deviating from the existing provisions for Board membership. If co option was compulsory, he pointed out, it could lead to netsmen of dubious credentials securing membership. As for tenant rods, since many of them had "little idea of what goes on" except for the few weeks of the year when they are fishing, the value of their contribution as Board members was open to question.

3. Amalgamated Boards

The final principal aim in Lord Gray's first objective, "provision for amalgamation of Fishery Districts", was the subject of much lively comment. All participants were aware that it related to a vital requirement: to provide for a complete and fully operative system of local fishery management throughout Scotland. With less than one-half (50 of 108) of Scotland's Salmon Fishery Districts as defined by the *1862-'68 Salmon Acts* having operative District Boards, there had long been problems, some very serious. In the absence of Boards in many West, North-West and North coast districts, in-river protection and management often posed difficulties. But of far greater concern to proprietors in most neighbouring Fishery Districts *with* operative Boards, for the maintenance of which proprietors often paid sizeable sums, the absence of coastal protection meant that local illegal netting led to alleged large catches from salmon heading for these (protected) home rivers. Furthermore, with no local Boards, and hence no local bailiffs and enforcement presence, there was no one to

INTERCEPTORY BARRICADES ... Solway Stake Nets—on the ebbing tide;

AT LOW TIDE ... Homing salmon heading for "top pocket" (Annan, Border Esk and Eden) Solway rivers, face over 100 similar barricades—and much more.

keep an eye on the operations, particularly of legal *coastal netsmen.* Those who paid to maintain neighbouring Boards were particularly sensitive because these netsmen paid "nothing to those Fishery Boards responsible for the maintenance of that stock which they freely harvest. And, of course, like all netsmen, [unlike angling proprietors] they pay no rates on their fishings to the [local District] Council".[5]

In an effort to meet an all-Scotland Salmon Fishery management requirement, the *Hunter Report* (1965) called for creation of 13 Area Boards which would incorporate and replace the 108 Salmon Fishery Districts.[6] No action followed. The issue was again raised in Government's *1971 White Paper.* This time 14 Area Boards were suggested.[7] Again no action. Thus the "District amalgamation" provisions in the 1986 Salmon Bill were the first indications of serious Government commitment. The problem was, and always had been, money! Supporters of Amalgamation contended that at least some state funding was needed to bring Amalgamated Boards into existence, and to assist in their maintenance during the initial years of operation. There also was the problem of securing the necessary statutory powers to ensure that Amalgamated Boards could be brought into existence. Salmon proprietors repeatedly baulked at statutory powers to effect *mandatory* creation of Amalgamated Boards.

The answer Government provided in the Salmon Bill was: if proprietors in a particular area (comprising two or more existing Fishery Districts) wanted to create an Amalgamated Board, legislation would be available to do this. However, as many proprietors remained unhappy about mandatory provisions, Government proposed that amalgamation could only be secured through *voluntary* agreement. As for funding: since Amalgamated Boards would be created solely by a *voluntary* arrangement amongst private proprietors concerned, it would be for them to provide the necessary finance. Lord Gray pointed out that "it would not be appropriate for public funds to be diverted" (col. 1051) to support such private voluntary ventures. Government, therefore, would provide no financial backing.

Lord Thurso, long troubled by illegal fishing in Fishery Districts close to his home river, and an ardent advocate of Amalgamation, was the first to voice loud criticisms. While acknowledging it would be a step forward in legislative provision for Board re-structuring, he asked "Where has the Noble Lord [Lord Gray] shown us the incentive? ...From where is the money to make it work to come?" (col. 1000). Referring to the *1971 White Paper,* he pointed to proposals which called for Exchequer grants to be made available to Boards to

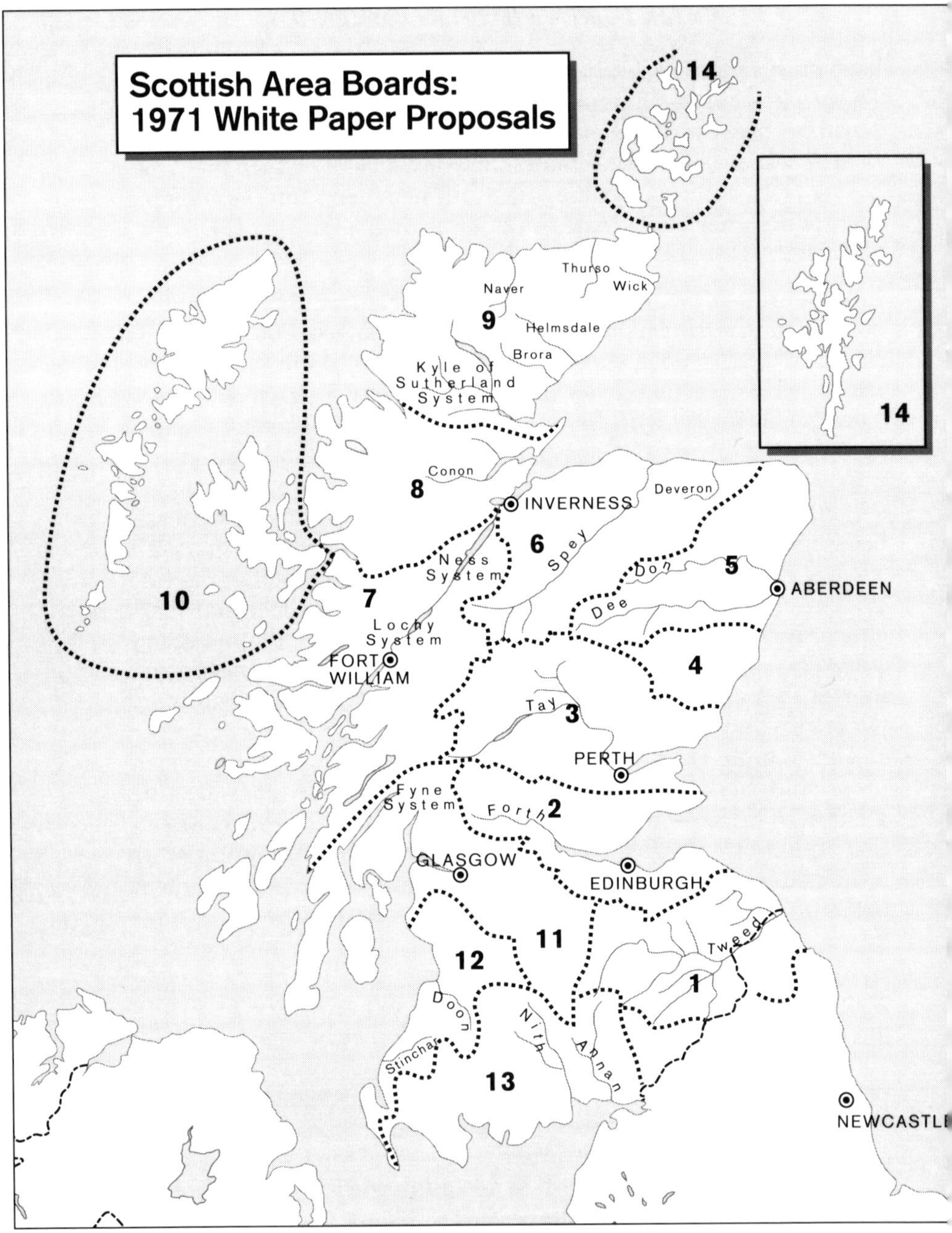

Scottish Area Boards:
1971 White Paper Proposals
14
14
Thurso
Wick
Naver
9
Helmsdale
Brora
Kyle of
Sutherland
System
Conon
8
INVERNESS
Deveron
6
Spey
Ness
System
Don
5
ABERDEEN
10
7
Dee
Lochy
System
FORT
WILLIAM
4
Tay
3
PERTH
Fyne
System
Forth
2
GLASGOW
EDINBURGH
11
12
Tweed
1
Doon
Nith
Annan
Stinchar
13
NEWCASTLE

help get them started. In terms of 1986 value, the amount suggested was about £1.29m. "Why is nothing available today?" Over £8m. of European Economic Community (EEC) money was available for agriculture and fisheries development. Why was some of this money not made available for development of salmon fishery infrastructure? The Boards' Amalgamation "enabling powers" were all very good, but what use would these be without at least some Government financial support?

Lord Thurso's views were strongly supported by Lord Lansdowne. Although conceding that inadequate finance was not a great problem in his own (Tay Board) area, it was a serious difficulty "in a great many parts of Scotland". (col. 1031) Lord Burton, having backed with equal vigour the requirement for an effective new Fishery Boards structure for all of Scotland, stressed "how absolutely vital" Government financial support was if this objective was to be secured. (col. 1036). Lords Massereene and Ferrard, Ross and Trenchard also maintained that quite apart from any new Amalagamated Boards which might be created, existing Boards had long needed much greater financial provision if they were effectively to perform increasingly costly functions—particularly bailiffing and protection.

JUVENILE FISHERY ... De-forestation damage reduces productive capacity of this South Esk spawning burn and its juvenile fishery.

4. District Boards: Greater Powers? While these specified points drew considerable comment from participants, it became apparent that there was a more basic issue of local fishery reform which concerned their Lordships. Whether or not Amalgamated Boards should be created, they stressed that Fishery Boards, whatever their future structure and composition, must have statutory powers over a much greater range of functions. As Lord Haig put it: "River Authorities should have powers over the construction of fish passes and of lade screens leading to fish farms, and powers over water abstraction and over the removal of gravel, as well as over all land and forestry developments which affect the river. River Boards should also have the right to sell forfeited fish." (col. 1026)

JUVENILE FISHERY ... Signs of health—one cast, two salmon parr on the upper Deveron.

Powers of District Boards, stated Lord Burton and others, should also extend to controlling the introduction of alien fish and species, the creation of fish farms—both of which raised the spectre of introduced disease, quite apart from the threat to native stocks posed by alien competitors.

Last, the emotive issue of low-water (drought) controls on fishing was raised. *Many Lords were adamant that local Boards, or if necessary the Secretary of State, must have powers to restrict estuary netting during periods of drought or extended low-water.* Rods too should be restricted during low-water—perhaps to fly-fishing only. Only Lord Lansdowne expressed a contrary view. During such periods, "nets are not always anything like as effective as one might imagine", he declared. In summarising, Lord Moran stated that he deeply regretted the omission of greater powers for Fishery Boards. Without them, Boards would be prevented from taking "prompt and effective action to conserve stocks in the light of local circumstances". (col. 1021)

'Flexible' Salmon Fishery Regulation

Moving to Lord Gray's second main objective in the Bill which sought "to introduce a greater degree of flexibility into the arrangements for salmon fishing", the DAFS Minister stated: "It is proposed that certain changes which at present require primary legislation may in future be effected by *statutory instrument,* subject to parliamentary approval where appropriate. This will allow proprietors and the Secretary of State to react more quickly to changing circumstances." (col. 992; Italics added).

Owners of Scottish salmon fishings had long sought legislation to deal directly with vital local matters such as problems of entry, passage and exploitation of salmon in rivers, estuaries and coastal waters of their Districts. It was, however, the Scottish Secretary who retained these powers—limited in extent as they were. More important, from the owners' viewpoint, there was no provision in the existing Salmon Acts which might permit the Scottish Secretary, on application from a local Fishery Board (or in the absence of a Board the proprietors concerned), to exercise his powers in a *specific* Fishery District. Any change in legislation—for instance, in the length of the Weekly or Annual Close Times—must apply to *all* Scottish Fishery Districts.

Limited Provisions It was hoped that the new Bill would change all this. It didn't. The "flexibility" introduced was minimal. There was only one provision which offered the prospect of "flexible response" to *local* circumstances. This concerned a minor—though not insignificant—provision which would enable the Scottish Secretary to specify for a particular Fishery District, or part(s) of the District, by Statutory Order, "the meshes, materials and dimensions of nets used in fishing for or taking salmon". (See *Clause 3*,(6), exercised in conjunction with *Clause 3*, (2) (d).)

Insofar as some measure of "flexibility" was to be introduced into the *general* powers of the Scottish Secretary, this was to be a loosening of "consultation provisions", as related to *Clause 3*. A new provision stated that he need only "consult such persons as he considers appropriate", thus releasing him from any specific obligation to consult solely with claimant District Boards, salmon fishery proprietors, or their representative bodies, normally the ASDFB. The implication of these new provisions was that *other* concerned elements—including tourism, angling, local government, conservation interests and bodies—might have *equal rights* to consultation. It would no longer be a totally "closed shop". The key provision to which these new powers of consultation were to apply was the *National* Weekly Close Time (Weekly Slap). Effectively, the provision in the Bill (*Clause 3*(3)) which concerned amendment to the Weekly Slap, allowed that: 1. The Scottish Secretary could change the duration of the National Weekly Close Time, after "consulting with those he considered appropriate"; 2. the Scottish Secretary could then implement this change by simple administrative *fiat,* or Statutory Order—subject to the parliamentary "negative procedure" which could be invoked by legislators representing objectors seeking nullification of the Statutory Order.

No fundamental change was proposed for provisions concerning alteration of dates or duration of the Annual Close Time. Changes applied *locally,* and could be secured only on application by a local District Board, or the relevant proprietors in the absence of a Board. However, *Clause 6* provided that so long as the 168-day minimum Annual Close Time requirement was met, then "different provision for different parts of a District" could be made in an "Annual Close Time Order". The provisions for implementing such an Order were set out in *Schedule 1,* paragraphs 3 to 9 of the Bill.

The lack of comment on these important "flexible provisions" suggested that participant Peers had some reserve about them. Lord Biddulph observed that *there was no provision for "imposing close times, other than on an annual basis"* (col.1004); thus excluding any provision for closure, particularly during periods of low-water or drought. Others, including Lords Haig and Lansdowne contended that under *Clause 3* provisions for General Regulation, clear definition of "netting methods" should be included. Lord Lansdowne and others also suggested that *Clause 3* should contain provision for regulating "baits and lures" used by anglers. Only Lord Thurso expressed opposition to the "flexible consultation powers" proposed for the Scottish Secretary. He asserted there should be specific provision for the Scottish Secretary to be *required* to consult with affected District Boards.

Anti-Poaching Measures

Concerning the third and final main objective of the Bill, to provide "further measures to combat poaching", Lord Gray stated:

> "...There has been much discussion over the past year about the possibility of introducing a salmon tagging scheme similar to the one in operation in Canada. We concluded that while tagging had certain attractions, it presented too many difficulties to be introduced in this country. However, we also considered further the possibility of having a system of dealer-licensing and decided that this would be worthwhile in Scotland, even though the circumstances in England and Wales make it inappropriate there. We have therefore made provision for the *possibility* of a *Dealer-Licensing scheme being introduced in Scotland* by an Order under the Civic Government (Scotland) Act of 1982.
>
> ...There is another anti-poaching measure to which I would draw your attention. That is the provision which makes it *an offence to be in possession of salmon, believing or having reasonable grounds for suspecting, that it has been illegally taken.* ...Though the Bill is essentially designed to deal with Scottish salmon matters, a similar anti-poaching measure is included for England and Wales. These

measures are intended to fill gaps in the legislation both North and South of the Border...

...The provisions in this Bill will allow us to take action against those who provide the outlet for poached salmon and will, I am sure have a significant effect on the level of poaching by making it more difficult to dispose of illegally caught fish". (cols. 992-993; Italics added)

1. Dealer-Licensing There was general approval of Government's proposed Dealer-Licensing provision. This, however, was qualified by the reservation that it *must* be applicable not just to Scotland, but to the *whole* of the United Kingdom. If not, as Lord Ridley put it: "I shall set up as an un-licensed dealer in Berwick-upon-Tweed [in the County of Northumberland, *England*] and I shall probably make a fortune!" (col. 1030). Many Lords also stressed that the scheme was far from water-tight. Lord Burton warned there was no reason to believe that Dealer-Licensing for salmon would be any more effective than Dealer-Licensing under the *Deer Act*—"a singularly ineffective [provision] so far". (col. 1038) The question of who would be eligible for a Dealer-Licence was queried by a number of Lords. Would "salmon smokers" be eligible, asked Lord Thurso? And would penalties "include loss of a catering or trading licence", asked Lady Saltoun? The main buyers of poached salmon, she noted, "are hoteliers and fishmongers who buy it cheap and so make bigger profits". (col. 1016). Lord Ross wanted much more detail about the licensing scheme, and how it would work.

2. Illegal Possession and Bailiffs' Powers There was general support also for the Bill's "illegal possession" provisions. But again there were serious reservations about details and how they would work in practice. Lady Saltoun expressed concern "about the task of proving what the accused 'believed', or had 'reasonable grounds for suspecting'". (col. 1015) Lord Trenchard asked whether the terms specified in the Bill concerning illegal possession "go as far as we reasonably can?" (col. 1018) Lord Gibson-Watt felt the new provisions would be of little use, no matter how strong they might be, if support from the Courts was not forthcoming. "It is a little galling", he said, "if on appeal the case goes to the Crown Court, and the judge cuts the penalty by half". (col. 1020) The "illegal possession" provision applying to England and Wales, stated Lord Moran, would need much clarification by amendment if everyone was to know "what it means and to make it more effective". (col. 1023)

One of the few clear party-political divisions emerged over the proposal for sizeably increased powers for bailiffs. Conservative

Lords Haig, and Massereene and Ferrard urged that bailiffs be given added statutory protection, and that their powers—to include search and arrest—should be extended. Labour Lords Carmichael and Ross, however, expressed fears about the extent of powers proposed. These, it was contended, were already extensive. The issues of "illegal possession", bailiffs' powers, and "reverse onus of proof" (that is, the requirement for the accused to "prove his innocence") were to prove perhaps the most contentious and divisive of all issues before the Bill had completed its passage. Insofar as there was an exposed raw nerve dividing the ordinary citizen from the legally and statutorily cocooned proprietor, these issues touched it. If deployed responsibly these anti-poaching powers would clearly have a deterrent effect. But if used irresponsibly, possibly by untrained or unsuitable bailiffs ignorant of their meaning and application, the ordinary citizen could find himself victimised and without normal legal recourse or redress.

ILLEGAL FISHERS IN TRAINING? ... Boy packs up monofil drift-net after a night's work on West coast sea-loch.

These were Peers' observations on the Bill's main objectives. In general they "welcomed" the Bill. Yet there was "no wholehearted support for the Bill from anybody".[8] "The Bill", declared Lord Tryon, was a disappointing, " half-loaf of bread"; Lady Saltoun of Abernethy "damned it with faint praise"; Lord Lansdowne dismissed it as a "wee tim'rous beastie"; Lord Burton lam-

HE AND HIS COLLEAGUE prepare to deposit nets and catch at nearby house.

ented that it only added to long-standing confusion created by the existing complex Scottish salmon fishery laws. Other Lords voiced similar sentiments. Only Lord Ross openly expressed the view which others seemed to imply, that the Government should have produced a White Paper. If Government then had "taken advice and made use of experience" available in the Lords, he contended, there would have been a "far better Bill". This said, Lord Ross joined with his colleagues in accepting the Bill, albeit with the reservation that "it be given a good keel-hauling when we reach the Committee stage".

BAILIFFS ON PATROL ... Checking anglers' permits and tackle on upper Tweed in October.

Thus, the stage was set, the nature and contents of the Bill known. It was a public Bill aimed primarily at promoting and protecting private interests—a Laird's Bill. Also the parliamentary response in the House of origin was revealed: the Bill was welcomed and would be supported. Henceforth, therefore, it was not to be a question of whether Parliament would endorse it: as a Government Bill it was now almost guaranteed passage. The important questions were: *what* efforts would be made, and by *whom,* to improve which sections of the Bill? *How great* would these efforts be? What could or would be *achieved*—both in the Lords and the Commons? And *who* would be the defenders of the *status quo?*

As for Government and the promoters of the Bill, they now could breathe a long sigh of relief. The Lords had "bought" it. Certainly, this acceptance eased greatly the need and extent of amendment which Government, its civil servants and legal draftsmen would have to consider. Yet there were interesting questions: what parliamentary strategy would Government adopt? Would it resort to any tricks to facilitate passage of the Bill, and/or to ensure maintenance of its initial form and content?

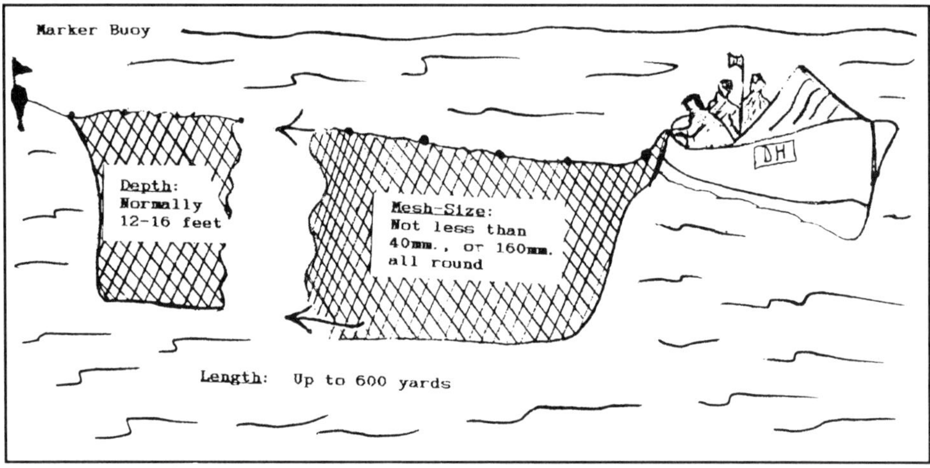

NORTH-EAST DRIFT NET ... Netsman and his 'consignees'.

Lords Demands and Reform Requirements

Peers had made clear which provisions they welcomed in the Bill. Equally they had made clear—mostly by their silence—which they would not welcome. There remained those few provisions which were not in the Bill, and which they thought ought to be included. Which were these?

Their Lordships shouted loudest about the absence of legislative provision to abolish, or at least greatly reduce, North-East English drift-netting. It was pointed out that promised minor Northumbrian Water Authority (NWA) bye-law restraints, together with a Review of North-East salmon fishing in three years, were no substitutes for restrictive clauses in the Bill.

The urgency and importance of such provisions were of concern not merely to the Scottish East coast fishery which continued to suffer from the heavy depredations of North-east English nets; there was also the international dimension to be considered. Without national legislation in keeping with an agreed National Salmon Policy to curb this "interceptory fishery", the basis of international co-operation and even the life of the NASCO Treaty could be seriously threatened. The need to implement a total ban on monofilament nets for salmon fishing in United Kingdom waters was repeatedly stressed. The absence of salmon tagging was queried by many Lords. Strong doubts were voiced about the adequacy of Dealer-Licensing without a supplementary tagging provision. How else were bailiffs, enforcement authorities and dealers to secure positive identification of poached fish?

Many Lords emphasised the importance of rod-fishing to local economies dependent on salmon in rivers. Lord Home admonished all salmon fishery interests to co-operate and exercise self-restraint: "Nets and rods", he said, "must reach agreement that to maximise the number of fish running up the river is to their mutual advantage". (col. 1007) Lord Ross stated that one of the most important measures which could be employed to achieve this objective would be quotas. "It is not good enough for the Noble Lord—I nearly said Marquess—Lord Kimball, to laugh at them [quotas]. I do not. We have [in respect of other fish species] been able to apply them, and we have the experience within the Scottish Office in respect of the organisation of quotas". (col. 1045)

Altogether participant Peers stressed that the facts were clear. There had been, as Lord Biddulph pointed out, "a dramatic decline in world catches of Atlantic salmon" from 10,400 tonnes in 1967, to 6500 tonnes in 1984. There was, therefore, a great need to change the existing law, not merely to curb this decline and acquire reliable statistics, but to meet what was now, as Lord Ross put it, "an entirely different situation so far as salmon fishing is concerned".

Yet, did the Bill address these pressing requirements? It did not. Instead, said Lord Ross, "We are hammering away at problems and a management structure that is out of date". In essence, declared Lord Carmichael, the Bill was merely "a defence and entrenchment of the rights of proprietors ... with little to say about meaningful long-term conservation". (col. 996). Indeed, "conservation", which should have been at the very root of the Bill had been virtually ignored.

Lord Ross perhaps best summed up basic criticisms of the Bill and general feelings of Peers: "On the whole, the Bill does good things in the wrong way, and it does not go nearly far enough in respect of the main concern, which is the decline in stocks, and an ability to prove to other countries with which we are seeking International quotas to allow the fish to get here, that once they reach here we will not so arrange it that we ignore the whole question of conservation." (col. 1048)

There was, he concluded, need for "a complete change of attitude in relation to those with interests" in wild salmon. "Everyone has to appreciate that changed importance from the point of view of the economy, from the point of view of justice, and above all from the point of view of the salmon itself".

References

1. Quoted from circular announcement to "Members of the House of Commons" (mimeo.), dated 6 November, 1985.

2. Scottish Information Office, *Salmon (Amendment) Bill: Non-Attributable Background,* (mimeo.), dated 6 November, 1985.

3. *Lords Debates,* 14 January, 1986, cols. 991-992. (Italics added). Further references to Hansard of this *Lords Debate* of 14 January will be included in the text, specifying only the column or columns.

4. It is interesting to note that in November 1987, at the first Tay District Board elections under the 1986 Salmon Act, the provision for a Chairman to be elected by *all* qualified proprietors had little effect in altering the customary outcome. On this river, "Tay Salmon Fisheries Co. Ltd.—who have automatically held the chairmanship since the Board was first formed—retained the post". Yet the contest was close. TSF's general manager, Ian Mitchell, edged out his Upper proprietor challenger, Alastair Duncan-Miller by 121 votes to 114. (See, *Taysider,* "Tay Angling Report", *Trout and Salmon,* (January, 1988), p.93). Subsequently, there were questions raised about sudden procedural changes then adopted by Chairman Mitchell in the voting for Upper members to the Board. It is alleged that the effect of these changes was to reduce the voting power of the smaller Tay proprietors, and hence influence the outcome of the vote. Perth and District Angling Association—the first club ever to be nominated for the board—failed by a narrow margin to place its mandatory, Association Secretary James Chambers on the Board. After the elections, *Taysider* reported that it was admitted that "the decision [regarding procedural changes] may have been wrong". Those elected to the Board remained.

5. David Shaw, "The Pillagers", *Trout and Salmon,* (January, 1985), p.64.

6. See *Hunter Report,* op.cit., pp.40-41; and Appendix B, for map showing proposed locations of proposed Area Boards.

7. See 1971 *White Paper,* op.cit., p.12; and Appendix for map.

8. *House of Lords: Parliamentary Debates (Hansard) Official Report,* Vol.469, No.26, (London: HMSO), 14 January, 1986, col.1043.

Chapter 4

THE POLITICS OF DIVERSION

"To the vast majority of anglers the aims and objects [of the Salmon and Trout Association] mean one thing only: that the Association exists and is worthy of their support because it seeks to promote and protect their interests. If they suspected there was any ambiguity about this, a high proportion of members could be lost overnight"!

Esmond Drury[1]

The national organisation claiming to represent United Kingdom salmon and trout anglers, with over 10,000 individual and 100,000 (club) affiliate members (in 1986), was the Salmon and Trout Association (S&TA). As noted briefly in previous chapters, with its Central Office at Fishmongers' Hall, London, it was ideally situated to lobby at Westminster (the Houses of Parliament) and Whitehall (the relevant Government civil service ministries). The recognised "trade union for salmon and trout fishermen",[2] the Association, until November 1983, supported both rods *and* nets—a fact not fully recognised by most of its 99 per cent angler-membership. However, hard-fought-for constitutional change secured at this time meant rods at last were "in", and nets "out". The primary aim was now "to protect and develop *angling* interests".[3] The Salmon Bill provided an ideal opportunity to put this new principle into practice.

The Association's leaders and parliamentarian advisers knew that the Bill was unacceptable to anglers as it stood. Outraged angling leaders alleged it would not put "one more salmon into Scottish, [English or Welsh] rivers".[4] Greater equity between the harvests of nets and rods must be secured.[5] Lord Home, the Association President and former British Prime Minister, along with Conservative MPs Cranley Onslow, Charles Morrison, Sir Geoffrey Johnson Smith and Labour's Roy Mason, all leading Council members, were active Bill participants. They knew that the Lords Second Reading was vital. If the *fundamental objectives* of the Bill were to be challenged and changed in favour of angler/tourism and conservation, this was the first and last chance. What would the Association do?

Many members feared that the Association might not do much. It was clear that the Scottish commercial establishment was interested only in "minimal reforms" aimed at enhancing their harvests. Others believed that the Association "meant business", and would press hard for the measures which must be legislated if netting was to be substantially reduced and more fish enabled to enter upstream waters.

The S&TA possessed considerable influence in the United Kingdom salmon and trout fishery world, and maintained a special interest in the Scottish salmon fishery. It was adaptable to marginal change, but few people were prepared for what happened in the early 1980s. A "revolution" took place which shook the Association to its foundations. This revolution, and the dramatic events that followed, bore directly on the position the Association would take during the Salmon Bill proceedings. Indeed, the drama played out at Fishmongers' Hall reflected the forces, interests and bitter conflicts that were to characterise the Bill's proceedings, and determine its eventual principles and content.

S&TA: Champion of the Status Quo

The Association was founded in 1903—and this was not without significance. The *Elgin Commission* in its 1902 Report recommended substantial changes to the salmon laws aimed principally at the Scottish fishery. If these had been accepted and implemented by Government, the rights and catches of netting proprietors would have been considerably reduced. Naturally this was vigorously resisted by the proprietors and commercial interests.

It was significant that S&TA made Fishmongers' Hall in London its headquarters. In keeping with its considerable role as a charitable organisation, the Fishmongers' Company was a generous patron as well as beneficent landlord. It provided the Association with annual funding, office space, venues for meetings, banquets and other gatherings, and all without charge.

As the City Company concerned with regulation of all aspects of the fish trade since the 13th century, salmon was an important source of revenue. In recent centuries Scotland supplied the bulk of salmon to Billingsgate market as harvests in England and Wales declined. Although the Company did not have authority to create or amend fishery laws—its role was mainly to see that existing laws were obeyed and fish were marketed "fit for man's body"—this did not mean that it had no interest in legislation. The Fishmongers' Company was well placed to ensure protection and promotion of commercial fishing matters, whether they dealt with shellfish, other marine species, or salmon and trout.

S&TA's initial membership was small, not exceeding a few hundred, and did not increase until after World War II. This membership was select, comprising many notable fishery proprietors of rank and wealth. In 1910 the President, 17 Vice-Presidents and nine members of the 18-member Council were Peers of the Realm. Three Council members were Baronets. Nearly all owned salmon fishings, many quite valuable, both rod and net. The Company placed appointees on the Council. By 1985, in a Council of 34, at least eight were Fishmongers, five of these Company nominees.

From the 1950s to early 1980s there were a few encouraging changes at S&TA. Efforts were made to broaden the base of the membership. The requirement for applicants to be proposed and seconded was dropped. Many anglers joined. By 1960, membership approached 2000. In the early 1950s two branches were started in London, and the South of England. By 1980 there were over 60 branches in England, Wales and Northern Ireland. In Scotland, there was a single branch for the entire Kingdom. In order to deal with specialised concerns a number of Standing Committees were eventually created. For salmon anglers—and netsmen and their mandated spokesmen—the most important was the Migratory Fish Committee. The Scottish Committee was also seen as vital to pursuing salmon issues.

Esmond Drury and Early Reform Efforts

Lieutenant-Colonel Esmond Drury was a leading post-war reformer. A keen (tenant) angler, angling instructor, and eventually an Association Vice-President, he saw the potential for S&TA serving the needs of a rapidly growing game-fishing community. With others, he played a prominent role in securing changes. Soon, however, it seemed that these might be more symbolic than real. Were salmon angling issues getting the S&TA Central Office support they needed? Should not recruitment literature clearly specify pro-angling issues?[6] Could the Migratory Fish Committee or Scottish Committee act effectively without clear terms of reference or objectives?[7] Could the Association defend and promote the interests of the salmon and the angler without a clearly stated policy? When approached for clarification, the response of the Association hierarchy was to ignore or dismiss these questions and the issues they raised. Even the (1965) *Hunter Report* was the object of Central Office scorn. Under pressure from

ESMOND DRURY (right) in action ... Instructing at Woburn Game Fair.

members to consider the Report and its many important proposals concerning the Scottish salmon fishery, Sir Hugh Lucas-Munro-Tooth, then S&TA Chairman, refused even to discuss the Report in Council or at the Annual General Meeting.[8]

In the 1970s angler frustration boiled over. In a Memorandum circulated in 1972, Esmond Drury spelled out what most informed angler-members felt about S&TA, but few could bring themselves to say. The points raised by Drury cut to the core of the problem.

> "One of the S&TA's problems is that compromise begins *within* the organisation. It is surely not in its best interests to seek to serve God and Mammon in terms of rod fishery interests and netting salmon fishery interests when to do so is to seek to reconcile the irreconcilable. There is bound to be a measure of conflict and *no single association can serve the interests of both except by a purely negative approach.*
>
> "The image of being a responsible body, which the S&TA has built up over the years, is a very valuable asset. But [the Association] must not be so mindful of its image that it *appears* to be neglecting its duty. It is *not* the function of the Association to see all points of view. It *is* its function to see all points of view in terms of the overall interests of its members.
>
> "For various reasons the S&TA holds a special position and is consulted, at top level, on game fishery matters. Its influence extends far beyond what the number of its membership would normally justify. There are times when the S&TA may find itself on a collision course with public bodies and fishery interests. In these cases the course of action must be dictated by what is right for its members and not what is expedient for its reputation.
>
> "For far too long salmon rod fishermen and [their] fisheries have been the Cinderellas of the Pantomime. They are regarded as over-privileged and unworthy of much sympathy. One rarely hears of the importance of salmon angling as an industry. Against this the netsmen have achieved a romantic image of hard-working, self-employed individuals who gain a meagre living by the toil of their hands and the sweat of their bodies. This image might have been

accurate in the distant past, but the situation today is very different. Salmon netting has become big business and a highly profitable one. It is a well-run and highly organised industry which exploits its franchise, generally within the law, to the limit.

"One can have no quarrel with its efficiency or profitability, except that the laws under which it operates are obsolete and inflexible and militate unjustly against the reasonable and legitimate rights of the rod fishing industry and to the detriment of sound conservation policy.

"Because of these basic conflicts between rod fishing and fisheries on the one hand, and net fisheries on the other, the two are incompatible bed-fellows whose interests cannot be served under the umbrella of one association, and the sooner the S&TA stops pretending that they can, the better.

"In recruiting literature the Association tends to gloss over the duality of its function in respect of salmon-interested members and to talk rather vaguely about 'game fishing', with our netting connections mentioned only in small type and ambiguously. The ethics of this are questionable, but if the Association were to declare its true dual allegiance the results in terms of membership and recruiting could be disastrous.

"The netting industry is well organised and has its own Association and powerful lobby to protect its interests. The S&TA should stand fair and square on the side of the interests of the majority of its members. The present position is illogical and unsatisfactory and, since the advent of the Atlantic Salmon Research Trust [which is to attend to the scientific and conservation matters concerning both rods and nets] no longer relevant".[9]

What Drury had to say fairly summarised the case for S&TA reform, and against what he termed the Association's prolonged "supinity" on vital angling matters. In 1973 and 1975 there were prolonged and passionate "salmon debates" in the columns of *The Field*. Arthur Oglesby declared "It is high time the S&TA got off the fence and declared its firm policy against netting". [10] F.S. Farrow demanded to know "What is the S&TA doing? The Association claims to advise Government departments, and to represent the game-angler. It solicits his support and takes his subscription—for what?"[11]

When the heat of debate had subsided the result was that there was no change at S&TA. The Chairman, Sir Richard Levinge, merely re-asserted its commitment to serving the needs of both nets and rods. And in response to William Baird's suggestion that another salmon group could perhaps "do better", Sir Richard warned that any more pressure groups would be counter-productive.[12] No new pressure group was created.

The initiation of a "National Salmon Policy" jointly sponsored by

T. DON THOMPSON . .Director, S&TA, 1983-'85.

J. DAVID SWATLAND ... Chairman, S&TA, 1982-'88.

the Atlantic Salmon Trust and S&TA in July 1981 briefly raised anglers' hopes.[13]. But on closer inspection the policy was a disappointment. "The only 'concession' to anglers", declared a distressed Scottish S&TA member, "was to suggest they be asked to contribute more via rod licences for less sport". [14] He deplored the Association's failure to include demands for legislation to reduce legal estuary netting.

Then something quite extraordinary happened: in December 1981, J. David Swatland was elected Chairman; and a year later T. Don Thompson became Director. Both men were keen anglers, neither had proprictorial fishery interests. Both were determined to advance the interests of anglers, and especially those fishing for salmon in Scottish waters. By June 1983 the first in a sequence of vital and dramatic actions had been taken.

The 'Revolution' of 1983-'84

Swatland and Thompson proved to be a potent combination. Swatland, aged 55, a wealthy Old Etonian and semi-retired solicitor with useful Establishment and parliamentary connections, was a Chairman of considerable arbitrative ability, a skill vital to maintaining unity amongst diverse, complex, often conflicting interests and forceful personalities. Thompson was a non-Establishment native of County Durham, and at 53 retired from Shell-International. He had built his career as a successful administrator and manager in the tough disciplines of commercial realism. With a cool, yet caring efficiency which characterised his incumbency, he had a commitment that won anglers' respect and support.

1. The Deveron Inquiry In June 1983, the new leadership undertook its first major initiative. S&TA, with support of many Scottish riparian owners, rendered full backing to the rods at the *Deveron Inquiry.*[15] Never before had the Association openly taken sides. On this occasion there was no alternative. S&TA must be seen to support its angler-majority membership. Netsmen were taken aback. Never before had they faced more than token opposition. The result of this initiative was a substantial increase in its credibility amongst anglers, and a 30 per cent membership rise, from 6000 to 8000, in the following 12 months.

In general the Inquiry revealed and confirmed for Swatland and Thompson—both of whom attended—the true positions of important interests. Briefly, it showed that the Department of Agriculture and Fisheries for Scotland (DAFS), the dominant Scottish proprietors who controlled the Association of Scottish District Fishery Boards (ASDFB)—almost all with netting interests—and S&TA's Scottish Committee leadership all supported the netsmen. It also revealed a new and potentially damaging internal conflict in the Association: between the angler/tourism and equity objectives of the new leadership, and the nets-orientation of the Scottish Committee headed by Derek Mills and Neil Graesser, proprietor of netting and angling beats. It was mainly this fundamental conflict, involving personality as well as policy differences, that triggered initiatives for profound changes in the Association in the coming year.

2. The Game Fair Petition In August 1983 the Association's Central Office launched a second vital initiative: a petition. Known as the Game Fair Petition, it was drafted by Drury, and addressed to the Scottish Secretary. It spelled out the new angler/tourism commitment of the Association; explained the reasons; and called for changes in the salmon fishery laws which would "better regulate exploitation of the resource in the best long-term interests of the Scottish economy".[16] Specifically, the Petition called for "urgent interim" measures: (1). to increase the Weekly Close Time (WCT, or Weekly Slap) to 66 hours; (2). to provide for a "compensatory [WCT] slap" on coastal nets when weather prevented weekend slapping; (3). to place river-side markers "to denote the river level below which all netting must cease"; (4). to examine and regulate fixed engines (nets), "on the principle that those who live within the environs of a particular river should be the beneficiaries of that river".

Bearing in mind the recent *Deveron Inquiry,* and the attempt of the netsmen to secure an increase in their back-end fishing by altering the Annual Close Time (ACT or Annual Slap) dates, the first measure specified in the Petition was of particular significance. It stressed that "any suggested alteration of close seasons should be considered under the following headings in order of importance: a) propagation and increase of the stock; b) enhancement of the angling/tourist infrastructure and its environs; and c) economic effects on the commercial market for salmon".

The Petition was an enormous success. It attracted more than 4000 signatures and many new members. Even more important, it greatly raised the credibility of S&TA as a body committed to advancing the interests of anglers, particularly those fishing Scottish waters. However, there were problems now made public which could block attainment of the new objectives. They had to be resolved. The leadership of the Scottish Committee was not in line with the new angler-orientated commitment at Central Office. S&TA's constitution contained a provision through which netting interests had long—and in terms of this constitution, legitimately—claimed equal representation and consideration with the angler-majority membership. Changes were needed urgently.

3. Pro-Anglers' Resolution Little time was lost. On 1 November, 1983, a third reform initiative which sought to make formal and official the Association's commitment to angler interests was brought before the Migratory Fish Committee.[17] It was proposed by C. Tom Waite, President of the Yorkshire Branch which had over 25 per cent of the Association's membership, and seconded by Leslie Stewart, the Consultant Biologist who recently had represented angling interests at the *Deveron Inquiry*. The Motion called for the Association formally to recognise that: "...whilst accepting that the overall conservation of salmon and trout is of paramount importance, [the Association] has as its *primary aim* the protection and development of *angling* interests".

After hours of heated debate the Motion was passed by a 6:5 majority. The close vote told the entire story. There remained powerful resistance within the Association hierarchy to the pro-angling commitment of the new leadership. Typical was Jonathan Stansfeld, director of the netting company, Joseph Johnston's and Sons of Montrose, and a member of both the Migratory Fish Committee and the Scottish Committee. He contended that Scottish salmon stocks had been "nurtured with loving care", and the "preservation of Scotland's salmon runs has been achieved through co-operation between nets and rods".[18] Scottish netsmen, he stated, were therefore "more than a little surprised at the recent outburst of the S&TA".

Neil Graesser also lodged strong objections aimed at the Director. He complained about the short notice Thompson had given of the meeting—which he was unable to attend since "people like myself have our diaries already full".[19] He deplored that seemingly it had become "the policy of the S&TA to support rod anglers in an intensive and completely unwarranted attack on the legal Scottish Net Fishermen". This, he warned, could have "far-reaching consequences, with the only possible benefit being a larger membership to the Association". He maintained that if the Petition's aims were implemented, they could "undermine the Scottish legal system governing the salmon fisheries".

4. Reform of the Scottish Committee and the Constitution Action at Central Office came swiftly. Steps four and five in the reform programme were initiated at the Association's Council Meeting of 19 January, 1984.[20] The first concerned a proposal to suspend or re-organise the Scottish Committee; the second to change the Association's constitution in order to give formal effect to the 1 November, "Pro-Anglers' Motion". The debate was lengthy, vigourous and tense.

Concerning the constitution: it was finally agreed that the proposed amendment should be made, subject to confirmations (which duly were secured) at the Annual General Meeting and a later Extraordinary General Meeting. The key change was in "Object b". To this point, S&TA had been committed "to protect and further the interests of all who fish for salmon and trout by fair and legal means". This was the loophole netsmen had long used to their advantage. After alteration, "Object b" now read, "to protect and further the interests of all who fish for salmon and trout within the United Kingdom with *rod and line* by fair and legal means". *The Association was now formally committed solely to anglers.* The Fishmongers' representative at the 19 January Council Meeting, Brian Till, proposed a supplementary Resolution calling for appointment of a "Netsmen's Liaison Committee" to aid in "improving relations with netsmen". The Resolution was approved.

An initial Resolution calling for the Scottish Committee to be given "28 days notice of dissolution" was rejected. An alternative Resolution fared better. It called for Central Office representatives to meet with the Scottish Committee in Edinburgh to discuss proposals for

DEVERON ENQUIRY ... Andrew Tennant, leader of S&TA objectors, in the box. ... From Left: S&TA Director, T. Don Thompson; DAFS' salmon scientist. ... , Willie Shearer; Andrew Tennant; netsman Patrick Sellar; and Sellar's fishery consultant, ASDFB Chairman, Neil Graesser.

the Committee's "re-organisation". The meeting was duly held. It was not a succss.[21] Eventually, following further meetings and negotiations, the Council agreed on 21 March, 1984, to suspend the existing Scottish Committee and substitute an interim "Working Committee" under the leadership of Andrew Tennant, proprietor of the premier Muiresk rod fishery on the River Deveron and leader of rods participants at the 1983 *Inquiry*. He was "empowered to form a new body to represent the interests of the Association in Scotland, and to assume Chairmanship of that body at a formal meeting to be held at the earliest opportunity". By 1986, no such body had yet been formed.[22]

Reaction and Retrenchment

The year 1983-'84 had seen remarkable achievements. Anglers and rod proprietors concerned with the Scottish salmon fishery were pleased. Swatland had shown great enterprise, tenacity and will in leading reform initiatives. He was ably supported by the new Director, Thompson. What few recognised, however, was that the chill wind of reaction was gaining strength. It did not bode well for the reformers or the changes they had achieved.

The new Director had not pleased everyone. He had pressed hard the various issues relating to the Central Office reform programme. Often this activity was undertaken by Thompson in the absence of Chairman Swatland. Also, since the Committees met formally only every three months, full consultations on swiftly moving events were not always possible.

Sir Richard Levinge, the Association President, was scathing in his criticism of the Director's preparation and presentation of the Game Fair Petition. He stated that "the petition had not been correctly processed through the Association's proper channels before its issue at the Game Fair". [23] He further maintained that "as a result [the Petition] contained elements which are inaccurate or inadvisable and which could reflect on the credibility of the Association". Thompson apologised for any embarrassment caused Sir Richard, and for any "intrinsic errors" in the Petition.

Sir Hugh Mackenzie, an S&TA Vice-Chairman, had vehemently and repeatedly expressed his opposition to various Central Office reform initiatives. Sir Hugh, who at the time also was Chairman of the AST and a Fishmongers' nominee on the Association's Council—while serving too on the Executive Committee, the Migratory Fish Committee, the Scottish Committee and on the ASDFB Council—was particularly critical of the basic "anglers only" objective of the new leadership. "He deplored the situation that had now evolved in which the Association was seen to be championing the anglers in a confrontation with legal netsmen. It was vital to avoid conflict with the legal netting interests and he emphasised that illegal taking of migratory fish is a much greater threat to the resource than are the legal nets".[24] Sir Hugh also took strong exception to the November, 1983 "Pro-Anglers Motion", and later to the proposed Resolutions concerning reform of the Scottish Committee.

Thompson found himself in repeated conflict with certain members—often the same persons—of the Executive Committee, the Migratory Fish Committee and the Scottish Committee. Much of this criticism emanated from AST quarters. S&TA's various Committees and Council contained a number of leading AST figures. Besides Sir Richard and Sir Hugh, these persons included Edward Davies, David Clarke, Director Gerry Hadoke formerly of the Foyle Fisheries Commission, and Fishmongers' Clerk Eric Earl. There were a number of prominent Scottish netsmen in the Trust leadership, including Stansfeld and Graesser, who held S&TA offices.[25] The Trust was formally committed to "fishery science", not to "getting more fish into and up rivers". Thompson felt the changes sought were fundamental and essential. If they were not secured, he made it clear he would regard his position as Director no longer tenable.

Thompson eventually found himself isolated. This was partly due to the enormous growth in desk work resulting from the great increase in membership, all to be administered from the Association's Central Office—two, small and very cramped rooms at palatial Fishmongers' Hall. There was also a seeming loss of communication between Thompson and his Chairman; and an apparent loss of support from key Executive Committee members. Executive action by the Director became increasingly difficult. Repeatedly Thompson asked for needed additional resources, staff and office space. These were refused. He became increasingly frustrated and distressed. In a letter dated 21 June, 1984, he made his final plea for support.[26] It was refused and his resignation—which he had offered if this support was not to be forthcoming—was accepted. He departed Fishmongers' Hall on 14 January, 1985.

With Thompson's departure, the "Revolution of 1983-84" came to an abrupt end. It was a tragedy for anglers and the salmon. Once gone, Thompson's name and achievements were virtually erased from the consciousness of the Association and Fishmongers' Hall. The forces of reaction now took charge.

Salmon Bill and S&TA Representations

Retrenchment of the "old order", a complex and difficult task, was achieved in a remarkably short period. By August 1985 Central Office had completed a comprehensive "restoration". The key element was a new salmon policy which blunted the pro-angling reforms of 1983-84. It stressed those secondary (1981) "National Salmon Policy" demands that had the backing of Scottish netsmen and anglers, including "the abolition of all drift-netting and use of multi—and mono-filament nets", and "vigorous action against all forms of illegal fishing". The policy evaded any commitment to reduction of Scottish netting.[27] The new Director, a retired Army Colonel, James Ferguson, was responsible for achieving this and many other feats. Shortly after assuming office, Ferguson was provided with the additional space, staff and resources Thomson had requested. Central Office and the salmon establishment were delighted with his efforts.

With the advent of the Salmon Bill in December 1985, the role and activity of S&TA was relatively straight-forward. It was not a matter of what would be advanced by Central Office—this was already set out in the new Salmon Policy. Rather it was how the Association's position would be advanced.

The Lords' First Reading was just before Christmas Recess. Second Reading came immediately Lords resumed in January 1986. Thus S&TA and other interested organisations had only one month to deliberate and make representations on this long and complex Bill. Meetings at best are difficult to convene during the Christmas holiday. Central Office representations were made to relevant Peers at Fishmongers' Hall immediately before the 14 January Second Reading debate. No written Brief was provided. [28]

It was only *after* Second Reading that a Special Meeting of the Association's ruling body on salmon matters, the Migratory Fish Committee, was convened. This meant that opportunity for *primary* amendment of the Bill already had passed. Furthermore, the meeting was not an exclusive gathering of Migratory Fish Committee members, more a "convocation" of disparate bodies concerned about salmon. In attendance at this gathering, held 21 January at Fishmongers' Hall, were representatives from: the National Anglers' Council, the Fishmongers' Company, the Fisheries' Committee of the Water Authorities Association, the Scottish (S&TA) Interim Committee, and the Welsh S&TA. Consideration also was given to submissions by the AST, Country Landowners' Association, British Field Sports Society, and certain detailed provisions set out by Lord

Hunter's *protegé,* Edinburgh angler and barrister, Michael Bruce. [29]

One veteran Migratory Fish Committee member who strongly objected to this convocational approach was Major David Pilleau. He warned Central Office that "there is a danger of getting bogged down with the views of other organisations—which, let's face it, have their own axes to grind—and a mass of [largely irrelevant material] before we ourselves coolly assess this Bill in the light of *our own members'* interests".[30]

MAJOR DAVID PILLEAU
... veteran salmon campaigner.

Pilleau stressed the paramount need to specify the S&TA formal policy position on the Bill, before considering proposed amendments. The Meeting Agenda called for amendments to be considered first. "From the viewpoint of members", Pilleau said, "the first and most important point is that this Bill *must* meet the need to put more *legal* fish up rivers either to spawn or to be caught on rod and line. As it currently stands the Bill totally fails in this respect. I just hope there is time to discuss these key issues before someone says, 'Well gentlemen, we have five minutes before the Fishmongers' lunch, when thereafter people need to depart to catch their trains or attend their next appointments'!"[31]

Pilleau's pleas were of no avail. The Migratory Fish Committee convocation was held. The representatives of other groups with "other axes to grind" were present and actively participating. There was much discussion. The Agenda was not altered. Consideration of amendments preceded S&TA "Salmon Policy" discussion. And since this policy excluded net-reduction provisions, prior discussion of policy and anglers' demands, even if it had been agreed, could therefore have served little purpose other than to embarrass Central Office and the Association's hierarchy. Indeed, Migratory Fish Committee members played little part at the Special Meeting, since the principal issues had already been pre-determined by others at a convocation held on 17 January at Edinburgh.

This earlier convocation, hosted by the British Field Sports Society (BFSS), also had been held *after* Lords Second Reading. The President, Lord Margadale, and former Chairman, Lord Kimball were owners of dual-interest (net and rod) Scottish salmon fisheries. The gathering was attended by representatives of the Scottish Landowners Federation, the Fishmongers' Company, Scottish Anglers' National Association (SANA), and the S&TA Scottish Interim (Working) Committee.

From neither the Edinburgh convocation, nor the Migratory Fish Committee Special Meeting did any clear statement of angler demands, and the amendments needed to meet them, emerge. In a subsequent News Release by Central Office, many criticisms of the Bill made by participants at the 21 January Special Meeting were noted.[32] However, not one amendment was specified. This was the first and last occasion when the primary demands of S&TA's angler majority, and the Salmon Bill amendments needed to meet them, could have been thrashed out. The opportunity had passed.

Diversionary Achievements

> "It is surely not in [the Association's] best interests to seek to serve God and Mammon in terms of rod fishery interests and netting salmon fishery interests when to do so is to seek to reconcile the irreconcilable".
>
> *Esmond Drury*

Things had moved forward considerably since Drury circulated his "bomb-shell" memo in 1972. Indeed, for one breathtaking moment, it seemed the "Revolution of 1983-84", had attained the unattainable. It seemed possible, contrary to Drury's principal maxim, the Association would actively support reform initiatives which would substantially "impinge on [existing legal or] legitimate netting rights".[33] But then came the counter-revolution and equally swift re-assertion of the authority of the salmon establishment, and "stabilising" of the Association. It was a vital diversionary achievement.

ANDREW TENNANT
... Chairman, Interim Scottish Committee of S&TA, 1984-'87.

With new Director Ferguson in place, a new salmon policy produced which excluded any nets-reduction commitment, and a firm hold re-secured on the restive rods-only Scottish Interim Committee, Central Office had set the base from which it hoped to make "exclusive" Salmon Bill representations. It was good news for the Scottish salmon establishment. It was bad news for angler members and the salmon. The battle, however, was far from over.

Although the Bill had survived Second Reading in the Lords, and emerged with its structure and principal provisions intact, not all Lords were happy. Many thought it essential to include much greater angling and conservation provision in the Bill. And while all remained keen to secure removal of the North-east drift-nets, there were some who felt strongly that Scottish netting too should be substantially reduced. Adjustments, they maintained, should be made to shift the historic imbalance to favour anglers and the sizeable, dependent, modern rod-tourism economy. New measures could be introduced. Others could be strengthened. The "wee tim'rous beastie" might yet be equipped with at least modest teeth.

Their Lordships had promised to give the Bill a proper "keel-hauling" in Committee. What reforms might they launch? How hard would they press? Furthermore, when the Lords had finished, the Bill would pass to the Commons. What might happen when Members "took the gloves off"? What then of rods-conservation demands and requirements? And what of the Scottish (S&TA) Interim Committee? Might not it seek to exercise some pressure of its own—regardless of imposed restraints from Fishmongers' Hall?

There was also the newly-created Salmon Conservancy.[34] Founded in 1984, it already had made an impact in influential quarters. The principal objective of this Glasgow and London-based organisation was precisely to get "more fish into and up Scottish rivers". If anglers were fed up with S&TA (London), might not the Conservancy do better?

There were interesting possibilities. But the immediate question was: what steps would Peers take in Committee, and indeed at Report and Third Reading stages that were swiftly to follow? What reforms would they attempt, perhaps achieve?

References

1. Esmond Drury, *S&TA Memorandum,* (mimeo.), 1972.
2. "Great Innings Hailed by the Former Chairman: Tribute to Francis Corbin", *Salmon and Trout Magazine,* No.207, (July 1976), p.10.
3. Circular Statement on the Outcome of the Extra-Ordinary Meeting of the Migratory Fish Committee of the S&TA, held 1 November, 1983, (copy).

4. See, *Parliamentary Brief by the Scottish Committee of S&TA: The Salmon Bill,* (copy), dated 2 March, 1986.
5. For details of needed angler/tourism and conservation legislative provisions, see the following by David Shaw: *Future Scottish Salmon Fisheries Legislation and Angler/Conservationist Provisions, (mimeo.),* June 1980, pp.18; *Scottish Salmon Legislation: Domestic Conservation Requirements, /A Brief Prepared for the Council for Environmental Conservation (CoEnCo), (mimeo.), London, August 1981, pp.8; A Brief on The Disappearing Scottish Salmon: Economic Effects and Conservation Requirements,* mimeo. Paper for Distribution to Scottish Members of Parliament and Other Interested Parties, October 1982, pp.9.
6. Drury took part in drafting the original S&TA recruiting leaflet, and protested at its ambiguity and vagueness. (See *Letter from Drury to the writer,* 18 March, 1984).
7. See *Letter from Drury to the writer,* 10 July, 1984.
8. See *Letter from Drury to the writer,* 16 December, 1984. The *Hunter Report* was concerned to a considerable extent with securing improved regulation of, and catch reductions in the legal Scottish net fishery. In an earlier letter, Drury had noted that "the S&TA, who are sponsored by the Fishmongers' Company—who are involved with the Scottish net fisheries—will only give token support [to any salmon fishery reform initiative] so long as this does not impinge on [existing legal or] legitimate netting rights". (*Letter from Drury to the writer,* 12 November, 1980).
9. Esmond Drury, *S&TA Memorandum,* (mimeo.), (1972).
10. Letters Column, *The Field,* 15 November, 1973.
11. Letters Column, *The Field,* 29 November, 1973.
12. Letters Column, *The Field,* 3 April, 1975. This extended correspondence (January to April, 1975) was stimulated by a series of four articles by Richard Waddington on the condition of the United Kingdom salmon resource. For a useful summary of this Correspondence, see, Glenbeg, "The Salmon Debate", *Flyfishers' Journal,* (Winter 1976).
13. The National Salmon Policy called for: 1. a ban on drift-netting for salmon; 2. a ban on the use of monofilament nets for taking salmon; 3. salmon dealer-licensing; 4. rod-licences for all who fish for salmon. (See *Salmon and Trout Magazine,* Autumn 1981, p.21.)
14. James A. Begg, "Letters to the Editor", *Salmon and Trout Magazine,* Spring 1982, p.85.
15. See above Chapter 2, pp.11-12 for background detail on the *Deveron Inquiry.*
16. *Petition to the Secretary of State for Scotland,* (copy), n.d.
17. See, *Extraordinary Meeting of the Migratory Fish Committee, 1 November, 1983,* (Circular Statement dated 14 November, 1983).
18. J.R.W. Stansfeld, *A Paper on Scottish Salmon Fisheries,* (mimeo.), 31 October, 1983, p.1.
19. *Letter from Neil Graesser to T.D. Thompson,* (copy), 19 October, 1983.
20. See, *Minutes of a Meeting of the Council of S&TA held at Fishmongers' Hall, 19 January, 1984,* (mimeo.).

21. See *Letter from J.D. Swatland to the Writer,* 16 February, 1984.

22. The "earliest opportunity", as it turned out, was to be January 1987! And at that time it was to be Lord Hunter—of *Hunter Report* fame—who assumed the Chair.

23. *Minutes of a Meeting of the Executive Committee of S&TA held 22 September, 1983.* (mimeo.), p.2.

24. *Minutes of a Meeting of the Migratory Fish Committee of S&TA, held at Fishmongers' Hall, 5 October, 1983,* (mimeo.), p.l.

25. Though frequently speaking in defence of Scottish netsmen, as at the *Deveron Inquiry,* few persons were aware of Graesser's personal netting interests. In a 1987 MAFF biographical reference, Graesser is described as a person who "owns both net and rod fisheries …". (See, *Joint Announcement by the Fisheries Departments in Great Britain: Membership of Salmon Advisory Committee Announced,* MAFF Press Release, 10 February, 1987.

26. See *Minutes of a Meeting of the Council of S&TA held at Fishmongers' Hall, 17 January, 1985,* pp.2-3.

27. Subsequent efforts to get a clear policy commitment to "reduction" of netting failed. (See particularly, *Minutes of the S&TA AGM's of 1986, and 1988*). Also see, David Shaw, "Behind the Scenes", *Trout and Salmon,* "The Gamefishers's Fellowship", June 1986, p.61).

28. See *Letter from S&TA Director, James Ferguson, to the writer, 10 March, 1986.* "There was no written briefing of their Lordships—we had a meeting here [at Fishmongers' Hall] at which various amendments were discussed and taken away".

29. See, S&TA Central Office Circular Notice of a Special Meeting of the Migratory Fish Committee, 15 January, 1986; and *Agenda for a Special Meeting of the MFC held 21 January, 1986, at Fishmongers' Hall,* together with appended copies of written submissions.

30. *Letter from Major D.M.G. Pilleau to S&TA Director Ferguson,* 19 January, 1986, (copy).

31. Ibid.

32. See, "Salmon on the Political Menu", *S&TA News,* 24 January, 1986.

33. *Letter from Drury to the writer,* 12 November, 1980.

34. See, The Salmon Conservancy, *Saving the Salmon —It's a Matter of Common Sense,* (brochure). For detailed provisions see, M. Vickers, *The Salmon Conservancy: A Future for Scottish Salmon,* (being the text of a Policy Briefing Paper presented at the First AGM of the Salmon Conservancy, held 3 December, 1984 at Edinburgh), (mimeo.) pp.8.

Chapter 5

THE LIMITS OF PRIVILEGE: I

> "The idea seems to me extraordinarily dangerous, that this House from its position of privilege and from its wide experience of owning and fishing salmon rivers, should pass a law which ... will look like very heavy sectional class interest, and that is something we should not in any circumstance tolerate".
>
> *The Earl of Onslow.*[1]

With Second Reading behind them, and the principal fishery representative groups "welcoming" the Bill, their Lordships now settled down to serious business. Twenty-three hours of debate over the three remaining Lords stages of the Bill—Committee, Report and Third Reading—were packed into a period of less than one month. There were repeated complaints about the tight parliamentary schedule. Peers had little time to consult with departmental officials, let alone with concerned fishery interests.

Yet despite all the rush their Lordships mustered their energies and set to work with a will. They were to focus their amending zeal on three principal concerns. These were: increased enabling powers for the Scottish Secretary over a range of District Board and national salmon fishery functions; increased functions and powers, including financial powers, for the District Boards themselves; and greatly strengthened powers, mainly through Dealer-Licensing and "Illegal Possession" provisions, to curb illegal fishing and poaching. As for reforms relating to conservation and equity, statutory provisions which would involve far greater state/Central Authority involvement in the control and regulation of the salmon fishery, these were hardly mentioned.

Their Lordships directed their main secondary efforts to securing maximum restraints on the North-east drift-net fishery and the use of monofilament nets; to creation of a "National Salmon Policy"; and to stressing the importance of attaining these objectives if United

Kingdom standing within NASCO—and indeed if the influence and authority of NASCO itself—were to be strengthened.

Given the limited framework of the Bill, the modest objectives that most Peers were aiming at, and watchful response of Government to amendment demands, what were their Lordships to achieve?

I Scottish Secretary: Quest for Strengthened Enabling Powers

While Peers were in general agreement that the powers of the Scottish Secretary over important District Fishery Board functions should be increased, they retained two principal reservations. First, these powers should be applicable to local Fishery Board conditions, rather than the whole of Scotland. Second, the Scottish Secretary must consult affected District Boards before taking statutory action.[2]

Efforts Unrewarded

Lord Burton pressed these demands most vigorously.[3] As it stood, Clause 3, he maintained, could mean that the affected District Boards could be omitted from consultation. There must be mandatory provision for the Scottish Secretary to consult such Boards. Lord Thurso supported this demand. For Government, Lord Gray replied that Clause 32 had been intentionally written to allow the Secretary of State discretion. On general issues he could consult the Association of Scottish District Fishery Boards (ASDFB) and hence preclude the need to consult local Boards individually. However, on matters which might bear on specific Boards, Lord Gray stated that they obviously would be consulted. As for Peers' repeated demands that the Scottish Secretary be vested with statutory powers to deal with purely local matters, Government remained adamant. It was not the job of the Scottish Secretary and Parliament, stated Lord Gray, to be required to legislate on specific local matters. To do otherwise would place an intolerable burden on both. (13 February, col.312) The intention of Clause 3 was to provide the Scottish Secretary with enabling powers to secure Statutory Orders that would apply Nationally—that is to all local District Boards.

Undeterred by Government's clear resistance, Peers pressed hard and repeatedly for extension of the Scottish Secretary's powers under Clause 3. Their principal efforts concerned the quest for provisions to secure control over Low-Water fishing; placement of farmed fish cages; and abstraction of water, sand and gravel.

1) Low-Water Restraints Most revealing, in terms of participant Peers' interests, were the debates concerning Low-Water fishing restrictions. Here angling and netting proprietors were divided into their historic opposing, if not overtly hostile, camps. Lord Ridley started off by asking that Government add to Clause 3 a provision which would allow for prohibition of "all netting operations in a river, if the flow fell below an agreed level, certified by the River Purification Board" (28 January, col.585). This also should be applicable to England and Wales. Just as shooting certain wild-fowl could be stopped during freezing weather so, he contended, net-fishing should be stopped, when there is insufficient water for salmon to run into and up rivers. There should, therefore, be statutory provision to enable each local Board to apply to the relevant Secretary of State.

Speaking in support of Low-Water restrictions for England and Wales, were Lords Moran, Trenchard, Gibson-Watt and Baroness White. It was essential, they contended, that such restraints be applicable to England and Wales, where stocks were "less plentiful and more vulnerable than they are in Scotland" (28 January, col.588). Speaking of the situation North of the Border, Lord Campbell of Croy stressed that the provision sought should not be seen as an attack on the nets. "It is in their interest, as much as anyone else's concerned with salmon, that stocks should be increased and conserved". Lord Chelwood agreed. Netting during Low-Water was "a self-defeating exercise". Since 1973, he pointed out, the Scottish net catch had decreased by 50 per cent. This surely indicated a great decrease in the numbers of fish trying to get up rivers. Reinforcing this contention, the Duke of Atholl stated that nets take an "enormous number of fish when there is a real drought". As for rods, he maintained, there was no need to stop rod-fishing during low-water, since rods seldom have any success during such periods.

The Earl of Onslow, supported Lord Ridley, but had certain reservations about rods. Referring to low-water practices on the River Helmsdale in North-East Scotland, he maintained that rod restrictions were needed. Lord Home supported the principle of Low-Water restrictions, but expressed concern about possible restraints on rods. These, he said, could lead to problems with tenants who let their fishings months ahead. Lady Saltoun asked whether the power should be given to the local District Fishery Boards, rather than the Secretary of State. Under such circumstances, swift action was vital. But for the Secretary of State to act, following an application, would likely "take far too long".

SUMMER LOW-WATER ON TAY. Tay Salmon Fisheries Company (TSF) netsmen reap the bounty. *Right*: The Marquess of Lansdowne, Chairman of TSF.

Opposing Lord Ridley's amendment were Lords Thurso, Kimball and Burton. Lord Thurso commented that on one occasion when nets on his river were removed during low-water, a large number of fish entered the river only to suffocate and die in up-stream pools. Rods, he added, did very poorly. "Full drought conditions are self-limiting and the idea of letting a lot of fish into the river in semi-drought conditions is an illusory one". Lord Kimball added that low-water netting restraints were simply not effective since during drought conditions fish "push off round the coast". He referred to a DAFS experiment which showed that 36 of 40 fish tagged in the Naver estuary during low-water turned up eleswhere on the East and West coasts. Finally, and "with regrets", Lord Burton registered his opposition. There were, he said, practical difficulties. Purification Boards would need more staff to undertake low-water monitoring. This would cost money. Yet there was no financial provision in the Bill. There was also the problem of notification which would probably best be done by newspaper notice. Yet by the time the notice appeared the water guage would likely be up again.

In the course of their presentations, the opponents of Low-Water restraints—all Scots, or Scottish salmon fishery owners—were subjected to a little polite badgering. The English Peer, Lord Trenchard, was the leading critic. He disputed Lord Kimball's "science". There was evidence that "the tagging and handling of fish alters their running habits. There is also enormous evidence that the vast majority of fish insist on returning to their own river". As for Lord Thurso's comments, Lord Trenchard stated that he (Thurso) was speaking of a small river. Others, however, were talking of rivers with estuaries "14 miles long". The situations were very different. Lord Trenchard entered a final plea to opponents of Low-Water restraints. He urged that they not destroy "what appears to be a totally unanimous view for Great Britain that there should be some such power in the Bill".

The efforts of Lord Ridley and his supporters were, in the end, of no avail. Although they appeared to win over Lord Lansdowne (25 February, col.980), Lord Thurso and his supporters did not see "any blinding light on the road to Damascus" (25 February, col.981). For Government, Lord Gray observed that if Low-Water restraint provisions were accepted, there might then be a need to dispense with Weekly Slap netting arrangements in high-water when nets tend to do poorly. Also, he did not see how Low-Water prohibitions could be enforced; and there were problems of effective sanctions and penalties. Before action was taken he thought it best to await the Report of the *1984 Drought Inquiry.* At Third Reading, Lord Belstead, the MAFF Minister, supported Lord Gray's position. There was "no scientific evidence", he said, to demonstrate damage to salmon stocks by commercial fishing during periods of low-water. "To write an amendment with the intention of meeting a need for which evidence has not been produced is really asking a lot" (25 February, col.985). Lord Ridley withdrew his amendment, having expressed the hope that the "door has not been finally shut".

2) Fish Cage Controls Their Lordships had strong feelings about the absence of provisions to control placement of fish cages. Lord Thurso called for the Scottish Secretary to be given powers under Clause 3 to control "the placing of cages to hold fish in any river, loch or estuary". (28 January, col.577) In the Committee debate that followed many Peers expressed their fears about associated problems of disease, pollution and cage escapees. Given the potentially lethal effect which these problems could have on wild salmon at either the juvenile or mature stage, and that neither the River Purification Boards nor the District Fishery Boards could exercise any powers in this matter, it was vital that the Scottish Secretary be vested with powers of "placement". While most Peers supported this position,

LORD MORAN

LORD HOME

THE EARL HAIG

Lord Onslow maintained that since such controls were concerned with "local matters", it was local Fishery Boards, and not the Scottish Secretary, that should be vested with the needed powers.

At Report stage, Lord Gray set out Government's position. (13 February, cols.307-8) Local Planning Authorities, River Purification Boards and the National Farmers' Union (on behalf of fish farmers) were all, he stressed, vitally concerned. To secure Planning Consent for the introduction and placement of cages in fresh-water lochs, the local Planning Authority first must consult with Purification Boards and others. Applications also must be advertised; this affording the opportunity for lodging objections. As for fish cages in the sea, they must be fastened to the sea-bed; estuaries were not suitable. The Crown Estate Commission (CEC) which owns and leases the sea-bed "can impose conditions". There was no evidence, said Lord Gray, of transmission of disease from caged to wild fish. The National Farmers' Union (NFU), he said, was concerned about the prospect of further controls on fish farmers. He concluded that while separate legislation to achieve these ends might be desirable, the Salmon Bill was the wrong place.

Many Peers were unhappy with this Government response. Lord Burton referred to the alleged origin of Ulcerative Dermal Necrosis (UDN) from fish farms in Southern Ireland. Purification Boards, he said, were sponsors of the "cage controls" amendment. Currently, he stressed, "they have no say".

As for the CEC, Lord Burton said it was concerned only with how much revenue it could get. It did not seem to mind "to whom [it] let fish farms", nor did it care where these were placed. (13 February, col.309) Lord Gray remained unmoved. On the understanding that Government was prepared to consider a separate Bill for fish farm and cage controls, Lord Thurso reluctantly agreed to withdraw his amendment.

3) Sand, Gravel and Water Abstraction At Report stage, Lord Biddulph, on behalf of his absent Tweed neighbour Lord Haig, tackled the vexed issues of sand, gravel and water abstraction. He strongly urged that provision be made under Clause 3 for the Scottish Secretary to have appropriate regulatory powers which could be deployed after due consultations with all legitimate interests, "and here I would most strongly include the District Fishery Boards". (13 February, col.301) Sand and gravel extraction, he said, often gave rise to serious damage. Spawning redds were destroyed, river life was desecrated, and for anglers dis-coloured, silted water often reduced

WATER ABSTRACTION DEVASTATION ... Tay's River Garry tributary, once home to 40-pounders.

fishing opportunities. While in England and Wales, the Water Authorities exercised control over these activities, in Scotland, there were no similarly empowered parallel bodies. As for local Planning Authorities, since their principal concern was with land development and building, they had to rely on others regarding "the conditions for protecting the river systems and how these are complied with".

Water abstraction, too, posed great problems. In Scotland there was no effective control. Although a remedy was available through Common Law, and River purification Boards could impose volume restrictions, in practice these procedures were unwieldy and seldom used. Water abstraction, he maintained, was directly related to pollution levels: the more the amount of water abstracted, the less the dilution and dispersal effect, and the greater the level of potential pollution. Particularly grave situations arose with river-side fish farms "where lengths of particular rivers were almost denuded by uncontrolled abstraction of water". (13 February, col.302)

In his reply to Lord Biddulph, Lord Gray merely stated that Government did not consider a Salmon Bill the place to deliberate on such matters. (15 February, col.303) Regarding the issues of sand and gravel extraction, what was suggested by Lord Biddulph offered no real advantages over the current system. Extraction and abstraction notices had to be advertised, and relevant District Boards were free to lodge objections. There was no point in making District Boards "statutory consultees" since there was no guarantee that their advice would be any more greatly heeded by Planning Authorities.

Concerning water abstraction, Lord Gray reminded Peers that the Common Law and specific statutory provision existed to ensure control. All affected river interests, he stressed, have extensive safeguards. And if salmon interests were allowed special consideration, then others would make justifiable claims for the same status. The 1978 *Report of the Scottish River Purification Advisory Committee,* he noted, concluded there was insufficient evidence to justify introducing a comprehensive system of licensing abstractions. Nevertheless Lord Gray said he would be quite willing to discuss all these matters with the ASDFB.

Lord Burton expressed extreme disapointment with Lord Gray's response. Not all planning applications, he noted, were advertised. The River Purifications Boards would welcome the Secretary of State taking on the suggested powers. Since Planning Authorities were not fishery or purification experts, it was "quite wrong" that relevant abstraction and extraction notices should not be required to go to affected District Fishery Boards. In concluding the debate on these issues Lord Gray repeated his offer to meet with the ASDFB. There was "no reason why, in due course, that might not lead to further legislation". Given these Government assurances, Lord Biddulph agreed to withdraw his amendment.

4) Annual Close Time Orders A modest effort only was made to extend the "flexible" powers of the Scottish Secretary under Clause 6 relating to the Annual Close Time (ACT). Lord Burton said provision should be made to allow only one proprietor, rather than two, to make application for an ACT "Designation Order". (13 February, col.313) This proposal was advanced on the grounds that the area concerned might have only one proprietor, or if only two, they might not agree. Lord Gray was not impressed. Proprietors, he said, must first sort out things amongst themselves. Indeed, he added, some might say they should have a Board formed before being permitted to make an ACT application.

Efforts Rewarded

There was at least some consolation for reforming Peers on these matters. Government agreed to extend the powers of the Scottish Secretary under Clause 3. A new provision (Clause 3(2)(f)) gave him general powers to regulate "construction, alteration and use [of] screens on off-takes from inland waters, [and] structures associated with such screens". (13 February, col.300) This was an important addition. It could provide for alleviation of long-standing problems in many areas where there is insufficient provision for passage of salmon up-stream, and smolts and kelts down-stream.

Furthermore, at Report Stage, Government introduced a new Clause (Section 21 in the *1986 Act*) on "Permitted Methods of Fishing". It did not change the lawful methods, but provided for the Scottish Secretary to give clear definitions of existing methods, thus ensuring against the introduction of any new methods. In addition, this new "regulation-making power would offer scope for changing the way in which nets are worked". More importantly, "the power could be used to regulate the use of adjacent nets so that they would not entirely block a river in the way described by my Noble friend Lord Lansdowne", observed Lord Gray. (30 January, col.801)

An important amendment to the Weekly Close-Time provision was also accepted by Government. As written, Clause 3(3) in the Bill empowered the Scottish Secretary to "alter" the length of the Weekly Slap. Lord Ridley pointed out that while this power might be used to increase the Slap, it could also be used to "reduce the close time below 42 hours ... a dangerous and retrograde step". (28 January, col.585) Lord Gray accepted Lord Ridley's amendment which specified that the Secretary of State might make regulations to alter the (National Scottish) Weekly Slap, "*provided always that such regulations shall not shorten* the periods specified" (Italics added) in Section 13 of the *1951 (Scotland) Salmon Act*—that is, 42 hours.

A final concession relating to the Scottish Secretary's regulation-making powers over angling "baits and lures", was extracted from Government. While this restraint provision was not secured until the final (October) stage of the Bill, nevertheless it was accepted at the Lords' stage under the principal advocacy of Lord Thurso. He first raised the question of a "baits and lures" restraints under Clause 3 at Committee stage. Now he called for the Scottish Secretary to be given powers to "adjust methods of fishing by rod and line" which would entail restriction of baits and lures to those "suitable for the occasion" (28 January, col.576). Having gained little positive response from Government, Lord Thurso pressed this demand at Report Stage (13 February, col.305-7); and with Lord Burton at Third Reading. (25 February, col.975) At this point, Lord Gray indicated that while Government was sympathetic to the amendment, he was not certain that Clause 3 was the right place for it. Any power provided must be applicable to *local* conditions. Clause 3 was concerned with *National* regulation-making powers.

In replying to Government, Lord Burton asked whether such a power might not best be given to local Boards. This provoked a rumble of discontent from other Peers. Lord Home observed that he favoured restrictions under low-water conditions. But if such restrictions were applicable under other circumstances, these could have "a pretty serious effect on tenants taking fishing. They might find themselves in great difficulty". (13 February, col.306) After further debate Lord Gray stated that DAFS officials were shortly meeting with angling respresentative groups, many of which were not happy about the prospect of restrictions. Following these consultations, the matter would be re-considered. In the event, provision was not made under Clause 3. Government introduced a new Clause which duly was incorporated (as Section 8) in the *1986 Salmon Act.* It enabled the Scottish Secretary to make *local* "baits and lures" regulations by Statutory Order for the whole or part(s) of a Salmon Fishery District, on application by the Board for that District.

Summary: Minimum Concessions

In this cat-and-mouse game with Government, Peers had comprehensively tested its commitment to a fundamental principle on which the Salmon Bill was founded: increased enabling powers for the Scottish Secretary. Peers wanted the Scottish Secretary to be able to act on a much broader range of important local functions than the

Bill provided. These might be exercised through general enabling powers, applicable to National or local matters, or sanctioned by the Scottish Secretary and implemented by local District Fishery Board applicants.

Government, however, showed its reluctance to extend either the general powers of the Scottish Secretary or those through which he might sanction local statutory initiatives. As ably expressed by Lord Gray, to do otherwise would increase intolerably the burden of the Scottish Secretary, involve Parliament in a vast quantity of business which effectively was concerned with local rather than national matters, and render favoured treatment to salmon interests. This was not only wrong and inequitable, but could lead to serious difficulties and claims for equal status by a variety of other affected interests.

Basically, Government demonstrated its commitment to adhere closely to its own conservative concept of "flexibility" and "extended powers" for the Scottish Secretary. Nevertheless, Peers had managed not only to define more clearly the boundaries of Government tolerance, but to demonstrate that with effort, determination and ingenuity, it was possible to extract marginal concessions, and even to secure from Government added commitments to discuss certain rejected amendments with a view to future separate legislation.

II District Boards: Quest for Increased Powers

It was during debate on District Board powers that Peers made perhaps their greatest efforts. These were directed at securing first, greater general powers through the initial clauses in the Bill relating to the creation of District Boards, amalgamation and finance; second, changes in the Bill's provisions concerning the composition and membership of the Boards; and third, a considerable increase in specific powers for them.

1) Creation and Amalgamation of District Boards Government's position on mandatory provisions for creating District Boards by amalgamating them was made clear at Second Reading. The basic aim of the Bill was to strengthen the Boards as "associations of voluntary members". Compulsion was not acceptable.

Lord Burton now led Peers' second effort. Regarding Clause 1, he proposed that, if after three years from the date of the new Salmon Act coming into force District Boards had not been created in all Scottish Salmon Fishery Districts, the Scottish Secretary should have powers, after consulting with "appropriate persons", to "review and make regulations" that *would* provide for the creation of individual or amalgamated Boards. (28 January, cols.546-7) This, he argued, was essential if the needed grass-roots salmon fishery management structure was to be achieved. Funding would be greatly assisted if there was provision for Salmon Fishery rates, currently paid to Local Authorities, to be allocated to District Boards.

Government's response was dramatic. It chose to regard this renewed demand for ill-disguised powers of compulsion (to create Boards) as a fundamental challenge to the entire Bill. Did Peers want the Bill withdrawn? Were they prepared to accept that further departmental work on the Bill would mean "yet a further passage of years" before a revised Bill "might" appear? Did they not recognise how difficult it was to secure parliamentary time for such legislation? In the debate which followed, details of proposed modifications were discussed. Some Peers argued that without amendment, "large areas will remain uncovered [by Boards] even after this legislation". Government, however, was unmoved: mandatory provisions were not acceptable. Reluctantly, Lord Burton withdrew his amendment. Other Peers fared no better.

2) Composition and Leadership of District Boards At Second Reading, Peers had expressed general support for the two principal "democratic advances" introduced in the Bill: election of Board Chairmen, and co-opted tenant representatives. But there were divisions. How and by whom should Board Chairmen and co-optees be elected—or in the case of co-optees, possibly appointed? Further, with regard to co-optees, how many should there be? What powers should they have; and most important, should the numbers of co-optees be balanced between nets and rods?

This was the sole section in the Bill that posed any serious threat to the exclusive and private control of proprietors who always had run and financed their District Boards. Yet at Second Reading they had shown they were prepared to accept tenant representatives on District Boards. The question was: how far were they prepared to allow "democracy" to go?

Lord Thurso expressed the strongest views on each issue. Basically, he favoured a more conservative approach for the election of Board chairmen, and a more liberal procedure for electing tenant representatives. Not to have the Chairman elected by Board members, he contended, could lead to built-in majorities for rods or nets if the vote were opened to include all proprietors. (28 January, col.639) Chairmen, therefore, should be elected only by Board members, and only after they had been elected to their Boards. Lord Gray, however, rejected this proposal. If the Thurso method were used, Boards would consist of equal numbers of upper and lower proprietors, and the Chairman would be chosen virtually by the "flip of a coin". It was this weakness, he said, that Schedule 2 was seeking to correct.

Turning to the issue of co-optees, Lord Thurso insisted that tenants should elect their own representatives, and Boards should then appoint these persons. (28 January, cols.635-41) It was "undemocratic" and unsatisfactory for Boards to dominate the nomination and co-option processes. A number of Peers supported Lord Thurso's concept of "democratic" co-option. Only Lord Burton took exception. District Boards, he contended, must retain the power to decide on co-option. To do otherwise was to risk co-option of certain netting tenants of dubious character. There could be particular problems in small, remote Board areas. In reply to these sensitive points, Lord Gray stated that the major provisions in Schedule 2 should remain as they were. He did, however, allow that Government would initiate amendments to provide absolute assurance that the balance between upper and lower interests was maintained.

Undeterred by Government's rebuffs in Committee, Lord Thurso pressed his demands again at Report Stage. It was imperative, he insisted, that there should be "tenant appointees", not "Board co-optees". (13 February, cols.325-9) This was "the democratic way": the tenant representatives "do not have to come to the Board, owing their appearance to the generosity of proprietors" but rather to the angling clubs and anglers who elected them. Such provision, he maintained, would ensure that tenant members did not become "second-class citizens".

This fresh assault by Lord Thurso generated new opposition. "Who", asked Lord Onslow, is an "eligible angler"? Could such a person be a "once a year visitor"? It was impossible, he declared, to have a "reasonable basis for an angler or rod-electorate". Hence, it was better that the Board should control the choice. Lord Kimball agreed. Only Lords Marnock and Lansdowne now spoke in support of Lord Thurso. And even Lord Lansdowne was careful to stress that the number of appointed tenants should in all cases be less than the number of proprietors, in order that proprietors on the Board would continue to have "the major say".

Lord Gray, still resisting change to Government's proposed system of co-option, was prepared to accept that provision be made to require Boards to "consult" with angling interests. But as for "who comes onto the Board as representatives of angling and tenant netting interests", this was for the Board to decide. Lord Thurso concluded with an impressive theatrical flourish:

> "Even if I withdraw these amendments, I shall not withdraw my adherence to the elective principle. There will be at least one District Board [the Thurso] where elections will take place to find out who the anglers [representatives] are. I hope it may prove a shining example to the Noble Lord [Lord Gray]". (13 February, col.328)

Lord Thurso then withdrew his amendment.

There was one final significant challenge to these Bill provisions. In the initial Bill, restrictions were placed on qualifications of angler-representatives eligible for co-option. The Duke of Atholl took strong

RIVER THURSO NETS
... fishing the afternoon tide.

Left: Lord Thurso: sole proprietor of net and rod fishing rights on the River Thurso.

exception to one of them. It was wrong, he contended, for angling club officials, if they were not paid, to be ineligible for co-option. (28 January, col.648) After all, it was often these very persons who were best informed and most concerned about angling and broader fishery matters. To the satisfaction of the Duke, Lord Gray in his reply indicated that Government viewed this issue with sympathy. A Government amendment would be—and was—made which enabled any angling club official, paid or unpaid, to be eligible for co-option.

Altogether, this section of the Bill emerged with Government's "democratic" provisions fully intact; provisions, it was noted that would enable proprietors to maintain dominant control. This was a rather special and extra-ordinary context in which to apply the term "democratisation", nevertheless it did correctly signify an extension of public participation—albeit within what was still a tightly, even secretively controlled private voluntary institution, the District Salmon Fishery Board.

3) District Boards: Definition, Finance and Powers Before joining battle in quest of increased specific management powers for local District Boards, Peers first gave attention to certain Board "definition" and "financial powers" provisions.

a) 'Definition' Queries Lord Carmichael called for Government to delete the provision in Clause 13 which stated there may be a District Salmon Fishery Board whether or not there are salmon in its waters. (28 January, col.607) If there were no salmon, why should there be a Board? In reply, Lord Gray explained that it would be useful to have this provision in the event that, given the introduction of salmon, there was a desire to form a Board. Conversely, he added, if the stock of a river was killed off, this provision would enable a Board to be retained by proprietors who wished to regenerate a salmon run A number of Peers spoke in support of Lord Gray. Lord Thurso mentioned the potential management advantages of this provision: it would enable small, non-salmon-bearing Districts not only to create Boards, but to be incorporated in any envisaged structure with which "we are hoping to cover the whole of Scotland, ...provided that the people in that area were not against it".

Some Peers appeared still somewhat bemused by the intricate wording in the Bill concerning the basic definition of a District Board. At Report Stage, Lord Lansdowne questioned the need for the term "association" prior to the formation of a "committee" which would assume the status and powers of District Board. (13 February, col.313) This prompted Lord Gray to spell out in clear and forceful terms what, in the view of Government, the Bill was all about. He stressed that under the existing Scottish Salmon Fishery Acts, District Fishery Boards

> "...enjoy a somewhat dubious legal status, and their powers are limited to what statute provides for them. ...In the new structure, we

expect a Board in its character as a Committee of a voluntary association, to avail itself of the Common Law powers appropriate to such a body, as well as the additional powers given to the Board under the Bill.

Likewise, the uderlying scheme allows for ease of transfer between Boards where Districts amalgamate. ...It is important, therefore, that the Board retains its capacities as the Committee of a voluntary association, and the Bill has been carefully drafted with that in mind". (13 February, col.315)

The meaning of this explanation was now clear. In essence, Government was clarifying and reinforcing the private rights of proprietors. It was emphasising their right to manage and control their fisheries under Board structures which the Bill now made very clear were to function under their private control. Where under the old Salmon Fishery Acts there remained certain questions as to whether these Boards were in fact *public statutory bodies,* the Bill now made their legal status clear. They were to be *private voluntary* bodies; but in addition to normal Common Law powers available to all bodies and individuals, they had special statutory powers—a privilege extended to few such voluntary bodies—to fulfil their various functions and duties.

What Lord Gray was implying was that Government was doing salmon proprietors a considerable favour. Proprietors were always fearful of state encroachment on their private rights. The Bill was simply confirming proprietorial rights through statutory provision. However, proprietors could not have it both ways. The further implication of Lord Gray's observations was that if they sought additional statutory powers which went beyond the limits set by Government in the Bill, and if they persevered in their quest for powers of compulsion, as in their demands for Amalgamated Boards, they would be inviting Government to remove Boards from their protected private status and place them under public control. Is this what Peers wanted? Lord Lansdowne made no further comment.

b) Financial Powers? Although seemingly chastened by Lord Gray's defence of Government and "public rights", their Lordships now probed for what minor statutory powers they could secure in relation to financing District Boards. Lord Burton pointed out there were often problems in collecting Board rates from proprietors. (28 January, col.611) He proposed that they should have statutory powers, not only to collect arrears but interest on them. This was the best way to ensure they paid up, and on time.

Once again, the question was: should a voluntary association have public statutory powers to compel proprietors to "contribute" to it? Lord Gray re-asserted Government's position. Boards had statutory powers to impose a fishery rate on proprietors. It was up to them to ensure payment. Statutory provision to require payment of arrears was therefore not acceptable. Lord Gray rejected Lord Burton's proposal, as well as proposals by Lord Ridley that District Board members were entitled to "travel expenses". At Report stage he dismissed Lord Burton's demand that Boards should be required to hold an Annual General Meeting; (13 February, col.317) to endorse such proposals would violate the voluntary principle under which the Boards were to operate. Still, he said, Government would give these matters further consideration.

At Third Reading, to the surprise of many Peers, Government relented. Lord Gray stated that Boards would be required by statute to hold Annual General Meetings. (25 February, col.976) Later, Government also conceded statutory powers to Boards to collect interest on rates arrears.

The only other serious query regarding "financial powers" for Boards was voiced by Lord Ross. (28 January, cols.611-14) The Bill allowed Boards to raise any sum in excess of double the annual assessment, "for carrying out their purpose", so long as proprietors controlling four-fifths of the District's ratable value, approved. Lord Ross said that a limit should be placed on the permissible amount to be borrowed. And what if one-fifth of the proprietors, by ratable value, opposed the mooted purchase? In order to provide some protection for the minority interest, Lord Ross said the Scottish Secretary should approve any such sum proposed by a District Board, to be used only for purchase of heritable property, including netting rights. This procedure applied to Local Authorities; it should also apply to District Boards.

The Duke of Atholl took strong exception to this proposal. Supported by two other Tay proprietors, Lords Ridley and Lansdowne, he asserted that to secure a four-fifths favourable vote on such matters was virtually impossible; therefore Lord Ross' proposal should be reversed. (29 January, cols.628-34) The Board should be able to carry out such a purchase, unless one-fifth of the proprietors by ratable value, objected. After further debate, Lord Gray summed up: the "four-fifths" requirement was an adequate safeguard. Even if the Scottish Secretary could "safeguard the smaller man", there was no guarantee that the proposed amendment would secure this position. (28 January, col.617) The four-fifths provision was duly incorporated in the 1986 Act.

c) Increased Powers Thwarted Still undeterred by Lord Gray's warnings and reminders, Peers continued to press hard, focussing their efforts on trying to secure increased statutory powers in the principal Clause (Clause 16) concerned with "General Powers and Duties" of District Boards.

i) Obstructions One problem that had long plagued many rivers, and up-stream proprietors in particular, was obstruction to fish passage. The Bill made provision that Boards should have powers to effect "removal of obstacles", but there was an important *caveat.* It could be done only "by agreement" of the proprietor(s) on whose waters the obstacles were situated. Lord Ridley declared that if the Board could only act "by agreement", the power would be toothless. (29 January, col.641) "No one riparian owner who refuses agreement", he said, "should be able to stop removal of natural or artificial obstacles to the passage of fish". He referred to a Ross-shire river "where some 14 miles of absolutely splendid spawning water is totally forbidden to salmon" because one proprietor would not permit the removal of a natural waterfall "which would not be difficult to do". The Tweed Commissioners (under the separate Tweed Salmon Fishery Acts) had such powers. Why then should Scottish Boards not be given the same? Lord Ridley added that the amendment he sought should also include power to put in passes at hydro dams. There were "many dams constructed which do not allow the fish to pass above them". Lord Gisborough innocently inquired whether Government would give Boards "permission to blow up a hydro-electric dam?"

HYDRO-ELECTRIC DAM OBSTRUCTION ... Fish "stacking" below Kilmorack Dam on River Beauly in Northern Scotland. How many get through?

Not only were these modest proposals resisted by

Lord Gray, who stressed the need to conform to the "voluntary principle" of the Bill, but also by the Duke of Atholl who on practically all other issues was in agreement with his fellow Tay riparian owner, Lord Ridley. The Duke referred to the River Inver, a tributary of the Tay. The National Trust for Scotland which controlled a scenic waterfall at "The Hermitage" on the Inver, was opposed even to a fish pass round this beauty spot. The Duke declared it would be "disastrous" if the words "by agreement" were removed from the Bill. Lord Ridley's only reply was, "Now I know why the Noble Duke's ancestors built a fishing lodge at this very point"! Lord Ridley then withdrew his amendment.

ii) Stocking and Ova-Planting Controls Another matter which greatly troubled their Lordships, and many District Boards, was the lack of control over planting ova and introduction of foreign fish. Lord Thurso reviewed the problem. The introduction of trout, pike and foreign ova/juvenile salmonids was not uncommon in many Fishery Districts. Also, fish farms were increasing on many freshwaters. District Boards should have specific powers to control these activities. Only in this way could control of competitors for space and food be ensured and disease risks reduced. (29 January, col.645) There was strong support for this position from Lords Moran, Onslow and Tryon. Lord Burton, referring to trout stocking practices by some angling clubs, stated "It is a case where salmon Boards must take priority over trout". In reply to Lord Thurso and his supporters, Lord Gray affirmed that the Bill's "voluntary principle" must remain paramount. To allow the amendment would violate the rights of private proprietors to do what they like with their waters—within Local Government, Planning Authority and Purification Board statutory limits. The amendment was withdrawn.

iii) Research and General Powers Lord Burton called for Boards to have powers to carry out "research into the state of salmon runs" in their Districts. (13 February, col.322) Lord Gray countered that since this was already provided for in the "General Improvement" sub-section ((1)(a)) of the Clause, there was no need for specific powers. A Board could carry out such research activity if it wished.

Lord Burton also suggested that Boards should have general powers to make bye-laws for District Fisheries, subject to confirmation by the Scottish Secretary. (29 January, col.328) Lord Gray, however, was quick and firm in his reply: such powers "which affect private rights should rest solely with the Secretary of State". The appropriate powers, he pointed out, were provided under Clause 3. It was, there-

VITAL RESEARCH TOOL ... DAFS' fish counter on the North Esk. Sadly, the counter is above highest netting station, hence count is only of those fish which escape intensive down-stream netting. (See also pp.29 and 31 above.) The counter therefore is of limited utility.

fore, neither necessary nor fitting for Boards to have bye-law powers for the purposes of this Clause.

Finally, Lord Burton suggested that Boards should be empowered to institute interdict (an "authoritative prohibition") proceedings regarding "any act which may be detrimental to the interests of any of the fisheries within its District". (13 February, col.329) He pointed to gravel extraction, which "should not be for an individual proprietor to sue for interdict, since all of the fishery is concerned". The Board should be so enabled. In reply, Lord Gray stated that when interdict was applied for, it could be that the Board makes the application, since there was no restriction on the "types of actions" it could institute. It would then be for the Court to consider whether the Board should sue for interdict. The Court might decide that the Board was so enabled; but, he added, there might be instances where the Court rejected this approach. Each case, he declared, would be decided on its own merits. The Court would decide.

Peers now had secured Government's response to their demands for District Board reforms. Politely but firmly, Government once again made clear its position. The Boards were voluntary associations, and in keeping with this status Government would not concede more statutory powers than they already had. Yet Government had been prepared to show some flexibility on financial provision, and Boards now would have statutory powers not only to collect rates arrears, but interest on them. For the rest, Boards would have to rely on the existing law and persuasion if they wished, amongst other things, to remove obstructions, control stocking and ova planting, or conduct research.

Limits of Privilege: I

Their Lordships had shown great ingenuity and determination in seeking to strengthen the powers of District Boards, either through increased enabling powers for the Scottish Secretary, or added substantive provision for the Boards themselves. It was not through want of effort that they had failed. There was simply a point beyond which Government was not prepared to allow Boards to go: if the "salmon Lords" and Scottish proprietors wished to retain the privileged position which Boards enjoyed as private voluntary bodies, then they must accept these limits.

Looking ahead: if reforming Peers now were to be successful in strengthening Dealer-Licensing and Illegal Possession provisions, even greater, and less self-interested efforts would be required. As for securing restraints on the North-east drift-nets, and incorporation in the Bill of a National Salmon Policy; given the resistance of Government and MAFF, herculean efforts could well be needed.

References

1. *Lords Debates,* 25 February, 1986, col.1003. The Earl of Onslow was here commenting on amendments being sought by Lords Trenchard, Denning and Moran to the "Illegal Possession" clause in the Salmon Bill.
2. For details of Peers initial stated positions on these issues at Second Reading, see above Chapter 3, pp.62-64.
3. See *Lords Debates,* 28 January, 1986, col.574. Hereafter, reference to Lords Debates will be included in the text by date and column. The relevant Debate dates and Hansard references are:

   Lords Committee: Parliamentary Debates, House of Lords, Vol. 470, (No. 34) 28 January, 1986, cols. 545-614; Vol. 470 (No. 35), 29 January, 1986, cols. 627-661; Vol. 470 (no. 36), 30 January, 1986, cols. 799-882.

   Lords Report: Parliamentary Debates: House of Lords, Vol. 470 (No. 42), 13 February, 1986. cols. 295-397.

   Third Reading: Parliamentary Debates: House of Lords, Vol. 470 (No. 50), 25 February, 1986, cols. 974-1035.

Chapter 6

THE LIMITS OF PRIVILEGE: II

> "[Illegal Possession of fish] is not a case where we are dealing with dangerous drugs, with firearms, or with any of the other things contrary to public safety, or to public health, or to morals. We are dealing with salmon. And they are not to do with public safety, and they are not to do with public health".
>
> *Viscount Colville of Culross*[1]

During Second Reading, there was general support for measures introduced by Government to bring illegal fishing and poaching under better control. However, strong reservations were expressed by Peers. Could Dealer-Licensing be effective if it were applicable only to Scotland? Their Lordships thought not. As for Illegal Possession of salmon, many Peers were certain this provision would be greatly diminished if the "onus of proof" was not placed squarely on the accused. An accused person found "in possession" of salmon under suspicious circumstances must provide a satisfactory explanation to establish his innocence.

As for curbing or eliminating the North-East drift-net fishery, Peers were aware of Government's resistance. This, however, did little to reduce their reforming zeal. At Report and Third Reading stages, Peers tried mightily to persuade Government to alter these provisions. They were determined to secure maximum restraints.

I Dealer-Licensing and Anti-Poaching Measures

1) Strengthening Dealer-Licensing

In earlier stages of the Committee's consideration of Dealer-Licensing, the silence of previously vocal Peers was notable. However, Lady Saltoun received clarification of the "permissive" powers of the Scottish Secretary in relation to Dealer-Licensing, and Lord Burton was reassured that "inspection of dealers' records" would be taken care of under the provisions of the *Civic Government (Scotland) Act 1982.*[2] Lord Carmichael remained unhappy about the provision for appointment of water bailiffs. He felt it was unsatisfactory that Boards should retain powers of appointment. (29 January, col.652) Referring to the case of a prison inmate appointed a bailiff by a Board which failed to check his credentials, Lord Carmichael maintained that nominees should be confirmed by the Scottish Secretary. Lord Gray, however, did not agree. Procedures, he felt, were adequate, and as this was purely a local matter, it should be dealt with by the relevant local Board.

Following this introductory sparring it was Lord Ross who raised the alarm. He was baffled by the failure of many leading Peers to participate on this key provision. "It is quite disgraceful. …I expected that at this stage quite a number of Noble Lords would draw out all the difficulties that will arise in relation to licensing". (29 January, cols.655-56) Lord Ross demanded details. Would the Regional or local District Council be the authorised licensing authority? How many licences would be issued in each local government area? Would the recipients be persons who already were dealers? And what of hotels, net and rod proprietors? Would they all be eligible? "We should not just let it [the provision] go through to suit Government's convenience, because it is late [in the evening], and they think they are clever in respect of what they have done hitherto". The response of Lord Gray was merely to recite the general provisions in the Clause which were subject to the relevant sections in the *Civic Government Act.*

Lord Ross was dismayed. "We are told [that Government] has no idea of what this scheme will be! None what ever! …They have been telling everyone in Scotland, 'Here is the way we are going to solve all the problems of poaching in Scotland'. And [yet] they cannot give us a single clue as to what they are going to do"! (29 January, col.659) Despite these strictures by Lord Ross and other Peers, the Dealer-Licensing Clause was accepted as proposed by Government.

a) Dealer-Licensing for England / Wales Two days later when Peers re-convened to consider the remaining clauses in the Bill, it became apparent that the battle over Dealer-Licensing was by no means over. Indeed, it had hardly begun. Peers had agreed on a tactic which they hoped would offer the best prospect of success.

Lord Ross led off. He called for a separate Dealer-Licensing scheme for England and Wales. (30 January, col.807) All participants now rediscovered their voices. There was full and strong support for this proposal.

Lord Trenchard proposed an amendment to Lord Ross's new Clause which would incorporate the idea of a "chain of licensing", similar to that operative for Game Dealers. The person who shoots game is licensed; the retailer/shop-keeper has a local authority licence; and the Game Dealer must have both a local authority and Excise Licence. (30 January, cols.811-12) Lord Trenchard contended that such a chain for salmon would enable "onus of proof" requirements to be more easily satisfied. Lord Trenchard also noted that implementation would involve "no added costs" to the fishery departments and Water Authorities, since the entire scheme would be under the control of the Local Authorities.

Lord Denning now entered the fray. The former Master of the Rolls stressed the need for a "uniform" system of Dealer-Licensing for England, Wales and Scotland. (30 January, col.814) Poached salmon were "taken in masses" both to London and Glasgow. As "The problem is the same, therefore, the law should be the same for dealing with it". The question was: should the scheme set out by Government for Dealer-Licensing in Scotland be followed? Or should the "ingenious suggestion" of Lord Trenchard "that we should adapt the Game Laws for England", be pursued? Clearly, Lord Denning felt the Trenchard scheme was far superior. "Whether in England and Wales or Scotland, cases arising from relevant prosecutions should apply the same principles".

In effect, a combined assault by Lord Ross and his English Peer supporters—with Scottish Peers maintaining a conspicuously low profile—virtually turned around Government's Dealer-Licensing Clause. The only other Peer who gave forceful support was Lord Moran. He felt this was an excellent opportunity not only for officials from England and Wales and Scotland to get together to decide on the best National scheme—Dealer-Licensing or tagging, or perhaps a combination of the two—but also, since such a scheme would be for "all Great Britain", to make the Bill a "UK Bill" by substituting "GB" for "Scotland" in the title. (30 January, cols.819-20) Government's reply to this comprehensive challenge was to defer comment to Report Stage.

b) Illegal Possession: Incorporation Efforts During earlier debates, poaching and Illegal Possession of salmon had caused their Lordships to wax wrathful. It was no different at Report stage. Lord Lansdowne asked that a provision be added to the Dealer-Licensing clause specifying "it shall be an offence for any person to be found in possession of salmon without being able to produce sufficient authority for such possession". (13 February, col.340) There was a buzz of approval amongst Peers—with one exception, the former Leader of the Liberal Party, Shetlander, Lord (Jo) Grimond. He urged Peers to show caution. Did they not recognise what it would mean if this amendment were adopted? Did they not appreciate that "established principles of British law" must be safeguarded? And was not one of these principles that a person was "innocent until proven guilty"?

Ignoring Lord Grimond's warning, Peers pressed on. Lord Lansdowne's amendment had raised the issue of "onus of proof". This amendment made clear, Lord Trenchard asserted, that the accused would be guilty of the offence of "illegal possession" if he could not "prove his innocence". (13 February, cols.340-43) Was this not the

ILLEGAL NET ... stretched across mouth of small West Coast river.

only possible way to proceed, he asked? "With no necessary identifying mark" on the salmon, there was nothing to show directly that it was not stolen. The Bill placed the "onus of proof" on the prosecution to prove "the mind" of the accused—that the accused "believes, or has reasonable grounds for suspecting" that the fish were illegally taken. But this was virtually impossible. Lord Trenchard added that if the accused were required to "supply specific information as to where and from whom the salmon were received" this would provide sufficient protection for the innocent.

Lord Denning agreed that Government's provision for a new offence, that of "handling, receiving, carrying, dealing" in salmon which had been illegally taken, was an important break-through. The problem with the existing Section 7 of the *1951 (Scotland) Salmon Fishery Act* was that it related only to the poacher. The new Dealer-Licensing provision would ensure that all those concerned with Illegal Possession activities could be brought before the courts. Yet there was a problem: the need for a "reversed onus of proof" provision.

Demonstrating a remarkable and detailed grasp of Scottish law, Lord Denning referred to a case brought before the Scottish Court of Session in 1963 under Section 7 of the *1951 Act.* The Appeals Court had ruled that given the "remote places" where poaching normally takes place, and the difficulty in producing "direct evidence" and witnesses, it was quite reasonable for the accused to be required to establish that the "suspicious circumstances have an innocent explanation", and that if the accused could not so establish, "then he can be convicted". (13 February, col.344) Lord Denning referred also to a similar 1963 Appeal case outcome in an English Divisional Court. The import of these decisions, he said, was clear: if a person was found with salmon in suspicious circumstances "it is up to [that person] to give an explanation". If not, then he could be convicted. The value of the new Dealer-Licensing Clause was that it would allow "the whole lot", and not simply the poacher alone, to be brought before the Courts, and convictions would follow if credible "innocent explanations" were not supplied.

Lord Gray stated that Government could not accept either of the amendments. "The existing [Dealer-Licensing] Clause", he declared, "is designed to allow conviction on an objective test, while retaining

MONOFIL DRIFT-NET ... stretched out to dry in a remote Wester Ross sea-loch.

the need to relate the suspicion to the individual accused". (13 February, col.347) He said mere "information regarding possession" was not enough; the Courts would require "records" of salmon caught. Government, therefore, could not accept that it was right to allow for "reverse onus of proof" in such circumstances. Insofar as the issue of Illegal Possession was being addressed, Lord Gray stated, "We in

Scotland believe that [the existing Clause] will be an effective weapon against both the poacher and the receiver". It was not appropriate that any provision concerning Illegal Possession be incorporated in the Dealer-Licensing Clause.

Twice rejected by Government, Lord Trenchard now sallied forth with a third and final thrust. He called on Government to consider an entirely new Dealer-Licensing Clause. (13 February, cols.354-56) which called for implementation of a "unified National Salmon Dealer-Licensing" scheme. Stress was placed not on Illegal Possession; but a 6-item set of provisions specifying the conditions under which any person might be defined as being legally in possession of salmon. Adoption of the replacement Clause, said Lord Trenchard, would make it much easier to bring an action against a person found in possession of salmon but who did not meet one or more of the six specified provisions. This, he contended, would establish the "licensing chain" of which earlier he had spoken.

It was a masterful effort. Lady Saltoun added that such a scheme should also provide that netsmen and riparian owners be ineligible to hold a Dealer-Licence. Lord Ross strongly agreed. (13 February, col.356) Lords Thurso and Burton, however, hotly opposed it. It was important, said Lord Thurso, "that people fishing should be able to dispose of their fish through legal channels". Proprietors "can do a great service by being able to handle fish for anglers". Lady Saltoun's amendment, Lord Burton stressed, would "very much limit the market". As there would be few licensed dealers in some areas, they could "corner the market, ...and the price of salmon would drop completely".

The reply of MAFF Minister, Lord Belstead, was polite but firm. The entire basis of the Bill's Dealer-Licensing (Scotland) Clause, he stressed, was based on the *1982 Civic Government (Scotland) Act*. To accept Lord Trenchard's scheme would be to remove the existing Clause from this carefully constructed foundation. This, Government was not prepared to countenance. (13 February, cols.357-59)

As a result of enormous efforts behind the principal initiatives by the two English Peers, Lords Trenchard and Denning, and with Lord Ross playing a vital role, the Government agreed to shift its ground. There would now be separate Dealer-Licensing schemes for England/Wales and for Scotland. A "unified UK" scheme was rejected.

One minor but important advance also was secured. While Lord Ross failed to persuade Government of the need to alter provisions concerning the eventual introduction of Scottish Dealer-Licensing from "permissive" to "mandatory", he secured confirmation from Lord Gray that any scheme ultimately formulated would be subject to "affirmative procedure", and hence must have the approval of both Houses of Parliament. (13 February, cols.333-35) As for renewed concern about the "extensive powers" to be given to bailiffs, as expressed by Lord Carmichael, Government once again was adamant. Lord Gray merely re-iterated that the relevant powers given to District Boards were in accord with the "permissive" provisions of the Scottish Dealer-Licensing Clause, and would be retained. While agreeing to accept Government's ruling, Lord Carmichael hinted—quite correctly—that the issue would remain "live", and subject to further consideration at Commons stage.

2) Illegal Possession: Valiant Efforts

Nothing if not determined, Peers now moved on to consider the separate (English/Welsh and Scottish) Illegal Possession clauses. Government was hard-pressed to justify its own position, much less argue away the tough persuasiveness of those who sought much stronger United Kingdom provisions.

a) Reversed "Onus of Proof" Demand During Committee Stage, Lord Moran, backed by Lord Denning, proposed that Government accept fundamental amendments to the Illegal Possession Clauses. These amendments would place on the accused the burden of proof for showing that salmon found in his possession, under suspicious circumstances, was not illegally taken. (30 January, cols.826-28) It would be for the accused, not the prosecution, to provide this evidence. "The onus ...shall be on the defendant". Lord Moran declared that the Water Authorities' Association, which was strongly critical of the Bill's Illegal Possession provisions, felt that such amendments would afford "robust and effective legal powers to pursue organised poaching". Lord Denning added that the value of Lord Moran's amendments was that there was no need to consider the accused's "state of mind", but only show there were "suspicious circumstances". Once this was achieved, it was "for the accused" to say how, why and where he had come into possession of the fish. If "he will not or cannot explain, then the Court can convict."

Their demands once again rejected by Government, Peers turned to secondary concerns. Lady Saltoun raised the issue of penalties. Provision, she said, should be made for removal of a licence to deal in salmon from any Licensed Dealer convicted of Illegal Possession. (30 January, col.838) This would be "almost as powerful a deterrent as the threat of a prison sentence". Lord Burton agreed, and added it was vital that the Court inform the District Council responsible for issuingthe Licence. However, Lord Cameron, Lord Advocate for Scotland (Government's Chief Law Officer for Scotland) rejected these proposals. These were matters for the District Council Licensing Authority. Lady Saltoun then suggested that loss of an hotelier's liquor licence would be the ultimate sanction in the event of an Illegal Possession conviction. Lord Cameron again rejected this proposal. He did, however, point to the "misconduct" provisions in the *Licensing Act (Scotland) 1976,* under which a liquor/spirits licence could be suspended.

Lord CAMERON of Lochbroom

LORD DENNING

LORD KIMBALL

b) "Onus of Proof": Government Concession? At Third Reading it was apparent that persistent pressure of reformists finally had produced results: Lord Cameron offered amendments to the Scottish Illegal Possession Clause in order to ease the burden on the prosecution, and increase it for the defence. He pointed out that the prosecution would still first "have to prove that the accused had salmon in his possession". (25 February, col.985) Instead of having to prove that the accused "believed", or there were "reasonable grounds for him suspecting" that the fish were illegally taken; the amended provision said that conviction could follow if it could be proven that "circumstances were such that it would be reasonable for the accused to suspect that those salmon had been illegally taken". The "onus of proof" was now shifted to the accused. The requirement that the prosecution must prove "the guilty mind" had been relaxed. So long as the prosecution could convince the Court that, given "the circumstances" in which the accused was "found in possession" of the fish, or that he "ought to have suspected" that the fish were illegal, conviction could follow.

Lord Cameron stressed that the Court would not be entitled to convict where it would be "unreasonable for the accused to so suspect". These amendments conceded, Lord Cameron made it clear this was the furthest Government would go to strengthen the prosecution's position. The new Clause was not concerned with any "poaching offence", but rather with an "offence much wider in its compass. It may be committed by any person", not simply the poacher. (25 February, col.987) Furthermore the Clause would be applicable wherever in the UK the offence took place.

Lord Trenchard was deeply disappointed with Government's concessions. It was basic to all the amendments that "others", including police and bailiffs, should be able to provide sufficient evidence for conviction. (25 February, cols.990-91) By employing this approach, what the accused might or might not have to say about his "possession" would not be sufficient to avoid conviction. It was a great pity, said Lord Trenchard, that Government was not prepared to meet this requirement. Without it, a "huge gaping hole in our enforcement laws" would remain. "What we are challenging is the difficulty of getting any real evidence [under Government provisions which run parallel to the *Theft Act*] bearing on whether the accused knew, unless you can at least confront him with all the circumstances, and unless, therefore, there is ...an onus on him to say where he obtained the salmon". Furthermore, there would be no threat to an innocent person "in possession"; because he would "readily and immediately" say where he otained the salmon.

Strong support once again was forthcoming from Lord Denning. Should not Government, he asked, accept the principles relating to the *1971 Misuse of Drugs Act?* (25 February, col.999) Under this Act, the accused "has to prove he neither believed nor suspected, nor had reason to suspect, that the substance in question was a controlled drug". Lord Denning maintained that the same procedure should apply to salmon: "Let the man be charged; let him get away with it" if he can prove that circumstances did not lead him to believe, or suspect, the salmon was illegally taken. "The circumstances are such that we want to catch the whole gang, from the drivers, all the way down. I want to catch those from the organisers, the chiefs at the top, all the way down. I want to bring them before the Court".

c) Peers' Reservations In subsequent comments it became apparent that Scottish—and one or two English—Peers had cooled in their enthusiasm for the proposed amendments. It seemed they were appeased by Government's amendments to the Scottish Illegal Possession Clause. Indeed, Lord Home was not convinced that the amendments sought by Lords Denning and Trenchard did not go too far. The accused must be given the opportunity to show he did not believe, or suspect, that the salmon found in his possession were illegally taken. Lord Onslow, who throughout debates expressed doubts about the alleged gravity of poaching and illegal fishing, agreed. The Government amendments went "absolutely far enough—I suspect even verging on the too far!" (25 February, col.1003) Lord Ross also counselled caution. It would be "far too easy for a miscarriage of justice to occur".

POACHERS' POOL
... Low-water and blocked-off pool can spell disaster for trapped fish.

Lord Moran expressed grave disappointment with the views of Lords Home, Onslow and others. He pointed out that "much legal opinion", and all Water Authorities, were adamant that the Illegal Possession Clauses were inadequate, and would not improve prospects for successful prosecution. The burden of proof remained with the prosecution. It was vital that this situation should be reversed if the proposed new provision was to work. Lord Trenchard agreed.

II North-East Nets and International Fisheries

Peers' most aggressive assaults were saved for the North-East drift-nets issue. Emphasis was not only on the domestic effects of this fishery—salmon bound for Tweed and Scottish rivers—but also its international implications. These problems were mainly outside the scope of the Salmon Bill. Peers knew this, but rather than discourage discussion it incited their reforming zeal.

During Committee Stage, it became apparent that all participant Peers agreed that drift-netting round the coast of England and Wales should be abolished and the netsmen compensated. There was, however, a difference of opinion on how this should be done. Lord Lansdowne was the most outspoken supporter of outright and immediate abolition. (30 January, cols.857-61 and 879) At the other extreme, a number of Peers led by Lord Moran, called for drift-nets to be phased out over a 5-year period. (30 January, cols.853-54 and 861-68) It was to the gradualist approach that Peers directed their principal efforts during the remaining Lords Stages of the Bill.

There also was recognition of the wider domestic parameters of the drift-net problem. Lord Ross was the first to draw attention to the underlying but seldom-stated issue: the Scottish estuary nets. He said:

> "Suppose we did stop [NE drift-netting] right away? Will it assist in any way with conservation if we leave as it is the ability to catch by the [Scottish] netsmen at the estuary? I can see the advantages for them right away. It is pure commercial advantage [for the Scottish netting interests]. ...I think the suggestion was that about 97 per cent of [the fish] ...if not drift-netted successfully, have gone into them. ...I shall be the first to agree fully to the cut-offs and to the stopping of the drift-netting, if we can ensure that we do not then proceed to accept that the [Scottish] netsmen can have their 90 per cent share of what is left, with very little going upstream." (30 January, col. 863)

Lord Ross and others strongly urged that restraints placed on North-east nets must be matched by similar restraints on Scottish estuary nets. Without complementary restraints there would be little or no true "conservation benefit".

Lord Ross also raised the sensitive issue of "quotas". Together with several other Peers, including Lord Lansdowne, he asked whether Government was prepared to incorporate relevant measures. Nets and rods would in future "almost inevitably" have to face up to a system of "quota regulation". There were simply "too many people chasing too few fish", declared Lord Lansdowne. "In the end, the commercial netsmen—of whom I am one—...and anglers—of whom I am also one—will have to accept quotas. One already has this in the United States of America". (30 January, col.873)

Altogether, the position of reforming Peers at Committee Stage was that a ban was essential on drift-netting not merely in NE English waters, but round the entire coast of England and Wales. The considerations primarily were "domestic conservation". United Kingdom salmon interests could not hope further to press international abolition initiatives on "interceptory fisheries", so long as little or nothing was done to abolish her own. Furthermore, since "conservation" was the object of Peers' reform measures, it was vital that Scottish interests should also accept appropriate restraints. In securing these objectives, rodsmen as well as netsmen must face the need for appropriate quotas. Incorporation of the word "conservation" in the long title of the Bill would provide International and other concerned fishery interests with an indication that the United Kingdom was concerned to "conserve salmon". (30 January, col.882)

Government's response to these demands was to re-assure Peers that it was fully alert and sensitive to the issues raised. Lord Belstead repeated Government's assurance that a new Clause would be introduced at Third Reading to provide for a "Review of Salmon Netting" on the North-east English and Scottish coast. It would be conducted three years after passage of the Salmon Bill, and would afford full opportunity to satisfy most of Peers' concerns. (30 January, col.870) In the interim, a new Bill provision requiring that the licence-holder "must be present when his net is being fished"; and three new Northumbrian Water Authority and Yorkshire Water Authority bye-laws specifying an 8-hour night-time drift-netting ban, a standardised 60-hours Weekly Close Time, and the introduction of alternative (fixed) netting; collectively these measures would not only effect increased restraints on drift-nets, but demonstrate Government's resolve on the issue. "Those controls must be given a chance to work", said Lord Belstead.

At Report Stage, Lord Moran provided the principal initiative in the form of a 3-part amendment, shaped partially to accommodate Government's position, and focussed on the proposed "Three Year Review" of North-east coast netting. The five-year phasing-out idea was dropped, while a decrease in Yorkshire and Northumbrian netting now was spoken of merely in terms of "gradual reduction". (13 February, col.575) The amendment further called on Government to secure the views of the North Atlantic Salmon Conservation Organisation (NASCO); and if envisaged decreases in NE netting were to be effective, to ensure steps were taken to bring Scottish nets into conformity with the objectives sought. All reforming Peers stressed the "background need" for a "National Salmon Policy" (NSP). Lord Onslow and others emphasised the need for complementary restraints on Scottish nets and flexible quotas. (13 February, cols.377-81) Lord Lansdowne agreed: "My own company [Tay Salmon Fisheries] would net less. ...There must be a scaling down all over". Lord Moran said that a "fair measure" for the permissible North-east drift net catch would be "about one-sixtieth of the total Scottish catch", or 6000 fish "in a normal year". Lord Perth maintained that if in due course a "salmon surplus" was produced, "the people who benefit must be rods. ...But above all, let us see that we conserve our salmon".

But was it not possible to ban drift-netting without complex new legislation? Must there be a further Act of Parliament? Could the Weekly Slap for England/Wales and Scotland be increased? Could Government act earlier than three years if necessary? Viscount Trenchard put these points to Government. (13 February, col.382) Lord Belstead replied that, drift-nets could be banned under powers available to it under the *1967 Sea Fish (Conservation) Act*. (13 February, col.385) "Secondary legislation would suffice. Primary legislation would not be needed". As for increasing Weekly Slaps, "Water Authorities have power for the Weekly Close Times to be extended". Finally, with regard to early action before completion of the 3-Year Review, Lord Belstead repeated what Government had stressed "again and again" to their Lordships: before any further action was taken the Report of the "full and fair" 3-Year Review to be completed sometime after 7 November, 1989 must first be received.

In concluding comments at Report Stage, Lord Moran expressed deep disappointment with Government's stubborn position on the North-east and national drift-net fishery. While Government now seemed prepared to accept "a rather vague commitment on conservation in some form of words which we have not yet seen", and while he welcomed "extension of the Review to cover the nets off the Scottish rivers", Government had in other respects failed abysmally. Since there was no recognition that the North-east fishery was taking "far too much", he wondered what was the purpose of the Review? "What are the terms of reference going to be? What is its objective? This is what we tried to spell out in this amendment". (13 February, col.387)

At Third Reading, Government, true to its word, introduced the promised 3-Year (North-east netting) Review and "endorsee" restric-

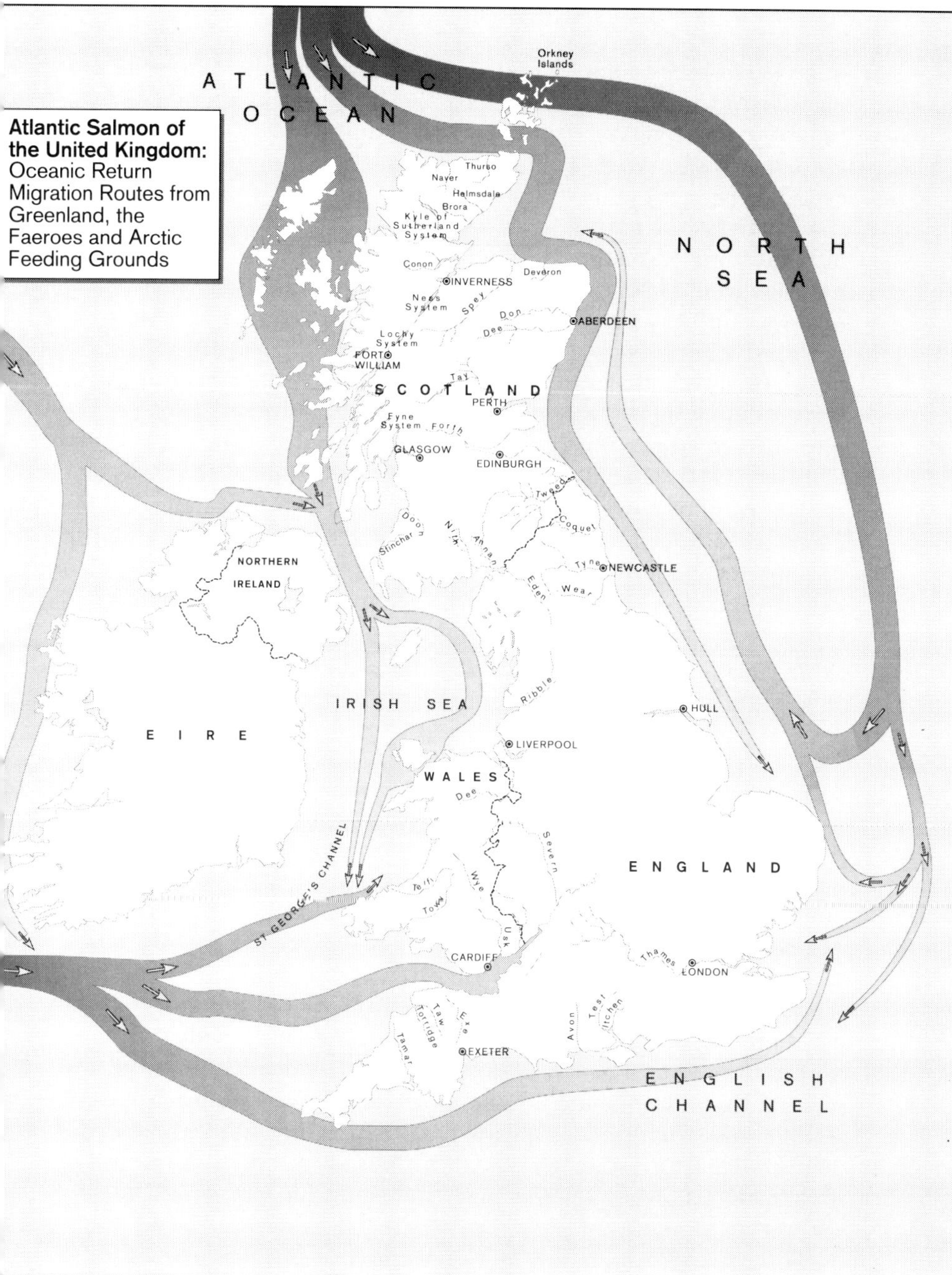

Atlantic Salmon of the United Kingdom: Oceanic Return Migration Routes from Greenland, the Faeroes and Arctic Feeding Grounds

tion clauses—Sections 39 and 36 respectively in the *1986 Salmon Act.* (25 February, cols.1014 and 1022). (The object of Section 36 is to reduce the intensity of drift-netting by requiring that "endorsees"—up to four persons listed on the licence of a netsman—no longer net, or land fish except in the company of the licence-holder). Thus Government was not totally insensitive to Peers' repeated demands at Report Stage. A concession had been made. The restrictions on "endorsees" would apply not only to North-east fishing, but "to all such fisheries" in the United Kingdom jurisdiction. While Lord Belstead declared that these new provisions served to fulfil the commitments which Government made at earlier stages of the Bill, reforming Peers were still unhappy. They made one last and vigourous effort to secure amendments they still regarded as vital.

Lord Lansdowne called on Government to abandon, once for all, its narrow commitment to a Review only of North-east net-fishing. "Her Majesty's Government have not yet addressed themselves to the problem of the British salmon fisheries as a whole". (25 February, col.1016) Lord Lansdowne stressed the need for a 3-Year Review which would afford the opportunity of "taking the necessary steps to conserve and enhance the stock of [all] United Kingdom-bred salmon". Furthermore, such a step was essential "if our partners in NASCO" were to be shown that "we wish to co-operate fully with them". Lord Moran and most other Peers endorsed these views. *It was imperative to establish a National Salmon Policy (NSP),* said Lord Moran, and "to take an overall look at the whole problem of salmon conservation". (25 February, col.1018) Had there been a national body "to co-ordinate and to recommend what our policy should be on all these matters, I am sure that the Bill would have started off in a very different shape".

Lord Belstead remained firm. It was, he said, "rather short notice to start a debate on the issue of a National Salmon Policy". (25 February, col.1020) Government was prepared to give its commitment only to a North-east Review, while "bearing in mind the international implications" when the Review was duly conducted. In agreeing finally to withdraw his amendment, Lord Lansdowne expressed hope that these matters might yet receive more favourable consideration when the Bill was examined by the House of Commons.

Following introduction of Government's new Clause (Section 39) calling for a 3-Year Review, Peers focused their final repeated efforts on securing inclusion of some reference to the international problem. Once again, however, Government remained adamant. No concession was granted. "I believe", said Lord Belstead, "that what we are doing in this Bill, despite certain remarks which have been made this evening, will be recognised internationally as enhancing our contribution. ...The fact of the matter is that we are taking action". (25 February, col.1028)

The Limits of Privilege: II

By the time Lords' Third Reading had been completed, Peers again had demonstrated that repeated, determined efforts could produce a measure of positive response from a recalcitrant Government. While it refused to allow amendments that would commit it to a "National Salmon Policy", or to NASCO , or even to a statutory "conservation" undertaking; and while it was equally adamant in rejecting Peers' demands either for the abolition, or the phasing out of the North-east drift-net fishery; nevertheless Government was prepared to grant two concessions. These included a "Servants and Agents" Clause—aimed at reducing netsmen at sea—and the provision for the North-east Review of netting (Sections 36 and 39 respectively in the 1986 Salmon Act).

The Salmon Bill was now to pass to "that other place", the House of Commons. Peers would not see it again for eight months prior to final passage in November 1986. What, then, had been attained by this lengthy and detailed phase of the Bill? One or two small improvements had been secured by arduous efforts of reforming Peers. But in the broader sense, had anything of significance been achieved?

Certainly, there had been an immense amount of informed and informative debate. Minor and major issues were raised—albeit the minor ones received most attention. All now were enshrined in the official record. The fact that such a record now existed which might prove of the greatest value to future salmon law reformers, was in itself a significant achievement.

But for the rest, the Bill remained a "wee tim'rous beastie". In relation to key reform provisions which might have rendered it "less tim'rous", including improved Central controls, an expanded Inspectorate with greatly increased powers, flexible quotas on harvests, and longer close-times, no progress was achieved. And while Peers directed their principal efforts towards enhancing and safeguarding their rights and privileges as salmon fishery owners, it was not for want of determination and diligence that these produced little statutory gain.

What had been identified in the Lords' debates as specific, acceptable reform measures—that is, increased powers for the Scottish

Secretary and District Boards, and new anti-poaching measures—would now be pursued in the House of Commons. In essence, the Lords' debates served to confirm and consolidate the "tim'rous" principles and legislative frame set by Government and DAFS. Nothing was done to guarantee measures which would slow down the relentless diminution of the wild salmon resource in the United Kingdom.

To the many of the un-informed in the "outside world", it seemed that Peers had conducted a comprehensive and masterful, even heroic reforming struggle against Government "baddies" determined to protect—and possibly enhance—the commercial interests. In fact, the dominant (Scottish) "salmon Lords" and Government were basically at one. The Bill fully protected private salmon fishery rights. Where Government and these Peers were at odds was over Peers' forceful demands to extend further these rights. Insofar as there were the "rights of the salmon" and the public to be protected, Government acted to ensure that the encroachments of privileged private interests were limited.

The interim Scottish Committee of the Salmon and Trout Association summed up what most informed observers and participants thought of the Lords performance: "Around 100 amendments to the Bill were tabled in the House of Lords, but most were withdrawn. The real issues have been ignored and the Bill, if passed in its present form, will allow the netting interests, including those of many of their Lordships, to again relax and continue their interests in estuary and coastal netting".[3]

In essence, the Bill was a "re-written netsmen's Charter". Anglers, conservationists and tourism interests deeply resented this. All wanted "more salmon in rivers", but the dominant Scottish "salmon Lords" either did not, or at best lacked the certainty needed to overcome their residual fears and reservations, to press for attainment of this fundamental objective.

Yet the Bill afforded basic protection not only to the rights of netting Lords, it also protected the private rights of angling Lords. In this sense the Bill could more correctly be termed a "Proprietors' Charter". Insofar as both angling and netting Lords supported the "private rights" *status quo*, as shown during the Lords debates, they were at one. Where they differed, was in the overwhelming statutory preference, and the legal right to continue taking the majority of the exploitable catch. The Lords with netting interests triumphed.

References

1. *House of Lords: Parliamentary Debates,* 25 February, 1986, cols.1001-02)

2. See *Lords Debates,* 29 January, 1986, col.655. Hereafter, reference to Lords Debates will be included in the text by date and column. The relevant Debate dates and Hansard references are:

   Lords Committee: Lords Debates. 28,29, 30 January, 1986.
   Lords Report: Lords Debates, 13 February, 1986.
   Third Reading: Lords Debates, 25 February, 1986.

3. *Parliamentary Brief by the Scottish Committee of the S&TA: The Salmon Bill,* (Amended Draft), (Aberdeen, 3 March, 1986), p.l.

Chapter 7

ACTION IN THE COMMONS

> "The [Salmon] Bill was seen as the greatest opportunity for many years to ensure that effective conservation measures are embodied in legislation, that control is not left in the hands of the commercial netting interests, and for the United Kingdom to develop a coherent National Salmon Policy. ...Unfortunately, the Bill fails to address these issues."
>
> *The Salmon Conservancy*[1]

The dominant Scottish salmon interests, by the end of the Lords debates, had attained the basic objectives they sought. The framework and principles of the Bill were now firmly in place. Still, reforming Peers too had secured achievements. The key issues had been identified, minor amendments had been secured, others were promised later consideration by Government. Given support from their allies in the Commons, it was possible that reform efforts which had failed in the Lords might succeed in the Lower House. This was reformers' hope.

While the dominant interests might be pleased and relieved with the position that had been secured, others were not. The Bill was condemned by angling and conservation interests as a "Scandalous outrage! Yet another sell-out! Triumph for the netsmen!"[2] Furthermore, if effective change was not achieved at the Commons stage, Government was aware it risked added condemnation by colleagues in the North Atlantic international salmon fishery community.

What would Government do? Were there not ways of rendering the Bill more acceptable to these interests and the wider public? What of the Scottish salmon barons? With their major objectives now safely secured, was there not something they too could do to appease, or at least temper the wrath of, their critics? Would it not be in their interest to do so? These, however, were matters for the future. The immediate challenge was clear enough. Government and its supporters must now muster a credible and convincing defence of the

"Landlords' Charter". The Fisheries Ministers and their departmental "salmon servants" faced more than a sporting challenge. How would they respond?

Preliminary Alarums

The success so far achieved by Government was partly due to skilful parliamentary manoeuvering. Judicious timing and swift sequence of the Lords stages meant that Peers, let alone lobbyists, were kept off balance and had little time to grasp vital details and formulate needed amendments. Partly this success was due also to effective tactics deployed by allies of the proprietorial *status quo*. These tactics had ensured that the more radical demands of steadfast minorities within leading conservation and angling groups were evaded or otherwise diverted and suppressed. Reference has been made to these factors in Chapters 3 and 4 above.[3]

Reformers were confident that things would be different at the Commons stage. They believed it "unlikely that the Bill would have its First Reading in the Commons before the end of March".[4] This would allow a welcome breathing space and ample time for interest groups to produce up-dated briefs and lobby targeted MPs.

In addition, members who were distressed by the "betrayal" of the angler-conservationist "cause" by Salmon and Trout Association (London) had made their own contingency plans for the Commons stage. By the end of February these were well-advanced. The Interim (and then still the un-official) Scottish Committee of the S&TA under its Acting Chairman Michael Smith, together with Salmon Conservancy Vice-Chairman, Colin Carnie agreed on two essential amendment demands: an increase in the Weekly Close Time for Scottish nets by three tides, from 42 to 72 hours; and an increase in the Annual Close Time for Scottish nets of about one and a half months, from 168 to 202 days, or 212 days (Salmon Conservancy).[5]

MICHAEL C. SMITH ... Acting Chairman, Interim Scottish Committee, S&TA, March 1986.

While these amendments were a long way from the thoroughgoing reforms which most members of the Scottish Committee and Salmon

Conservancy wanted, nevertheless, if achieved, they would help greatly. Furthermore, if these committed reformers did not take these urgent actions, no one else would. At least there would be enough time to prepare the parliamentary ground.

It came, therefore, as a profound shock to these reformers, and many others, to learn two days after completion of Lords Third Reading (25 February), that "Government, with total contempt for concerned salmon interests, [had] quietly slipped the Bill the very next day (26 February) into the Commons for its First Reading! By the time most were aware that the Second Reading, when any extended debate can normally be expected, was to be held the following Tuesday (4 March), rod and conservation lobbies found themselves with less than one day to get hold of and brief relevant MPs!"[6] Swift action was needed.

Suddenly other problems loomed. When S&TA (London) learned of the Scottish Committee's proposed initiative a fierce and frenzied reaction came from Fishmongers' Hall. "Mr. Smith, and clerk to the Scottish Committee, Guy Bentinck, were subjected to a sudden fierce volley of abuse and threats" from the London office of the Association.[7] And why was Director James Ferguson and S&TA (London) kicking up this almighty fuss? It turned out that the London office "had released its own brief... [which] said nothing about reducing netting [and] made no clear amendment demands. It was simply another bit of public relations waffle".[8]

There was equal uproar in the Salmon Conservancy. When Harriet Comfort, now (joint) Salmon Conservancy Secretary/S&TA (London) public relations officer, learned of the Smith/Carnie initiative, she warned that the "whole Conservancy initiative could be ruined!"—though what damage could be done was not clear, since the "official" Conservancy brief contained little more than additional public relations waffle.

In the event, the Scottish Committee's brief went to the local and national press on the Sunday evening. The "un-official" Conservancy brief went to MPs on the Monday in ample time for next day's inaugural Commons debate.

On 4 March, with the alarums of the preceding days safely behind them, Salmon Bill reformers settled down in the Commons Gallery to follow the proceedings. In fact "debate did not commence till the House had first exhausted its after-dinner energies on a Scottish Housing Bill. That was 9 pm."[9] Then suddenly these observers became aware that their problems were far from over. "A quick survey revealed the worst! A grand total of not more than 30 Members (15

Government and 15 Opposition) settled on the benches. And not a single MP from Scotland's immensely valuable Northern and Highland salmon fishery constituencies was to be seen. From John O'Groats, all the way down to the Firth of Clyde [with the exception of Bill Walker, Tayside North], salmon interests were totally without representative spokesmen! ...Where were these salmon-area parliamentarians? Why did they not at least raise their voices and get their statements on record?"[10] Had they been warned off?

Establishing the Battle Lines

1. Government: Salmon and the Local Economy

To John MacKay (Member for Argyll and Bute), Under-Secretary of State at the Scottish Office (and Commons Minister for Agriculture and Fisheries), fell the unenviable task of guiding the Salmon Bill through the Commons. In his opening address he appealed to the aggrieved angling interests. "Angling in general", he said, "is the biggest participation sport in this country". It was a multi-million pound industry. "Figures [for the value of salmon angling to Scotland] have been put variously at between 22 million and 140 million per annum. While those employed directly or indirectly in the salmon industry may not add up to a lot of people in Glasgow or West Central Scotland terms, they [do] add up to a lot of people in the remote rural corners of Scotland, often in the most fragile economic parts of the countryside. In addition to ghillies, boatmen, and keepers directly employed, hotels, self-catering, shops, restaurants and all parts of the rural economy benefit from the angler. The angler will come, and continue to come, only if he feels he has a reasonable chance of catching fish, and that depends on how well we conserve the stocks of salmon."[11]

MacKay spoke cautiously of netsmen. "The legitimate netsman", he said, "is equally an important part of the rural economy. Netting forms a very important part of the annual fishing cycle. Their survival is linked, critically, to the survival of the salmon, and in sufficient numbers, to allow them a reasonable catch". The Bill therefore had a "direct impact on employment in the countryside". Its aim was to "improve the protection of the salmon so that the legitimate netsman and the angler" could enjoy "continuing livelihood and sport".

TABLE 3

SALMON BILL: LIST OF MPs (BY PARTY/NATIONALITY) SPEAKING IN THE COMMONS SECOND READING DEBATE AND THEIR SALMON INTERESTS*

Number of Speakers at Second Reading = 25

PARTY PARTICIPANTS:

Conservative—12

Labour—9 Liberals—2 Scottish Nationalist Party—1 Plaid Cymru—1

SCOTTISH CONSERVATIVES (5):

John Corrie (Cunninghame North); owner of salmon rod fishing on the Solway Dee.

Michael Forsyth (Stirling); no known salmon interest.

John MacKay (Argyll and Bute); salmon angler; no proprietorial interest.

Sir Hector Monro (Dumfries); no known salmon interest.

Bill Walker (Tayside North); no known salmon interest.

SCOTTISH LABOUR (4):

Norman Buchan (Paisley South); no known salmon interest.

Tam Dalyell (Linlithgow); no known salmon interest.

John Home Robertson (East Lothian); owner of Lower Tweed net fishing.

Martin J. O'Neill (Clackmannan); no known salmon interest.

ENGLISH CONSERVATIVES (7):

John Selwyn Gummer (Suffolk Coastal); no known salmon interest.

Sir Geoffrey Johnson Smith (Wealden); salmon angler; no known salmon proprietorial interest.

Hon. Charles Morrison (Devizes); elder son of dual-interest salmon proprietor, Lord Margadale. (See Table 1, Chapter 3, p.49)

Hon. Peter Morrison (City of Chester); son of Lord Margadale.

Cranley Onslow (Woking); salmon angler; proprietor of salmon rod-fishing on a Welsh river.

Sir Michael Shaw (Scarborough); no known salmon interest.

Neville Trotter (Tynemouth); no known salmon interest.

ENGLISH LABOUR (3):

Dr. David Clark (South Shields); no known salmon interest.

Roy Mason (Barnsley Central); salmon angler; no known salmon proprietorial interest.

James Tinn (Redcar); no known salmon interest.

* *Source*. See *Parliamentary Debates* (House of Commons), 4 March, 1986, cols.232-258; and 5 March, cols.259-286.

WELSH LABOUR (2):

John Morris (Aberavon); no known salmon interest.

Ted Rowlands (Merthyr Tydfil and Rhymney); no known salmon interest.

OTHERS (4):

Alan Beith (Berwick-upon-Tweed) (Liberal); no known salmon interest.

Richard Livesy (Brecon and Radnor) (Liberal); salmon and sewin angler; no salmon proprietorial interest.

Rt. Hon. Donald Stewart (Western Isles) (Scottish Nationalist Party); no known salmon interest.

Dafydd Wigley (Caernarfon) (Plaid Cymru); no known salmon interest.

MacKay then outlined the three principal objects of the Bill, and noted both the various amendments and the leading issues which had been raised at Lords stage. Concluding on a conciliatory note, he declared that "Government's approach to the Bill", had been characterised by a "...willingness of Ministers and our Departments to listen to the views of salmon and other interests, and where possible to take these into account. That has, I think, been acknowledged as a constructive and essentially non-political approach, and I very much hope that this attitude will be reflected in our debate". (col.240)

To a considerable extent, MacKay's hopes were not in vain.

2. The Opposition: Salmon and the Public Interest

John Home Robertson (East Lothian), Opposition Leader on the Bill, moved an intial amendment which summed up not only the partisan position of the Opposition, but seemed also to represent the non-political views of angry and disillusioned anglers, tourism interests and conservationists—indeed, all but the small and vociferous minority of Scottish netting and dominant proprietorial interests. Home Robertson called for the House not to give the Bill a Second Reading, "...on the grounds that it would extend the powers and privileges of private proprietors of salmon fisheries without making adequate provision for anglers or for the wider public interest, and that it is an inappropriate and inadequate measure to deal with the urgent need to conserve salmon and other fish species, and to protect the environment of rivers and estuaries for the benefit of the whole nation's sporting, recreational and environmental interests." (col.240)

Home Robertson moved swiftly to the offensive. "It is amazing", he declared, "...that in this day and age, legislation should entrench the powers of absentee landlords, foreign investors, and in this case a Labour Member of Parliament [Home Robertson himself being the

JOHN HOME ROBERTSON ... Commons Opposition Leader on the Bill.

JOHN MacKAY... Commons Government Leader on the Salmon Bill.

owner of Paxton Policy, a netting beat on lower Tweed], while doing practically nothing for local fishing interests. That is absurd." (col.241)

Government, he said, had the opportunity to bring Scottish salmon legislation into the 21st century. Instead, it was "building on failure by re-adopting the dis-credited framework" of the 1860s Scottish Salmon Fisheries Acts. Government had spoken of "democratising" the District Fishery Boards", yet the franchise would be extended "only to the people who own the fisheries. How that can be called democratisation is beyond me!" As for the extended coercive powers of Boards, he warned that "bailiffs appointed by such Boards" would be bound to continue to be seen "as landlords' men". This "fundamental inequity" in the constitution of Boards was "a significant factor in the lawlessness afflicting so many rivers in Scotland." What was needed was "genuine representative river boards" which would "command the respect of all concerned". The Bill failed to do this.

Dealer-Licensing, and Illegal Possession provisions, he accepted, could prove useful. But in terms of prosecuting poaching offences the provision for corroboration by one witness (instead of two) was a violation of a fundamental principle of Scottish law; while the apparent presumption of guilt "until he [the accused] can prove he is innocent" was repugnant to the very principles of British justice.

Home Robertson also had mixed feelings about the North-east drift-net fishery. Although accepting that its catch had risen dramatically between 1965 and 1981, and that "something will have to be done", he expressed "some sympathy" for these netsmen. It "should not be necessary to hound [them] out of existence." (cols.243-44)

Having said nothing to this point with which most angling and conservation interests could seriously disagree, the Opposition Leader launched a concerted attack on "rich seasonal [angler] visitors" and "my old friends, the riparian owners". The latter were making "strong representations [to secure] the closure of licensed net fisheries." He characterised comments made by Peers during the Lords debates—"a fascinating catalogue of vested interests"—and suggested that while many "might not put it in writing", it was evident they "would like to do away with the netting operation." He "would like to see considerably more public access to salmon fishing and rather less emphasis on the exclusive rights of the very rich on some rivers."

What did Home Robertson actually *mean* by these remarks? Members had many queries. Were they not aimed at that long-archaic stereotype, "the rich salmon angler visitor"? But were not most modern salmon anglers persons of ordinary means? And even though there remain many "rich angler visitors", was it wrong that they should be "rich"? Were they not important contributors to the Scottish angler-tourism economy? Did they not bring much business and benefit to ordinary local people? Furthermore, was it wrong that Scottish, as well as North-east netting, should be reduced, phased out

NETS AT TWEED-MOUTH ... Netsmen set out on a sweep.

or simply banned? Had not Scottish legal nets taken far too many fish for far too long? Should they not be curbed by law—particularly estuary and river nets? (col.279)

And while many rodsmen might not object to the idea of "improved access", what precisely did Home Robertson mean? What were the limits he was setting? He did not say. As for his summary comment, that he hoped the Bill would "provide a fair share of the available catch to all legitimate interests", how would he define "fair shares"? Did this mean that netsmen should be permitted to retain the legal right to extract their customary 85-plus per cent of the catch? Home Robertson did not elaborate.

Ideologies and Issues

1. The Ideological Divide

The division between private and public interest, as represented in the Salmon Bill had not escaped the notice of Peers during the Lords debates. As we have seen in Chapter 3, Lords Ross and Carmichael ensured that things were put in a fully-rounded perspective. However, even these observations on the Bill by Labour's solitary duo had been made gently, courteously, as befitted Members of the Lords. Furthermore, their comments were made within the context of "welcoming" the Bill, and seeking to secure improvement in the existing provisions.

In the Commons "the gloves came off". In short order, all subterfuge and camouflage were stripped away. The Bill, its central purpose and its wider ideological meaning, were nakedly exposed. Donald Stewart (Western Isles) applied the principal scourge: "The Bill is tailored for sectional interest. The owners of the estates have real power. No marches or demonstrations for them. They intercede with the Government to defend their interests, and a Bill is provided for them. The Bill has nothing to do with conservation. It is offensive to natural justice. It is a Landlords' Charter with oppressive and despotic connotations." (col.263)

Norman Buchan (Paisley South) took his turn with the lash. "We know what the salmon means in Scotland, and especially in the Highlands. The salmon means privilege. It has meant privilege, and it has been maintained for the purpose of privilege, and the purpose of the Bill is to maintain that privilege. That is what it is all about in the Highlands, where King Salmon still rules." (col.276)

With rather more than a hint of bitter irony, Martin J. O'Neill (Clackmannan) noted that recently he spent many days attending "debates about the defence of the realm". (col.270) But in the Lords it seemed that "more interest is generated in the defence of salmon fishing interests" He conceded the need for a Bill which would meet public interest and conservation requirements, "...but we [the Opposition] are always suspicious when the vested interests which the Government nakedly and openly represent greet legislation with the enthusiasm that this legislation received in the other place [Lords]". (col.271) In summing up, Home Robertson put the Opposition's position simply and clearly. "The fundamental flaw in the Bill is that it is a Landlords' Bill". That, he declared, was "why it will fail, and that is why we intend to press our amendment to a division." (col.280)

To these stinging criticisms and rebukes there was little basic defence. The Bill was a Landlords' Charter. The MAFF Fisheries Minister, John Selwyn Gummer, admitted as much. But the Bill, he stressed, had other basic objectives. "[It] is a major step in the control of poaching, the conservation of salmon and the protection of the proper demands and rights of those who live from and enjoy catching fish." (col.284) And there was another issue at stake. The Opposition talked of greater public access and control. The Bill itself introduced measures of "democratisation". But, as Charles Morrison (Devizes) implied, would this mean that the salmon and Scottish fisheries would be assured better protection and management under a public, rather than a private system of control? (col.259) This was not an issue which the Opposition sought to explore.

For the rest, Government supporters adopted varying postures of hurt and outrage. Sir Hector Monro rebuked the Opposition and reminded them that if it were not for the District Fishery Boards, and the "volunteers" who agreed to serve on them, there was "nobody else" who would look after "most of the rivers of Scotland". (col.250) Cranley Onslow (Woking) spoke out strongly. "It would be quite wrong", he declared, "to suppose that the Bill is a Landlords' Charter. It sets out to protect, and does protect, the interests of ordinary anglers as well as riparian proprietors". (col.263) As for the alarums of Home Robertson, the Minister dismissed them out of hand. To the considerable merriment of all concerned—excluding Mr. Home Robertson—he pointed out: "We all know why he did it. It is his annual speech of re-selection. Every year the Hon. Member has to come up with something to show the selectors that he is not what he seems to be [that is, a Scottish landowner and salmon fishery proprietor], and he chose today to do his Militant rain dance"! (col.281)

ALAN BEITH

In the end it was Alan Beith (Berwick-upon-Tweed), a seasoned parliamentary campaigner in the "salmon wars", who brought the debate back from this brief flourish of competing ideologies, to the grass-roots realities with which the Bill was concerned. The Bill, he declared, was "…not primarily a party political matter." Indeed, it required "considerable effort to work up a party political argument about any of these matters which [in fact] cut across almost all party issues and party lines". (col.253) The real core of any conflict generated by the Bill, he contended, arose from the incendiary emotions which salmon fishing unfailingly generated. "Broadly speaking, all those who fish for salmon think that all other categories of people who fish for salmon should not be doing so." (col.257)

2. Principal Issues and Competing Interests

Once the battle clangour of partisan political self-interest had subsided, what then of the the principal issues about which Members were concerned? What Regional interests, what political party interests were revealed?

While only 25 MPs, including Ministers, spoke during the Second Reading debate, and for the majority salmon was hardly a leading constituency interest; nevertheless, by the small hours of 5 March a fairly clear indication of the issues which participant Members considered important, together with the party and Regional lines along which positions on these issues appeared to divide, had emerged. These eight principal issues are listed in *Table 4, a) and b)* below.

a) Poaching Poaching was of greatest concern to political party and Regional groups. Government supporters and most Opposition Members regarded the situation as grave. They appeared to support Cranley Onslow's contention that the anti-poaching provisions in the Bill would assist considerably in "the war against poaching [both] North and South of the Border". (col.264) There were, however, political and Regional parameters to this concern. Martin O'Neill, expressing a basic concern of Scottish Labour Members throughout the Commons debates, stated that while he accepted that the Bill's provisions might be aimed at "the large poacher", there was nothing to suggest that the "small poacher" would be excluded. The "one-for-the-pot-man" could well have "an unhappy awakening, no matter how sentimentally or affectionately we view [him]". (col.270-71) It was the small man who needed protection, yet the Bill did nothing to assure this.

In Regional terms, it was the North-east English Members who expressed the greatest concern about large-scale poaching. They were adamant that the Bill's provisions and proposed Water Authority bye-laws would do little to correct this evil. The proposed night-ban on drift-net fishing, declared James Tinn, would effectively assist poachers. (col.265) Without the presence of legal netsmen at night, the problem would only be compounded. Much more expenditure on "policing and protection" was needed if "sea-poachers" were to be stopped. Alan Beith added that the Bill afforded little prospect of reducing "serious poaching" along some sections of the Scottish coast, and in Tweed's 120 square miles river-mouth "Conservation Box". (cols.253 and 257)

TABLE 4

SALMON BILL: COMMONS SECOND READING
PARTICIPATION ON PRINCIPAL ISSUES BY PARTY AND REGION/NATION*

[*Legend*: Conservative = C; Labour = Lab; Liberal = Lib; Scottish Nationalist Party = SNP; Social Democratic Party = SDP; Plaid Cymru = PC; Scottish Highlands = SH; Scottish West Coast = SWC; Scottish Borders and Lowlands = SBL; Wales = Wa; North-East England = NE; Southern England = SE. *Numbers of Party and Regional/National MPs participants is given in brackets) after headings.*]

a) Party Participation on Issues

ISSUE	C(12)	Lab(9)	Lib(2)	SNP(1)	PC(1)	TOTALS (25)
1. Anti-Poaching	5	4	2	-	-	11
2. NE Drift-Netting	5	3	1	-	-	9
3. Dealer Licensing	5	2	2	-	-	9
4. NASCO	5	2	-	-	-	7
5. NE Review	5		1	-	-	6
6. Rod/Tourism	3	1	2	-	-	6
7. "Illegal Posses'n"	-	2	1	1	-	4
8. Low Water Limits	4	-	-	-	-	4
TOTALS	32	14	9	1	-	56

* *Source:* See *Parliamentary Debates* (House of Commons), 4 March, 1986, cols.232-258; and 5 March, cols.259.

b) Regional / National Participation on Issues

ISSUE	SH(1)	SWC(2)	SBL(7)	Wa(4)	NE(6)	SE(5)	TOTALS (25)
Anti-Poaching	1	-	3	1	4	2	11
Pro-NE Drift-Nets	-	-	-	-	4	-	4
Anti-NE Drift-Nets	1	-	2	-	1	1	5
Pro-Dealer Licens'g	-	1	2	-	3	3	9
Pro-NASCO	-	-	2	-	1	4	7
Pro-NE Review	-	-	1	-	3	2	6
Pro-Rod/Tourism	1	-	3	1	1	-	6
Pro-Illegal Poss'n	-	-	1	-	1	-	2
Anti-Illegal Poss'n	-	1	1	-	-	-	2
Pro-Low Water Lim'n	-	-	1	1	-	2	4
TOTALS	3	2	18	2	17	14	56

b) North-East English Nets and Dealer Licensing The issues of North-east drift-netting and Dealer-Licensing drew the next greatest interest of participant MPs. In political party terms, Members showed about equal concern over North-east nets, but an assessment of Regional interest predictably revealed a sharp division. While all North-east spokesmen strongly opposed any further restraints on drift-nets, all other Scottish and English representatives were resolved that the drift-net fishery, at the very least, should be reduced to its mid-1960s catch level, and use of monofilament nets banned. Supporters of North-east netting questioned the effectiveness of Scottish protection of returning migrant stocks, and called for much improvement. Nor did they overlook the legal Scottish nets. What was the "conservation significance", they asked, of permitting continued "huge catches" by Scottish nets—about 85 per cent of the combined Scottish and NE catch? (col.268) A substantial proportion was taken by estuary nets, which afforded "far less chance of fish escaping", than did sea-nets.

Dealer-Licensing was welcomed by all, Government supporters and Liberals showing rather more enthusiasm than Labour Members.

Regionally, greatest interest was registered by North-east and Southern English Members. All were relieved that Government had agreed to extend Dealer-Licensing to cover both Scotland and England/Wales.

Salmon Tagging remained a particular concern, for Welsh, Scottish and North-east MPs. Most felt strongly that tagging should be incorporated in any Dealer-Licensing scheme. Mention was made of the Welsh Water Authority's readiness to undertake an "experimental tagging scheme" in the Principality, if a national scheme could not be agreed upon. (col.255) There was concern also about "what machinery there is to be to operate a Dealer-Licensing system", and the need for effective sanctions. (col.264) Would a Dealer found guilty of "back-door transactions" have his licence suspended? (col.249) Was it right for the Bill seemingly to provide the Minister with powers "to create criminal offences"? (col.254)

c) North Atlantic Salmon Conservation Organisation (NASCO) The importance of "putting our own house in order" to meet NASCO requirements, and hence improve prospects for strengthened regulation and further quota reductions on the Danes and Faroese who levied a heavy toll on British salmon in the North Atlantic, was stressed by several non-North-east Members. South-east Conservatives raised key issues which extended well beyond the customary attention given to North-east drift and United Kingdom "interceptory netting". In order to make a "positive and conscious" contribution to conserving the North Atlantic salmon, Cranley Onslow suggested that "quotas" might well be needed, "difficult as it may be to apply quotas to a mixed fishery such as we have in the United Kingdom". (col.264) Geoffrey Johnson-Smith observed that reduction of netting "in the estuarial waters of Scotland" was also important if the Danes were to be persuaded to reduce their Greenland catches. (col.273)

d) Angler-Tourism and the North-East Review Angler-tourism and the North-east Review emerged as (equal) subordinate issues during Second Reading. Government supporters and Liberal Members gave particular attention to angler-tourism. Regionally, it was the voices of Scottish and Welsh Members that were heard. Labour and Liberal Members emphasised the need for "more public access" to salmon waters. (cols.244 and 278) Government supporters were at pains to stress that salmon angling was a "popular recreation", rather than a sport for the "well-off and the privileged" (col.278); that many jobs depended on angler-tourism in Scotland (cols.250 and 279); and indeed that angler-tourism made a large contribution to Scottish and local economies. (col.279)

Government's provision for a North-east Review of net fishing was strongly welcomed by several Government supporters and the Liberal Member, Alan Beith. No Labour Member, and only one Scottish Member (Sir Hector Monro) spoke to the issue. Regionally, North-east Members voiced their satisfaction that the Review was to be based on "scientific data". Beith was confident this data would provide strong counter-arguments against those who wished to phase out North-east drift-netting. (col.256) North-east Members also were pleased that Scottish East coast netting would be included in the Review (col.268), and hoped that poaching "at the source of the rivers"—and not just at sea, and in estuarial and coastal waters—would also be dealt with. (col.277) Other spokesmen stressed the need: to shorten the three-year period of the proposed Review; to extend it to the whole United Kingdom coast (col.252); and to ensure that "optimum", rather than mere "sufficient numbers" of salmon to meet "spawning needs", be enabled to ascend rivers. (cols.260 and 273)

e) Illegal Possession and Low-Water Limitations Government's Illegal Possession provisions, and the absence of Low-Water fishing restraints in the Bill drew least comment during Second Reading. The sole Scottish Nationalist Party spokesman, Donald Stewart, dismissed the Illegal Possession provisions as "repugnant to natural justice", and warned they could be the "recipe for real trouble". (cols.262-63) The two Scottish Labour Members to speak to the issue also expressed concern about the potential threat to "civil liberties". As Norman Buchan put it, "The proposals were a major step backward" and seemed to provide "fresh reasons for sending people to Botany Bay"! (col.275) The sole North-East spokesman on the issue, Alan Beith, also warned of the need carefully to consider the issue of civil liberties. He was, however, prepared to give the measure a cautious welcome.

As for Low-Water (net) Limitations, the four Government supporters (two Scottish and two South-east Members) who spoke to the issue agreed that provision must be made to restrict netting during low-water conditions. It was pointed out that the proportion of net-caught to rod-caught salmon "increases dramatically" in drought years, from 3:1 at normal water levels, to between 6:1 and 11:1 during low-water periods.

All things considered, Members participating in the debate performed with surprising credit. Considering that most knew little about "salmon issues", debate was remarkably informed and relevant. If Government had thought it might be able to get away with deceiving Opposition MPs about the basic objectives of the Bill, it had been badly mistaken. It was perhaps to be expected that Government's supporters would dominate proceedings. But as shown in *Table 4, a)*, Labour, together with its minority party allies, managed to achieve a collective contribution which was only marginally less in numbers than its opponents. And so far as Regional and National contributions were concerned, *Table 4, b)* shows that participation was about what was expected. Even allowing for the inexplicable and critical absence of Highland MPs, Scottish Members made the major contribution, followed by North-East, Southern English and Welsh Members. Given the advantage of hind-sight, it is possible to say that personal dis-interest in salmon was to prove a considerable asset both to those Members who took part in Second Reading, and those who would be participating in the forthcoming Committee stage.

Summary: A Successful Defence

When finally debate concluded at 30 minutes past mid-night on 5 March, the House divided and a vote was taken on the Opposition amendment which John Home Robertson had moved at the start. The Opposition called for the Bill not to be given a Second Reading. Did Members agree?

Had the vote been taken then and there, with only those six Government and five Opposition Members remaining at this late hour, the amendment might have been carried. However, the Party Whips had been busy, and a considerable throng could be seen impatiently milling about behind the leaded windows of the lobby doors. When the Division was called they filed into the Chamber to do their duty. The result was a foregone conclusion. The amendment was rejected by a vote of 125 to 43. (col.284) It was interesting to note that two of the most vocal Members during the debate, Labour's Roy Mason and Scottish Nationalist, Donald Stewart, did not vote, also that the two Opposition Liberal participants, Alan Beith and Richard Livsey, voted with the Government. This was good news for Government as it now set about preparing for the mid-April start of the Commons Standing Committee on the Salmon Bill.

Government and the dominant Scottish salmon interests had emerged from Commons Second Reading relatively unscathed. True, Government had been subjected to an intense ideological assault which laid bare the essential motivation, direction and ultimate beneficiaries of the Bill. But it had been braced for this assault: the price to be paid for seeking passage of a *Government* Bill which basically was concerned with promoting and protecting *private* rather than *public* interests. The fact was that the ideological rhetoric, once spent, allowed attention to be turned to a number of the main issues. Opposition Members were prepared to concede that paltry, inadequate, even dangerous as most of the Bill's provisions might be, nevertheless they, along with certain unhappy Government supporters, were now reconciled to pursuing their reforming activity *within* the framework of the Bill.

But what of the last-ditch amendment initiatives by Salmon Conservancy and S&TA Scottish Committee reformers? Had their efforts borne any fruit? Mention was made during Second Reading of their demands for increased Weekly and Annual Close Times for Scottish nets. But nothing resembling a collective demand by Members for these vital amendments had emerged. Indeed, the apathetic behaviour of Members on these key issues merely confirmed what Government had learned as long ago as 1979, when it had issued its *DAFS Consultation Document*. Just as it had then discovered "what omissions—including vital increased Weekly and Annual Close Times—would be acceptable or at least tolerated" by the various non-dominant salmon interests[12]; so now it could feel re-assured that similar key "omissions" were again "quite acceptable" and posed no threat to the relevant Government provisions—Clauses 3 and 6—in the Bill.

MPs had paid little attention to the first two principal sections of the Bill concerned with "streamlining" the administration of Scottish salmon fisheries, and creating a "more flexible system" of fishery regulation. In addition, there had been only passing comment on the main provisions relating to substantial increases in the powers of local District Boards—and hence salmon proprietors—and the Scottish Secretary. Would these vital sections of the Bill be subjected to closer scrutiny in Committee?

Finally, there was the matter of Government concessions. Did it feel that appeasement initiatives were necessary? Certainly, nothing so far had been forthcoming. But might not a Government concession on Low-Water net limitations, or perhaps tough sanctions applicable to transgressing Licensed Salmon Dealers, or possibly provision for an "experimental tagging scheme" to be introduced in Wales only; might not any or all of these serve substantially to appease vociferous critics and enhance the *public* credibilty of the Bill? As for the dominant Scottish salmon proprietors: was there not some *private voluntary* initiative *they* could produce which might ease the task of Government; some initiative which also might provide convincing evidence that they too—like the salmon reformers—were committed to "getting more fish into and up rivers", and to enhancing conservation and the angler-tourism economy?

As far back as October 1985 parliamentary mention had been made of one sure way of getting more fish into Scottish rivers: buy off the nets.[13] So far, however, during Bill debates this issue had not been raised. Would some kind of voluntary buy-out scheme emerge at Committee stage?

References

1. "Chairman's Letter", *Safe Passage: The Newsletter of the Salmon Conservancy,* (Spring, 1986).

2. David Shaw, "Salmon Salvation or a Sell-Out?", *Trout and Salmon,* (February, 1986), p.50.

3. See above, Chapter 3, pp.45-46; and Chapter 4, "The Salmon Bill and S&TA Representations", pp.83-85.

4. See *Minutes of a Meeting of the Steering Committee of the Salmon Conservancy, held on Wednesday, 26 February, 1986, at Glasgow Chamber of Commerce,* p.1.

5. See *ibid.*, and personal communications of the writer with Carnie and Smith.

6. David Shaw, "Behind the Scenes", *Trout and Salmon,* (April, 1986), p.61.

7. *Ibid.*

8. *Ibid.* See also *Salmon and Trout Association: Salmon Bill (H.L.), Second Reading—House of Commons, 4 March, 1986,* (mimeo.), dated 28 February, 1986.

9. Shaw, "Behind the Scenes", *Trout and Salmon,* (April 1986), *op.cit.,* p.61.

10. *Ibid.* Among absent "salmon area" Members were Robert Maclennan (Caithness and Sutherland), Charles Kennedy (Ross, Cromarty and Skye), Sir Russell Johnston (Inverness, Nairn and Lochaber), Alex Pollock (Moray), Albert McQuarrie (Banff and Buchan), Gerry Malone (Aberdeen South), Robert Hughes (Aberdeen North), Alick Buchanan-Smith (Kincardine and Deeside), Peter Fraser (Angus East), Nicholas Fairbairn (Perth and Kinross), David Lambie (Cunninghame South), George Foulkes (Carrick, Cumnock and Doon Valley), Ian Lang (Galloway and Upper Nithsdale).

For a listing of those Members who were in attendance at Second Reading, see *Table 3,* below, pp.132-133.

11. *Parliamentary Debates* (House of Commons), 4 March, 1986, col.232. Hereafter, references to Second Reading debate will be included in the text, and by column only. It should be noted that Hansard coverage extends through the separate *Parliamentary Debates* for 4 March, (cols.232-258), and *Parliamentary Debates* for 5 March, 1986 (cols.259-286).

12. See above Chapter 2, p.14.

13. See *Parliamentary Debates* (House of Commons), 28 October, 1985, col.775.

Chapter 8

POLITICAL THEATRE AND LEGISLATIVE REALITIES: I

> "This has been a truly memorable debate in several ways. First we had the Liberal spokesman [Alan Beith] saying that he endorsed both sides of an argument between Conservatives, which to many of us seemed entirely appropriate. Then we had the splendid spectacle of the Minister defending someone else's brief. ...[And then] leading the attack [on Government] was none other than the Chairman of the 1922 Committee [Cranley Onslow]! We could live for a very long time before we next saw an onslaught of that nature! ...We look forward with fascination to see whether he decides to go through with this exciting rebellion"!
>
> *John Home Robertson*[1]

Traditionally, the Commons Standing Committee stage on any Bill performs two principal functions. First, it permits detailed scrutiny of the Bill's provisions. This is vital. While by this stage the basic principles and structure have been accepted and established, and hence the opportunity for fundamental amendments has passed; nevertheless, there is always the chance that minor amendments and perhaps added provisions, given diligent effort, may be extracted from Government. Second, Committee debate provides an opportunity to tidy up drafting, while providing a detailed account for the official (Hansard) record. Hansard of Committee Proceedings can provide essential information, particularly for lobbyists and legislators who may wish to use it for later legislative or other purposes.

Informally, Standing Committee performs at least three main functions for Members taking part. First, it provides their greatest opportunity for challenging and useful work. Back-bench activity in theHouse itself normally is extremely limited. Only in Committee can the ordinary Member hope to make a meaningful contribution. Second, Committee work affords Members the chance to "perform";

to display their parliamentary and debating skills; to demonstrate their capacities for often lengthy, detailed and exacting exposition; to keep their rhetorical "tools of the trade" in trim. Party Whips are known to use Committees as "examination rooms". A Member's career prospects—up, or down the party ladder—may well be influenced by his performance.

Finally, Committee attendance performs a third important function for Members—at least so far as this novice observer was able to establish. It offers an excellent opportunity to catch up with mountains of constituency post! Indeed, the more enterprising Members leave the Committee room at frequent intervals to dictate letters to secretaries who attend them on the corridor benches outside, or to use corridor telephones, and/or to conduct other "corridor business".

So much for the formal and informal functions of Committee work. What of the observer? What can be gained from sitting through week after week of Committee proceedings? First, regular attendance afforded this observer at least, the opportunity not only to increase greatly his knowledge and understanding of the Bill's provisions, but his appreciation of the issues and problems of salmon fisheries legislation in general.

Second, it provided a fascinating and most re-assuring insight into the unique and wondrous workings of our Westminster system operating under the full strain of "battle conditions". Effective operation of this system is as dependent on the style, nuance and subtlety of what is essentially the distillation of English (*not* Welsh or Scots) culture, as it is on its capacity to encompass the broad sweep of wider issues, right down to the incisive detail of closely argued provisions. No matter how successful the Westminster "export model" has been, the true genius of these parliamentary institutions can only fully be appreciated in the rooted context peculiar to their origins. As an American lady who attended one of the livelier Committee sittings rather wistfully put it: "Those Committeemen cover so much, so quickly! And wow! I could see they sure did have their differences! There was calculated cruelty and outright assault there! But it was all done in such a *civilised* way. Humour, wit, under-statement. ...In our Congress they just get up and bawl at each other. No style, no finesse. Clubs, not rapiers. ...It was marvellous."

And there was a final bonus. The proceedings of the Salmon Bill Committee provided "live entertainment" of the highest order. Indeed, given the "serialisation" of Committee activity through 15 Sittings, it assumed the status of ongoing "political theatre". Mostly, this was reserved for the subtle and meaningful wry comic thrusts, with occasional interspersions of slap-stick and pure farce. But there was the underlying current of tragedy too, for the entire Bill was designed to ignore or evade urgent realities. Yet this sombre mood occasionally was lightened by brief, exhilarating moments of triumph when Members managed to shift Government from an established stance. Throughout, a form of dramatic tension was maintained. Could Government be forced to concede any amendments which even marginally met vital conservation, equity and rod/tourism requirements? Would any Government initiative be taken to effect any reduction in netting? Was it really possible that the Bill would place no restraint on the archaic right of the Scottish netmen to take up to 97 per cent of the Summer catch?

Preliminary Logistics and Assessments

Initial prospects for a useful Committee stage looked anything but promising. There were the logistics of Committee composition. Since representation on parliamentary Committees must accord with party standings in the House, this meant that of the 18 appointed Members, 61 per cent must be Conservatives, 33 per cent Labour, and six per cent Liberals and others. Accordingly, the Tories placed 11 persons, Labour six, and Liberals one Member only. This put Government in a very strong position. If voting followed the lines of Second Reading—and if certain unhappy Tories could be kept in check—then it was virtually assured of a 12:6 or 14:4 majority on most issues, should these come to a Division or vote.

In terms of National/Regional composition, the situation looked equally grim. It showed the Committee to comprise: Seven Scots, three Members from North-East England, seven from the South-East, and one only from Wales. It seemed still quite incredible that for a Bill which was principally a Scottish Bill, that Scottish membership on the Committee should comprise less than 40 per cent.

What then of the Committee Members themselves? Comprised, seemingly of "place-men" and others who knew little about salmon or the complexities of salmon politics, it seemed likely the Committee would simply go through the motions.

And yet there were one or two glimmers of hope. Tam Dalyell (Member for the Scottish industrial constituency of Linlithgow), arguably Parliament's most searching and meticulously demanding—and feared—participant, was present. So too was his Scottish Labour colleague, the member for West Falkirk, Dennis Canavan. Canavan was well known as a tough and abrasive performer. He had strong views on private rights and game-fishing in

CRANLEY ONSLOW

SIR GEOFFREY JOHNSON SMITH

SIR HECTOR MONRO

Scotland and he was not shy about expressing them. The utterances of Canavan always were guaranteed to put a shiver down the back-bone of the Tory salmon fishing establishment. And then there was the eloquent Alan Beith (Berwick-upon-Tweed) champion of the North-east drift-netsmen. Finally, there was the contradictory figure of John Home-Robertson (East Lothian), the Scottish socialist land-owner who had spoken forcefully and well at Second Reading. He again was to lead for the Opposition. Given determination, luck, with perhaps a little timely cross-party support, it was possible that this curiously assorted Opposition four-some might engineer a degree of effective amending pressure on Government.

On the Tory benches, along with Scottish Fisheries Minister John MacKay, and England/Wales Fisheries Minister John Selwyn Gummer, there was, amongst others, the party's premier back-bencher, Cranley Onslow (Woking), Chairman of the Tory *1922 Committee*—the "trade-union" of Conservative back-benchers. Onslow was an established campaigner for salmon conservation and the rods/tourism cause. Also present was Onslow's South-east colleague, Sir Geoffrey Johnson-Smith (Wealden). The Scottish-born Sir Geoffrey, a knowledgeable, courteous and articulate Member and a keen angler, was one who often had expressed views on salmon fishing which did not co-incide with Government's. The same could be said of his Committee colleagues, Nicholas Soames (Crawley), grandson of the late Sir Winston Churchill and a keen salmon fisher with Nith (Cowhill Estate) interests; and Sir Hector Monro (Dumfries), the former Minister of Sport, who on occasion, also expressed views on salmon matters at variance with Government.

So there were possibilities. If these Opposition and Conservative Members and their respective casts performed to expectations, things could prove interesting.

The Politics of 'Provision Modification'

Leading off for the Bill's critics, Cranley Onslow declared that "Many members of the Committee find it a fault that the Bill is not a conservation measure, [and] I suggest to the Minister [John MacKay] and his colleagues, that they should seriously attend to the task of making the Bill better. ...The representative of the left-wing lairds [John Home Robertson] may hanker for his smoked salmon, but I want us to do a job of work. ...We are not likely to get the luxury of Government time again for a while". (cols.3-4)

It is not often that a member of the governing party, let alone the "shop steward" of its back-benchers, leads off with a warning to his political masters. Yet this is what Cranley Onslow did. He was closely supported by his colleague, Sir Geoffrey Johnson Smith, who, alluding to the UK's unsatisfactory position within the international salmon fishery community, stressed that "our reputation is not good. If we are to take action internationally for the conservation of Atlantic salmon, we must put our own house in order. The Bill is a golden opportunity so to do".

It was clear that Government was to face demands for modification—in some instances for removal of, or additions to the Bill's provisions— and not from the Opposition alone. Sir Geoffrey and Onslow were but two Conservative Members determined to "have a go" at securing changes they felt to be desirable.

How then were those who wanted to secure "mini-reforms" to the Bill to fare? Would Government continue to stone-wall? Would it make concessions? If so, in what form? And while it was possible that all-party support for certain issues might cause Government to ease its resistance to amendment demands; nevertheless on most issues, including salmon conservation, there were clear and often competing views held by the principal factions, which sometimes did, and sometimes did not, conform with political party divisions.

Second Reading had revealed that there were four principal factions or groups whose positions now were represented in Committee:

1. The Tory rod/conservation element (led by Onslow) which wanted provisions more favourable to getting fish into rivers, keeping them there, and conserving them in the coastal sea-passage to their home rivers;

2. the Tory element which rendered near-total support to the Government and the Bill (Michael Forsyth and others);

3. the Labour element (led by John Home Robertson, Tam Dalyell and Dennis Canavan) which sought greater public access to fishings, broadened representation on the governing District Fishery Boards, greater accountability of the Scottish Secretary, and removal or reduction of what it regarded as draconian anti-poaching provisions in the Bill; and

4. the North-east (England) element comprised of Alan Beith, Stuart Randall and others on the Opposition benches, that was determined to ensure that provisions which threatened the North-east drift-netsmen would vigorously be opposed.

Successful reforming pressure on Government would require resolute united effort by all or most of these elements. Could this be achieved? The reforming capacity of the Committee was first put to the test in relation to the substantial powers that the Bill proposed for the Scottish Secretary.

1. The Scottish Secretary: Powers and Duties

a) General Amendment Demands The main criticism which had earlier been levelled at the Bill related to the powers given the Scottish Secretary. Reformers pointed out that there was, 1. no mandatory provision requiring him "to consult with all affected interests" before making an Order, and 2. no provision that would require him to subject a proposed Order to the "affirmative resolution" procedure—that is, to bring it before both Houses and thus secure the approval, or dis-approval of Parliament. They thought that the Bill gave the Scottish Secretary far too great authority which could be used arbitrarily, and that if and when these two powers were exercised, serious damage to affected salmon interests could result. Peers had tried to secure alteration to both and failed. Would the Commons Committee fare any better?

In the debate on "Designation Orders" (Clause 2), the Opposition probed Government on both these issues. Government's response, as expressed by Minister MacKay, was that "statutory consultation" was unnecessary since other interested parties, through advisory or consultative committees, could make their views known to the Scottish Secretary *via* the District Fishery Boards. (cols.25-26) As for the use of the Affirmative Procedure, MacKay stressed that since Designation Orders concerned only local, not National matters, these should be effected by Statutory Instrument, and not brought before the House. (see col.38)

i) Statutory Consultation Having established that Government was determined to stand firm on these two issues insofar as local matters were concerned, the Opposition next tested Government commitment to these positions in relation to national matters as provided under the provisions of Clause 3 (General Regulations). Taking issue with the Bill's provision that the Scottish Secretary need consult only "such persons as he considers appropriate", John Home Robertson demanded thatthese requirements be widened: "We are constantly asked", he said, "to give credit to the [Scottish Secretary] for being reasonable, and the Minister renewed that appeal a minute or two ago. However, it will be possible for the Scottish Secretary to make such regulations without consulting the very people who have the most direct interest". (col.51)

After listing a number of bodies which he contended should, by statutory requirement, be consulted, he referred specifically to the Scottish Secretary's proposed powers "to make regulations with regard to the meshes, materials and dimensions of nets without necessarily taking the advice of tenant netsmen whose livelihood could be affected". He warned that the Opposition would press their amendment on "statutory consultation powers" unless the Minister could provide an assurance "that such people will be consulted before regulations are made". Messrs. Beith and Randall strongly supported this demand, Beith contending it went "to the heart of the anxiety felt by many fishermen". (col.52)

Speaking up for Government, was Sir Hector Monro. "We must ask ourselves", he declared. "where we start and where we stop in deciding which bodies should be consulted. The Bill makes it clear that the Scottish Secretary must consult those whom he considers appropriate". This statement triggered renewed Opposition outrage. Who, or what bodies, might the Scottish Secretary consider "appropriate"? After further heated exchanges, MacKay summed up Government's position. The words "as he considers appropriate", were to be found "in just about every Bill that goes through the House. ...Opposition members [therefore] will not be surprised that the furrow I shall plough is the one that all Ministers, of whichever party, have ploughed over many years whenever the subject has been debated". (col.55) The words would remain.

Distressed at this stone-wall response, Home Robertson flayed Government for its inflexibility. "We fear the over-riding interests and influence of proprietors. For proof of the strength of proprietorial influence over the Government on salmon fishing regulations and legislation, we need look no further than the Bill. This is a Landowners's Bill"! Unimpressed, Nicholas Soames quipped, "The hon. Gentleman is the landowner"! In swift riposte, Home Robertson countered that "The animal noises from the hon. Member for Crawley (Mr.Soames) confirm my argument nicely. Why on earth are Conservative Members going to such lengths to resist the suggestion that there should be wider consultation on the regulations to be made under the clause"? The resistance of Conservative members, however, remained solid. The Opposition amendment went to division. The result was a 9:6 vote on a straight Government party vs. Opposition alignment. (col.60)

ii) Affirmative Resolution Procedure Taking up the issue of deployment of the Affirmative Resolution Procedure under Clause 3, Beith pointed out that here one was not talking about local matters. The concern of many Members was with the extensive (national) powers relating to the entire Scottish fishery, powers which could have a profoundly damaging effect on the livelihoods of netsmen in particular. It was essential, therefore, that any Order which the Scottish Secretary might wish to make under Clause 3 should not be made "unless a draft Order has been laid before, and approved by, each House of Parliament". (col.83)

On this issue Conservative Members broke their silence. Cranley Onslow strongly urged Government to "resist the amendment, despite the Opposition's emotional arguments". (col.85) Then using a little emotive language of his own, he declared in a thinly veiled reference to the North-east drift-nets that sea-fishermen "must realise what will happen to them if they continue to use those barbarous nets, and recognise that we have no desire to protect their livelihoods at the expense of such damaging waste. Good conservation", he stressed, " is not achieved by dead fish washing about at sea, and dying fish coming up rivers"! These words inflamed North-east Members. Stuart Randall was outraged. "The hon. Member for Woking [Cranley Onslow] has just said he has no desire to protect the livelihoods of netsmen. ...He has shown his bias by going on to talk about his concern—as he did implicitly—for the rodsmen, rather than those who earn their living ...using nets"! (col.86) Onslow objected: "Nothing that I said indicated a bias in favour of rodsmen, and my emphasis was in favour of conservation. If the hon. Gentleman feels that he must put words in my mouth, I hope that he will use accurate words"!

The skirmish continued with Nicholas Soames and Sir Hector Monro lending firm support to Onslow and the Government position, while John Home Robertson weighed in behind Opposition colleagues Beith and Randall. When partisan views on this issue had been exhausted, MacKay summed up the position of Government. Should there be strong feeling against any Order under Clause 3, Members concerned were free to "table a Prayer"—the method used (the "Negative Resolution Procedure") to request that the Order be brought before the House for approval or rejection. But Opposition Members demanded to know how many Prayers actually reach the floor of House? "The issue we must face", declared Beith, "is whether the Government [will] allow time for the Prayer either on the floor of the House or in Committee". (col.91) Not content with Government assurances, the Opposition forced the Committee to its second Division. With voting once again following strict party lines, the Opposition amendment was defeated by an 8:6 tally.

b) Specific Amendment Demands Turning to specific amendment demands under Clause 3, Committee members directed their principal energies to the Weekly Close Time (Weekly Slap). Here the principal factions clearly emerged. Some extraordinary bed-fellows in most curious, camouflaged clothes were revealed!

i) 'Compensatory Slap' Attention first was directed to an amendment proposed by the Opposition leader John Home Robertson calling for Weekly Slap "compensatory periods" for fixed nets. This was an issue strongly favoured by the Tory rod/tourism element. It offered the prospect of getting more fish into rivers. Yet here was the Labour leader in Committee proposing it! Furthermore, the amendment, had been suggested by the Salmon and Trout Association. Two S&TA Council members on the Committee were Cranley Onslow and Sir Geoffrey Johnson Smith—a third was Charles Morrison. Yet these two leaders remained silent during the entire "compensatory period" debate. All this was most interesting. What was more interesting still was the way in which this essentially Tory rod/tourism issue was dressed up in a most convincing Labour disguise.

It was proposed that "compensatory periods of close time" should be made operative "where legitimate constraints, including severe weather, make it impossible to observe the regular Weekly close time". (col.60) Was it not absurd, observed Home Robertson—now revealing the Labour disguise—"to expect netsmen to risk their lives to take down fixed nets" under such conditions? Would it not be best to leave these nets in place, and then slap them for the appropriate period during the following week?

There was strong resistance from one Member on the Conservative benches. Michael Forsyth contended that such a provision could have a serious effect on "some people's livelihoods. ...Netsmen would be tempted to make sure that their nets were slapped during adverse weather conditions when they were not expecting a run of fish". And "how could [the measure] be enforced? ...And who will decide what is meant by 'legitimate constraints' and 'severe weather'"? Sir Hector Monro endorsed the views of Forsyth.

This seeming "callous" regard for the "health and safety" of working netsmen caused Dennis Canavan to sally forth on the first of many "salmon tales" which were to enlighten and greatly entertain the collective Committee gathering. Few were aware that Canavan himself had been a netsman. Fewer still were aware of the harrowing conditions under which the men on the nets labour. Canavan proceeded to educate us:

> "More than 20 years ago when I was an impoverished student I got a holiday job with the Tay Salmon Fisheries [Company]. It was one of the most dangerous jobs that I have ever been asked to do. I got 5 shillings an hour, which even then was slave labour.
>
> "Moreover, the conditions in the middle of the Tay, in the Firth of Tay between Perth and Dundee, were downright dangerous. The gaffer never even asked me whether I could swim. He gave me a pair of waders ...and sent me out to take my turn at laying the net. The Tay is very fast flowing, deep and dangerous. We went out at all times of the night and morning. Because of the tides in the Tay we had to do shift-work, five hours on and five hours off. We lived in a bothy on the banks of the Tay. By the weekend we were so disoriented that we did not know whether it was night or day, let alone what day of the week it was"! (col.62)

This said, Canavan went on to state that he was in fact "not a wholehearted supporter of the amendment as worded". Instead of introducing "more flexibility for the close time, it would be preferable to ensure better health and safety regulations, implemented and enforced by an inspectorate". Certainly, "slave labour and dangerous conditions whereby workers are exploited and their very lives put in danger", he declared, "should not be allowed to continue"!

After the Committee settled down following Canavan's moving address, some sympathy was expressed for the issues he raised. But it was for Canavan himself, that the most grave concern was reserved. "I am sure we all often wonder why such a reasonable man as the hon. Member for West Falkirk joined the Labour Party", observed Minister MacKay. "Clearly after a week working on the Tay for a netting company, he was so dis-oriented that when he came home at the weekend he joined the Labour Party". This provoked a round of Committee merriment. "The Tay fishery people may have something to answer for", the Minister opined, "but it seems to have done the hon. Member for West Falkirk no harm. He is trim and fit, obviously as a result of his hard work on the estuary of the Tay"! (col.63) More Committee merriment.

After further debate, Home Robertson finally accepted defeat. Despite the impressive performance by his colleague Dennis Canavan, the convincing deployment of the Labour disguise, and the silent presence of the Tory rod/tourism faction—silence which just might have been converted into cross-party voting support had a Division been pressed for—the Opposition leader, showing a rare willingness to accept Government's contentions, agreed "it might be impracticable to enforce such regulations". Accordingly, he withdrew his amendment.

ii) Sunday Salmon Angling A second Weekly Slap amendment was brought forward; this time, by Sir Hector Monro. It was suggested by the Association of Scottish District Fishery Boards (ASDFB), and was a most curious one. During the Lords debates on the Bill, the Weekly Slap provision had been amended to provide that nets must maintain a minimum 42-hours weekly close period. This provision was introduced mainly to ensure that nets would not be enabled to reduce this minimum period, and hence further reduce the weekend passage of fish past nets and into rivers. Yet here was Sir Hector bringing forward another amendment which, if accepted, would cancel the Lords amendment. He called for removal of the 42-hours provision to make possible "Sunday rod fishing for salmon" (col.78)—rods are slapped for 24 hours each week (Sunday) throughout the season. The fact that it equally would afford netsmen the opportunity to secure a reduction in the current 42-hours Weekly Slap was a point not raised by Sir Hector. Following a short, tense debate focused on the "conservation failings" of the amendment, MacKay observed that just as the 42-hours period ensured no fishing by nets, so the 24-hours (Sunday) period within the Weekly Slap was aimed at ensuring no rod fishing. This he thought was "re-assuring to conservationimsts". Sir Hector withdrew his amendment.

iii) Dams and Dykes The "dams and dykes" provision in Clause 3 also was the target of renewed reform efforts. Again Sir Hector called for the Scottish Secretary to have powers not merely to authorise "alteration" but "removal" of dams and dykes. MacKay, however, simply repeated that dams were "private property", and hence removal was a matter for negotiation with the proprietor concerned. He pointed out that under Clause 15 (General Powers and Duties of District Boards) powers existed which would enable District Boards "by agreement, to purchase dams to remove them". (col.65)

BREACHED DYKE on Lower Doon ... *Up-stream fishing improved markedly.*

iv) 'Materials, Meshes, Net Dimensions' The provision enabling the Scottish Secretary to regulate "materials, meshes and dimensions of nets" was the cause of considerable alarm to many Scottish fishermen. Use of lightweight materials, in particular, had enabled greatly increased efficiency and intensity of modern net fishing. Hence to restrict or ban use of certain materials like nylon multi-filament—let alone increase mesh size while perhaps reducing the dimensions of nets—could have serious effects on the size of catch taken. "Exercise of these powers could wipe out the entire river net fisheries of Scotland", warned Alan Beith. (col.67) People's livelihoods could be at stake. MacKay, however, indicated that Beith was being too sensitive on this issue. The intention, he said, was to bear in mind that the 1980s were very different from the 1860s; and that it was only reasonable "on conservation grounds" to provide for control of nets in this way, and enable the

Scottish Secretary to have "the power to react to new materials and methods". (col.69)

v) Lures and Baits What then of the Scottish Secretary being empowered to regulate "the use of lures or bait in rod fishing"? This issue which now was raised, and yet again by Sir Hector, initially had been debated vigourously in the Lords. At that time Government had given an assurance that the matter would be "sympathetically" considered. Was there still Government sympathy? After all, it was only right, as Beith observed, that if netsmen stood to be restricted through exercise of the "meshes, dimensions, methods" provision, that rods too should be subject to "lures, baits" restraints. (col.71) MacKay informed the Committee that consultations with affected bodies were still in progress, but that he would bring forward an amendment at Report Stage "that will certainly embrace the principles that he [Alan Beith] and other Members...support". (col.78)

vi) Low-Water Net Limitations Finally, yet another attempt was made to persuade Government to accept a Low-Water netting restriction under Clause 3. This issue was long-established and hotly advocated by the Tory rod/tourism element. But did a Conservative move this Low-Water amendment? No. It was the Opposition leader who called for a provision "to make regulations having temporary effect during periods of drought". (col.82) These difficult low-water conditions, observed Home Robertson with masterful under-statement, "must make life particularly difficult for fish trying to swim up river. Salmon swimming in river estuaries could be subject to the depredations of fishing activities".

Indulging in further under-statement, Sir Geoffrey Johnson Smith briefly surfaced to indicate that "while there is no amendment or sign of support from Government Members, many Conservative Members are interested in the proposal". MacKay, however, was not impressed. "Even if it were possible to do something practicable at national level—and I am far from convinced that it would be—this would not be the way [under Clause 3] to do it". Still, he hinted he might consider this very important issue in another context: "...We shall come later to the obvious and appropriate place to discuss drought more fully". With this assurance, Home Robertson withdrew his amendment.

The debate on Clause 3—running to 46 columns of Hansard, the second lengthiest in Standing Committee—provided encouraging promise that cross-party reforms might be achieved. Both the "general issues", concerning "statutory consultation" and "affirmative resolution", were firmly backed by many Conservative Members. Yet when the respective Divisions were called, Government managed with ease to secure the votes of even its most reluctant supporters. The result was that no cross-party vote was secured and these principal provisions remained fully intact.

LOW-WATER ON TWEED ... *Netsmen at work.*

2. Annual Close Time: Extension Initiatives

Short of scrapping the entire Bill and trying to induce the Department of Agriculture and Fisheries for Scotland (DAFS) to bring forward something more in keeping with modern requirements, there were two vital provisions which, if incorporated in the Bill, could serve to get more fish into and up rivers: an increased Weekly Close Time; and an increased Annual Close Time (Annual Slap).

The Committee already had dealt with the Weekly Slap. No amendment had been advanced to secure an increase, despite urgent demands by the "reform wings" of both the Salmon Conservancy, and the S&TA (interim) Scottish Committee for a 30-hours (two and one half tides) increase to 72 hours.[2] The failure of any Opposition element or Conservative "reformer" to propose any substantive change did not augur well for envisaged initiatives under Clause 6. A welcome surprise, however, was in store.

a) Extension or Compensation? Sir Hector Monro demanded that the statutory National (Scottish) Annual Slap be increased from 168 to 196 days. (col.118) Sir Hector declared that here at least was an opportunity to incorporate a "true conservation" measure in the Bill. "The Annual Close Time", he said, "has been 168 days for no less than 120 years, yet during that period great improvements have been made to nets, boats, the method of propulsion and weather protection which has given more time for fishing. ...If more salmon do not get up rivers to spawn, the salmon population will drop even more dramatically, and no one, whether netsmen in the rivers and estuaries, hotel keepers and those interested in the tourist industry, or owners of the fishing will get a livelihood".

While Sir Hector was determined that one way or another the Annual Slap must be increased, it quickly became apparent that there was precious little of the unity needed to achieve it. Beith and Randall registered their strong opposition. "It is not sensible to alter, at one stroke", contended Beith, "the scope for fishing with river nets throughout Scotland without regard to the circumstances of each river". (col.123) Randall stressed the need for "scientific evidence"—a theme oft-repeated by all factions throughout the Committee proceedings. The Tory rods/conservation leader, Cranley Onslow, strongly supported the *principle* of getting more fish up Scottish rivers, but was not certain that increasing the Annual Slap was the best way. "We should redress the balance in favour of ensuring that [more] fish get up rivers", he said, "if necessary making financial compensation to the netsmen who could lose part of their livelihood". (col.120)

Sir Geoffrey Johnson Smith agreed. "If a new balance is to be struck, someone has to pay for it. It will not come free". (col.124) Underlining this position, Charles Morrison stressed that the current problem is "over-exploitation". A new balance must be struck. "There should be some equality of misery"! (col.126) Both netsmen and anglers "must be prepared to accept some control and limitation on their activities", but to increase the Annual Slap was "not necessarily the right way to do it". He opposed "removing the rights of netsmen without compensation".

With the majority on the Committee opposed to the 196-days amendment, what then was the stance of the Labour Opposition? Dennis Canavan indicated he was inclined to support the amendment—at least in regard to the Tay. Arguing on the basis of "jobs support" and "up-stream equity", he noted that a recent survey by the Tay Advisory Committee showed that "35 jobs on the river, and many more in hotels and the tourist industry in the area have been lost because of excessive netting, especially by companies such as Tay Salmon Fisheries". TSF was "...raping the lower reaches of the river and leaving practically nothing for anglers upstream. That is having a detrimental effect on the rural economy in areas such as Pitlochry, not only for rod fishing but for the tourist industry, such as hotels and service industries". (col.128)

Canavan accepted that if a net fishery was to be phased out, there was a just case for compensation—though not perhaps for companies like "that cowboy outfit" Tay Salmon Fisheries. "The lot that run it are not exactly impoverished: I understand that a dividend of 45 per cent to 47.5 per cent a year is paid to shareholders, who include members of the other place whose political affiliations are well known—for example, Lord Mansfield, the former Minister of State at the Scottish Office, and Lord Lansdowne". Furthermore, "the way TSF treated their employees was a disgrace, and if the company went out of business altogether, I should not shed any tears". (col.127)

Given that TSF was a "bad employer", that it was "spoiling the sport of others", that "no health and safety legislation operated then, and probably is not enforced now", there were, declared Canavan, strong grounds for saying that the Annual Slap should be extended. These contentions were applauded by his colleague Home Robertson. But he then went on to ask whether any Annual Slap extension should not be based on "scientific evidence"? The 168 and 196-days figures, he observed, "seem to be magic figures plucked out of history". (col.130)

With each Committee faction taking a separate stance, and with divisions even within these groups, it was easy for Government to dismiss Sir Hector's amendment demand. Minister MacKay merely reminded the Committee that legislation should allow for increases in Annual Slaps only in those fishery districts "where they are appropriate". (col.133) To seek to increase the Annual Slap to 196-days nationally was the wrong way to proceed. Changes could be made by Statutory Order, on application by local District Fishery Boards.

But what then was Government's position on the increasingly topical issue of "compensation"? It was an option frequently advanced by campaigners in relation to securing reduction or removal of the North-east drift-net fishery. About these initiatives Government in the past had been decidedly un-responsive. But what of the Scottish net fishery which took an equally heavy toll of the salmon that managed to escape the drift-nets? What was Government's view concerning compensation in relation to this fishery?

MacKay, with timely prompting by the Tory rods/conservation faction, made the Government's position clear: "I was asked about the possibility of buying out netsmen and compensating them", he said. "There is nothing to prevent District Fishery Boards from doing that at present. I think that four or five netting operations have been bought over and gone out of existence on the Spey estuary. That can be done, and I hope that in time more of that will be done by District Boards. That is the right way to proceed." (col.132)

Cranley Onslow, then made a vital interjection: "I am encouraged to hear what the Minister says. I hope he means that he will give them the money".

MacKay's reply was equally vital: he did not think that "people should look to the taxpayer for assistance with their sport and recreation. ...That is not the right way to go about it. Some Taxpayers disapprove of sports such as angling, and they may not be happy about subsidising it".

This was an important Government statement on what was to become a key issue. The message was clear. Government was not against the reduction or removal of Scottish nets in principle, but it would provide no money. If, however, local District Boards or voluntary groups wished to raise money to buy out the proprietorial rights of Scottish netsmen who were prepared to sell, that was their business. Government would not stand in the way. In view of certain developments which shortly would break, this brief exchange between the Minister and Onslow was of considerable significance.

b) District Boards and 'Unreasonable Behaviour' Rebuffed on his 196-days amendment, Sir Hector now approached the issue of Annual Slap alteration or extension from another direction. He called for the Scottish Secretary to be given powers to take independent action "when he thinks that a Board is acting unreasonably"; in other words, he could act as the majority of District fishery owners might wish and increase the local Annual Slap. (col.136) The Minister was courteous but dismissive in his response. "As I have said, our principal aim is to achieve any changes in the Annual Close Time through local initiative. ...We should leave it there".

Nothing if not determined, Sir Hector tried another tack. Suppose the Scottish Secretary should say to himself: "This Board is being unreasonable. All the proprietors have the same interests and therefore they [the Board] are not looking fairly at the Annual Close Time". (col.144) It would be helpful, stated Sir Hector, to secure clarification of the Scottish Secretary's powers under such circumstances. There was strong support for this position from Sir Geoffrey Johnson Smith and Charles Morrison. MacKay, however, was reluctant to respond directly to the issue raised. Sir Hector, therefore, resorted to a little plain speaking. "A Board", he said, "could consist, for various reasons, entirely of netsmen, or of upper river angling proprietors, who would have total control, irrespective of anyone else's interests, over the Annual Close Time, as only they could ask the Secretary of State for a variation".

"All that I am asking for—I cannot understand why the Minister will not reconsider it positively—is that in such circumstances, in which unfairness was obvious to all, the Secretary of State should be able to step in and say, 'Look here, this is wrong, but the Act prevents me from doing anything about it'. ...It may only arise once in a hundred times, but both netsmen and anglers have the right to know that the Secretary of State could step in if their interests were being treated unfairly". (col.150)

Sir Geoffrey now chipped in. "We are talking about mavericks. ...[Cases] involving difficult people with vested interests". These persons "do not represent the locals, they represent themselves and no one else. Can we not have a system whereby an appeal could be triggered against the inaction of the Board, so that the Department could consider the matter"? (col.151)

Nothing could be plainer. Allegations were often made that District Boards dominated by the netting interests, as on the Tay, Spey and Deveron, used this control either to block initiatives which the vast majority of local fishery proprietors wanted, or to promote changes which the majority did not want. Was there not some provision which could be made to enable the Scottish Secretary to act in accord with the majority's demand under such exceptional circumstances? Sir Geoffrey had the wholehearted support of Charles Morrison. Once again, however, MacKay merely observed that while he did "appreciate my hon. Friend's arguments, [nevertheless] they have not pointed to an obvious case for extending the Annual Close Time". (col.152) MacKay did add, however, that he would "consider the points raised". In fact, Government was not to be budged from its established position.

These Annual Slap and Weekly Slap amendment proposals provided the key statutory opportunities for shifting the Bill in the direction of reforms which would bring it slightly closer to modern conservation, equity and economy requirements. And yet, despite persistent and skilful pressure which clearly had involved some measure of cross-party and cross-faction co-operation, no progress had been made.

The Committee now was to consider the clauses concerning the District Boards themselves; their composition, representation, powers and duties. Whether there would be much prospect of cross-party and inter-factional co-operation seemed doubtful. Conservative Members largely were content to accept the Bill's provisions which placed almost all authority in the hands of proprietors. Opposition Members, on the other hand, wanted Boards to be more widely representative, and their powers, which some regarded as draconian, to be substantially reduced. Little attention was given to the need for better management of salmon rivers, control of harvests to sustain the runs, and other conservation measures.

3. District Boards: Membership, Composition and Powers

During Lords' consideration of this section of the Bill (Clauses 10 to 17), consistent efforts were made to extend the rights and powers of proprietors. Government resisted these efforts. Lord Gray made clear that District Boards, as provided in the Bill, were already in a very privileged position as "private voluntary bodies" with extensive public statutory powers. During Commons Committee stage, reforming initiatives were to have almost entirely the opposite aim. Behind

CELEBRATED SERVANT OF THE SALMON ... Former Dee Board Superintendent, Willie Irvine, inspects the redds.

what now was a united Opposition front, vigourous efforts were to be made to reduce District Boards' powers, increase public representation, and make Boards more publicly accountable.

a) Proprietors and Representation John Home Robertson commenced the Opposition assault. Government promoted this Bill on the basis it was "democratising" the 1860s system. One of the basic precepts of modern democratic systems is "one man, one vote". Yet under the provisions of Clause 10 (Qualified Proprietors, and Upper and Lower Proprietors) not only was "weighted voting" to continue, but each ballot would be worth from one to four votes, depending on the size of Rateable Value (RV) of the fishery concerned; also proprietors could vote more than once if they owned more than one eligible fishery, and in both Upper (angling) and Lower (netting) categories.

Moving one of many Opposition amendments designed to limit proprietors to the "one man, one vote" principle, Home Robertson stated that it should be regarded as "one small step in the interests of democracy—not that there is anything remotely democratic about the Boards proposed by Government. That is one of the great fictions of the Bill"! (col.158) The amendment was supported by Stuart Randall. MacKay, however, was unmoved. The Government position, he contended, was "fair". The proprietors "have a major interest in the river. They are expected to pay money to the Board. ...If [they are] elected in both capacities they should be able to represent the interests of their electorate". (col.160) Straining his own credibility and that of the Bill a trifle, he added, "I should have thought that that was a democratic position"! With a sorry wag of the head, Home Robertson merely observed that his amendment had been "useful in highlighting a shortcoming" in a section of the Bill which was "beyond human aid". He agreed to withdraw it. (col.161)

In the concluding debate on Clause 10, Randall and Home Robertson spelled out the Opposition's fundamental criticism of the Bill. Home Robertson declared, "We have come to the fundamental principle. Qualified proprietors and upper and lower proprietors are the 'constituencies' that this so-called democratic institution is to represent".

"Under Clause 10 there is no provision for direct representation for the workers on the river, for those who go in for angling for enjoyment, or for those who earn their living out of netting on the river. Only those who own the rights will be represented".

"I shall not go on at length. The point is glaringly simple. We completely reject the principle of total proprietorial control, whether by the proprietors on the upper reaches or by the lower classes of proprietor further down. I believe that Clause 10 is unamendable, and we shall reject its entire principle by voting against it". (cols.161-2)

Stuart Randall stated that the "main worry" of the Opposition was "...the awful representation in the Bill. ...Fishing is one of the largest sports in Britain—yet those who fish for sport, and are members of our massive angling clubs and associations are deprived of representation by a Government who have squandered the opportunity to put forward a Bill which would amend the ancient legislation based on inequity and unfairness".

"The Minister has no right to use the word 'democratic' here. ...(Interruptions) Conservative members may jeer. We know that they are in the hands of the proprietors. We know that they have been selected to serve on the Committee, and that someone is pulling the little strings, or cracking the whip to ensure that the right amendments are accepted. Conservative Members are not men, but mere tools of the system. I still hope that the blood will boil in their veins, they will see the light and realise that we have the opportunity to introduce a tiny change that would make the system fairer". (col.162)

MacKay, by no means immobilised by this savage assault, responded with a few barbed rejoinders. With a handsome back-handed compliment to Dennis Canavan, he contended that Home Robertson and Randall, clearly lacking the courage of their colleague's socialist convictions, had failed "to bring forward a nationalisation amendment". (col.164) Instead, all they had done was "a bit of tilting at windmills". He also was pleased to note that the Opposition appreciated the "virtue of field sports, and the freedom of people to pursue them. That is splendid news from the Labour Party"! (col.163) MacKay turned finally to Government's concept of "democratisation". So far as Clause 10 was concerned, it simply underlined the point that "The people who have a major interest in the salmon fishings are the people who own them. ...Those people sign the cheques that fund the District Board to improve the fishing for the benefit of all".

Home Robertson, yet again, could only sorrowfully wag his head. The Minister's comments, he said, "nearly brought tears to my eyes with his ringing declaration of the democratic principle of the rights of property"! MacKay, he added, made the point that the proprietors pay for the fishery. But "who pays them? The poor old anglers pay—through the nose, in many cases, to fish, and the netsmen on the lower reaches pay rent for netting rights". Government, he declared, was determined "...to leave in the Bill the anachronistic principle that exclusive power should remain in the hands of the owners of the water. That is fundamentally wrong. ...Boards should be properly representative to command the respect of the public. That means representations not only for proprietors but for elected local authorities, for anglers, for netsmen and for environmentalists where appropriate. Without that representation, the legislation cannot work". (col.164)

SOUTH ESK SUPERINTENDENT, Donald McIntyre ... One of the many unsung miracle-workers of Scottish local fishery management and salmon conservation.

Home Robertson now called for Clause 10 to be dropped from the Bill. On the Division, his amendment was defeated on a straight Government:Opposition, 8:4 vote.

b) Sole Proprietors and Mandatories Opposition Members, now well settled in their assault upon the "private interest" and "exclusive" under-pinnings of the Bill, proceeded to step up the pressure. The very existence of some Boards, where each was effectively a single proprietor (Clause 11, *Sole Proprietor in a Salmon Fishery District*), afforded new opportunities for the expression of Opposition outrage. A conciliatory Government amendment which called for powers of appointment of bailiffs in "Sole Proprietor" Districts to be authorised by the Scottish Secretary, only elicited further howls of protest. Why should not the principle of "bailiff vetting"—an issue about which the Opposition was sensitive—be extended to apply to all bailiff appointments? Home Robertson then used this opportunity to recount alarming tales concerning the activities of over-zealous bailiffs responsible for protecting certain angling waters, including the renowned Grimersta in the Western Isles. (cols.170-71)

That there should be such a thing as "sole proprietors" was, in Opposition eyes, bad enough. But that these privileged proprietors should also appoint "mandatories" to act for them (Clause 12, Mandatories) was nothing short of iniquitous! Indeed this allegedly scandalous situation was further compounded by a Government amendment which sought to extend the role of mandatories. "It is bad enough", exclaimed Home Robertson, "that we are letting proprietors appoint mandatories to elect the Board, but if the people who then are elected can appoint people to stand in for them, that would seem to make a mockery of the whole system! Whatever else it may be, it is not democracy"! (col.181) Despite this and other Opposition outcries, no Division was forced, and the Government amendment "to include Board members and chairmen" as eligible to appoint mandatories to serve for them was agreed.

c) Representation, Accountability and Finance As the Opposition was unhappy with the representation which the Bill offered, what then did it favour? Under Clause 13 (*District Salmon Fishery Boards*) Home Robertson proposed an amendment calling for the "founding local Associations" (comprised of all fishery proprietors in the local fishery district) created under the Bill, and from whose numbers local District Board members would be elected, to include not only proprietors but also representatives of "local authorities and persons who exercise a right to fish for salmon—that is, clubs, anglers, tenant netsmen and the like". (col.183) As Stuart Randall put it: "Where there is an Association and its membership which will make up a District Board, we want the interest to be as broad as possible". As for "balance", Home Robertson maintained that the only balance that existed on Boards was that "between Upper and Lower proprietors", with mere "token representation" of other interests through co optees. (col.186)

In reply to these Opposition indictments, MacKay explained that the the object of these Clause 13 provisions was to "retain the [1860s] system where appropriate, and to improve aspects which are inconsistent with modern thinking". (col.185) But, he went on to ask, suppose one were to follow the line suggested by the Opposition that "persons who exercise a right to fish for salmon" should be eligible as Association members. "Who are these people? What sort of right do they exercise"? Should there be a requirement "to exercise the right for a week, or a month? How is the [District Board] Clerk to know?" The Opposition amendment, the Minister declared, was clearly a "wrecking amendment. ...Only disorder can result".

Home Robertson hotly denied that his, and similar amendments, were "wrecking amendments"; this implying that the existing system worked well. "He [the Minister] does not need to look hard at what happens in Scotland to see that it does not work well"! (col.186) Forcing his amendment to Division, the vote once again followed strict Government vs. Opposition lines and was defeated by 9:5.

The Opposition, with Home Robertson continuing to carry nearly the entire load of amending initiatives, pressed Government on a number of other points of principle and substance in Clause 13. Having secured a "major triumph for socialism", as Home Robertson put it, in picking up Government on a drafting fault, the Opposition ran into an uninterrupted series of Government rejections.

Should not angling associations share in the assets of a Board being disbanded? No—proprietors finance Boards, so only they should share. Should not the "founding local Associations" of proprietors bear responsibility for District Boards' actions, and conversely should not these Boards be accountable to their "founding Associations"? No—"Association members" would have the opportunity to influence Board activity, through changes in Board membership, every three years. Should it not be that where there are no salmon in a river, there should be no Board? No —it was possible in future there could be.

In addition to these Opposition amendment demands, Conservative members themselves brought a measure of pressure on Government. Might not Government contribute money to "pump-prime" new Boards or Amalgamated Boards, asked Sir Hector Monro? No—Government money, as indicated during Lords debates, was not available for these purposes. Not even European Community funding, inquired Cranley Onslow? Not likely, replied Minister MacKay. What then about Scottish Development Agency (SDA) and Highlands and Islands Development Board (HIDB) funding, asked Home Robertson in a final sally? The Minister was doubtful, but would "make inquiries".

This sequence of cuts and thrusts—with most of the decisive "thrusts" executed by Minister MacKay—continued through the debate on Clause 14 (*Financial Powers and Duties of District Boards*). Sir Hector Monro managed to secure Government's agreement that "audited" accounts should be presented to District Board Annual General Meetings, rather than unattested financial statements. Home Robertson did not find the Minister so accommodating in response to his demand that "salmon anglers and tenant netsmen" should have a statutory right to attend Board Meetings and Annual General Meetings. Becoming a little weary of the Opposition's repeated "improved representation" demands, MacKay merely noted that co-optees already would be in attendance, as of right; but that Boards also could open meetings to anglers and netsmen, if they (the

Boards) should so wish. (cols.200-201) Striking a note of caution in relation to the Bill's new financial provisions, Home Robertson demanded to know whether new "expenditure ...accruing from any other source [other than proprietors' rates]" was in fact not a back-door method for bringing in rod-licensing in Scotland? No—"Any other source ...does not include a rod levy", declared MacKay. (col.206) Was there no chance of securing Scottish Development Agency or Highlands and Islands Development Board finance? No—There was now no such need since Boards would have their own borrowing powers.

Under Clause 15 (*General Powers and Duties of District Boards*), Home Robertson pressed on with the Opposition's amendment demands, and with equally little success. Should not there be "Access Orders" to improve the access of ordinary anglers to salmon fishing waters? No—proprietors paid high rates, and often secured very little profit, even from "exclusive beats", hence they "paid" for the right to "control access" as they chose. In any event, there was plenty of good low-cost fishing available. (cols.209-11) But if Boards were to be effective in their management role, should they not have powers at least to "monitor acidification in waters"? And what of "forestry and drainage", inquired Onslow? No—these were jobs for the River Purification Boards and relevant agencies, not District Boards. (cols.212-13) In a final plea to the Minister, Sir Hector called for the Bill to include powers to create a long and urgently sought "Joint Solway Board". MacKay rejected this idea, observing that with no existing agreed Joint Board plan linking rivers in the English North-West Water Authority area with the Scottish Annan and perhaps the Nith, it would not be possible. (cols.216-20)

In completing the Opposition's pursuit of these minor but significant amendment proposals, attention was now directed to the vital position of Chairmen of District Boards under the provisions of Clause 16 (*Proceedings of District Boards*), and Schedule 2 (*Election and Co-option of Members of District Boards*). First, should not the Chairman be barred from exercising a "casting vote", in the event of a tie? Home Robertson was prepared to concede that where the Chairman is "impartial" and independent, this would pose no problem. "But ...the Chairman we are talking about here will be anything but impartial in many cases". (col.235) The Minister was adamant: No—similar practices operate elsewhere, he stated; the Chairman must retain the right to a casting vote to avoid dead-lock. Second, the perennial demand voiced frequently by Lord Thurso during the Lords debates on Schedule 2 now was aired in Committee: should not the

Board Chairman be chosen by (newly elected) Board members, rather than by the Board's "founding Association"? No—it was better that all proprietors participate in electing the Chairman, declared MacKay. This was the fairer, more balanced and "better way to proceed". (cols.237-39)

Consideration of this vital first and substantive section of the Bill was now complete. While Opposition reformers made little amending progress on the issues targeted—pressing four to Division—nevertheless they exposed a number of the more extraordinary anomalies in the system. While the system of District Boards was to remain whole-heartedly and unashamedly private, this section of the Committee's proceedings at least provided a clear public record of those features germane to re-trenchment of this archaic structure of a by-gone age.

Political Theatre and Provision Modification: Act I

Given the limits of party, interest and region within which they were constrained to operate, Committee members had made the best of their opportunities to amend and tidy up the substantive clauses in this the first and principal substantive section of the Bill. That the changes they had secured were few and minor was not the fault of the reformers who proposed them. Government once again clearly demonstrated it was determined to use its position of numerical dominance to retain this antiquated legislation virtually in the form in which it had been introduced.

Still the Opposition, and some Conservative members, had successfully achieved what it was their duty to do, and with considerable flair and flourish. The Committee's "political artistes" had performed to expectation. Recondite terminology and verbiage had been translated into everyday language; intention and meaning had been exposed and explained. Use of tightly reasoned argument, combined with generous measures of repetition; judicious application of hyperbole, humour and dramatic exposition; all ensured full and clear elucidation not only of complex detailed provisions, but also of the fundamental principles of the Bill. And it had all gone into the official public record (Hansard).

The Committee now moved on to the second and subsidiary section of the Bill—principally those clauses dealing with Dealer-Licensing and Illegal Possession. They offered the best remaining opportunity to build into the Bill at least some measure of effective "salmon conservation".

To this point, Government had managed to fend off most changes to these provisions sought by reformers. During Lords debates, Conservatives together with Liberal and Independent Peers, endeavoured to strengthen them. During Commons Second Reading Opposition Members tried to weaken them. Both failed. Would either side now fare better during the "Second Act" of this Standing Committee political drama?

References

1. Quoted from, *Parliamentary Debates: House of Commons, Official Report, Standing Committee D,* (Salmon Bill [Lords]), (April-June, 1986), col.700. Hereafter, reference to Commons Standing Committee Debates will be by the relevant column, entered in the text.
2. See above Chapter 7, pp.129-130.

Chapter 9

POLITICAL THEATRE AND LEGISLATIVE REALITIES: II

> "Before I shut up, I want to say that, as I make more inquiries, I become curiouser and curiouser"!
>
> *Tam Dalyell,* (col.268)

> "Somebody might deposit a salmon at the door of a poor crofter woman, perhaps in the Minister's [John MacKay's] constituency. She takes the salmon as a gift from God. (Interruptions) Members may laugh! Many people in the Highlands and Islands believe that salmon comes directly from God, and are certainly not the property of the Minister!"
>
> *Dennis Canavan,* (col.492)

There was now a perceptible change in the atmosphere as the Committee moved into the "Second Act" of its proceedings. To this point, the prevailing mood had been one of moderately-charged disquiet. Now the tension sharply escalated. Each sitting was transformed into a rivetting theatrical event. What new surprise would the Opposition—perhaps Government's own "supporters"—spring? Could Government keep its nerve? Was it really possible that in the face of repeated embarrassment and humiliation, it still would hold to its bizarre defence of the "archaic order"? Would the Minister finally crack?

Those who knew MacKay as a fair and considerate person began to wonder how much longer he would tolerate the brief to which, in the name of Government, he had allowed himself to be shackled. Perspiring freely in the sweltering heat of a late May morning, he mopped a furrowed brow and shot a daggered glance at Robert Williamson, Scotland's Chief Inspector of Salmon and Freshwater Fisheries, one of the "salmon servants" (officials) who had passed to him yet another of a seemingly un-ending stream of "briefing notes". It was clear that

MacKay did not now regard the Opposition—along with such Tory mavericks as Cranley Onslow—as his only tormentors!

A lively—even malicious—sense of anticipation, together with mounting anger and frustration, contributed to increasing tension. But there was more to it than this. First, there were the vital and sensitive principal provisions, Dealer-Licensing and Illegal Possession, to be debated. "Subsidiary" though these might be, they were crucial to achieving any effective "conservation" in the Bill. There was, therefore, a considerable sense of urgency about these provisions which had generated the greatest contention during earlier phases of the Bill's passage. If the "heat" had been "hot" during the Lords debates, what would it be in the rough and tumble of a Commons Committee?

Debate on the first section of the Bill had been a learning experience for most Committee members. All now had a firm grip on the Bill and its key weaknesses. These weaknesses were to be targetted and attacked. But effective attack is seldom achieved by a collective front; individual leadership is needed. It was Government's bad luck that this leadership was to be supplied by Parliament's acknowledged "chief inquisitor", Tam Dalyell. It was Government's further bad luck that he was joined by Parliament's most fiercely outspoken Scottish Socialist, Dennis Canavan.

As Dalyell and Canavan were to feature prominently in the high drama of the remaining proceedings, it is perhaps appropriate here briefly to describe the "presentation method" used by each, and to touch on the highly individualistic personalities of these two Members, personalities which gave their respective presentations great vitality and force.

Dalyell's method is unique. To the unwary, his manner is disarming; not unlike that of the classic absent-minded professor. His grave, be-spectacled face registers a permanent expression somewhere between shock and surprise; an effect enhanced by an unruly mop of short-cropped grey-black curls. Can this be a serious politician, one asks? Is it possible this is the Member who threw Government into such a spin by his damning revelations about the (Falklands War) "Belgrano Incident"? * Until one is transfixed by those magnified black eyes at close range; there is no hint or warning of the intensity which burns within. His presentations followed a set pattern. Prior to speaking, Dalyell would rummage through the sizeable stack of papers

* The Argentinian battleship, the Belgrano, was sunk, with heavy loss of life, by the British at the start of the (1982) Falklands War. Dalyell—amongst many others—vigourously queried whether the "rules of engagement" had been properly followed prior to the attack.

TAM
DALYELL

DENNIS
CANAVAN

and "brown envelopes" on his bench-end desk—which happened to be placed immediately opposite that of another Old Etonian, Cranley Onslow. An envelope would be extracted. Dalyell, his jacket often discarded to display a splendid system of belt and braces infrastructure, would then rise, adjust his spectacles, and examine the contents of the envelope. Total silence. Government supporters would eye him apprehensively, even Opposition members would shift uneasily.

Dalyell always began with an elaborately courteous introduction. Sometimes it identified the victim, sometimes not. Members held their breath. Then suddenly, with swift and deadly accuracy, the rhetorical stilettoes flashed out. Once, twice, thrice they found their mark! Dalyell then would move on, seemingly unaware of the alarm and consternation left in the wake of his remarks. He duly would close his presentation with as elaborate a flourish of courtesy as he had started, and would take his seat. It was all over—until the next attack. Persistence and determination, as all Members were well aware, also were hallmarks of his method. A few moments of shock-recovery were required before business would re-commence.

Often, Dalyell's assault was followed up by a cross-party hue and cry. But it was another Opposition "weapon" which did the real damage: this was the Member for West Falkirk, Dennis Canavan. Short and wiry, sharp-featured, with a full head of grizzled ginger-grey hair, and a neatly-trimmed beard, Canavan did not actually speak his words; rather, in a deep, resonant bass which had the clear truculent ring of Clydeside, he released them, one by one, from behind grinding teeth.

If Dalyell's rhetoric appealed to the intellect, Canavan's was directed at the emotions. Passionate language, artfully interspersed with humour of the most outrageous and comic nature was deployed. What became known as Canavan's "salmon tales" was the device he most commonly used to convey his points. And yet while on occasion his performances reduced us all to tears of laughter, he carried on in the same dour, growling mono-tone, except for the odd twitch of his moustache. In this severe and sober manner outrage was piled upon ridicule, which in turn was heaped upon insult, and no one was spared.

Yet "Committee Clown" though he was, a role that often brought welcome relief to us all, his presentations were apt and relevant, tightly packed with fact, and as cleverly constructed as those of his more cerebral colleague. As artful as Dalyell was with his "stilettoes", Canavan was brutally effective with his tragi-comic "clubs". Together, Dalyell and Canavan packed a very powerful one-two punch—as Government was soon to learn.

Salmon Bill Basics: Information, Evidence and Interests

During the "First Act" of the Committee's proceedings there had been little opportunity for members to do other than concentrate on detail—with occasional detours into lively embellishment. Many questions had been asked which raised doubts about the amount, relevance and accuracy of information upon which Government had constructed the Bill. But these questions were scattered. They had not been focused. It was here that Dalyell and Canavan performed the vital function. They targetted queries and led the attack on what they and others had come to regard as the key underlying commitment of Government to the Bill: defence of the commercial netting interests.

This attack followed two lines. First, there was the question of evidence in support of the netting interests. What exactly was it? How did it justify built-in dominance for them in the Bill? Second, there was the sensitive issue of "interest". It was no secret that certain powerful proprietors had vested interests which they sought forcefully, and quite legitimately, to advance and protect. But what about Government and departmental personnel responsible for shaping the Bill and its key provisions? Was it possible they had informal or hidden "interests"? If so, what were these interests?

1. Government Evidence and the Netting Interests

Dalyell led off the attack. "I am prompted to ask a candid question. I had imagined that the various interest groups had been thoroughly consulted before the Bill arrived in the Commons. ...I must now tell the Committee that we are getting endless communications of dissatisfaction from serious people who say they have never been properly consulted. ...People are extremely worried. ...Would it not [therefore] be sensible for Government ... to take another look at the whole structure and to ask this constant stream of complainants, what they are on about, and to try to meet them? ...I must confess that I started out some weeks ago under a very different impression and did not realise the size of dis-satisfaction". (cols.221-22)

Would Mr. Dalyell care to specify what the Bill was lacking, and what was "the nature of the representations ... being made to him", inquired Sir Geoffrey Johnson Smith?

Dalyell put it bluntly. "The nature of the representations is that the Bill does very little to protect the salmon: the Boards have insufficient authority to stop netting in particular, which absolutely ruins the angling industry in Scotland and, for all I know, in parts of

England. I had not realised the extent of the feeling, but I see the honourable Member for Dumfries nodding ...and I suspect that he knows exactly the kind of complaints that we are now getting".

In defence of Government, Minister MacKay contended there had been many consultations "since the [DAFS] Consultation Document was produced in 1979". (col.224) He made no comment on structural re-considerations.

Dalyell now moved on to the key issue raised by many who had been communicating with him: favouritism towards the nets. The Minister, he pointed out, was constantly speaking of "equity" and "balance", but the Bill merely strengthened the position of the *status quo*. Under these provisions, the nets would continue to catch most of

KYLE OF SUTHERLAND NETS AT WORK ... Netsmen at Bonar Bridge making the most of the turning tide just below mouth of the River Carron. (right) Neil Graesser, proprietor of Kyle District net and rod fishings.

the salmon. Furthermore, the netting interests "apparently employ very few people, and that very few ...depend on netting for their livelihood", while the Scottish angling industry was "being wrecked ...thanks to an ever more efficient and frankly greedy" small number of netsmen. (col.225)

Dalyell now came to the crux of the matter. "I have been told that the netting interests are important, and I have taken that on trust. I ask a simple question. ...How many folk are actually involved in this netting"? The Minister's reply was evasive. This provoked the dour Canavan. "Will the Minister stop laughing and answer the simple question put to him by my honourable Friend. What is the Scottish Office estimate and Department of Employment estimate of the number of people in Scotland who are dependent upon net salmon fishing for their livelihood? If the Minister cannot tell us, he has not done his home-work"! (col.226)

This direct query finally elicited a direct response. "I do not have that information to hand" admitted MacKay. "We know what the [reported] catch is, but not the number of people employed".

Dalyell looked visibly shocked. With an air of incredulity he now extended his appeal to the Committee as a whole. "My honourable Friend [Mr. Canavan] and I are asking a very simple question. ...Some of us who do not represent netting communities want to ask our colleagues who do, how many people are affected? ...If I am told by my honourable Friends and colleagues that this is very important to hundreds of people ...and that they would go out of business if we pursue this line of argument, then we will listen. But I am becoming very sceptical about the assertion we have heard time and again that the netting interests are very important. I have to be persuaded, and so does my honourable Friend".

This appeal brought an immediate cross-party response. Charles Morrison, who amongst his many posts was also Prime Warden of the Fishmongers' Company, declared that the "most accurate guesstimate—more of an estimate than a guess—is that between 500 and 550 are involved". (col.227) That said, Morrison stressed that these netting jobs were "relatively important because of the limited employment opportunities" in the affected areas; that netting was a "traditional" activity; and indeed that Dalyell was "hitting at the wrong target"—the North Atlantic and North-east netsmen were, in his view, the real culprits. Home Robertson was prepared to allow that Government did face a very difficult problem in trying to "keep accurate statistics" regarding employed netsmen, since the work itself was "seasonal, part-time". (col.227) Sir Hector Monro suggested it might be useful to try to secure figures from the Crown Estate Commissioners (CEC), given that they "must be one of the most important netting operators in Scotland". (col.228)

Dalyell remained bemused. Turning first to the issue of "tradition", he noted that modern Scottish netting certainly was "...not traditional, in the sense that what went on for hundreds of years was far less efficient than the modern operation of netting. ...I am not an expert, and it is no use pretending that I am, but I am told ...that certain companies have got the netting down to an efficiency and an art never contemplated before. They use scientific techniques and far more effective materials. The fish do not have a chance". (col.228)

But what was the effect, the damage done by modern netting operations? Dalyell continued. "Some of us are told that the future of fly-fishing in rivers is now in jeopardy ... [Yet we are told by the Minister and others that this net-fishing] affects communities all round Scotland. Do not let us exaggerate. If there are only 500 altogether—and I suspect the honourable Gentleman's figures are correct, and that comparatively few people are involved—it is an exaggeration to

"TRADITIONAL" SWEEP-NETS on Tay Estuary ... assisted by power winch, lightweight nylon nets, motorised cobles and night lights.

say that communities all round Scotland are affected by not being able to net. It is, [however], not an exaggeration to say that communities all round Scotland are affected by their tourist industry and all that goes with it ...being reduced to ruin. A great many remote communities are likely to be affected".

MacKay finally agreed that he and his officials would see "what statistics we can produce". (col.229) It was suggested to the Minister that the Crown Estate Commissioners (CEC) and the Salmon Net Fishermen's Association of Scotland (SNFAS) might be worth contacting, as each might be able "to come up with something quantifiable". (col.232)

While grateful for the Minister's apparent willingness to produce figures, Dalyell remained distressed. To a chastised and now briefly silent Minister he expressed his dismay and concern. "I am genuinely taken aback that after all this time, the Government do not have some quantifiable statistic of what they mean by 'the netting interests'. Before embarking on a Salmon Bill, surely they had some precise idea of what these assertions about the netting interest amount to". (col.231)

Canavan took this opportunity to lend his own forceful support. "The Minister", he pointed out, had "painted a rosy picture ...where all the wee crofters were trying desperately to make a living by doing a little net fishing at certain times of year, and that if we deprived them of that opportunity, they would be in the poor-house". (col.231) The matter, he contended, was not quite like this. "Let us get things straight. We are not just talking about the livelihoods of such people, although that is important and should be a priority. We are also talking about people like Lord Mansfield and others with vested interests in the Tay Salmon Fishing Company who line their pockets from it".

It was now the turn of Dalyell to follow up. Mention of Lord Mansfield raised another serious issue relating to the Bill: ministerial vested interest. "My honourable Friend put this in more colourful and looser language, but I would like to ask who was in charge at the time of the original formulation of this legislation. Was Lord Mansfield in charge? All sorts of things are being said in Scotland and all of us, under privilege, have to be exceedingly careful. But I ask a factual question. When the Bill was in its embryo stages, was or was not the Earl of Mansfield in charge"? (col.231)

The Committee, declared Dalyell, would await "with considerable interest" what the Minister and his department would come up with concerning this and other vital issues raised.

At the next Committee sitting, MacKay needed a reminder from Dalyell that he had promised to make one or two important explanations to a more than usually attentive Committee. First MacKay turned his attention, and that of the Committee, to figures.

In a written response to Dalyell's request for nets-employment figures, the Minister provided some departmental statistics. These showed that in 1973 it was estimated that 1300 people were employed as netsmen in Scotland; while in 1981 "the corresponding estimate ...is about 1000". (col.267) Dalyell thanked the Minister for his assistance, and inquired whether he had been able to find "any up-dated statistics"? MacKay did not reply immediately. When eventually he did, he was able only to say that "the best estimates ...give a range for netting which is about 1000 at peak times". (col.285) No attempt was made to reconcile these figures with the 500 given earlier by Government and the Fishmongers' Company's Prime Warden,

Charles Morrison. This, it appeared, was the best MacKay and his department could do.

2. Government Evidence and the Angler / Tourism Economy

What then did these official estimates mean? What did they suggest about the importance of netting jobs in Scotland? What about the relative importance of jobs supported by rod/tourism? And what about revenue generated by netting, compared to revenue from rod/tourism in Scotland? What "balance" between the two should be represented in the Bill's provisions? The Committee took a firm grip on these issues, and a lengthy, often heated, sometimes ill-tempered debate now followed.

By the time the Committee had finished with these issues, one thing had become clear. In terms of jobs and revenue, commercial salmon netting in Scotland was a minor industry. Figures showed that netting supported about "600 full-time jobs generating about £5m. annually, whereas tourist and recreational fishing provide about 30,000 jobs and up to £210m. a year". (col.268) As Sir Hector Monro put it, "We are now getting somewhere nearer the facts. ...We are probing for information about the relatively small number of fishermen who genuinely net for a livelihood, as opposed to the vast number of people who are dependent on angling for a livelihood". (col.269)

Some Members expressed dismay that these figures had come not from Government, but from an article by the writer published the previous day (21 May) in the *Glasgow Herald*. "When the Minister was asked how many people worked in the various sectors of the industry", observed Stuart Randall, "he said that the statistics did not exist. Yet a newspaper columnist seems to have been able to produce figures, which I find remarkable". (col.280) The figures used were in fact taken from a March 1983 study, conducted by, this writer and colleagues: *A Survey of Salmon Angling and the Scottish Tourism Economy: Revenue Input and Employment Support.*

When confronted with these figures, MacKay was neither clear nor enthusiastic in his response. "Salmon angling is important, both for sport and for tourism. I have said before that we must try to keep the balance. Netting has interests; it gives people employment in many parts of my constituency". (col.284) This vague and equivocating language was too much for Dennis Canavan. Angrily, he confronted MacKay. "Does the Minister accept David Shaw's figures in the *Glasgow Herald* that the jobs ratio between net fishing and angling is 600 to 30,000"? (col.285)

MacKay was not about to be jostled into a direct reply. "I read those figures. ...All I know is that there is a large number of jobs. I freely concede that tourism generates more jobs than netting. There is no argument about that". These newly revealed figures and the debate which revolved around them, demonstrated that the "jobs balance" between netting and rods/tourism overwhelmingly favoured the latter. The "revenue balance" showed a similar lop-sided ratio. And yet with nets taking an average of 80 per cent of the annual total rod and net catch, and up to 97 per cent during the summer peak-holiday angling period, the "catch balance" overwhelmingly favoured the nets. It was this 1860s "catch balance" which was built-in to the Bill and indeed stoutly was being defended by Minister MacKay and the Government.

At earlier stages, the "ideological bias" of the Bill had been brutally exposed to the public gaze. Dalyell and Canavan now had exposed the naked bias of the "netting interest". Even the most conservative reading of statistics showed that it was the rod/tourism interest which deserved legislative support, yet the netting interest continued to enjoy dominance and favour. This bias was not only unacceptable to Dalyell and Canavan, it was extremely puzzling. What little evidence the Minister produced had shown that his department (DAFS) had long been aware that the netting interest was negligible in terms of its size and contribution to the Scottish economy. And yet this department was prepared to support its continued dominance in the legislation they drafted. Why had they done this?

3. Ministerial Interest: Lord Mansfield and the Nets

Dalyell and Canavan earlier had expressed concern about the role of Lord Mansfield in the Bill's formulation. They were about to discover some important "salmon realities".

Canavan addressed Minister MacKay. He reminded him that at the previous sitting of the Committee, Dalyell had mentioned "the vested interests of Lord Mansfield" and requested some factual information about his financial interests. (col.277) So far, the Minister had not replied. Canavan now jolted the Committee with revelations from researches he had carried out.

"My information is that the Tay Salmon Fisheries Company is not only Scotland's, but Britain's biggest salmon net fishing company, and that Lord Mansfield holds 5000 shares in the company. I am told that Scone estate, his family seat on the Tay, also operates nets on the river and that those nets are owned by the Trustees for Viscount Stormont, the son of Lord Mansfield". (col.277)

NETS AT SCONE ... *drying out after a hard night's work.*

Silence descended on the Committee. Canavan continued. "As we all know, Lord Mansfield was Minister of State [for DAFS] at the Scottish Office when there was a great deal of lobbying for more conservation of salmon fishing in Scotland. Many of the angling interests rightly pointed out the massive decrease in the catch over the past decade or so, and asked for more radical conservation measures".

He paused and fixed the now freely-perspiring MacKay with a truculent glare. "It is hardly surprising that Lord Mansfield stood in the way and resisted lobbying from the angling interests ...because he and his family have considerable interests in salmon netting"! (col.278)

Canavan now put his question. "I wonder whether [the Minister] ...will confirm the information I have just given to the Committee? I understand that the House of Lords does not have a register of interests such as we have in this House. But I think that the Committee is entitled to an explanation of the interests of Lord Mansfield, who was instrumental in the framing of the Bill at a pre-legislative stage. He is no longer in the Scottish Office, but his hand is undoubtedly on the Bill"! MacKay remained mute.

When the Committee had recovered from the shock of these revelations, Members on both the Opposition and Government benches busied themselves in the pursuit of several matters which had no bearing on the dramatic issue raised—all Members but one. David Harris (St. Ives) took umbrage at the "slur" cast on the name and reputation of Lord Mansfield. He felt that "the personal remarks" made by Canavan "should not go unchallenged". (col.280) He deplored these "attacks", and considered them "cheap". He expressed his hope that "other members of the Committee will show their disgust too". Other Members remained silent.

Dalyell then spoke up. With customary courtesy, he first commended Lord Mansfield. "I shall say quite openly that, when [Lord Mansfield] was a Scottish Office minister, he was very helpful in a number of constituency cases". (col.281) He felt Canavan's comments were "not a question of a cheap attack. I am not even sure that 'financial' is the gravamen of it".

That said, Dalyell turned acutely to the point at issue: "A Minister who has to make decisions at the embryo stage of a Bill must be seen to be whiter than white". Venturing further along this rhetorical tight-rope, Dalyell stated that his "honourable Friend", Dennis Canavan, was "undoubtedly right ...in saying that Ministers in the House of Lords do not, so far as I know, have to declare interests as we do in this House. I suspect that in Lord Mansfield's case it is not a matter of pounds, shillings and pence, but possibly a feeling of obligation to people he knows very well. At least a statement ought to be made on it. I ask the Minister, in the light of what the honourable Member for St. Ives has said, to make a Government comment on what went on on Tuesday [the previous sitting]".

Though still much rankled by Canavan's attack, Harris was somewhat mollified—"The honourable Gentleman has put it in a reasonable way".

Finally, MacKay spoke up. After a few humourous asides at the expense of Canavan—"after a little while one gets used to him and almost comes to enjoy his contributions. ...We all know that he has a well-known habit of having a go at the Scottish peerage when he runs out of things to say"—the Minister addressed the question. He confirmed that "Lord Mansfield was the Minister at the Scottish Office when the Consultative Document was issued in 1979, and during the period when observations [on it] were being made". He stressed, however, that Lord Mansfield had "left his post at the Scottish Office at the general election of 1983, and the preparation

DAVID HARRIS

of the Bill has been undertaken by Lord Gray in a ministerial position. I hope that makes it perfectly clear".

As for the "interests" of Lord Mansfield, MacKay referred the Committee to a statement in the House of Lords Hansard for 23 January, 1980. At that time Lord Mansfield stated that he owned "a somewhat undistinguished tributary of the Tay so far as fishing is concerned". He also said "he was a trustee for his son, who owned a substantial interest on the Tay".

Harris then made a fatal error. He chose not to leave well enough alone. He called on Canavan to withdraw "the slur which he has cast publicly on the noble Lord". With a rueful grin, MacKay tried to warn his colleague. "It may be a pointless exercise to attempt to pursue that course". Then noting Canavan rising to speak, he added, "Perhaps I am about to be proved wrong"! The Minister was not wrong. Canavan spoke his mind. "For the record, I told the Committee that I had been given information that Lord Mansfield holds 5000 shares in Tay Salmon Fisheries Company, and the Scone estate, his family seat on the Tay, also operates nets in the river which are owned by the trustees of Viscount Stormont, the son of Lord Mansfield. If the Minister can tell me that this information is wrong, I am sure that all members of the Committee, including myself, would be grateful for as much useful information as we can get. But I shall certainly not withdraw anything unless I am convinced that I have been giving false information"! * With this statement, followed by a few further efforts at forced humour by the Minister (and some lively coverage in the Scottish press), the curious and unsettling issue of "Lord Mansfield and the Netting Interests" came to an end.

While many Members continued to harrass MacKay and MAFF Fisheries Minister Selwyn Gummer about the quality of information, indeed in many instances about the very existence of evidence upon which the Bill had been constructed, it was again Dalyell who cut through this plethora of complaints to focus on the source of facts and figures. It was clear that Lord Mansfield had a "vested interest", but what of the Ministry (the Department of Agriculture and Fisheries for Scotland—DAFS) itself? Like all fisheries ministries, its officials were thoroughly imbued with the "food-producing" ethic, and hence—as noted above in Chapter 2—long had manifested what many regarded as an inevitable bias towards the commercial netting interests. But was there really more to it than this?

* The Annual Company Return (1982-83) for Tay Salmon Fisheries Company, shows the Earl of Mansfield (A21 in the List of Shareholders) with a holding of 5000 shares in the company.

4. Departmental Interest: DAFS and the Nets

Briefly, it seemed DAFS had a clear vested interest in protecting the nets. If so, could not this have a fundamental bearing on the Bill and its provisions which DAFS officials were responsible for formulating?

Tam Dalyell quoted from a letter he and other Committee members had received from Salmon Conservancy Vice-Chairman, Colin Carnie. It said that "because of the size of catches by the netsmen, and indeed, because the concentration of such catches are at individual locations, netting stations provide very good settings for research programmes into the life of the salmon". (col.655) The letter continued, "As a result, the research programmes by DAFS are carried out by courtesy of the netting companies, and inevitably the direction and emphasis on such programmes take cognisance of the importance of salmon to the netsmen".

According to Carnie, "Research is inevitably linked primarily with issues of food production, and not necessarily to upstream stock enhancement, which would have quite a different thrust". He concluded with an observation which summed up the theme of his contentions: "If a research scientist wishes to be known as an authority on salmon, he has to co-operate with the netting interests to obtain access to significant statistics which also leads to mutual interest in the research programmes". Dalyell expressed his dismay. "I ask the department whether [this] is fair"?

There was no response from the Minister, nor from any other Member. Repeated efforts by Dalyell to elicit response or explanation met with no greater success. The conclusion to be drawn from this total non-response seemed obvious enough. Clearly, this issue both Government and Opposition regarded as too sensitive to explore. Dalyell had touched a very raw nerve. Public exploration of "departmental interest" was not to be tolerated.

Summary: Salmon Bill Basics Revealed

The value of the contribution by Dalyell and Canavan to the work of the Committee—and to the official Hansard record—was very great. They pin-pointed the basic determining issues underlying the Bill. They led and persevered with a series of vital assaults that produced crucial revelations. These virtually confirmed what many had long suspected, that it was not influential netting proprietors alone who were responsible for the archaic, nets-dominated Salmon Law provisions remaining intact. Ministerial and departmental vested interests also played important roles. If, to this point, salmon law reformers had come to regard the Bill merely as an extra-ordinary and bizarre vehicle for defending archaic principles and proprietorial interests, the Bill now could fairly be described as little short of parliamentary fraud. Many Members were angry and resentful.

Principal Subsidiary Issues

Mostly, the remaining proceedings of the Committee were dominated by two issues: Dealer-Licensing and Illegal Possession.

1. Dealer-Licensing Liabilities

During the debate on Clause 19 (Dealer-Licensing in Scotland), Committee members turned their attention to some well-aired issues. If the Bill was to be effective in controlling movement of illegally-caught salmon, and discouraging poaching, must not various loop-holes be closed? Should not "salmon smokers" be licensed? And what of hoteliers? Would not Dealer-Licensing be more effective if jointly-operative with a salmon-tagging scheme, as many Members advocated? Was it right that sea-trout should be excluded? And what of the proposed exemption of live salmon, or salmon which has been preserved or processed? Did not all this open up endless opportunities for the unscrupulous? (cols.241-43) MacKay could only reply that each and all of these matters had been considered, and that the Bill in its current form offered maximum opportunities for control. Issues of tighter restriction and flexibility would be given "great consideration ...when we decide how to implement the Dealer-Licensing provision". (col.244) The provision for exemption of "live" and "preserved or processed" salmon was later removed from the Bill.

Both Canavan and Home Robertson took particular exception to the penalty provisions in Clause 19 which rendered malefactors liable to up to two years' imprisonment and a fine of £2000. This was "very heavy", objected Canavan. "I have heard of people mugging old ladies and not receiving a sentence anything like that"! Home Robertson stressed that the special "powers of search" given to bailiffs could lead to serious trouble and should be removed. Encroachment on civil liberties by bailiffs was already great enough, said Canavan, and they should not be given further powers to go "poking their noses in here, there and everywhere". (col.249) MacKay again could only reply that the scale of poaching called for serious penalties, and "powers of entry and search" would only be used "if it is thought appropriate". The Opposition pressed amendment demands on both of these issues. Both were lost. Subsequently, however, Government relented on "powers of search". (col.520) A sub-section was duly added to the final Act making specific provision for bailiffs in "hot pursuit" to enter, without a search warrant, any land other than a "dwelling house, or any yard, garden, outhouses and pertinents belonging thereto". (Section 20, (1)(f))

Opposition concern over Dealer-Licensing again arose during Committee consideration of Clause 28 which set out separate provisions for its introduction in England and Wales. There was some repetition of earlier contentions that penalty provisions were "draconian", and that the "innocent person" was exposed to considerable risk. Two new Opposition criticisms, however, raised important procedural points. Beith stressed that under the existing provisions Parliament would be enabled only to accept Clause 28 in its entirety, or not at all. This was unacceptable. (cols.566-67) Minister Gummer replied that Government would ensure that full consultations would produce a proper and acceptable Order; but if the House should object, then Government would take the Order back and set to work again. (cols.567-68) Not satisfied, Beith pressed this demand to division and the Opposition amendment was defeated by an 8:5 vote.

More vital was a demand by Randall that Dealer-Licensing "shall" be introduced: that is, that its introduction should should be mandatory. (col.547) This would be a statutory guarantee that Dealer-Licensing would be implemented simultaneously in England, Wales and Scotland. Any "time lag", observed Home Robertson, could create great problems, particularly concerning "cross-border" (Scots/English) salmon traffic. (col.549) In reply, Gummer pointed out that the "permissive" word "may" was used in order to allow time for Orders to be developed. "The most important thing", he said, "is for me to repeat what my noble Friend, Lord Belstead said in another place, that we [are] committed to the introduction of the scheme. As the progenitor of the scheme, I am committed to the scheme not only because I am a member of the Government, but because I think it extremely important." (col.550)

2. *Illegal Possession Perils*

The provisions of Clause 21 (Illegal Possession of Salmon In Scotland) the Opposition regarded as outrageous. These provisions revealed what they alleged was the fundamental injustice, even danger of the Bill. The arguments brought forward were similar to those which repeatedly had been advanced during earlier Lords and Commons debates. The difference was the dramatic force and theatrical flourish with which they were driven home.

It was essential, declared an emphatic Canavan, that "he believes" and "reasonable for him to suspect" be struck from the clause. "It is incumbent upon the Minister to explain why on earth it is necessary to introduce statute law which is even more stringent than statute law relating to any other goods or articles, including the Crown Jewels"! (col.289) These provisions were another grave encroachment on civil liberties. "One of my favourite meals is poached salmon", said Canavan. "Several good friends of mine are very good at catching salmon, and, as far as I know, catch it legally. On occasions, when I have come back from London, I have found fish at the door. If I am not in, they will leave the fish inside the door".

"If the clause is passed unamended, the Minister will be putting pressure on people such as me to go around to my friends and say, 'Where did you catch this salmon?' As the Minister says, sometimes it is difficult, unless one is experienced, to know the difference between a salmon and sea-trout. One would have to go along to a person and say, 'Is this a salmon or a sea-trout? Where did you catch this salmon? Did you have permission to catch this salmon? Let me see your permission.' I wonder whether all this nonsense is necessary... ?" (cols.289-90)

Canavan then jumped on an amendment proposed by Sir Hector Monro which sought to delete "for him" from the Government provision of "reasonable for him to suspect". This was totally outrageous, exclaimed Canavan. It would mean that if a person were found "in possession of a salmon [in circumstances] in which it would be reasonable ...for the police, the water bailiff, the procurator fiscal, a judge or a jury... to suspect" that it was "illegally taken", then conviction could follow—"even if the person may not be home when the salmon is delivered to his door"! (col.291) Randall agreed that this provision was "exceedingly alarming". Beith added it meant that conviction could result even though the person had no knowledge (mens rea—that is, "no knowledge of the thing or matter") he was committing an offence. (col.292)

Like his ministerial predecessors at Lords stages, MacKay then had to explain that the purpose of the provision was to enable the law to bring before the courts not only the poacher himself (as provided in Section 7 of the *1951 Act*) but also others who might be engaged in handling, transporting or distributing these fish. Clause 21, said MacKay, made what often was an impossible task for the prosecution, somewhat easier. It provided two options. First, it would give the prosecution the chance to prove that the accused "believed" the salmon was illegally taken. Alternatively, it would provide an opportunity for the prosecution to prove that circumstances were such that the accused "ought to have suspected" the salmon had been illegally taken. (col.293)

Again, as at earlier stages, this explanation only further incensed Opposition spokesmen and disquieted one or two Members on the Government benches. A Queen's Counsel consulted by Beith had expressed the view that establishing guilt on the basis of "criminal intent", or that the accused "should have known", was simply "outrageous". (col.489) What ever would happen, he added, if this "waffly objective test" were applied "to handling stolen goods"?

Sir Geoffrey Johnson-Smith tried another tack. Might it not be a sufficient defence for the accused to say "from where" he acquired the fish? (col.491) Indeed, observed Cranley Onslow, might not the accused construct a satisfactory defence by saying "from whom" the salmon had been obtained? (col.495)

Totally exasperated, Canavan—with a supporting cast—now treated the Committee to another topical "salmon tale".

"My amendment ...suggests that it should be a basic principle of justice that if a person can show that he did not know that a relevant offence had been committed, it should also be an adequate defence. ...Somebody might deposit a salmon at the door of a poor crofter woman, perhaps in the Minister's constituency. She takes the salmon as a gift from God or whomever put it at her door. (Interruption) Members may laugh! Many people in the Highlands and Islands believe that salmon come directly from God, and are certainly not the property of the Minister"!

Gummer: "Are there many people who believe that salmon arriving at their door come directly from God? That is the issue we must address".

Canavan: "The poor crofterwoman has been virtually starving to death because of the iniquitous policies of the Tory Government, and she is down on her knees praying for food for herself and her family, when suddenly a salmon appears at the doorstep. She may think it is a gift from God".

Randall: "Whether the salmon arrives on the doorstep or in the river, is it not right that God moves in mysterious ways"?

Canavan: "Yes, indeed. My hon. Friend is perfectly correct. I did not know that he was a theologian. ...Any way here is this poor woman preparing her salmon, and along comes a gamekeeper, the water bailiff, the warden or even a policeman. Although he is not allowed into the croftswoman's house without a warrant—we should all go down on our knees to the Minister for that assurance—the nosy gamekeeper or policeman may go round the back and look in the kitchen window, and may see the poor croftswoman preparing the salmon. He might suspect that the salmon has been taken illegally or that an offence has been committed in relation to it. Before she knows where she is, the poor croftswoman finds herself in Oban Sheriff Court being interrogated by the procurator fiscal".

"It is all very well for the Minister to say, 'We don't want the clause to apply in such cases', but innocent people could get caught up. I have been on Standing Committees before, and Ministers give these assurances. ...Yet sometimes, when the law has been passed, it is used against people [whom initially it was stated the law would not be used against]. Therefore, I am certainly not in favour of giving the prosecuting authorities such draconian powers as the Minister suggests". (cols.492-93)

Gummer (who now filled in for MacKay) again explained the Government's position. Clause 21 was not aimed at the poor croftswoman; but if Canavan's objections were accepted by Government, "there would be no more successful prosecutions for poaching than there are now". (col.496) As for suggestions made by Sir Geoffrey and Onslow, Gummer reminded the Committee that the accused's right to silence could not be removed, as would result if the accused was required to say "where", or "from whom" the salmon in question was obtained. In conclusion, Gummer maintained that Clause 21 "...strikes a reasonable balance between the impossibility of proving an offence in most cases of poaching, because one is not present when the fish is taken out of the water, and, on the other hand, placing the onus of proof on the defendant in such a way that one distorts the normal arrangements in the English or Scottish Courts. ...I do not claim that this is a perfect answer. ...But this would seem to be the way which is closest to precedent and comparison, which gets the right sort of balance, and will achieve the end that we want". (cols.497 and 499)

Not persuaded by Government's explanations, the Opposition pressed Canavan's amendment (requiring the prosecution to prove that the accused knew the salmon was illegally taken) to division. The amendment was narrowly defeated on an 8:6 vote.

Nothing if not determined, Canavan tried again. On the basis that Clause 21 penalty provisions were "draconian", and "out of all proportion to the possible seriousness of the offence committed", he called for deletion of these penalty provisions. When this time it came to division, Canavan found that only his colleague Tam Dalyell was prepared to render support—with Beith voting with the Government. The division was lost by a 9:2 vote. (col.506)

The unusual provision in Clause 21 that conviction could follow on the evidence of only one witness also aroused the Opposition. In fact, this provision breached the requirement of "corroboration" under Scots law whereby the evidence of the witness must be corroborated by a third party. Home Robertson, though affronted by this provision, was prepared to compromise. He called for an amendment which specified that evidence presented by one witness would be acceptable if that witness "has no direct or indirect interest in the fishery on which the offence is alleged to have been committed". (col.507) Without such a provision, there was risk of bias in the evidence—if the witness should be a bailiff, gamekeeper, etc.—and a further risk of "malicious or mischievous" prosecution. MacKay, however, stood firm. At division, Home Robertson's amendment was defeated by another narrow 7:5 Government majority.

Altogether, the "Illegal Possession" Clause had caused the Opposition the gravest concern. Canavan sought to convey to the Committee what, from a recent personal experience, implementation of Clause 21 could well mean to the "innocent angler" out for a "quiet day's fishing". Committee members relaxed. MacKay looked uneasy.

"During the Whitsun Recess", said Canavan, "I did a bit of investigation work [up in the isolated West coast penninsula of Ardnamurchan] to check [MacKay's] assertion that the peace-loving citizen is entitled to a quiet day's fishing in the Minister's [former] constituency, provided he pays a reasonable sum of money. As the Minister said, it is not much—one does not have to be a millionaire to do a bit of quiet fishing in Argyll. ..."

"[Now] the Minister has told us that innocent people have nothing to fear, ...but he ought to bear in mind the experience last week of myself and two friends, one of whom, incidentally, is a respected civil servant".

"When we asked some local people where we could fish, we were told that Loch Mudle, which was along the road, was a good loch for fishing. ...We started fishing on opposite sides of the loch, and a person with an Alsatian dog appeared on the far side and spoke to my friend. The man said that he was a gamekeeper, or water bailiff or something, and demanded £3 from my civil servant friend. (Interruptions) ... My friend did not want to argue with the Alsatian and so, faced with such intimidation, he handed over the £3. I was not approached, either because the Alsatian could not swim across the loch, or because he had heard of my reputation! (Laughter) ...[Should] it not be possible, in the peaceful Highlands, for ordinary people to fish without being accosted by someone with an Alsatian who is trying to extort money? That man did not get any money out of me, but then, I did not catch any fish"! (Laughter and Interruptions)

"When we got back to the hotel and I told others of our experience, we heard that Loch Mudle was very cheap at £3. ...When I asked why that was thought comparatively cheap, I heard that fishing on the [nearby] River Shiel can cost £1000 a week! ..."

"[Now] the Minister, presumably, thinks that £1000 a week is a fair price. ...If he is looking for bandits and criminals, he should get a grip on [these] people who are fleecing the tourists! ..."

LOCH MUDLE ... A quiet day's fishing.

"I would be all in favour of the draconian penalties set down in Clause 21 [being] imposed on the greedy landlords who charge such extortionate fees, and on those responsible for sending out bailiffs with Alsatian dogs to terrorise innocent civil servants who have gone out for a quiet afternoon's fishing! ..."

"But the Minister seems to imagine that the real criminal is the poacher, and what he calls the poacher is someone who is merely taking advantage of the Common Law of Scotland. ...That person may not even be fishing for salmon; he may be more interested in brown trout, and, as I explained earlier, under the Common Law in Scotland, the trout and salmon in free-running water belong to no one, and become the property of the catcher when caught". (cols.522-23)

Canavan maintained that MacKay and the Government had their values and priorities badly confused; that they were colluding in a perverse and dangerous interpretation of Scots Law, one which violated the root principle of British justice and basic civil rights. He called for the Committee to reject Clause 21. However, the Committee, though clearly appreciative of the refreshing contribution Canavan once again made, resisted his advice. It voted by a 10:5 margin to keep the Clause in the Bill.

Committee debate on the parallel provision for England and Wales (Clause 29, *Handling Salmon in Suspicious Circumstances*) provided Opposition members with the opportunity mainly to re-emphasise

RIVER SHIEL ... in high summer.

their reservations about "draconian" penalty provisions.

Particular concern was expressed about any person found in possession of "suspect salmon" being considered guilty "until he proves himself innocent". (col.575) This was regarded as intolerable, a clear "breach of civil liberties", and must not be allowed. In reply, Gummer repeated that Government had "sought to provide that a court can say someone is guilty of the offence, if a reasonable person in his position, having his knowledge and background, ought to have been suspicious". (col.576) Conversely, he stressed that Government "wanted to protect against... the situation in which [someone], although he ought to have been suspicious in the circumstances, he can prove that the salmon he bought was caught legally". The difficulty was that "salmon do not come with their names and addresses on them. ...Nor, if I may say so very delicately to some members of the Committee, do they come in tartan trews"!

Opposition members were unimpressed by the Minister's earnest efforts at plausibility. As Alan Beith put it, "the words [concerning illegal possession, and the penalty provisions relating to it] are dangerous and do not provide for a satisfactory defence for a genuinely innocent person". Despite their strong feelings on these matters, the Opposition appeared to accept that Government was not to be moved; thus no amendment vote was forced. Clause 29 was accepted without a division.

The provisions of Clause 22 (*Power of Court in Trial of One Offence to Convict of Another*—this Clause also applicable only in Scotland) provoked further strong, but brief, Opposition outrage. As Home

Robertson put it, Clause 22 was a "Catch 22": "It means that if the court does not get the offender on one count, it will get him on another". (col.525) This could mean that the accused ended up being convicted without any advance notice of the charge. This was not only "inequitable and wrong" but "flies in the face of established law". Beith inquired whether the inequity might not be slightly eased if the accused initially was charged on several counts. Canavan, however, would have no truck with this compromise on basic principles. He made a straight-forward demand: the accused should be acquitted if the court is not satisfied he is guilty of the offence charged. And if the accused then was to be brought before the courts on another charge, there must be a new charge and a new trial. (col.528)

Once again, MacKay rejected these demands. They would, he stated, make the situation "unnecessarily elaborate". Alex Pollock (Member for Moray, and a Scottish barrister) supported the Minister. A new trial on a new charge would "in some circumstances ...be prejudicial to the accused". (col.529) He suggested there was precedent for bringing an "alternative charge": this had been known to happen when a defendant was acquitted of murder but the court brought in a verdict of "culpable homicide". Even MacKay was prepared to recognise that murder and salmon poaching were not quite of identical gravity! He sought—and failed—to re-assure Home Robertson and the Opposition that the court powers were "permissive" and no conviction would follow if the court thought it unfair to convict on another charge.

Despite another demand by Canavan to "call in the Solicitor-General" to explain more clearly the complexities of Government's reasoning, MacKay stood firm. He was not prepared to make any change unless he could be convinced there was a "real problem". On the division, Government secured an 8:2 majority.

3. Legal Fishers and Illegal Acts

To this point, attention had been focused on "poaching and illegal fishing". Clauses 23 (*Unauthorised Introduction of Salmon or Salmon Eggs into Certain Waters*) and 24 (*Exemption from Certain Offences in relation to Certain Acts*) considered briefly the position of "legal fishing and illegal acts" in the Scottish salmon fishery.

In relation to Clause 23, Home Robertson merely observed that it seemed ironic that while the Committee had spent "several days discussing a range of measures to stop people from taking salmon out of rivers, [now we have] Clause 23 which makes it an offence to put salmon into rivers! What are we doing"? (col.534) MacKay hastened to explain that the purpose of Clause 23 was to ensure that "no person should introduce salmon or salmon eggs into the inland waters of any District for which there is a Board, unless he has the consent of the Board". Government, he said, considered Clause 23 a "sensible precaution ...compatible with good management of the fishery". This explanation appeared to satisfy Home Robertson.

Clause 24 was a different matter. Once again, Home Robertson led the Opposition challenge. The Clause, he maintained, set out provisions which could "drive a coach and horses through not only every aspect of this legislation, but other relevant legislation" as well. (col.537) Why had it been included? The exemptions proposed could have a grave and damaging effect on "whole, or parts of, rivers, depending on the types of activities envisaged". (col.538) He directed his comments to the alleged principal object of the Clause: creation of a "Salmon Ranchers' Charter". "It has been suggested that it is designed to enable salmon ranchers to set up on lochs and rivers around the Scottish coast". This was "a matter of some anxiety", as it would mean the "blocking up of a river to facilitate an extended form of salmon farming" which would "kill the river from the point of view of sport", and "exclude wild salmon from the river, and could have far-reaching effects on the water" (col.538).

He referred to a specific instance.

"It has been drawn to my attention that the Clause will afford commercial fishmongering interests, such as those carried out by the Honourable Edward Davies on the river Polly near Ullapool, to block up legally salmon bearing and non-salmon bearing rivers and burns with fish-traps. That would completely obstruct the up-stream passage of salmon and sea-trout..."

"Much of the Bill is designed to protect and promote the stocks of wild salmon in Scottish waters. So why is the Minister apparently seeking a let-out that could sterilise a river after an approach to the Secretary of State?" (col.538)

These were astonishing observations, not only on the proposed "exemptions from offence of certain forms of legal fishing", but also on the alleged "fishmongering" activities of Davies. Vice-Chairman of the S&TA and a Management Committee member of the AST, Davies was known to most only as an ardent champion of the angler.[2]

Clearly ambushed by these alarming allegations, MacKay quickly rallied. He reminded Home Robertson that one of the proposals in the *Hunter Report* stressed the need to "phase out netting", and institute trap-fishing to secure the commercial catch. Clause 24 was in keeping with this proposal. Also it would enable scientists and fishery managers to secure a variety of much more accurate and reliable statistics on the commercial catch, as well as the movement of migratory stocks into and out of the river. This, declared the Minister, made up the "background" to Clause 24. "To allow any development, such as single-trap fishing, some exemption powers are required. Obviously, that would be illegal at the moment, but this is what we want". MacKay made no comment on Davies' River Polly trap.[3]

Not prepared to let the matter rest, Dalyell now raised the issue of what, in informed salmon fishery circles, was regarded as the notorious "Lochmaddy Salmon Trap". This trap on North Uist in the Western (Outer Hebrides) Isles, was part of a "salmon ranching" business operated by North Uist Estates, and owned by the wife of

THE POLLY SALMON TRAP ... Total obstruction of up-stream escapement on River Polly near Ullapool on the Scottish North-West Coast.

Earl Granville (Granville James Leveson-Gower), the Queen's cousin. It had been of some considerable concern to visiting anglers. Placed at the sole exit to the sea from the Loch Skealter system, it blocked up-stream passage of salmon and sea-trout. Most visiting anglers who stayed at Lochmaddy Hotel—also owned by North Uist Estates—came there to fish for salmon and the renowned Hebridean sea-trout. Those who learned of the ranching trap at the outflow of Loch Skealter were not amused. Dalyell referred to a letter from an angler, Donald Boyd, with photographs of the "illegal trap" taken "the third Sunday in September 1982". (col.539)

After outlining the method by which salmon ranches operate, Boyd said he had gone to Lochmaddy "on an advertised fishing holiday in a well-known salmon and sea-trout fishery which has for a hundred or more years provided the public with holiday game angling. As I found, to my cost, it was no more, and I had been conned".[4] The situation "as I see it, is as follows:

a. There is no Kings (or Queens) Gap at all as required in the common law.

b. The Grills are so close that even an eel can hardly get through. About half an inch. The law lays down MESH sizes for *nets,* for obvious conservation reasons, which surely should or ought to be made applicable to grilles in traps.

c. These traps operate seven days a week, including SUNDAYS. Of all illegalities this is the one which bugs me as an angler barred from angling on Sundays, as the worst of the various crimes for which the operators have never been prosecuted". (col.539)

This was another nasty bouncer for MacKay to handle. Seemingly overt illegal acts by reputable legal fishers had been committed. In fact, however, Boyd was not correct about the operators "never having been prosecuted". A prosecution had been brought against North Uist Fisheries in 1983, but no conviction had been secured.

Home Robertson remained unhappy about Clause 24. He pointed to the Polly and "the activities of Mr. Davies". Far from "fulfilling what the Minister cited as Lord Hunter's intention of allowing a number of fish to get out, [the trap is] blocking up the river with salmon ranching activities. That is also happening at Lochmaddy. ...If this is happening now, why has nothing been done about it? Is it the Minister's intention that this provision may be used in future to legalise such methods of salmon ranching which could have a detrimental effect on the passage of wild salmon"? (col.540)

MacKay did not respond. The "Salmon Ranchers' Charter" was duly accepted. It became Section 27 of the *1986 Salmon Act.*

Political Theatre and Subsidiary Issues

The Committee had dispensed with the Bill's subsidiary clauses. Could Government now be persuaded to recognise the need for "conservation provisions" to be incorporated in the Bill? And what of a full National Review of salmon fishing and institution of a National Salmon Policy? Would Government introduce any measure to accommodate modern "equity, economy" and rod/tourism demands? Would it finally concede there was a crucial need for statutory net-reductions?

References

1. *Daily Express,* 11 February, 1990.

2. It might be noted that Davies is a member of the Worshipful Company of Fishmongers.

3. See also, David Shaw, "Netsman for Chair [of S&TA]?", *Trout and Salmon,* (January, 1986), p.45; and "Letter to the Editor" from Davies in reply to this item, *Trout and Salmon* (March. 1986), p.22.

4. Letter from Donald Boyd, to Tam Dalyell, dated 30 May, 1986.

Chapter 10

POLITICAL THEATRE AND LEGISLATIVE REALITIES: III

"If the position of critics of North-east [drift-nets] nets [is] that more fish should be conserved for rods, then 'the fishery which is catching the largest proportion of the fish, which otherwise would be available to the angler, should be stopped—that is, the Scottish net fishery'!"

Alan Beith, (see p.208 below)

"We do not need to work to eight places of decimals and indulge in enormous scientific research to establish [the] simple connection ...that salmon caught on their way to the Scottish rivers through the North-east drift-net fishery will affect that [Scottish] fishery"!

Cranley Onslow, (col.618)

"By its nature, a net is interceptory, because it catches something on its way to somewhere else. Fish move in particular directions, so [not just drift-nets, or fixed-nets, but] any fishing net is interceptory".

Minister Gummer, (col.600)

"Some of us think... we are in danger of conniving at some kind of netsmen's charter"!

Tam Dalyell, (col.595)

The Challenge of Modernity and Government's Final Response

This third and final "Act" of Committee proceedings was ripe with dramatic opportunity and promise. The "substantive" and "principal subsidiary" provisions in the Bill had been dealt with in "Acts I and II". There now was the opportunity for Government to end on a climactic note. But would it? Did it have any intention of meeting "conservation" and "net-reduction" demands which were just as insistent now as at the start of the debates?

In fact, as we have seen, Government was not totally unresponsive. Some accommodations had been made and "enabling provisions" incorporated in the Bill. In relation to netting reductions, Government had introduced certain amendments. Clause 32 (*Servants and Agents Authorised by Fishing Licences*) and Clause 33 (*Review of Certain Salmon Net Fishing*) had been introduced at Lords' Third Reading. Clause 32, which now was to be examined in detail, proposed restrictions applicable to licensees and their "consignees" throughout England and Wales. Clause 33 would provide the opportunity for consideration of reduction—possibly abolition—of the North-east drift-net fishery and/or East coast Scottish netting. And then there were the three recently enacted Northumbrian and Yorkshire Water Authorities' bye-laws—these providing for an 8-hours night-time drift-netting ban, a standardised 60-hours Weekly slap, and inducements for drift-netters to switch to land-based coastal fixed netting.

In relation to securing Scottish net-reductions, Government had repeatedly stressed there were several provisions equipped with "enabling powers". These included: Schedule 1 and Clause 2 (Designation Orders—including the setting of Annual Close Times), Clauses 3 (Weekly Slap, and regulations with respect to "meshes, materials and dimensions" of nets used), 6 (Alteration or Increase of Annual Close Time), and 20 (Permitted Methods). And should any Scottish-based boats be tempted to risk a little inshore fishing with monofilament nets, the new Statutory Instruments (SIs) 59 and 60 "banning use of gill nets", and "carriage of monofilament nets in Scottish inshore waters" respectively, contained punitive provisions which would make it costly for convicted perpetrators.

Government was happy to commend voluntary buy-outs of Scottish nets. Indeed, another salmon conservation body recently had come into existence with a remit to do just this. Entitled the Atlantic Salmon Conservation Trust (ASCT), its inauguration had been announced at the Committee Meeting of 13 May. (col.203) Already the ASCT had "concluded arrangements to take over 53 interceptory salmon netting points off the Moray Firth coast". Though of somewhat worrying origins—prominent Moray netsman Hon. James Stuart was its principal spokesman—and with a policy that seemed rather "back to front" (that is, priority was given to removal of coastal fixed nets, rather than the more orthodox "top-down"—from river, to estuary, to coast—approach) the ASCT nevertheless did offer the prospect of promising if limited and selective reductions.[1]

As for "conservation", Government maintained that the entire Bill with its up-dated provisions was a "conservation" measure. Its clauses provided needed provisions which could be employed to ensure improved salmon conservation in local, regional and national contexts. It was merely that it was up to local Fishery Boards and Water Authority Fisheries Committees to use the new powers in the Bill. These provisions and accommodations provided solace to some critics. But most, on both Opposition and Government benches, were not satisfied. The onus remained on Government to devise some means of enhancing the Bill's credibility, some plausible device which would demonstrate its commitment to meeting the demands of modernity. What would it do? What course would it pursue?

1. Net Reductions: The North-East and Scottish Issues

First indications were that Government, far from making serious concessions, was determined to brazen it out. During the debate on Clause 32, Beith and Randall objected strongly to further restraints proposed for English and Welsh netsmen and their "small but historic industry". These representations in turn provoked an angry and heated protest from critics of Government and the North-east drift-net fishery. The patience even of the scrupulously courteous Tam Dalyell was severely strained. He put a sharp question to Minister Gummer: "How damaging are the North-east fisheries?" (col.595)

He then put bluntly the basic position of Government's critics. "Some of us think... we are in danger of conniving at some kind of netsmen's charter, that the Bill is too biassed towards netsmen, that wild Atlantic salmon is not a food resource, and that [it is wrong for] people to do what netsmen have traditionally and understandably done. I am entitled to answers to those questions".

Gummer replied in an equally sharp, even ominous manner. The Bill, he asserted, was "in no sense... a charter for netsmen". Indeed, netsmen "should be congratulated on the degree to which they were prepared to accept the very considerable restrictions we [already] have placed on them". The fact was that "North-east [drift-net] fishermen catch less than one-third" of the total North-east coast (English and Scottish) net catch. It was very difficult to "get the balance right" between nets and rods, but Government was "trying". The proposed North-east Review would assist greatly towards this end by providing objective data and scientific material that would enable judgements to be made on the nature and level of restraints to be placed—or maintained—on drift-nets. (cols.596-97)

Far from satisfied with this response, Dalyell pressed his point:

"Am I [then] being told that the drift-netsmen of the North-east, whose present methods are more efficient than their traditional methods, do not threaten the conservation of salmon as a species? Am I being told that although it is difficult to obtain precise statistics the North-east drift-netsmen are not a threat to the conservation matters before the Committee? Is that the expert view of MAFF [the Ministry of Agriculture Food and Fish]?"

Seemingly oblivious to Dalyell's pressure and the under-current of feeling within the Committee, Gummer spoke up with equal asperity. While "expert advice and scientific evidence" from competing interests might produce "diametrically opposed" conclusions, he declared, "I believe that, if properly controlled, the fishermen of the North-east do not present any danger to the conservation of salmon". (col.597) The proposed Review would enable these views to be tested.

Alex Pollock, referring to the ban on drift-netting in Scottish waters since 1962, emphasised that depredations by North-east English nets on Scottish stocks was "demoralising to Tweed fishermen", and that the North-east fishermen contributed nothing to the maintenance of this stock. (cols.598-99) This pointed assault went too far for Gummer. He struck back, and this time at the Scottish "vitals".

> "I do not accept an attitude to fishing for salmon with nets which believes that it is possible to discuss the North east drift-net fishermen without discussing the [Scottish] estuarial nets, which is what [Mr. Pollock, referring to a brief from the Scottish Landowners' Federation (SLF)] has done. How can one talk about the depredations on the salmon stock when they amount to one-third of those netted, without reference to the two-thirds that are netted by [Scottish] estuarial nets? *Those nets sometimes stretch right across the mouths of rivers, and if they do not catch salmon going up, they catch them [on the turned tide] coming down...*" (col.600, italics added)

He went on to add a few home-truths about the concept of "interceptory nets", a subject about which Scottish, and particularly Tweed interests were extremely sensitive. "I have been beaten about the ears by those who have felt that one has dared to raise the question, whatever the technical meanings... of the word 'interceptory'. By its nature, a net is interceptory because it catches something on its way to somewhere else. Fish move in particular directions, so [not just drift-nets, or fixed-nets, but] any fishing net is interceptory".

Finally, Gummer targeted the one issue which petrified the Scottish "salmon establishment", the sole issue which they and their representatives had gone to such lengths to obscure or evade: ban-

DOUBLE-BANK NETTING on Tay ... Sweep-netting by competing operators on opposite banks (TSF and Insch [Mark Clements] Fisheries) virtually shuts down up-stream escapement.

ning the *Scottish* nets. "I must say to the [Scottish interests], that if it were true on conservation grounds that this [NE drift-net] fishery had the damaging effect some fear, but have not proved, I would have no hesitation in recommending to the Committee that we should find a way to phase out that fishery. I want to make that absolutely clear. ...[By the same token], if the same were true about the private netting interests on the estuaries of Scottish rivers, I would hope that the Scottish [interests] would react in the same way". (cols.600-01)

Seeking to stem this dangerous—to anti-North-east nets *Scottish* interests—tide, Pollock interjected. On what basis were the Minister's above "interim conclusions" based? Were they in fact based on information from the MAFF-commissioned "Solomon Report"?

This Report on the North-east fishery by the fisheries consultant Dr. David Solomon, was known to have been recently completed, but the Ministry refused to release it. Critics of the drift-net fishery were convinced it contained information and "scientific evidence" which would support their case; that it would provide useful, up-dated counter-information to dis-prove and reject the only other systematic "scientific evidence" produced on the North-east fishery. This information was contained in a 1982 MAFF scientific report.[2]

Gummer, however, in his reply to Pollock indicated that his Ministry's position on the Solomon Report had not changed. While he was prepared to "consider the question that was raised about the Report", he was not prepared to allow Committee members or the public to see it, principally for reasons of "commercial confidentiality". Indeed, despite persistent demands during the Committee debates, and in the years since, it has remained secret.

Beith now added further blunt observations on highly sensitive Scottish issues. The North-east drift-nets, he asserted, do contribute to stock protection and conservation. Policing the sea-fishery and river stocking is funded by netsmen's licence revenue and monies from ratepayers. Indeed, "only... the rivers in Northumberland [show] clear evidence of the salmon stocks increasing". (col.602) This increase, he stated, must be due partly to to the efforts of the Northumberland Water Authority and the policing—and "self-policing"—of the drift-net fishery. In general, there were "more resources for [English/Welsh] rivers,... than for Scottish rivers"; and in relation to poaching, "there is more effective prevention... in areas where there is drift-netting, than in areas where there is not".

Beith stressed that "the absence of the [drift-net] fishery in the wide area around the Tweed [known as the 'Tweed Conservation Box'], although it is a good conservation measure, adds to the difficulty of policing within that area". As for Tweed river netting: not only was the "largest proportion of netted fish taken" this way, but there was plenty of evidence of abuse where this method was used. Beith referred Committee members to an early-1980s Tyne-Tees television programme, which had caused something of a furore at the time, that showed a tractor towing a net on Tweed. Tweed protagonists on the Committee shifted uncomfortably.

2. Net Reductions: Conservation and National Review Demands

It was in an angry and contentious mood that the Committee proceeded to debate Clause 33 and Government's proposed (3-year) North-East (NE) Review. Home Robertson led off, advancing a theme which had been popular with critics of the Bill: the need for a National review of "coastal salmon fisheries throughout the United Kingdom". (col.612) A review of North-East netting was not nearly enough.

Sir Hector Monro and Roger Thomas (Member for Carmarthen) strongly agreed. Any such Review, they said, should also cover the West coast of Scotland and Welsh fisheries. (col.614) Sir Hector declared *there was "virtually nothing" in the Bill about conservation.* Yet there was urgent need for "stricter measures" to assure the long-term future of salmon fishing.

As for the continuing "imbalance" between net and rod interests, Sir Hector added: "I believe we have failed in the Bill to deal with the equation between the livelihood of the netsmen, and the livelihood of tens of thousands of others involved with salmon". Those affected, warned Sir Hector, "will feel cheated if the interests of the majority are not given more emphasis" in the remaining deliberations. As for the netsmen, Sir Hector stated that "some may lose a percentage of their livelihood, [so] we have to look at compensation".

Adding fuel to these fires, Thomas pointed out that the angling community in Wales was "very concerned". Conservation provisions for Welsh fisheries in the Bill were "totally inadequate". While the Welsh Water Authority (WWA) said that commercial catch statistics showed "no appreciable decline in local fisheries", many informed persons strongly disagreed and held that in fact there was "a decrease which is continuing inexorably, year by year". The rod-fishing season was being "gradually narrowed" from more than seven months to a "late summer fishing only", because there was "no fair catch in our rivers" in the early part of the season. There was also much evidence of over-netting. If grave conservation, social and economic effects were not to follow, "a fairer regard to the overwhelming power and influence which nets are having in our estuaries" must be established. (col.615)

WHEN ALL ELSE FAILS ... Tweed netsmen and fish merchant, Ralph Holmes (left) provides the writer with a fine Spring salmon and sea-trout.

The reaction of Beith, principal spokesman for North-east and English and Welsh commercial netsmen, was swift and fierce. He turned the full force of his counter-attack on Sir Hector, Dalyell and the Scottish salmon interests. If there was "an argument for banning anything", he declared, "it [was] an argument for banning all net fishing in Scotland".

Putting his finger squarely on the central issue, he declared: if the position of critics of the North-east nets is that more fish should be conserved for rods, then "the fishery which is catching the largest proportion of the fish, which otherwise would be available to the angler, should be stopped—that is, the Scottish net fishery". (col.615)

If this was the only way "employment in Scottish hotels" could be preserved, then, declared Beith, the arguments of the net-reductionists "must relate to paying compensation to all the net fisheries in Scotland".

But this argument, he contended, hinged on the assumption that there is "conclusive evidence that the rod fishery is about to collapse, either generally, or in a number of specific rivers". And if that were so, and the correct remedy was considered to be "banning fishing", then "...all kinds of fisheries on rivers ought surely to be stopped. I am talking not only about drift-net fisheries at sea, but about the net fishing in the estuary and river, and angling in the river itself. If [Sir Hector] can point to a river where there are virtually no salmon left and any kind of take is preventing spawning, [then] there should be no fishing whatsoever in that river—unless he accepts the more complex arguments which are advanced in scientific discussions on the subject which suggest that cropping is a perfectly reasonable way of ensuring that a stock remains in the river". (col.616)

Sir Geoffrey Johnson-Smith interjected. He was amazed that Beith should imply that "just a cropping exercise" was taking place in the North-east drift-net fishery. "I have seen no figures which substantiate that it is a cropping exercise".

Beith hit back hard. "The majority of fish that would otherwise go into Scottish rivers are not caught in the North-east drift nets, but in the rivers and by estuarial nets used by Scottish netsmen. ...Why is [Sir Geoffrey's] attention not directed at the section of the industry which is catching the majority of fish that would otherwise go into Scottish rivers? I do not see the logic of his argument".

> "All the figures produced by the Ministry so far", [Beith went on], "have shown a very small impact on Scottish rivers, and that, as I know only too well, is concentrated mainly on the Tweed. The day that [Sir Hector] can convince me... that the state of the salmon on the West coast [of Scotland] is gravely affected by the North-east drift-net fishery, ...I shall know that his arguments are striking home. I find that argument astronomically absurd, and I wait in eager anticipation for some convincing evidence".

Having laid out the "North-east defence", and terrified the representatives of Scottish interests into a stunned and sullen silence, Beith now laid out what he and the North-east netting interests considered a "sensible and constructive" approach to this highly sensitive matter. "All the arguments point to the desirability of making sensible scientific assessments of what the stock levels in various rivers are, how they can best be maintained, and how a balance can be maintained by those who have additional involvement in the fisheries and whose livelihood is dependent upon them… ".

> "My conviction is that the North-east drift-net fishery has nothing to fear from a proper scientific assessment of the situation. I would therefore welcome any steps by the Minister to ensure he has the widest possible advice at his disposal. …If he does that, the case for maintaining an extremely well-regulated fishery off the North-east coast, and for ensuring that net fisheries throughout Scotland are properly regulated will be well demonstrated". (cols.616-17)

This "gloves off" exchange on this most sensitive of issues triggered the most heated, and in many ways the most informative debate of the entire Bill proceedings.

3. Net Reductions: 'Scientific Evidence' vs 'Common Sense'

The central issue around which battle now raged was the seemingly harmless factor of "scientific evidence". Government and nets supporters contended that any alteration to the existing "balance" in net and rod catches must only be undertaken after first establishing the need for such changes on the basis of the "best available scientific evidence".

Opponents of this view dismissed this contention. They claimed that no one—and no Government department—possessed accurate figures, or were vested with powers, resources or the will to secure them. Hence all catch and other statistics, relating to stock levels both within and outside of rivers, could be regarded as "guesstimates" only, and "scientific evidence" used in this context was a misnomer. They maintained that "common sense" should prevail. And common sense, in their view, made clear that the existing "imbalance" between nets and rods must be re-adjusted; that the North-East English drift-nets—and most were prepared to allow that the Scottish nets too—must be substantially reduced; and finally that there was no need for "scientific evidence" to establish that these things must be done.

Amongst those speaking up on behalf of opponents were Conservatives Messrs. Onslow, Morrison, Pollock, Sir Geoffrey Johnson Smith and Sir Hector Monro, with Scottish Labourites, Messrs. Home Robertson, Dalyell and Canavan rounding out this interesting "marriage of convenience". Backing Government and its Ministers Gummer and MacKay were two equally interesting bed-fellows: Messrs. Beith and Randall.

Onslow led off. The basic point made by opponents of the North-east drift-nets, he stressed, was that salmon passing through waters off the North-East coast of England on their way to Scottish rivers were caught by these nets; and that this had a definite negative effect on the Scottish fishery. Dismissing the issue of "scientific evidence", he declared, "we need not work to eight places of decimals and indulge in enormous scientific research to establish that simple connection"! (col.618)

As for the emphasis which North-east nets supporters gave to the importance of "livelihoods"; this issue, he contended, was not the paramount consideration. As with restraints placed on herring fishing, "the resource can come first, and the jobs can come second". Indeed, Onslow was prepared to concede—and for the first time on the public record, so far as the writer is aware—this priority should apply not only to the North-East drift-nets, but to Scottish river nets as well—"We may well come to that... I do not rule out that possibility".

There followed a lively exchange between Onslow and Messrs. Gummer and Beith on the vexed issues of illegal catches, undeclared catches, and night-fishing in the drift-net fishery. "No one", declared Onslow, "knows what goes on at night... however well-policed it may be by day". (col.619) Gummer expressed great interest in these views, and said he would welcome any supporting evidence. He added that there were similar "arguments about how much netting, legal and illegal, goes on [in Scottish] estuaries"; but that while these were "strong presumptions", he had "no evidence whatsoever". Onslow replied that if he obtained any such evidence, he would let the Minister have it at once!

Turning to the broader "common sense" issues of conservation and netting—legal and illegal—Onslow urged the Minister to extend the proposed North-east Review to a full National Review, thus rectifying a "fundamental omission" in the original Bill. In the North-east, the North-west, and Wales there was a threat to salmon stocks, he said. The same applied to a dozen other rivers. "Anyone who knows the state of the Towy and the extraordinary decline in the number of salmon in that river over the past 20 years, must be worried". Indeed, one could go "all the way round the coast, even to the Avon in Hampshire and see that there has been continuing and growing cause for concern about the decline of salmon stocks, for a variety of reasons". (col.620)

There was strong support for these views—if with differing emphasis—from both the right and left in the Committee. Morrison acknowledged that "scientific evidence" had, as yet, not proved anything. A National Review would, however, greatly "improve the general level of knowledge. ...[Indeed] I find it odd that the Government was not prepared to introduce a more all-embracing clause in the first place". (col.621) At the other end of the political spectrum, Canavan took a more robust line. He declared that already there was enough "scientific evidence" to measure the "balance—or rather imbalance"—between the catches of nets and rods. Referring to official catch figures in Scotland for the period 1979-'83, he noted there had been a reduction of 20 per cent in the rod catch. "We do not need a three-year Review to start counting up [these figures] all over again. ...Why we need a postponement... before taking adequate action is beyond me"! (col.624)

The "other important balance", said Canavan, was "the balance of jobs". The Minister had not refuted the figures recently published in the *Glasgow Herald.* These showed that nets provided only 600 full-time jobs, while generating £5m. annually in revenue. Rods, on the other hand, pumped "up to £210m. annually into Tourism-linked Highland enterprises", while providing employment for more than 30,000 people. The official catch statistics, however, clearly showed "that it is the *angler* who is being discriminated against, rather than the netsmen". A thorough Review of all salmon fishing in Scotland was needed, and Canavan was prepared to accept that this Review should apply "to the whole of the United Kingdom". (col.626)

The Bill, "and particularly this part", declared Canavan, was "a lost opportunity". What was required was "a more comprehensive and radical review to bring about a fair solution in the interests of those who enjoy fishing as a sport, and in the interests of those whose livelihood is connected with it, directly or indirectly".

A somewhat exasperated Randall, a firm defender of the North-east nets, said he was in full agreement with the demand for a full United Kingdom Review. But on one matter he was adamant: any decisions must be made on the basis of "proper scientific evidence", and this only could "come from the Ministry. The various interest groups have ground their axes and over-stated their case. I am suspicious of the information". (col.623)

It fell to Dalyell to sum up this section of the debate. The key issues relating to conservation and a National Review hinged on reliable information about nets. He referred to figures which showed that in England and Wales, in certain areas, there had been increases in nets employment; and yet in others there had been decreases. The key point was, how many of these netsmen were "full time, really depending on it for their livelihood"? —or as Onslow put it, "how many are professional fishermen,... and how many of them are amateurs or hobby netsmen, which is a developing trend?" (col.627)

The situation concerning the salmon fishery, declared Dalyell, was perfectly clear to any informed and sensible person: *"Conservation of a priceless asset" depended on netting reductions, and yet "after 29 or more hours of debate in the House of Lords, Second Reading in the House of Commons, and all the sittings of this Committee", Government had not yet accepted a single amendment to secure this objective.* (col.628)

Why was it "that the interests of a few wealthy proprietors of netting rights in Scotland and their [nets] employees, amounting to [no] more than 1000 people, are favoured at the expense of upwards of 20,000 people dependent on the angling tourist industry for their livelihoods"?

And, equally important, why was it that "...drift-net fishing [has] been allowed to operate off the North-east of England 20 years after drift-netting was banned in Scotland"?

Finally, he probed Government on the one item of "scientific evidence" which opponents believed could shed new light on North-east drift-net realities: the *Solomon Report.* "Why", demanded Dalyell, had this "Report prepared for MAFF not been made public"? (col.628) Was it not merely common sense that this seemingly vital "scientific evidence" be made available at least to Committee members to assist them in their deliberations? The Minister was no more helpful in his response than he had been to earlier requests.

4. The Minister's 'Rabbit': The Salmon Advisory Committee

Dalyell really said it all. The opponents' case had been put in a nutshell. "Conservation", "balance", "scientific evidence", "common sense" reform, a proper Review, netting reductions in the North-east drift-net and Scottish fisheries, the enormous value of salmon rod-tourism to the Scottish economy; these were the issues which Government was challenged fully and finally to face. Time was fast running out. Would Government attempt to meet these basic criticisms? Would it do anything to raise the Bill's credibility?

Minister Gummer rose to speak. The usual *soto voce* buzz of Committee discussion subsided. Members looked up. Was he at last going to take up the challenge? There was an air of expectation.

"Perhaps this is an occasion", he began, "to make my own view clear. I came first to consider the Bill when it was ready, when last Autumn I took the job [as Minister of Fisheries] I now have. I came to the Bill with two profound prejudices. The first is that conservation is paramount. I admit that prejudice because it has to do with a fundamental view about life and one's responsibilities. The second—I

ALL QUIET ON SPEY ... Ghillie Colin Thompson in pensive mood.

... AND DEMONSTRATING the art of Spey-casting on Tulchan water.

represent a rural constituency—is that often the interests of rural employment are less well considered than those of urban employment. ...Poverty [all too often] is considered excusable when it comes thatched. ...We must all admit our prejudices, because otherwise we shall not make balanced judgements". (col.628)

He acknowledged there had been from both sides rather more "sharp words", and "rather less of facts, figures and evidence". The result was that members had "to try to balance" the relevant issues for themselves. He accepted "there are three things" about which they "might legitimately be unhappy".

First, major salmon legislation is a rare parliamentary concern. "This is the first Bill... we have had for a long time, and people might think that if they did not get into the Bill all that they might want or need now, it would be a long time before they had another opportunity. That seems a reasonable fear. [But also] it means that when one argues, reasonably, that we should not make a decision now, because we do not have the evidence, they [the critics] say, rightly: 'That is all very well, but by the time you [do] have the evidence, there will not be a Bill. What will happen? We shall have to hang about waiting for another opportunity, and if it comes as quickly as this one has, there will be no salmon left!' I accept that argument". (cols.628-29)

Second, there was the issue of "conservation". "We [all] are supposed to be in favour of conservation: the Bill should do a great deal for conservation, yet it has not addressed itself as sharply as it should to some of the fundamental arguments within the salmon fraternity ...if one is to meet conservation demands. ...The hon. Member for Falkirk West (Mr. Canavan), in his permanent attack on my noble Friend Lord Mansfield, illustrates for us those tensions within the salmon fraternity, and the fact that different groups, in fearing for the future of the salmon, tend to put their interests above those of others, for the best of reasons. I believe strongly that it was important not to ignore the nets and angling disagreement; I put it no higher than that".

Third there was the issue of a National Salmon Policy, or a National Review of United Kingdom Salmon Fisheries. "Some people believed—partly because it is a Scottish Bill, and most of the salmon are in Scotland—that the Bill did not amount, as they would wish, to a National policy for salmon stocks. There is some truth in that... It would be sad, would it not, if the Bill could protect salmon in Scotland, and [yet] do nothing for some of the other areas that have been mentioned"?

The Committee was unusually, silent. Members were guardedly impressed by the Minister's generous and reasonable summary. But where to from here? Gummer provided a hint. "We must [now] consider how to meet these three reasonable demands of those who believe the Bill does not do what they want". While noting that he "did not necessarily agree" with these demands, Gummer made his position very clear: "The three points are so important, that we must try as far as possible to meet them". (col.630)

The question was: how was this to be done? What did the Minister and his "salmon servants" have in mind? The Committee did not have long to wait. After further brief debate, Gummer, with all the polish and panache of a professional magician, finally pulled the "rabbit" from Government's "hat".

> "I want to announce to the Committee today, that the Government has decided to establish a Standing Advisory Committee on Salmon Conservation". (col.635)

This Advisory Committee, to be known henceforward as the *(UK) Salmon Advisory Committee,* would "report to the fisheries ministers [MAFF and DAFS], so it will be National". It would concern itself with the salmon in Scotland, England and Wales. And as a Standing Committee, he added, it would "be able to continue its view on a number of issues". It would sit under an "independent chairman". Government, he declared, had agreed on the formation of the Salmon Advisory Committee "because we are committed so strongly to conservation, and because we accept that from time to time we [may have] to take severe measures, both by changes in the statute, and by actions under the statute".

Committee members now set about trying to discover just what kind of "rabbit" this Advisory Committee was to be. First, it was not a statutory committee and was not included in the Bill. While it would have an independent chairman, it would not be an independent Committee of Inquiry. It would be directed by, and accountable to, the MAFF and DAFS Ministers. Further there was no provision enabling, or requiring the Fisheries Ministers or Government to act on Advisory Committee decisions or recommendations. The 20-person Committee, said the Minister, would have a proper "balance of interests concerned, so as to reflect the salmon's status as primarily related to leisure, conservation and other such issues, rather than as a food resource". (col.661) As for its powers: it would be able to consider any issue—including seals and other predators, acid rain, agricultural drainage, water abstraction, forestry planting, collection of statistics, status of stocks, and, of course, nets and rods concerns. The Committee would be funded by Government, and extra funds would be available, though the precise amount would only be known when the Committee had started work and its full needs had been assessed. It also would be required to publish its reports "so that people will be able to see what advice has been given". (col.658)

In the course of the lengthy debate which now followed, the Advisory Committee, while in general welcomed as a "step forward", was seen to have numerous weaknesses. At worst, it was regarded by cross-party critics as a "sop", a "departmental poodle" likely to be comprised of "Yes men"; at best, a ministerial agency with no statutory basis and no powers or requirements to act on issues or recommendations which it might find urgent or desirable.

Minister Gummer, however, firmly held his and Government's ground. The Advisory Committee was not a "sop" or a "poodle", he said. It was an "action Committee". It would not "slow things up", but rather "accelerate and encourage things and make action more possible". (col.640) There was nothing to stop it picking up "all sorts of matters", (col.656) depending on what issues were considered serious by salmon fishery interests. It was even possible that issues raised by the North-east Review might be further examined by the Committee. All in all, Gummer declared that the decision of Government to create the Salmon Advisory Committee was "Probably the most important change we have considered". (col.661)

This, then, was the "climactic accommodation" which Government finally was prepared to concede in an attempt to appease its critics. Briefly, after debate had stripped away all its impressive trappings, it was not much; yet it did offer hope. Here at least was a permanent formal agency through which important salmon issues could be kept to the fore of Government's consideration. But would the Advisory Committee be able to persuade Government to act?

5. Denouement and the Advisory Committee 'Loophole'

Introduction of the Advisory Committee at this final juncture achieved at least two important Government objectives. First, it lifted the spirit and temper of these concluding Committee theatrics. Committee critics, though by no means fully content with the shape the Bill had taken, were now at least somewhat appeased. The second objective was more immediate and practical: the Advisory Committee provided Government with a most convenient loop-hole; a useful device for deflecting and de-fusing remaining demands by Committee reformers.

Things now moved swiftly. Clauses 34 (Interpretation), and 35 (Amendments and Repeals) were quickly agreed. As for Schedule 4 (Minor and Consequential Amendments), Minister MacKay brought some measure of satisfaction to Sir Hector Monro by securing Committee approval for certain amendments which assured full protection for the Borders/Solway fishery. Though these amendments fell far short of Sir Hector's quest for a "Joint (English/Scots) Solway Fishery Commission", they were at least something. Under these provisions, the (English) North-West Water Authority (NWWA) would continue to be responsible for the administration and protection of these Borders/Solway waters under the (English) *1975 Salmon and Freshwater Fisheries Act.* Nevertheless, any prosecution would be initiated in the National jurisdiction where the fishery offence was alleged to have taken place. The Minister noted that 80 per cent of the River Border Esk, to which this specific provision applied, remained in Scotland. (col.678-79)*

MacKay also had good news for Cranley Onslow and Sir Geoffrey Johnson-Smith. He announced that Government had agreed to amend Clause 30 (Introduction of Fish into Fish Farms Without Consent); and that this amendment (relating only to England and Wales) would be tabled at Commons Report stage. The Government position now was that the exemption of fish farms from Water Authority (WA) permission for release of fish/spawn "into *any* inland water", should be restricted *only* to *fully-isolated* fish farms or inland waters; or to such waters connected with other inland waters by conduit or pipe "constructed for this purpose". (col.683) When pressed by Onslow and Sir Geoffrey to include an added provision to ensure improved control of fish farm effluent discharges, Minister MacKay resisted. Such matters, he stated, could be dealt with by the appropriate WA, deploying powers under the provisions of the *Control of Pollution Act, 1974.*

Minister MacKay now turned to more delicate matters. It was here that the potential value of the Advisory Committee to Government and to its long-suffering Ministerial advocates in Committee became apparent.

Three immediate issues were considered: Control (in English and Welsh waters) of "incidental" salmon and sea-trout catches by coastal sea-fishermen; the introduction of fixed-net fishing for salmon and sea-trout in England and Wales; and the need to extend the powers of WA bailiffs in England and Wales, to permit control and protection of coastal sea-fisheries where migratory fish were known to be present. These issues, though applicable to England and Wales only, had obvious overlapping significance for Scottish fisheries, and the Solway/Borders and North-east coast fisheries in particular. They

* See map of Main Salmon Rivers of Scotland, p. 21 above

were specifically raised by Onslow in his proposed amendment (clause) to Government's new "Bye-Laws Under Sea Fisheries Regulation Act, 1966" Clause.

Government had arrived at a clever compromise on the first two issues. Basically, it placed the onus on the concerned local Water Authorities and their counter-part Sea Fisheries Committees to sort out their own agreements. MacKay explained that while the relevant Sea Fishery Committee must make the first move in relation both to tightened controls on "incidental" catches, and in relation to the "introduction of fixed-nets"; nevertheless, the local Water Authority *must consent* to any such initiative(s) for the proposed provision(s) to be legally binding and operative. (cols.685-87)

The implication of this approach, given a little thought, was clear enough. If sea-fishers wanted to provide more fishing, by means of fixed-nets, for their fellow sea-fishermen; then they must be prepared to accept what rods/conservation interests wanted. And what rods/conservation elements wanted was tighter controls on sea-fishermen operating in coastal waters where migrant runs of salmon and sea-trout were known to pass. The point was: only by such a "brokerage of interests" would it be possible for either party/element to get at least a part of what it wanted.

Messrs. Onslow and Beith took strong exception to Government's approach. The Water Authorities should have more powers. (cols.685-88) If not, there likely would be a "stand-off"; and in such a case, the only other alternative was that the "Minister should decide", as set out in Onslow's amendment (clause). The sea-fishers, however, had their "champion" too. David Harris (St.Ives) objected to the range of powers already proposed for the WAs. He called for what he termed the "WA veto" to be removed. (col.691) Despite considerable pressure from both sides, Minister MacKay refused to be swayed. The issues concerned were "local matters"; and it was up to the local official bodies—the relevant WAs and local Sea Fisheries Committees—to sort it out between themselves.

But suppose, as envisaged by Onslow, a satisfactory sort-out proved still not to be possible. What then? If all else failed, Minister MacKay indicated there was one last possible avenue to remedy. And what was this "possible avenue"?

Yes, the Salmon Advisory Committee. "If the proposed system proves with the passage of time" not to be working as intended, then "I hope that... the matter can be sent to the [Salmon] Advisory Committee. That is a promise I can give my hon. Friends". (col.692)

The last of these three issues, that of "extended powers for WA bailiffs" into sea-fishery areas, again strongly urged by Onslow, gained a similar rebuff from Minister MacKay. While Onslow made an earnest plea, noting the abuses which were known to take place in the coastal waters of South Wales and round the mouth of the River Usk—though, interestingly, no mention was made of the alleged massive abuses off the North-east English coast—the Minister remained unresponsive. Sea-fishery protection was for Sea-Fishery protection officers, not Water Authority bailiffs.

But suppose these alleged abuses continued, and the Sea-Fishery protection officers were either unable or unwilling to take appropriate regulatory action? What then? Once again, the Minister's answer was simple and straight-forward: call in the Salmon Advisory Committee! "If problems appear to be arising, my right hon. Friend, the Minister of State [Mr. Gummer], wil be prepared to ask the Advisory Committee for its advice". (col.701)

When debate on these issues was concluded, Government secured the agreement of the Commons Standing Committee to its three new clauses. These were duly incorporated in the *1986 Salmon Act,* becoming Section 37 (Bye-laws Under Sea Fisheries Regulation Act, 1966); Section 25 (Fixed Engines in the Solway); and Section 33 (Placing and Use of Fixed Engines).

Committee reformers now made a last-ditch effort to secure three new amendments (clauses) which, in their view, were vital to the effective operation of the Bill. (cols.704-27) These were: 1. "Control of [net] Fishing in Time of Drought"; 2. "60-Hour Weekly Close Time" for the Scottish net fishery; and 3. "Tagging of Salmon". There were lengthy, often impassioned exhortations by the critics, but MacKay's response was uniform. While it would not be appropriate, he said, to include the suggested new clauses or provisions in the Bill, there was an alternative. Yes, each, he suggested encouragingly, could well become the subject of consideration by the Salmon Advisory Committee.

Canavan's Finale: The Alternative Scenario

> *"[My] aim is to restore to the people of Scotland what is morally their rightful property, and to open up freshwater fishing under controlled conditions. I do not want a free-for-all, but the rules should be decided democratically by those who participate in Scotland's favourite sport, ...[and not by] us in Committee, or, even worse, the Minister in his office, or the landlord in his castle".* (Dennis Canavan, col.672)

Canavan was not only the Committee's leading humourist, lightening many a drab morning and afternoon sitting for members and observers alike, he was the leading critic when it came to rhetorical assault with "blunt and extremely damaging instruments". He consistently, and with great dramatic force, brought forward issues which Government and "salmon establishment" elements least wanted exposed to the light of Committee scrutiny.

And there was another side to these unfailingly impressive performances. The issues he raised were close to the hearts of the vast majority of ordinary anglers in Scotland—a majority, which in terms of the bulk of the Bill's provisions, one could be forgiven for believing did not exist at all!

Two months earlier, Canavan had started his Committee theatrics with a performance which put a chilling shudder down the collective "salmon establishment" backbone. He now concluded in a similar vein. In keeping with his unwavering political stance as one of the few remaining "un-reconstructed" socialists in Parliament and with his uncompromising commitment to the people of Scotland, he nailed his colours to the mast.

The popular banners of "free fish", and "free fishing" for the people of Scotland, were now unfurled. He gave both a prolonged and vigourous flourish. And lest Committee members had forgotten what the realities of Scottish politics are (the most relevant fact being that the Conservative Party is a "minority in perpetuity" in Scotland, where in 1986 it governed with but 10 of Scotland's 72 parliamentary seats) he now gave us all a sharp and sobering reminder: the overwhelming Labour Party majority in Scotland is a fact of political life, and any attempt by any vested interest to ignore or evade this reality is a course fraught with danger. Certainly, Canavan had saved his best, and in many ways his most important performance, for last.

1. The Banner of 'Free Fish'

Canavan first directed his attention to the age-old popular Scottish issue of "free fish". He called for an amendment to Clause 33 which would ensure "respect for the common law of Scotland, whereby fish in freely-running water are not the property of anyone until caught, and become the property of the person who catches and lands such fish". (col.666) There was a ripple of subdued laughter from both benches. The dour Canavan remained deadly serious. He produced a well-known 1981 letter from Lord MacKay of Clashfern, then Lord Advocate for Scotland (now Lord Chancellor).

> "The common law position in relation to both salmon and trout, [the letter read], is that they are not the property of anyone until they are caught. Thus brown trout in waters not protected by an Order under

the *Freshwater and Salmon Fisheries (Scotland) Act, 1976,* do not belong to anyone whilst they are in the water, but become the property of the fisherman or person who catches and lands them, whether or not that person owns the fishing rights, and whether or not permission has been given".

Canavan expressed his view that this was "a very good letter". He had distributed it "widely throughout the angling fraternity in Scotland—so much so that I have had telephone calls at weekends from landlords who have come upon people fishing in their alleged territory". These landlords, when confronted with the former Lord Advocate's letter had been, he stated, "left without a leg to stand on, because the common law position, as stated by the Lord Advocate, is correct". Canavan added that "recently", the Solicitor-General at the Scottish Office had confirmed the Lord Advocate's statement.

The basic purpose of his amendment, Canavan explained, was to prevent statute law (the Bill) from "absolutely contradicting" the Scottish common law. "Sympathetic" treatment by Government of his "reasonable amendment" would establish this position, and would prevent "confusion" and making "the law into an ass". (col.667)

In his response, MacKay showed he was neither "sympathetic", nor did he consider the amendment at all "reasonable". Indeed, like most anglers in Scotland, MacKay confirmed that he knew "all about that letter... from my noble Friend and fellow clansman, the Lord MacKay of Clashfern". To another ripple of Committee merriment, MacKay added that he knew about this letter "because some of my constituents, when they have suggested that people should leave their front gardens—not grand estates, but front gardens fronting on the haugh-side—with their six bait rods and so on, this letter has been thrust in their face".

With tongue partially in cheek, the Minister sought to chastise an unmoved and unrepentant Canavan: "I should like to think that he does not approve of this kind of behaviour. ...Secondly, I hope that he does not approve the method of fishing [with multiple bait rods] that bedevils so many lochs of Scotland. ...In addition, those people cause a fair degree of havoc to the trees and surrounding countryside of the lochs".

Now touching "with some trepidation" on the principles at stake, MacKay agreed that under Scottish law, "wild fish" are indeed *res nullus* (belonging to no one) and belong to the captor when caught. But "the right" to fish for and catch salmon and trout, he reminded the Committee, was a very different matter. "From earliest times", these rights had belonged to the person or proprietor who owned them. Canavan's amendment, he declared, was in any event "irrelevant" to Clause 33. "There is no free access to the public to catch salmon and trout in the area to be covered by the [North-east] Review and the common law principle".

Sir Hector Monro sought to bring support to the Minister's position. He referred to the *1971 White Paper* on Salmon and Freshwater Fisheries in Scotland. This White Paper stated "there is no public right to fish for either salmon or trout in Scotland, with the exception of tidal waters". As for the "right to fish for brown trout", this belonged "to the riparian owner".

Canavan was outraged. He expressed deep resentment at this "bitter attack" on the former Lord Advocate. He suggested Sir Hector "take the matter up" with Lord MacKay and "the present Solicitor-General" to secure confirmation of the common law position "as enunciated by [Lord MacKay] in his letter to me". (col.669) With a dramatic flourish, Canavan declared that what was here at stake was "respect for the common law of Scotland. Do Committee members respect the common law of Scotland, or do they not"? Committee members remained silent. "I do", he said, "and I shall vote accordingly"! On the division, Canavan's amendment was defeated by a vote of 10:1.

1. The Banner of 'Free Fishing'

Bloodied, but not at all bowed, Canavan moved on to his second amendment to Clause 33. This called on the Scottish Secretary to ensure "that all freshwater fishing rights in Scotland be deemed to be the property of the people of Scotland, and that they be administered for the people of Scotland by a democratically constituted Scottish Anglers' Trust". (col.670)

He explained that while his previous amendment dealt with the "ownership of wild fish, including salmon", this one dealt with the "ownership of salmon fishing rights". There was a difference between the two. The owner of "the fishing rights on a river is the riparian owner", often a big landowner who had "simply inherited the fishing rights along with the land" from his ancestors. Canavan did not dispute the right to fish should belong to the person who owned the land/riparian rights. The question was: should this be certain historic, titled owners of large estates and fishings; or should it be "the people of Scotland"? This brought Canavan onto his favourite topic: the enormous rights, privileges, authority and influence of the Scottish landed nobility. Committee members, for their part, could see what was coming. Somewhat uneasily, they settled back. Canavan proceeded.

"It is interesting to look at the passage of the Bill through another place [the House of Lords]—it may be no coincidence that the Government chose to introduce the Bill in that place—and at some of those who took part in that debate". He then noted who some of these Peers were and reeled off a list of 20 lords. "Not many working class lads in that lot"! It seemed to Canavan, "looking through that list, that many vested interests in land ownership and the consequent ownership of fishing rights" were represented there. Indeed, he reminded the Committee, "the whole history of land ownership in Scotland is tied up with the ownership of ancillary rights such as fishing rights, shooting rights, and so on".

Canavan settled on the instance of Lord Home of the Hirsel. "It would not be so bad", he said, "if people such as Lord Home of the Hirsel, or the 14th Earl of Home, as he used to be known before he renounced that title in order to become Prime Minister, had fishing rights through hard work or effort on their own part". However, he went on, "examination of the past shows that the 14th Earl of Home obtained his rights because the 13th Earl had them before him; and he had them because the 12th Earl of Home had them". Indeed, suggested Canavan, "If one goes right back, one will probably find that the 1st Earl of Home stole them from the people"! This interesting supposition stirred the Committee from its repose. There were interruptions and cries of "shame"!

Canavan explained. "All that I am trying to do is to restore the ownership of those rights to the people of Scotland". He accepted it was "perhaps... unfair to pick on the 14th Earl of Home, the former Prime Minister", because there were, of course, "many such families in Scotland" whose ownership and attendant rights dated back "centuries to the Battle of Bannockburn". (The village of Bannockburn is about three miles from Stirling. It was here in 1314 A.D. that Robert the Bruce by defeating the forces of Edward II reasserted and secured Scottish independence.)

Warming to his subject, Canavan became a little more expansive. "That battle", he confided, "was fought just down the road from where I stay". (col.671) There was another ripple of Committee mirth. He continued: "I do not pretend to be an expert, but some soldiers who fought that battle changed their jerseys at half-time when they saw that they would be on the losing side, and as a result, acquired land from Robert the Bruce, the captain of the winning side". (col.671)

The Committee erupted in general merriment—but not for long. Canavan went on: "It has now reached the ridiculous stage where in the 20th century there are people with property simply because of a bloody battle fought over six centuries ago, ...and the part played by some who fought it was none too glorious"!

Canavan now came to his point. "Under my amendment, we would restore to the people of Scotland one of their basic rights—namely, the right to fish their own waters. Ownership of fishing rights would be vested with the people".

And what form of popular ownership was Canavan proposing? He explained.

"The style of people's ownership which my amendment proposes—I am thinking also of the Private Member's Bill which I have tried to introduce several times, the Scottish Anglers' Trust Bill—is a de-centralised form of people's ownership. It could work in harmony with the District Boards. Any angler would be free to join a *bona fide* angling club, and any such club would have the opportunity of affiliating itself to the Scottish Anglers' Trust and sending delegates to the Trust's annual general meeting. The members of the Trust would be elected, and the exact constitution could be set down by statutory instrument, subject to parliamentary approval".

The value of this approach, he further explained, would be that: "Instead of the Minister, his advisers and the landowners deciding policy on freshwater fishing, the anglers themselves would decide, through their representatives on the Trust. They would decide on such matters as access. There may be a case in some areas, for conservation [purposes], to have limited or no access. They would decide on prices—what is a fair price, and an extortionate price, ...[for instance] the bandit who owns the [River Shiel] fishing rights [and charges] the extortionate price of £1000 a week! That also applies to regulations about permitted and forbidden tackle. It would all be discussed in a democratic, de-centralised way, instead of us in Committee, or even worse, the Minister in his office, or the landlord in his castle, deciding what the rules should be and what is fair and unfair". (cols.671-72)

Canavan stopped briefly to assess the impact of his presentation. David Harris made an inquiry. Did Canavan's "great plan" call for compensation to those people "who would lose their rights"? Certain Conservative members shook their heads and cringed.

Canavan expressed his gratitude to Harris for raising this important issue. "There may be", he said, "a case for compensation for those who have put work or financial investment into fisheries. But if someone had inherited freshwater fishing rights with his land and done nothing to conserve the fisheries or make them more open to recreation, I would not give him one penny in compensation"! If, however, "the rights were taken into public ownership, it would be feasible to say, 'That person has put in a bit of work in stocking the water and administering the fishing rights for many years, so let us give him, and perhaps his family, so many rods per year, either in perpetuity, or until the death of [that] owner'. ...That would be more reasonable than financial compensation. [Indeed] we hear so much bleating from some of the owners about the high rates they have to pay for their fisheries, that they might be glad to be rid of them"!

Canavan now summed up his case. "Like all my amendments, this is reasonable, moderate and modest. Its aim is to restore to the people what is morally their rightful property, and to open up freshwater fishing under controlled conditions". He went on: "I do not want a free-for-all, but the rules should be decided democratically by those who participate in Scotland's favourite sport, instead of their running the risk of being terrorised, as was my good friend in the civil service, by a man with an Alsatian dog who demanded money, or having to go to the River Shiel and spend as much as £1000 a week. That is unfair by any standard, and my amendment would help to eradicate such unfairness".

Canavan's amendment was not warmly received by Conservative Members. Sir Hector declared—albeit cautiously—that the amendment did "a dis-service to angling in Scotland", where "thousands of miles of first-class fishing is available at modest cost... [as little as] £5 per day—less than half the price for a round of golf"! (col.673) Harris, directing his comments to John Home Robertson, proprietor of the substantial Paxton Estate on Tweedside, asked why this colleague of Canavan and supporter of his amendment did not "hand over his fishing rights voluntarily to a Trust, as his hon. Friend advocates"? (col.674) Home Robertson replied that the Scottish Anglers' Trust was first recommended by the 1965 *Hunter Report*. "It is sensible to have local organisations that control locally, look after fishing interests and ensure sufficient and adequate access to fishing rights throughout Scotland". As for "handing over his fishing rights", Home Robertson stated that he looked forward "to the day when such Trusts exist so that that will be possible. My Party is in that business"!

Minister MacKay chose to respond in true partisan spirit. He dismissed Canavan's "Socialist Valhalla". He reminded the Committee of the "many miles of the banks of rivers owned by angling clubs"; that the payment of £1000 per week on the River Shiel covered the cost of "not just one, ...but a number of rods"; indeed that many Scottish football fans were travelling to the (1986) World Cup competition in Mexico "for which they cannot have had much change out of £1000"! (col.676) Again he reminded the Committee that Clause 33

MODEST COST FISHING ... Veteran Nith-Fisher, Fred McKune, stalks an Autumn "Greyback" (large back-end salmon) on the Mid-Nithsdale Association Water.

was concerned with the North-east fishery, not with the general and controversial issue which the amendment raised.

After further exchanges concerning whose ancestors were, or were not, present at the Battle of Bannockburn, and what their role was, or was not, Dalyell in his role as "sweeper" for Canavan, spoke up. His observations, not for the first time, brought a deadly serious issue into realistic perspective. He explained why, despite initial reservations, he would vote in support of Canavan's amendment.

> "I am a believer in Anglers' Trusts which perform a service, [he stated, and] there is a matter which Conservative Members must take into account. ...In general terms, up to 30 or 40 years ago, most of the large proprietors looked after their rivers. Whatever else may be said about them, on the whole they believed in conservation, stocking and good management. Some of the present owners are exemplary, and no one could fault their management or general custodial relationship with their property. I do not doubt that Lord Home of the Hirsel is among them. ...However, many estates are not properly run. For financial pressures or for other reasons, a quick buck has to be made. So stocking has not been properly carried out, and financial corners have had to be cut. I am not passing moral judgement, but that sort of ownership is not satisfactory by any criterion. Therefore, my hon. Friend has a far stronger case than many Conservatives may believe".

Whether it was a measure of Dalyell's judiciously selected and eminently plausible observations, or not, this amendment of Canavan's fared better than the first. It was defeated by only a 10:6 margin on a straight party division—with Beith absent.

Political Theatre and Government Concessions

Government's critics at last had received their answer. Net-reductions and conservation, in the end, had not been ignored. Gummer, in particular, had given a most impressive performance.

Government was prepared to act. North-east (English), Scottish and indeed UK net-reduction issues as a whole could be addressed by the new Salmon Advisory Committee. As for conservation issues; these too, along possibly with even rods-reduction issues, could be raised within the remit of the Advisory Committee. Creation of the Advisory Committee—the "rabbit" produced from Government's "hat"—was a minor stroke of genius. It offered the *promise* that those things which the different elements within the salmon fraternity wanted, *could* be achieved. Persistent effort could bring statutory and other sought-after reforms. And yet, in terms of binding statutory requirement, Government was committed to nothing more than was already in the Bill.

This was the principal concern of Government's critics. These critics were further concerned that the Advisory Committee was subject to the direction and will of the MAFF and DAFS Ministers. It would be for the concerned Minister to decide what issues would, or would not, be referred to the Committee. In addition, Ministers Gummer and MacKay had made clear that as unreliable and inconclusive as salmon fishery "scientific evidence" might be; it was this evidence which would take precedence over evidence of the "common sense" variety. And if there was to be a correction of the existing historic "imbalance" which continued strongly to favour the netting interests; then this, it clearly was implied, would only follow on the basis of, once again, appropriate and convincing "scientific evidence".

In short, Government yet again had evaded and deferred the central and vital issues. If anything eventually was to be sorted in relation to these issues, this would have to be achieved outside the remit of the Bill, and the future Salmon Act. The Advisory Committee could assist in the consultative process under such circumstances. It provided the promise of a narrow opening of the door to future reforms.

Thus in making provision for the Advisory Committee, Government not only had deflected primary responsibility for change away from itself; it also neatly had deflected any future intitiative back to those elements whose pressure had caused Government to produce the Bill in the first place. Once again, Government could congratulate itself on a clever, complex and effective exercise in parliamentary engineering. The Advisory Committee could well prove a most effective instrument in blocking any future reforms threatening the ancient and comprehensively protected salmon fishery *status quo*. Attempts to modernise the Scottish salmon fishery had come full circle.

"Act III" of these Committee proceedings also revealed clearly the positions of the leading Government and Opposition actors. Statements by Gummer and Beith in particular, clarified not only what these positions were, and how these related to key issues with which the content of the Bill was concerned, but also what confidently might be expected of them, MAFF and Government in future.

As for the "Alternative Scenario" provided by Canavan: in a Bill and a debate which had very little to do with "game-fishing reality" as it exists and is perceived by the vast majority of the Scottish people, Canavan's finale contribution served to bring the Committee face-to-face with what this reality actually is. It was an important reminder and a vital warning. In essence, it caused all to reflect on the dire consequences which legislation as narrow and exclusive as the Salmon Bill was, does threaten and openly invite.

All the major substantive and principal subsidiary issues bearing upon the Scottish salmon fishery had now been addressed. It had been hard slogging for salmon reformers on both Opposition and Government benches. The rewards for these sustained, often enormous efforts were sparse, in terms of amendments secured. In other respects, however, these efforts had produced useful, important results. Foremost was the fact that the "secrets" of the Scottish salmon world, so long and artfully concealed or obfuscated, were exposed to the public gaze. Although some Committee members were uncertain that anything useful had been achieved, they could rest assured. Together with their colleagues in the House of Lords, Committee members had constructed the most comprehensive parliamentary documentation on Scottish salmon fishing in nearly 700 years of legislative concern. This was no small attainment.

There now remained only Commons Report Stage and Third Reading to be completed before the Bill was returned to the Lords for final *pro forma* endorsement. Not yet prepared to accept defeat, the Bill's critics set about preparing one last stand.

References

1. See, David Shaw, "ASCT: Warning Light", *Trout and Salmon,* (July, 1986), p.55; also *Trout and Salmon,* (February 1987), "Comment: Prayers Answered" (p.2), and David Shaw, "A Word In ASCT's Ear" (p.77).

2. See E.C.E. Potter and A. Swain, "Effects of the English North-East Coast Salmon Fisheries on Scottish Salmon Catches", *Fisheries Research Technical Report, No.67*, (Lowestoft: MAFF Publication, 1982).

Chapter 11

A FINAL CHALLENGE

> "The Bill represents probably the last chance in the foreseeable future to legislate for salmon. [The Salmon Advisory Committee is therefore perhaps our best hope for needed future action. But] as we all know, if the British can fumble and fudge anything, they will do so by setting up a committee. The fear is that, if we set up a committee which is not statutory, that is just what will happen".
>
> *Sir Geoffrey Johnson Smith* [1]

There were rumours, first in late June and then in July, that the Bill would be given its final parliamentary Readings before the House rose for Summer Recess. Reformers busy constructing a final challenge were alarmed. Would there be time to complete preparations? Summer Recess came and went. It was not until Parliament re-convened in the Autumn that it was announced that Commons Report and Third Reading of the Bill would be undertaken on 23 October.

The extra time afforded by this four-month reprieve was used to advantage. The principal elements of the reform challenge were now in place. A complex and promising plan which included strategically-timed international pressure had been evolved. Vital cross-party alliances had also been constructed.[2]

The target of reformers' initiatives was Government's proposed Salmon Advisory Committee. Government had "sold" it to Members as the key engine and instrument of future change. Many Members, however, had reservations about its capacity to measure up to its Government billing. Added provisions, they contended, were essential.

The principal requirement was that the Advisory Committee be included in the Bill and have statutory powers. The points supporting this position had been detailed in Standing Committee. (See Chapter 10 above, pp.216-17). There was guarded optimism amongst reformers. Government and reformers were agreed that such an official agency was needed. They were divided only on the form that the Advisory Committee should take. Certainly, an Advisory Committee with "teeth" could only enhance the credibility of the Bill and Government. Other similar adjustments earlier had been conceded. Before joining battle on this last-stand issue, there was other business to be tidied up.

Challenge and Response: Preliminaries

Many conservationists and rod/tourism elements hoped that more than the Advisory Committee provisions would be challenged at Report Stage. It was rumoured that initiatives would be launched to increase the vital (Scottish) Weekly Close Time (WCT), and Annual Close Time (ACT). A 30-hour increase in the former was thought to be a real possibility, while an 18-hour increase to 60 hours was regarded as a near certainty. Similarly, it was believed that the 168-day ACT might be extended to 221 days, and failing this almost certainly to 196 days.[3] Even before debate began, however, these hopes were dashed. The (Amendment) Order Paper revealed that neither Weekly nor Annual Close Time would be considered.

As for the rousing challenge which many hoped for on the issue of the Advisory Committee itself, a head-count of MPs in the Chamber showed that anything which might be achieved would have to be done by few. As at Second Reading, the turnout was disappointing. Present for the 6:40 pm start were 12 Conservative and 10 Opposition Members. More disappointing still, of these only six were Scots: two Conservatives and four Opposition—and this for what remained basically a Scottish Bill.

Yet there was some consolation. Many faces in the near-empty Chamber were familiar. Along with Ministers Gummer and MacKay, leading Conservative "salmon politicians" Cranley Onslow, Sir Hector Monro, Charles Morrison and Sir Geoffrey Johnson Smith were present. Leading Opposition Members included John Home Robertson, Alan Beith, Stuart Randall and Dennis Canavan—Tam Dalyell was absent due to urgent "Westland Affair"* parliamentary business. At least, therefore, debate should be informed. And small numbers can be an advantage in achieving cross-party objectives. Certainly, little would escape the equally small—and informed—audience in the Public Gallery. Six persons were present. These included from Fishmongers' Hall, Salmon and Trout Association

* The 'Westland Affair' was a major public issue, and concerned alleged 'dirty tricks' in placing contracts for supply of helicopters. 'Westland' was one of the competing helicopter makers.

Chairman David Swatland and Director James Ferguson, in company with Tay Salmon Fisheries' Managing Director Ian Mitchell; and from the Welsh Salmon Trout Angling Association, officers Michael Matthews, Artie Jones and "Moc" Morgan.

The first two "preliminary" issues raised in debate afforded little opportunity for Members to work up their reforming energies. During earlier Bill proceedings Government had promised amendments concerning fish farming and angling restraints. It now presented them. New Clause (NC)10 (Disclosure of Information Furnished Under the Diseases of Fish Act, 1937) was Government's response to demands by Cranley Onslow and others for better control of fish farms in (England/Wales) freshwaters. (See Chapter 10, p.218). Onslow, supported by Alan Beith, was however, still unhappy. Fish farms were fast proliferating; fish diseases and fish farm discharges were dangerous to marine life, with risks of contagion far beyond home rivers. Stronger controls were needed. Onslow proposed an alternative, NC2 (Measures Relating to the Prevention of Disease Among Fish) which had the full support of the Water Authorities. Minister Gummer, however, was not responsive. NC10, together with other minor statutory adjustments, were as far as Government was prepared to go. Admonishing the maverick 1922 Committee Chairman, he reminded Onslow that "*De*-regulation [not increased regulation] forms an important part of Government policy". (col.1342) NC10 was agreed.

NC7 (Use of Baits and Lures) was Government's response to Committee (and Lords) demands for restrictions on angling in Scottish waters. Minister MacKay explained that while the Scottish Secretary would have the powers to authorise NC7 restraints, he would act only on the properly executed application of a District Board, or boards. NC7 was supported by both S&TA and the Association of Scottish District Fishery Boards (ASDFB), while Scottish Anglers' National Association (SANA) expressed concern about a ban on all natural baits—the worm being a preferred, and often the only effective bait on many lower-quality waters available to local and association anglers. Sir Hector Monro, on behalf of Conservative supporters welcomed the new clause. Even John Home Robertson was prepared to support NC7. While expressing doubts that such restrictions would be equally applicable to "the hierarchy" and the "common local angler", Home Robertson joined by Beith was prepared to endorse the measure so long as it was enforced "fairly". Anglers, Beith agreed, must take their share of increased control. (See cols.1347-48).

The final preliminary issue concerned the Scottish Opposition's, and more spcifically Dennis Canavan's demand for a Scottish Anglers' Trust (SAT). Although there was no prospect that the Opposition's NC3 (Scottish Anglers' Trust) would be any more palatable to the House now than on previous occasions, it did provide an opportunity to lift the tempo of proceedings—though hardly strengthening fragile cross-party links.

Introducing NC3, John Home Robertson explained that "A new clause such as this is necessary because in many areas of Scotland salmon fishing is virtually exclusively retained. ...The new clause seeks to achieve at least some balance". (col.1350). Donald Stewart, Scottish Nationalist Party Member for the Western Isles, agreed. NC3 would partially offset "the main thrust of the Bill [which] is to set proprietorial rights in concrete". (col.1351). Norman Godman, Labour Member for Greenock and Port Glasgow underlined the main object of the new clause which was to increase "access to this very fine sport [which] should not be [virtually] confined to a small group of very rich people". And while Liberal Malcolm Bruce rendered support for the SAT which fell short of full endorsement, he agreed with the principle. "if the Bill ensures that there are more fish in Scottish rivers, we should then take measures to ensure there are more fishermen to take advantage of the fishing. ...What we should be looking for is expansion of liesure fishing".

Finally, Dennis Canavan rose to speak. After outlining the historic background to NC3 and highlighting its merits, he turned to one of his favourite Salmon Bill themes: ownership of fishing rights. There followed a final, brief "salmon tale"—albeit that it was quickly apparent that the impact of his customary delivery did not carry nearly so well in the near-empty House as in the closer confines of Committee Room D.

"I remember", said Canavan, "the story of a man who was caught by the local landlord, allegedly for poaching. The landlord said, 'Get off my land!' The poacher replied, 'Who said that it's your land?' The landlord said, 'I'll tell you this, my boy, my ancestors fought for this land! That is how it is my land!' The poacher replied, '[Alright then] get your bloody jacket off now and I'll fight you for it!' ...(Interruptions) Hon. Members may laugh, but it goes back to the battle of Bannockburn. That is the morality of land tenure in Scotland. ...It's about time that the balance was restored, and that we returned land and fishing rights to the people". (col.1153) While prepared to accept that "not all hon. Members agree with my radical ideas"—and NC3 in fact "does fall short of my ideas"—Canavan nevertheless hoped that "the Minister and the House will sympathetically consider accepting the new clause".

The Minister and the House, needless to say, showed no such sympathy. MacKay merely noted that he at first thought Canavan "had lost the tape to his usual speech", but he had been re-assured when Canavan got "back on-stream" during the second half. The Government, he said, "could not accept what is essentially a doctrinaire proposition". NC3 was rejected.

The preliminaries were now complete. It was time for the "main event". Reformers turned their attention to their principal concern: the Salmon Advisory Committee.

Challenge and Response: The Advisory Committee

The issues to be resolved in the debate on the Advisory Committee were clear and simple. Could reformers persuade Government to accept that the Advisory Committee should be a *statutory* body—that is, that it be included in the Bill? Could they convince Government that the Minister or Secretary of State should have *enabling powers* so that he could take—indeed, might be required to take—appropriate action in accord with Advisory Committee decisions? Finally, could Government be induced at this last hurdle to accept that the Minister be vested with powers to implement *salmon tagging*?

The Advisory Committee, although initially "welcomed" by Members, was regarded with suspicion. "Departmental poodle", a "sop" to reformers, another "quango refuge" for Government "good boys" and "Yes men"; this was hardly flattering language, and it came from both Conservative and Opposition benches during Standing Committee. Much unflattering language, however, had been used during all stages of the Bill. None of it had caused Government to do more than occasionally to alter its course. Could reformers now do better?

Government and Ministers were pleased with the "rabbit" they had produced in Committee. It had got them off the hook. In principle it promised everything, yet in practice conceded nothing. It would require a mighty effort if Government was to be shifted from this position.

Welsh interests played a prominent role in shaping the reform challenge on the Advisory Committee. At each successive stage of the Bill, the Welsh Water Authority (WWA) had sought changes it considered imperative. The Bill, after all, was supposed to be a UK Bill, even if nearly all emphasis was on the Scottish fishery. Welsh interests were particularly concerned about Government's sole "conservation" provisions: Dealer-Licensing and Illegal Possession. They felt these to be inadequate at best, and virtually useless at worst. Salmon tagging, they were convinced, could greatly assist both in strengthening fishery regulation, and improving catch data and statistics. A detailed "Salmon Sales Group" Report for MAFF had strongly recommended that tagging be introduced. MAFF, however, remained unconvinced. Despite repeated requests by Welsh, and many other UK interests and salmon bodies, it refused to make provision for salmon tagging in the Bill. Feelings were running high. Nor was it only in relation to these key provisions that Welsh interests had suffered rebuffs.

Provisions to improve protection of salmon-bearing coastal waters, combat pollution, abstraction and fish disease had been sought. After persistent pressure, Government had addressed most of these issues. Little satisfactory provision, however, had been secured in the Bill. Changes to the Advisory Committee, therefore, provided a final chance to secure the main legislative provisions they wanted, and possibly many more. But to achieve these changes, co-operation with non-Welsh MPs, and on both sides of the House, was needed. Given the level of cross-party criticism of the Advisory Committee following its introduction in Committee, such co-operation seemed possible. It was a last chance worth pursuing.

To strengthen this initiative, a National "Public Petition of Parliament"—a rarely used procedural device—was organised by the Welsh Salmon and Trout Angling Association. Under the leadership of its fisheries officer and veteran activist, Llandysul's D.A.M. (Artie) Jones, 23,000 signatures were gathered nation-wide for a Petition that specified two general objectives: 1. "endorsement, in principle, of UK-wide salmon-tagging"; and 2. "parliamentary endorsement of legislative enabling powers to be given to the responsible ministers in order that Government's proposed Advisory Committee may have greater assurance that recommended initiatives may be acted upon".[3]

Finally, on the very day of Third Reading, further support emanated from International quarters. At the conclusion of the Third International Salmon Symposium held at Biarritz, France, a number of important resolutions were agreed. The first specifically concerned salmon-tagging, and called for NASCO to investigate "the value of a salmon-tagging scheme such as is in operation in Eastern Canada and Spain, and that it recommend the adoption of [salmon-tagging] by all member countries, for both a more reliable collection of catch data and a more effective control of illegal fishing".[4]

Altogether, salmon reformers had constructed an impressive range and depth of well-timed support for their Advisory Committee challenge. While Welsh interests had performed the detailed tasks to formulate the initiative, the petition and Biarritz resolutions provided convincing evidence of UK-wide and International support. Would it be enough? Would Government be convinced that changes to its proposed Advisory Committee were needed?

SALMON CHAMPIONS ... WSTAA's Artie Jones (right) congratulates Torridge's Joe Chappell on Salmon Conservation award.

A Statutory Advisory Committee?

At the (23 October) afternoon Whitehall Press Briefing prior to the evening Salmon Bill debate, Minister Gummer was in confident, ebullient mood. The Bill, he enthused, was "Historic, reforming and consolidating" and heralded "a very, very major change in the management of salmon". The Advisory Committee, he declared, was a vital addition. Since it applied to "all of the United Kingdom", it was "national". Furthermore, it would act as a "continuing agency" to keep important issues of "salmon management and conservation under review".

For those inclined towards optimism, Gummer's words were encouraging. Yet what did they mean? Similar words had been used by the Minister in Committee. Had Government finally conceded statutory provision for the Advisory Committee? Was it to be written into the Bill? Was this not what the Minister's up-beat language implied?

Debate now commenced on the first of the Opposition's three

Advisory Committee-related new clauses, NC4 (Advisory Committee on Salmon Conservation).

NC4 provided that the MAFF and DAFS Ministers create a Salmon Advisory Committee within three months of the new Salmon Act coming into force; that the Committee consider "such matters relating to the conservation of salmon" as the Ministers may refer to it; that the Committee present its first Report within 12 months of the Salmon Act coming into force, and "thereafter annually"; and that in its First Report the Committee consider whether the Ministers should be "conferred with powers which would enable a scheme, or schemes, to be introduced for the *better regulation* of salmon fisheries, including the more effective collection of catch statistics". (col.1355)

NC4, therefore, provided the platform from which envisaged reform measures, principally salmon-tagging, could be pursued in NCs 5 and 6 to follow. As the WWA Brief put it: "NC4 ensures that the Committee at least considers the question of 'more effective collection of catch statistics' (and implicitly, therefore, tagging), and NCs 5 and 6 provide Ministers with the necessary enabling powers, NC5 for *better regulation* of salmon fisheries generally (including tagging), and NC6 limited solely to tagging for the purposes of *improved catch data*".(5)

First, however, it was important to know whether Members were prepared to endorse the concept of a statutory Committee; a Committee which would recommend whether the relevant Ministers should, in fact, be empowered to consider and introduce possibly a wide range of measures—including tagging—relating to improved fishery regulation, data collection and, of course, conservation.

Leading on NC4, Stuart Randall, declared that "in June we were delighted when the Minister announced that he intended to establish an Advisory Committee". (col.1357) The Bill had been "in trouble", and despite the fact "we had been working on it for some weeks", Members on both sides were not satisfied that "the issue of conservation" was being fully addressed. When, therefore, the Minister came to the Committee and announced the Advisory Committee, it was, said Randall, a welcome relief and the source of great encouragement to all. Yet there were problems. These had been voiced then and since. Government's stated purpose for the Advisory Committee was "to collect more accurate information, and to establish effective fishery management regimes". But did it have adequate powers to do this? Reformers believed it did not. Only if the Advisory Committee were written into the Bill, and Ministers given enabling powers to act on any recommendations the Advisory Committee might make; only if these requirements were met, Randall maintained, could the Advisory Committee fulfil its stated objectives. All reformers wanted the Advisory Committee to be "durable and effective", and for these reasons it must be statutory. (col.1359) "The Minister's credibility", he warned Gummer, "is at stake. We expect him to deliver"!

Randall's Welsh colleague, Ted Rowlands agreed. The principal reason for the new clauses was "to inject a sense of urgency into the process". (col.1361) All were in agreement that "*Time was not on the side of the salmon, or on the side of conservation*". The WWA, "was surprised and shocked by the decline" shown by a 1982 Inquiry by the Authority. A severe decline had since taken place, and "it has not been properly discovered and charted. The establishment of the Advisory Committee cannot be a genteel, liesurely affair". Reformers hoped it would be "set up within three months". (col.1362)

Dafydd Wigley stressed the extent of cross-party concern about the lack of conservation in the Bill. People in Wales, he said, were particularly distressed about the lack of attention to Welsh problems. Over 200 letters from constituents and a detailed representation from WSTAA confirmed the widely held complaint that "conservation provisions contained within the existing Bill are totally inadequate as far as Wales is concerned". (col.1364) In order to tackle these problems what was needed was a Committee "with teeth" which would address Welsh as well as Scottish and English problems. It was for these reasons that "the people of Wales" supported the proposed statutory Advisory Committee under NC4.

Other than Randall and the Welsh Members, the only other Opposition Members to speak on NC4 were Norman Godman—the sole Scot—and Alan Beith. Both accepted the need for statutory provision; the details of NC4, as Beith put it, serving "to firm up" the Advisory Committee. (col.1377)

While the Opposition were united on the principle of a statutory Advisory Committee, and firmly backed NC4 to secure its implementation, what of the positions of their cross-party Conservative colleagues? Sir Hector Monro conceded that "whatever action the Government have taken, they will have to go a great deal further". (col.1360) The Advisory Committee "must take the strongest possible measures in recommending to the Government the appropriate course of action. ...We do not want a ghost-like Committee, making reports that are shelved, and nothing happening". (col.1361) Half measures would not suffice. Members wanted Government action.

Sir Geoffrey Johnson Smith also took the "Government action" line. "In Committee", said Sir Geoffrey, "Conservative and Opposition

Members expressed concern about the need for further action. ...[Perhaps that is] the main reason why Opposition Members want a statutory Committee". He was dismissive of non-statutory committees. "As we all know, if the British can fumble and fudge anything, they will do so by setting up a committee. The fear is that if we set up a [Salmon Advisory] Committee which is not statutory, that is just what will happen". That said, Sir Geoffrey strengthened his support for the "Government action" line. "There are strong grounds for believing that further action is needed, and we would expect that Committee to be able to report with authority, and in a way that would morally bind the next Government to take action". (col.1366)

"The Bill", agreed Charles Morrison, "does not do enough for conservation. ...The need for an Advisory Committee is self-evident". Contrary to his fellow Conservative reformers, however, Morrison made (nearly) clear his view on statutory powers: "I am not convinced that we should make the Committee a statutory body". (col.1368) Indeed, expressing a view very close to Government's position, he added, "If it is not statutory, it may retain more flexibility, and perhaps could stray into areas that need looking at which it might not be able to examine if it were a statutory body". Morrison contended it was "much more important" that the Committee be "established quickly, and act quickly".

The one Member from whom there had been much Advisory Committee talk, but no discernible comment on the vital NC4, was the reform alliance leader and Tory maverick—"who tonight probably became the first chairman of the 1922 Committee to be described as the Opposition"!—Cranley Onslow. All Conservatives claimed Onslow to be the sole originator of the Advisory Committee concept. He now spoke much about the need for clarification of provisions concerning the composition, staffing, membership, activities, resources, duties and responsibilities of such a Committee. He said nothing, however, which could be clearly interpreted as supportive of NC4.

Was there, or was there not cross-party support for a statutory Advisory Committee (NC4)? Opposition reformers supported it, but the position of their Conservative cross-party colleagues was ambiguous. The WSTAA officers in the Public Gallery were, understandably, concerned. In meetings and communications with Onslow over the past six weeks, they had received "cast-iron guarantees" of support for the Welsh tagging and statutory initiatives. Reformers and WSTAA observers suppressed their fears. No doubt this lead would be forthcoming. They remained hopeful.

Salmon Tagging and Enabling Powers

New Clauses 5 and 6 were straight-forward enabling provisions. Each was linked to NC4, but could stand on its own. Both were cleverly constructed and afforded Members and Government ample scope for choice. NC5 (Measures for Conservation of Salmon) sought *general powers* for the relevant (English/Welsh and Scottish) Ministers to implement statutory measures, *including tagging*, to improve conservation and the regulation of salmon fisheries in the *United Kingdom as a whole*. NC6 (Measures for the Better Regulation of Salmon Fisheries) sought Ministerial powers for the implementation of *salmon tagging alone*, for "more effective collection of catch statistics", with any such scheme applicable to *one region only*—for instance, Wales—if the Minister should so decide.

These New Clauses, therefore, comprised a framework of "gentle persuasion". If Government and the House, in the end, could not be persuaded to accept NC4, then there was always NC5 with its general enabling powers. But if even NC5 was not acceptable, then there was the final fall-back position of NC6. The WWA and Welsh interests were convinced of the value of tagging. In the last resort NC6 would at least enable them to get on with an interim or pilot tagging scheme in the Principality. Government could accept any of these provisions with no loss of face. All would improve fishery regulation, conservation and the quality of information upon which these must be based. After all, these were, as Ministers frequently repeated, the main objectives of the Bill. Acceptance of one or more of these NCs could only enhance the credibility of the Bill and the Government.

Stuart Randall set out the basic reasoning behind NC's 5 and 6, and their integral tagging provisions. NC5 sought "tagging for regulation purposes". (col.1358) In any "salmon transaction", the salmon "would have to be tagged or labelled. There would be exceptions, but that would be the general thrust", he explained. As for NC6, "the major short-term interest of Wales is to develop a more effective system for creating catch statistics". NC6 would meet this requirement. While extolling the virtues of NC's 5 and 6, Randall emphasised that both were fall-back provisions. The "improved statistics" objective of NC6, and the "improved conservation/regulation" aims of NC5 could be met through the actions of the statutory Advisory Committee proposed in NC4. That might be the simplest and most flexible way to proceed—if NC4 were approved. "Is the Minister sympathetic to using tagging techniques purely for developing statistics", he asked?

"Will he encourage the Advisory Committee to give fair and due consideration to the matter"?

If acceptable, tagging, Randall added, could also be used in a "pilot scheme"—perhaps in Wales. If the pilot scheme duly proved successful, and the Advisory Committee should so decide, then tagging could be introduced, possibly on a UK-wide basis, for "licensing and regulation schemes". Randall made a final plea: "Will the Minister keep an open mind about the use of tagging for catch statistics as a pilot scheme"? All were agreed on the need for improved conservation. "The reason for tagging", he said, "is simply to conserve fish". (col.1359)

All that reformers were asking in NC5, said Ted Rowlands, was that "the Minister takes the power" to enable him to implement, if in future he should so decide, any number of possible conservation measures, including tagging. (col.1362) The value of NC5 was that the Minister could create a tagging scheme by Statutory Instrument; there would be no "need to come to the House for a full-scale new Bill". Without this provision, and "even with an early realisation" by the Advisory Committee of the need for tagging, it could be "two, three or four years before legislation could be enacted to give the Minister power to enact such a scheme". Certainly, within the Principality, he stressed, there was a "consensus bordering on unanimity" in support of tagging. "With the popular support there is, we could run a pilot scheme". Alan Beith strongly agreed. "It is a perfectly reasonable request that this experiment should be carried out". (col.1377) Indeed, such an initiative would put the UK and Wales in the forefront of International fishery developments.

Rowlands referred to the Biarritz tagging resolution, and to the Symposium announcement that the French Fisheries Ministry "intends to introduce a full-scale nation-wide tagging system" in 1987. The French scheme would cover "rod and line, commercial fishing, commercial fishing at sea, and imports". The reasons given by the French for introducing tagging were "conservation and better catch statistics. That double purpose is contained in NC5 and in our fall-back position in NC6".

But what of practical matters relating to the introduction of tagging? These, Richard Livsey assured Members, would pose no problems. "I am closely associated with agriculture, where all stock is tagged". (col.1369) Salmon, "whether they are farmed or taken in the wild", could readily be tagged. There was also the example of successful salmon tagging in Canada. "We [in the UK] are in the stone age in our recording of salmon. We know very little about the true catch.

Tagging will enable us to know how many salmon are caught, and that will enable us to improve our fisheries". Dafydd Wigley added that the WWA's Chief Fisheries Officer, Warwick Ayton, in his brief to Welsh Members, stressed that tagging was urgently needed to get this information which was vital to their work. "They are the experts, and surely we ought to listen to them". (col.1371) Indeed, this position had been repeatedly and forcefully stated. Alan Beith reminded Members that those with "a great deal of experience" were convinced that tagging "would make prosecution easier and would ensure that the provenance of salmon held or transported in Wales had to be demonstrated". These advantages would apply equally to farmed fish produced in Wales. "Wales is not an area in which there has been a great expansion in fish farming". (col.1377)

There was one further advantage to tagging. Tagging, said Rowlands, would complement dealer-licensing, not "duplicate or contradict" it. "If a fish is presented with a tag, the dealer will know it was legally caught. If not ...the dealer can question the *bonam fides* character of the person". (col.1373) Together, dealer-licensing and tagging would comprise "an effective system of conserving [salmon] and collecting statistics, which we in Wales feel are woefully inadequate". He appealed to the Minister "not to turn his back on the petition signed by more than 18,500 supporters right across the country".

This, then, was the case advanced by Opposition reformers in support of NC's 5 and 6, and salmon tagging in particular. All stressed the National and International support for tagging. As for implementation: whether operative Nationally or regionally was not important. The main objective must be to act quickly. And if it would not be acceptable to Government and the House to initiate a National scheme, then Welsh Members were adamant that in keeping with WWA scientific advice and strong popular support, it must be implemented—even if only as an interim pilot project—in the Principality.

It was now the turn of Cranley Onslow and Conservative reformers. Support for tagging had been promised. Would they deliver? The WSTAA representatives did not look happy. Matthews and Morgan slumped glumly on the Gallery benches. Beside them a flushed Artie Jones was engaged in an animated exchange with one of the Welsh MPs who had appeared in the Gallery.

Sir Geoffrey Johnson Smith gave full and generous credit to Welsh interests for their vigourous initiative. "I share the concern of the Welsh Members". And although the problems raised were not exclusive to Wales, nevertheless, "judging by what we have heard tonight", he said, "the problem is even more serious there than in some Scottish rivers". (col.1365) But what of tagging? What of a Welsh pilot scheme?

Preferring to address the wider issues, Sir Geoffrey explained that he was "not convinced that tagging in the *United Kingdom* would fulfil the objectives that have been ascribed to it as successfully as some of the hon. Members think". The alternatives proposed by Government, he said, went "a long way towards meeting the fears" of Members. Dealer-licensing was one such measure. "When the Bill was first introduced [dealer-licensing] was limited purely to Scotland". It was now nation-wide. "This was one of the big changes Government made in its thinking". It was a "most helpful" measure.

Turning to "statistics", Sir Geoffrey veered sharply off on a tangent. In Scotland, he said, there were problems. "It has been extraordinarily difficult to get hold of statistics to prove to doubters that we are facing a serious situation". (col.1366) Still some figures were available, and "although not accurate to the last decimal point", these showed that the number of Scottish netsmen varied between 520 and 1177 "at peak periods". Relating available catch figures to the numbers of netsmen "the average earnings per man amount to just over 1000". There were, however, "wild fluctuations", with 70 netsmen in the North of Scotland taking around 86 per cent of the regional catch, while producing average earnings of about 6000 per man. The Advisory Committee, he suggested, should in due course "look at the figures carefully and take action accordingly". All figures indicated that "salmon and sea-trout have much more economic value as a sporting resource to the economies of Wales, England and Scotland than as a food".

HIGHLAND RIVER IN SPATE ... Searching for salmon.

Returning to the "conservation and regulation" themes of the New Clauses under discussion, Sir Geoffrey, in conclusion, expressed forcefully his general concern. "Some of us believe we are approaching the point of no return in the damage being done to a great natural resource. The factor uniting fishermen and others is that we want to conserve the salmon".

Sir Geoffrey's contributions on tagging did little to quell concern in the Welsh and "new clauses reform" camp. Always fair and courteous, he had given full credit to the Welsh for their "conservation initiative". But he had clearly stated he was "not convinced" about the benefits of UK-wide tagging. Did this mean he also had reservations—perhaps was opposed?—to Welsh tagging? What about tagging under the provisions of NC4? Until very recently he had been a firm supporter of tagging. Why had he suddenly changed his view? Did he still believe that tagging could play useful statistical and regulatory roles? Could it serve as an effective complement to dealer-licensing? Sir Geoffrey had said little that was addressed directly to the points at issue, and what he had said was extremely unsettling to fellow reformers.

Other Conservative reformers, including Sir Hector Monro and Charles Morrison expressed views on various matters relating to conservation, regulation and the Advisory Committee. They made no mention of tagging. Unease was visibly growing amongst Opposition reformers on the floor, and Welsh onlookers in the Gallery. Nor was there encouragement in the tagging reservations voiced by the Scots Opposition reformer, Norman Godman. "However, admirable a practice", he said, "tagging would present formidable problems" for small fish farming enterprises, and many "in the islands off the coast of Scotland" were "very small" indeed. (col.1373) But would it really? Had not the points raised by Wigley and Rowlands made clear that fish farmers—and small producers in particular—had nothing to fear from tagging; that it was a procedure, as with cattle, involving little fuss and bother?

Finally, the espoused champion of Welsh tagging and statutory demands, the Tory maverick Cranley Onslow, rose to speak. Members and onlookers took a deep breath. Onslow first commented briefly, and non-committally, on the Advisory Committee. He then engaged in one or two knock-about exchanges with the Opposition. Finally, he turned to tagging.

First came the body-blow. "It is extremely difficult to understand how it can be said that salmon tagging will be an aid to more accurate statistics"! (col.1370) Then came a vicious upper-cut. "I do not see how a requirement to tag fish [when they are taken] out of the water will have the slightest effect on the accuracy of statistics or will be of assistance to the Welsh Water Authority"! There was consternation in the Public Gallery. This was their "champion"?

Onslow now launched a full-scale attack on tagging. Referring to Richard Livsey's observations on the ease of tagging, he was dismissive. "Would he [Livsey] put a tag on a fish before returning it to the water"? This was a puzzling query by Onslow. Did he really believe that tagging in this context was meant to apply to catch-and-release fish? Undaunted, he went on to contend that if Livsey were to "think this through, he will understand that salmon are not like cattle. One cannot have fish swimming round in a river with tags in their gills, in the way that cattle walk around the market with tags in their ears. ...What possible benefit is contained in NC6"? (col.1371)

As for the regional application of tagging: why, asked Onslow, should "this clause [NC6] also be applied to England and Scotland"? Seemingly overlooking the fact that NC6 was specifically designed to be applicable to Wales—or to either of the other two national regions—alone, and forgetful of the support for tagging recently rendered by the Association of District Salmon Fishery Boards in Scotland, the Atlantic Salmon Trust, Scottish and English netsmen, as well as a very large number of rodsmen and conservationists nation-wide, he added, "There has been no argument to show why it should be so applied". Continuing in this vein, he noted that while tagging "may be and probably is a Welsh idea"—which it wasn't—"that does not automatically mean that it is a good idea to apply to the whole of the United Kingdom. ...Even the Welsh Nationalists may understand that point of view"!

Turning now to NC5 and its tagging provisions, Onslow stated that it was "not a conservation or statistical measure". Rather it was "designed to make it possible to catch poachers". Showing yet again a remarkable lapse of memory in relation to the triple-role of tagging (that is, improved statistics, anti-poaching and sales-control functions) Onslow exclaimed that he was "extraordinarily surprised that we have not heard more about *that* purpose, because *this* scheme is designed to prevent the sale of illegally caught salmon".

And what did Onslow make of the practicability of tagging? "I know that Ministers looked closely at it. I discovered from conversations with them that they were not convinced that it was practicable". Acknowledging his conversion, he admitted he was "disappointed to learn that, but ultimately I was convinced they were right". And what of the weaknesses? "These became quite clear quite soon", he said.

There would be many tags in circulation, so "a man with tags can apply them to fish he has caught illegally. That is the major weakness in the scheme".

Reformers were bemused. Had not the Salmon Sales Group's Tagging Report shown that this weakness was minimal? Plastic tags, with different colours for netsmen and anglers, and each coded to identify the specific fisherman and date of issue had been shown in Canada to be effective in curbing abuse. Had not Onslow read this Report? Had he suffered yet another lapse of memory on details? There was every reason to believe such a system would be equally effective in a Welsh pilot scheme, for a start.

And what of the boundary problem? "In respect of Wales", said Onslow, "the major flaw is that the rivers are so close to England, if they do not actually form the boundary." Hence, "if there were not a tagging scheme in England ...that would be an open invitation to poachers to take their illegally caught fish across the border as quickly as possible". Yet again, Onslow appeared to have been mentally absent when proof and viability had been discussed: that, for instance, it was accepted that some poachers would escape detection; but that for those who were detected "it would be the end of the story"; that successful prosecutions would increase the effectiveness of tagging and strengthen anti-poaching restraints, which in turn would be reinforced by dealer-licensing controls; and that all this could be undertaken within the provisions of a flexible, interim Welsh tagging pilot scheme which WWA officials, backed by International specialists, were convinced would be effective.

Bearing in mind the tenets of his new "faith", Onslow declared, "Whatever long-stop scheme is being considered, the important safeguard is enforcement on the river, and prevention of an illegal catch on the spot". (col.1372) And how was this to be achieved? More water bailiffs, said Onslow. This would be far better than "an elaborate bureaucracy built round the movement of tags", which would not be anything like as "efficient as a man and a dog on the river bank". Once again, Onslow failed to recall the basic purpose of tagging. This was, in fact, to *assist* "baillifs with dogs" in "identifying what is legally or illegally caught fish". Repeatedly, in the House and Standing Committee, Members had heard from those "in the front lines", that tagging was not merely important, but a "vital and integral part" of modern regulatory and enforcement functions. (col.1371) Onslow, however, had apparently forgotten these details.

Insofar as any regulatory system deserved the attention of Members, this was, said Onslow, Government's proposed dealer-licensing.

This system should be set up, put into operation and monitored. "It is premature to insist upon the introduction of tagging". Furthermore, he stated, "the provisions of NC's 5 and 6 go much further than was originally suggested". (col.1373) In conclusion, he urged Minister Gummer to ensure that the Advisory Committee, when in operation, should consider a range of ipstream and other problems; problems which he contended were just "as serious for the conservation of salmon stocks" as anything discussed during the evening's debate.

And so concluded the contribution of the cross-party alliance reform leader, Tory maverick and "champion" of Welsh statutory and tagging initiatives, Cranley Onslow. As one bitter Welsh Member later put it: "Some maverick! Some champion"!

Reformers' Challenge: Outcome

Minister Gummer now summed up Government's position on the proposed new clauses. Adopting his most earnest and compassionate mode of presentation, he turned first to tagging. "I started with the clear view that salmon tagging was the right way to solve the major problem of the poacher and make a major contribution to conservation—for this is a conservation Bill!", he explained. (col.1379) However, after close examination, he now believed that tagging had within it "inherent difficulties that would make the problem worse". And why worse? Because, he said, "it would make people rely on tags, and by relying on the tags, have a false sense of security".

As for Welsh tagging: "If it is wrong to tag nationally, …then it becomes even more wrong to tag regionally, or even in the Principality alone". (col 1384) Gummer, however, was quick to re-assure Welsh Members that this did not mean he had "closed my mind to tagging for ever". The matter might well be an early subject for consideration by the Advisory Committee. Indeed, so swift might action be, "we might not [even] wait for the Water Authority [to ask] …but tell it that if it wishes salmon tagging to be considered the Advisory Comittee will look at the matter"!

The Minister urged tagging supporters and and Welsh interests to be patient. When dealer-licensing had been implemented, and the Advisory Committee had asessed its effectiveness, that would be the time "to look at the Welsh Water Authority's tagging proposals—if it then has any". He urged reformers to bear in mind that tagging of fish was not the same as "tagging sheep". The Authority, he gently suggested, "could considerably help its case if it considered the number of water bailiffs and others available" for fishery and river protection work.

The news from the Biarritz Symposium was heartening, said Gummer. Not only had the Symposium been "carefully considering" tagging, but also "a policy, which in almost every particular, the Bill already is applying" and which would "provide exactly the sort of National salmon policy which the discussions in Biarritz lead us to want". (col.1384) He was, however, not sanguine about the French tagging initiative. As it would apply only to "some salmon", it "will not wash. ...Consider the danger"! (col.1384)

On the key issue of NC4 and its proposed statutory powers, the Minister confirmed he still preferred the Advisory Committee to be non-statutory, for "flexibility" reasons. (col.1380) As for membership and composition, Gummer announced that George Dunnet, Regius Professor of Natural History at the University of Aberdeen, had agreed to serve as Chairman. Committee Members would be appointed soon, with Dunnet taking part in the selection. Regarding composition, he stated that "a majority of those on the Committee will represent Scottish interests, because most salmon are caught in Scotland". (col.1381) However, the Secretariat, because the Committee "is national", would have a "London focus", with a MAFF Secretary and DAFS Deputy, with a "Welsh input".

The Advisory Committee would meet "before the opening of the new season", and early consideration would be given to assessment of "statistics and their reliability". And might this involve tagging? Gummer agreed that "it would be absolutely natural for the Committee to discuss that issue at an early date".

In response to repeated queries concerning the Advisory Committee and the North-east drift-net fishery, the Minister stated that the Advisory Committee would not consider North-east matters, as this would be the job of the North-east Review. If, however, during the course of the three years before presentation of the *North-east Review Report* "the Government has evidence which shows we must take further steps, we shall have to do so. ...I give that undertaking. ...conservation must come first"!

In conclusion, Minister Gummer stated that Government had "presented the House with a mix of a dealer-licensing system, an Advisory Committee, and a Chairman who will clearly have the support of all salmon interests. ...We have thus changed the way in which the salmon industry is viewed". (col.1386) He asked finally that "a fair wind" be given to "our major proposals", and that the House would accept that "the amendments are unnecessary".

In a brief response to Gummer, the proposer of the new clauses, Stuart Randall, noted Government's continuing "doubts and uncertainties about tagging". In Wales, however, "there is unanimity that it is essential to an effective system of conservation". He reminded the Minister of "successful schemes in other parts of the world", and declared that "we too should gain some practical experience". The new clauses would simply allow the Minister "to take powers, and we could then see what the Advisory Committee has to say about the technicalities of tagging. That is the best way forward, and it will ensure that we have a good system of conservation".

The time had now come to vote on the new clauses. Technically, there was still a chance reformers might succeed. In the House Chamber there were only 14 Members: seven Conservatives, and seven Opposition. Only one maverick Tory was needed to swing the vote. Could this possibly happen? It was, after all, only an amendment concerning an issue (the Advisory Committee) upon which all, in principle, agreed.

Alas, this was to be but a brief and bootless hope. A division was called. The lead-paned Chamber doors duly swung open and in paraded the respective Government and Opposition "troops", summoned from their various entertainments and activities within and outside the House—and clearly anxious to return at the earliest moment. It was no contest. Government secured an easy victory. The new clauses were rejected by a 128:32 margin, with voting following strict Government vs. Opposition lines.

And so ended the reformers' "final challenge". It had been an enterprising and vigourous effort. In the end, however, the cross-party alliance had not held up; and neither the Petition of Parliament, nor the Biarritz resolutions had caused Government to alter its course. For whatever reasons, stated or unstated, Government was not prepared to endorse an Advisory Committee with statutory "teeth". Neither would it endow Ministers with enabling powers, nor endorse salmon tagging, either nationally or regionally. Not even a Welsh interim pilot tagging scheme was acceptable.

The Welsh (WSTAA) contingent was deeply distressed. What had gone wrong? Venting his feelings afterwards, Artie Jones said he could, with difficulty, accept rejection of NC5, even NC4, as "both had complex national implications". But NC6 was "tailored specifically to Welsh circumstances. Yet Gummer knocked it on the head too. Why"? Was it really Government reservations about a Welsh scheme? Was it resistance from certain sectors of the farmed salmon industry? On the other hand was it covert resistance from salmon netsmen, MAFF and DAFS? Was it political fears amongst Scottish elements that success for tagging in Wales could mean introduction of tagging in

Scotland with complementary rod and net licensing by the "back door", and all the furore this would mean?

And there was equal distress and bemusement about the failure of the cross-party alliance, and in particular its leader, Cranley Onslow. It was, said Jones, the contribution of Onslow which applied the *coup de grace*. "As the debate progressed, we were becoming increasingly concerned. But it was not until Cranley said what he did that we knew the cause was lost". It was, said Jones, "a return to the lessons of Welsh history". Once again, an English "champion" had broken faith. "I had some sharp words with Cranley. But why had he led us on? Why had he promised support during these last weeks when clearly he opposed the very things we were seeking"? There were no ready answers. It could only be surmised that, in the end, Onslow's allegiance to Government was greater than his allegiance to the cross-party alliance on Advisory Committee reforms. The "maverick" had come to heel.

Would the Advisory Committee turn out to be simply a de-fusing "fumble and fudge" device? Would Government's preferred alternative, dealer-licensing—still only an uncommitted proposal—fulfil expectations? Only the actual implementation and operation of dealer-licensing, and the outcome of Advisory Committee deliberations in the years to come, would tell.

The Curtain Descends

Government's ministerial representatives having demonstrated their paramountcy, and with all combatants showing visible signs of fatigue in what was now the early morning of 24 October, the debate was brought to a close. Magnanimous in victory, Government provided salve for reformers' wounds.

Minister MacKay announced he had accepted reformers' criticisms of Clause 10 (Qualified Proprietors and Upper and Lower Proprietors) and was amending it to ensure that a qualified proprietor could serve in an Upper and Lower capacity in relation to only one fishery each—there would be no "multiple memberships" on Boards. (col.1400) Reformers were also reassured to hear MacKay confirm that Clause 19 (Additional Powers in respect of Licensing and Regulation of Salmon Fishing) was being amended to ensure that bailiffs would *not* have powers of "entry to dwelling houses" in search and pursuit activity, and further that the exemption on "preserved or processed" salmon was being removed to close any possible Dealer-Licensing loop-hole. (col.1405) Finally, Minister Gummer brought a nod of approval from Cranley Onslow when he confirmed that Clause 33 (Introduction of Fish into Fish Farms without Consent) would be applicable only to unconnected inland waters, or to an inland water connected to another by conduit or pipe. (col.1421)

At nearly 1 am, 24 October, some eight months after it had entered the Lower House, Commons deliberations on the Bill ended. It was read a third time to the 13 remaining Members in the House, and passed. The S&TA and Welsh contingents in the Public Gallery gathered up their belongings and departed. Members on the Floor virtually vanished. I packed up. It was time to go home.

Lords Finale

As the Bill had originated in the House of Lords, it now was returned one week later (30 October) for final endorsement of amendments introduced during Commons stages. This did not take long. About 50 amendments were approved in as many minutes. Starting at 7:15 pm, the eight Government supporters and seven Opposition Lordships—many clearly anxious to get off to dinner or other pressing engagements—were by 7:25 already at amendment 20.

Principal consideration was given to: powers to "collect interest on arrears of fishery assessment" (Clause 14); removal of bailiffs' powers of "search and entry" to dwelling houses (Clause 19); Government's new "baits and lures" Clause; and the requirement that the Scottish Secretary must approve the appointment of bailiffs by sole proprietors (Clause 10). Each of these amendment concessions was welcomed with varying degrees of warmth by their Lordships.[6]

Attention also was directed to the sensitive issue of "improved control and regulation" of the English and Welsh salmon net fisheries, with particular relevance to the North-East of England. MAFF Minister, Lord Belstead, explained the *quid pro quo* arrangement which had been worked out between the Water Authorities and the Sea Fishery Committees. Under the provisions of Clause 32 (Placing and Use of Fixed Engines), and Clause 36 (Byelaws Under Sea Fisheries Regulation Act, 1966), Sea Fishery Committees could introduce fixed nets—which are prohibited under the *1975 (England/Wales) Salmon Act*—but only where the consent of the relevant Water Authority was first secured. Similarly, strengthened fishery controls in salmon-bearing coastal waters sought by a Water Authority could be introduced, but only where these were first agreed and then ultimately implemented by the Sea Fishery Committee—or the Water Authority where no local Sea Fishery Committee existed. (cols.880-83)

Though not generally recognised at the time, this initiative to legalise English/Welsh fixed-nets was to be a particularly vital tactic in the Scottish/Tweed initiative to reduce North-East drift-netting. The drift-nets mainly catch Scottish salmon seeking to return to Tweed and Scottish East Coast rivers. Fixed-nets exploit mainly sea-trout and salmon trying to return to Northumbrian and Yorkshire rivers. Hence by encouraging Water Authorities and Sea Fishery Committees to shift fishing effort from drift to fixed-nets, the result would be a gradual increase in the numbers of salmon enabled to return to Tweed and Scottish rivers further north. This fixed-net enabling provision was to produce fireworks in the North East before a year had passed. The 1987 *Wear Inquiry* was dramatically to demonstrate that it was one thing to attempt to introduce Northumbrian fixed netting, and quite another to achieve it. (See Chapter 13 below, pp. 273-74.)

Finally, there was the matter of Government's proposed Salmon Advisory Committee. Lord Thurso agreed it was an important "conservation" initiative, but why had their Lordships been given no opportunity to debate it? (col.876) Was Scots representation on the Advisory Committee satisfactory? And what of Welsh representation, asked Lord Moran? Responding for Government, Lord Glenarthur (who, in September, had replaced Lord Gray as Scottish Fisheries Minister) repeated Gummer's Commons assurances: the Scots interest was "acknowledged", and there would be a "Welsh Office input". (col.878) As for issues: he confirmed that early consideration would be given to the availability of information on salmon stocks, and the influence on stocks of predators and low-water.

Lord Moran, having raised the issue of national salmon policy, now drew the attention of their Lordships to the Biarritz Symposium resolutions. The Symposium's General Resolution represented an historic and vital break-through. It stated:

> "In view of the greater income and employment potential of salmon angling and its appreciably smaller harvest of limited salmon populations, each national government of salmon-producing countries is urged to declare a salmon policy which will institute conservation measures within its area of jurisdiction, a management programme to reduce commercial harvesting of salmon with a view to increasing stocks and improving recreational salmon catches". (col.877)

Having commended the General Resolution to Government and their Lordships, Lord Moran turned to the Symposium's four specific recommendations. These were:

1. that NASCO investigates the value of a *salmon-tagging* scheme such as is

in operation in Eastern Canada and Spain, and that it recommends the adoption of this by all member countries for both a more reliable collection of catch data and a more effective control of illegal fishing.

2. that *all methods of enmeshing salmon*, such as drift nets and fixed hang nets (excepting the operations off Greenland) should *be phased out* and that fishermen relying on these methods should be given other opportunities to participate in the salmon fisheries of related industries, including salmon farming and ranching.
3. that we should support the recommendation of the rapporteur to the European Community Sub-Committee on Fisheries that European Community funds should be made available to *improve and co-ordinate national salmon fisheries inspectorates*.
4. that following the action taken by Canada, the recommendation was that each nation, through its salmon conservation bodies and sport fishing organisations, should encourage the introduction of a reasonable daily and season *rod-catch quota, prohibit the sale of the catch, and consider the adoption of a 'catch and release' philosophy*".

Adding that the UK Government had been the subject of sharp criticism at the Symposium—"drift-netting is condoned and illegal operations continue unabated"—Lord Moran sought clarification of Government's position.

Lord Glenarthur's terse and chilly response from a written text provided a summary confirmation of what critics had said of the Bill from its very outset 10 months before. On the General Resolution, he said that Government accepted "the importance of game-fishing for salmon", and was "fully committed to a conservation policy which includes [but not as its principal aim] the limiting [not reducing] of the commercial catch". On the specific recommendations, Lord Glenarthur made no comment on 1. On 2 he commented that "in Scotland the use of drift nets for salmon fishing is already prohibited"—with no mention of drift-netting in North-East England, or any wider nets-reduction commitment. On 3 he merely noted that Government was "aware of the recommendation and that the Symposium supported it". Recommendation 4 received similar short shrift, Lord Glenarthur stating that Government would be "interested to see what comments the various sport-fishing organisations make". (col.879)

Government had contended throughout the Bill's duration, that its primary aim was to build modern conservation requirements into existing antiquated salmon legislation. The Biarritz recommendations —unanimously supported by Scots, English and Welsh Government fisheries officials, as well as by officials and representatives of all other salmon-producing and exploiting nations attending the Symposium—set out what these requirements were. And what now was the response of Her Majesty's Government? It ignored one, dismissed one, and evaded two.

Though hardly re-assuring to salmon reformers and conservationists, Lord Glenarthur's observations provided an accurate and honest concluding statement of what the Salmon Bill was *not* about. "A sad waste of a potentially valuable opportunity to legislate for the future of salmon and freshwater fisheries". This was the concluding assessment by the Commons Opposition leader on the Bill, John Home Robertson. Alas, no serious salmon law reformer or conservationist could disagree. After receiving the Royal Assent on 7 November (a formality applicable to all new legislation), the *1986 UK Salmon Act* came into force on 7 January, 1987.

References

1. *Parliamentary Debates*, House of Commons, Volume 102, Nos.161 and 162, 23 and 24 October, 1986, col.1365. (Hereafter reference to this Commons Debate is by column entered in the text of this Chapter).

2. See, David Shaw, "Waterloo at Westminster", *Trout and Salmon*, December 1986, p.54

3. David Shaw, "Salmon Bill: Moment of Truth", *Trout and Salmon*, (October, 1986), p.62.

4. *Parliamentary Debates*, House of Lords, Vol.481, No.160, 30 October, 1986, col.877

5. Welsh Water Authority, *Salmon Bill: Briefing Note*, 2 October, 1986, p.4.

6. *Parliamentary Debates*, House of Lords, Vol.481, No.160, 30 October, 1986, cols.867-73. (Hereafter, reference to this Lords Debate is by column entered in the text of this Chapter).

Chapter 12

TRAGEDY OF THE SALMON

> "We are hammering away at problems and a management structure that is out of date. [There is need for] a complete change of attitude in relation to those with interests [in wild salmon]. Everyone has to appreciate that changed importance from the point of view of the economy, from the point of view of justice, and above all from the point of view of the salmon itself. ...The Bill does not go nearly far enough in respect of the main concern, which is the decline in stocks, and an ability to prove to other countries with which we are seeking internatonal quotas to allow the fish to get here, that once they reach here we will not so arrange it that we ignore the whole question of conservation".
>
> *Lord Ross of Marnock*[1]

At the turn of this century, Lord Elgin and his Commissioners had spelled out the basic requirements for a restored and healthy United Kingdom salmon fishery.[2] In relation to Scotland these were three in number. First, a Central fisheries authority with the powers to "do" as well as "talk" must be created. Second, in order to ensure more fair treatment of *all* fishery owners, and to provide for adequate conservation of spawning stocks, river nets above an established point must be removed—with compensation—and a minimum 48-hours weekly close-time (Weekly Slap) implemented. Third, the District Salmon Fishery Boards (District Boards) must be re-constructed. In order to encourage open and equal participation of *all* salmon fishery owners, the system of distinctions and privileges must be abolished. It was only through such re-construction, the Commissioners held, that the necessary goodwill and harmony might be achieved, and that the interests of the fishery, rather than those of rival net and rod factions, could become paramount.

The great Calderwood wholeheartedly endorsed these proposals and worked tirelessly for nearly 30 years to secure their implementation. He failed.[3] Thus it was that the 1986 *Salmon Bill* offered the first major opportunity both to complete the task which in 1902 the Elgin Commission had started, and to bring finally to fruition the dedicated efforts made by Calderwood.

And what was the result?

These primary reform requirements, as we have seen, yet again were evaded or ignored.

It is in this modern-day failure to act on these long-recognised and clearly identified needs that the true tragedy of the Scottish and United Kingdom salmon lies.

So where did things go wrong, and why? What did the Salmon Bill proceedings reveal? What was achieved? Were there any signs of promise?

Central Authority: Instrument of The Food-producers

In fact, since Lord Elgin's time there has been change in the representation of fisheries interests at the Centre (Whitehall). Today the fisheries of England/Wales do have separate Whitehall and Cabinet representation, albeit that they occupy an embattled inferior status to the influential and wealth-generating powerhouses of agriculture and food in the Ministry of Agriculture Fisheries and Food (MAFF).

The Scottish fishery, however, still does not enjoy equal access and status. Fishery matters are dealt with by the Edinburgh-based Department of Agriculture and Fisheries (DAFS) for Scotland. The sole representative of all Scottish interests at Cabinet level is the Secretary of State for Scotland, and with more than six portfolios with which to grapple he has very much more than fishery matters—let alone the tiny salmon fishery interest *within* the remit of DAFS—to occupy his time.

In this respect, therefore, things in Scotland are no different than they were in the time of Elgin. Fisheries together with Agriculture must queue up with Education, Environment, Home and Health, Industry, Central Services and their many important departmental sub-units for their share of scarce ministerial time. There still is no one whose specific job it is to fight their corner at Whitehall and in Cabinet. And given the insignificant status of salmon within the overall framework of responsibility of the Scottish Secretary, one might only observe it was good fortune indeed—and likely only the result of special pleading by certain titled and other influential persons, including the former Prime Minister Lord Home, with access to the Thatcher Government—that a major Government Bill was in fact brought forward.

So far as a body which can actually "do" things to assist the Scottish salmon, DAFS is the responsible authority. Administrative, research and field officers with a level of professional and scientific expertise which no doubt would greatly please and surprise Calderwood, attend to salmon scientific and other matters assigned by ministers. What would greatly distress Calderwood, however, is that DAFS (and MAFF) have deployed their resources vigourously to resist those very changes which Lord Elgin and his Commissioners so strongly recommended. These ministries are mainly concerned with the requirements of food-production. Hence their principal efforts consistently have been given to protecting, and where possible enhancing commercial fisheries. It is the netsmen who carry out commercial fishing for salmon.

Indeed what this book has demonstrated clearly is not only the strength of this commitment, but the determination of Government fisheries officials to ensure this support is maintained against all conservation and economic logic. Exchanges over the issue of North-East drift-nets between MAFF (Lords) Minister Lord Belstead and Lord Lansdowne ("Outright abolition now"!)[4] and sharper exchanges on the same subject between MAFF (Commons) Minister John Gummer and Cranley Onslow ("No need to work to eight places of decimals" to prove that these nets should be reduced!)[5] perhaps best exemplified this posture. Given this entrenched attitude, combined with the close and mutually beneficial links that fisheries scientists and officials have long retained with the netting interests in the UK salmon fishery,[6] the explanation for their casual even patronising regard for the increasingly vociferous demands of modern rod/tourism interests seems clear enough.

In their view, commercial fishing is concerned with the serious professional business of food-production; rod fishing is a mere recreation for angler-hobbyists—even if today it does produce staggering levels of revenue and employment. Certainly the level of economic contribution by the rod/tourism industry was not about to cause these officials to advise changes to the 1860s exploitation *status quo*. Far from it. Fisheries Minister John MacKay's response to rods/tourism pressure applied by reforming Members was typical of Government's stance. "Salmon angling is important", he conceded. But netting had "interests", and gave "many people employment. We must try to keep the balance".[7] It was of course the 1860s nets-dominant "balance"—or "im-balance"—which MacKay and Government stoutly defended. No adjustment need be made to accommodate the burgeoning rod/tourism sector. And when challenged by reformers' contentions of "stock decline", insufficient "up-stream escapement", or "inadequate protection", Ministers and supporters of the *status quo* merely replied with appropriate "scientific evidence" supplied by Government scientists, or with a polite request that a particular critic produce his "scientific evidence" in support. Indeed, on those few occasions when critics did produce such evidence, the fact that it was largely notional or anecdotal, made rejection by ministers easy.

Altogether, therefore, such involvement of a "Central authority" as there now was in Scotland, was shown clearly to be used *not* to secure change in the direction of the Elgin Commission's equity and conservation requirements, but rather to support the *status quo*, and hence the unaltered dominance of the commercial fishing interests. As an exasperated Tam Dalyell put it in the later stages of Commons Committee: "Conservation of a priceless asset depends on netting reductions, and yet after 29 or more hours of debate in the House of Lords, Second Reading in the House of Commons, and all the sittings of this Committee, Government has not yet accepted a single amendment to secure this objective. ...Why is it", he asked, "that the interests of a few wealthy proprietors of netting rights in Scotland and their netsmen employees, amounting to no more than 1000 people, are favoured at the expense of upwards of 20,000 people dependent on the angling industry for their livelihoods"? And equally important, why was it that drift-net fishing had been allowed "to operate off the North-East of England 20 years after drift-netting was banned in Scotland"?[8] The simple answer was that departmental and commercial fisheries interests were happy with things as they were. Any attempts at encroachment they would resist.

Netting Reductions: Enabling Glimmers

The Elgin Commission had received massive evidence concerning over-exploitation by net fisheries. In Scotland, interestingly, the Commissioners came to the conclusion that the major damage was being done *not* by fixed-nets on foreshores round the coast—the main target of many modern-day conservationists—but by estuary and river nets which primarily harvested stocks native to the rivers in which these nets operated. The problem was most serious in premier fisheries, including those on Tweed, Tay, North Esk, Spey and Findhorn. Insofar as this was the single issue which most inflamed relations between upper (rod) and lower (net) proprietors; since it most directly concerned conservation of river stocks; and since resolution of this issue might render possible the growth of more harmonious relations between upper and lower interests; it was for these reasons that the Commissioners called for mandatory river nets reductions and an increase in the Weekly Slap to 48 hours.

These recommendations died with the 1902 Report. They have seldom been raised since. They must rank as one of the best kept "secrets" of the Scottish salmon fishery.

The 1986 *Salmon Act* did not violate this secrecy. There was no mention of river nets reductions. There was no increase in the (42 hours) Weekly Slap to 48 hours. Neither was there direct statutory provision for any other kind of netting reduction. There were, however, a few glimmers of hope offered by "enabling powers" in the Act, and by private actions initiated at the same time.

While the *1986 Act* failed to provide directly for an increase in the length of the Weekly Slap, it did provide "enabling powers" for the Scottish Secretary to take the necessary action—if he could be so persuaded.* These powers were set out under Section 3(3) in the Act. It was, therefore, now possible, if proprietors and conservationists could agree on the necessary initiative, to secure an increase in the national (Scottish) Weekly (netting) Slap without having to resort to the unwieldy process of primary legislation.

Section 3 also afforded other enabling opportunities. These, however, were two-way. They could be used to provide an increase, or a decrease in netting. The Scottish Secretary could for instance implement Statutory Orders increasing the size of net meshes, banning lightweight materials (in keeping with the netting industry's desire to remain "traditional"), and altering or reducing the dimensions of nets; these powers applicable nationally or locally [Section 3,(2)(d)]. Such regulations could have a profound effect on netting effort and intensity, and hence on catches—a point which netsmen's spokesmen during the Bill were quick to pick up. "Exercise of these powers", declared an alarmed Alan Beith, "could wipe out the entire river net fisheries of Scotland!"[9] What Beith failed to mention was that the Scottish Secretary's powers under this part of Section 3 could as readily be used to provide for an increase in net catches.

There was also Section 21 (Permitted Methods of Fishing for Salmon). Under its terms, the Scottish Secretary, "after consulting such persons as he considers appropriate", could implement new regulations which could affect catching capacity and hence catch levels through "definition" of existing netting methods—that is, stake net, bag net, and net and coble.[10] The primary intention of Section 21 was to provide, where necessary, improved definition of existing net fish-

* See *Figure 1*, below, pp.261-63, for *Summary List of Key Provisions* in the 1986 Salmon Act.

ing methods so that they might be regularised and to ensure against introduction of new methods. New regulations could produce an increase or decrease, or no change in netting activity and catches.

FIGURE I

THE 1986 (UK) SALMON ACT

Summary List of Key Provisions

I. *Provisions Applying to Scotland Only*

1. *Amalgamated Boards* (Sect.2 & Sched.1) The Scottish Secretary may, by "Designation Order", create one Area or Amalgamated Salmon Fishery Board from two or more existing Salmon Fishery Districts.
2. *Weekly Close-Times* (Sect.3) The Scottish Secretary, "after consulting those persons he considers appropriate", may *increase* the national (Scottish) Weekly Close-Time(WCT) for nets—currently 42 hours—and/or rods—currently Sundays only. *He may not shorten the existing (42-hour) WCT period.*
3. *Regulation of Nets* (Sect.3(2)(d)) The Scottish Secretary may make regulations with respect to "the meshes, materials and dimensions of nets" used in fishing for salmon.
4. *Annual Close-Times* (Sect.6) The Scottish Secretary, *only* on application by a District Salmon Fishery Board(DFB), or by 2 salmon proprietors in a Fishery District without a DFB, may *alter* the dates at which the Annual Close Time(ACT) for nets or/and rods in that District, or a part of it, shall start and end. Subject to the same conditions of application, he may *increase* the ACT for nets or/and rods. *He may not shorten the current statutory minimum ACT of 168 continuous days.*
5. *Rod-Fishing Restrictions* (Sect.8) The Scottish Secretary, *only* on application by a DFB, may make regulations restricting the use of angling baits and lures during specified periods, and in specified area(s) within that District Fishery.
6. *Elected DFB Chairmen* (Sect.14 & Sched.2, para.3) Each DFB Chairman is now to be *elected* at a meeting open to all qualified salmon proprietors in that District. The election of a DFB chairman will take place *prior to* the Triennial Election of members to serve on the DFB for their respective District.
7. *DFB Membership* (Sect.14 & Schedule 2, paras.3,4 & 6) DFBs, together with their elected Chairmen, will continue to comprise an equal number of elected Upper (normally 3 rod) and Lower (normally 3 net) salmon proprietors. *Board Chairmen will continue to retain a deliberative as well as a casting vote.*
8. *DFB Co-opted Members* (Sect.16 & Schedule 2, paras.5 & 6) Persons who may be tenants or representatives of salmon interests in a Salmon Fishery District, may be invited by a DFB to join that Board as "Co-

opted Members". The number of co-opted rods representatives shall be equal to the number of co-opted nets representatives, and together shall not exceed the total number of Qualified Proprietors on that Board.

9. *Permitted Methods of Fishing* (Sect.21) The Scottish Secretary may "by regulations, define" fishing for salmon by: net and coble; bag net, fly net, or other stake net; whether by reference to "anything used" for the purpose, or to "the circumstances in which, or method" by which it is so used, or to "any combination" thereof.

10. *Persons Exempted from the Salmon Laws* (Sect.27) The Scottish Secretary may give to a salmon proprietor written permission to contravene certain provisions of the Salmon Act. Such contraventions may include non-compliance with WCT and ACT provisions, taking salmon out of season, and total obstruction—by river trap or weir—of ascending salmon. Before the salmon proprietor—for instance, a West Coast aspiring "salmon rancher"—makes his application, he must first have secured the consent of every "affected" salmon proprietor in that District, and the DFB, if there is one.

II. *Provisions Applying to Scotland, Wales and England*

1. *Salmon Dealer-Licensing* (Sects.20 & 31) *Only* a person holding a Salmon Dealer's License may buy salmon from, or sell salmon to another person not having such a license. Penalties for contravention of this law include up to 2 years' imprisonment and/or a fine of up to £1000+.

2. *Illegally Caught Salmon* (Sects.22 & 32) A person found in possession of salmon "under suspect circumstances", and on the evidence of *one witness only*, may face charges bringing a maximum penalty of 2 years' imprisonment and £1000+ fine.

3. *East Coast Salmon Fishery Review* (Sect.39) The Scottish Secretary together with the MAFF Minister, "as soon as practicable" after *November 1989*, will prepare and present to Parliament a Report. This Report will give special consideration to the adequacy of spawning stocks, and the management of salmon net fishing in East Coast fisheries extending from South Yorkshire in England to North Aberdeenshire/Buchan in Scotland.

III. *Provisions Applying to England and Wales Only*

1. *Introduction of Fixed Nets* (Sects.33 & 37) Fixed nets (which are illegal under the *1975 England / Wales Salmon Act*) may now be introduced by a Water Authority (now the relevant Regional NRA), and/or by a Sea Fisheries Committee through bye-laws authorised by separate enabling provisions/procedures in the *1986 (UK) Salmon Act*.

2. *Restraints on North-East Netting* (Sect.36) The "licensee" must be present at all times when his net is being fished. None of the (up to four) "consignees" (helpers) endorsed on his licence may operate the net alone—except where the licensee produces a validated "sick note". (Sect.36 was accompanied by Northumbrian WA and Yorkshire WA bye-laws providing for a standardised 60-hours WCT, an 8-hour night-time drift-netting ban, and the introduction of fixed nets).

►

3. *Protection of Salmon in Coastal Waters* (Sect.37) Where the local Water Authority (now Regional NRA) "consents", the local Sea Fisheries Committee may introduce bye-laws "for the purposes of protecting salmon and of preventing any interference with their migration" in coastal/sea waters adjacent to their home rivers.

Finally there was Section 6 (Annual Close Time). Once again, it was a two-way provision. A simple alteration in the starting and ending dates of the Close Time—as was sought by the Deveron netsmen, as noted above in Chapter 2—could lead to increased catches. On the other hand, an increase in the length of the Close Time might result in reduced net catches.[11] The Scottish Secretary could use his "enabling powers" only on submission of an appropriate application; and in this instance in relation only to individual Districts. It was to be noted that the existing 168-day Close Time could only be increased; it could not be decreased.

These then were the enabling powers which the Scottish Secretary could use to effect a decrease or increase in the amount and intensity of net fishing. The message to reformers was that changes could be achieved, but that these were few, limited, and likely require great collective effort to secure the needed consensus let alone persuade the Minister and his officials.

Apart from these enabling powers available under the *1986 Act*, the Atlantic Salmon Conservation Trust (ASCT), a private voluntary body, was formed for the express purpose of reducing netting by purchase and termination of netting rights in Scotland. [12] Certainly any reductions were welcome. There was however a problem. The Trust did not direct its main efforts to reducing river and estuary netting. On the contrary, it concentrated on reduction of coastal netting. The result was that a large number of coastal nets in the Moray Firth area of Northern Scotland were removed. The problem was that without removal or reduction of estuary and river netting in the rivers affected—most notably the Spey, Findhorn, Nairn, Ness, Beauly and Alness—the majority of homing salmon thus saved would merely further swell the catches of the major estuary and river netsmen operating in these localities. Thus it was unlikely that ASCT reductions would produce more than very marginal up-stream benefits both for angling interests and spawning requirements; these benefits furthermore applicable only to those very few fisheries in Scotland's 106 Salmon Fishery Districts where these purchased reductions had been achieved. This was *not* what the Elgin Commission had in mind, nor was it a substitute for general statutory provision.

Local Management: Regress Or Progress?

If local management of the Scottish salmon resource was to be effective, the Elgin Commission had stressed that District Boards must be re-constructed. The system of "distinctions and preferences" relating to Board membership served only to reinforce faction between lower (net) and upper (rod) interests, and must be abolished.[13] It must be replaced by a system which would encourage common commitment amongst all concerned salmon interests to maintain, protect and improve the *fishery*. Two options had been suggested.

The first called for "*all* proprietors to meet and together elect a *common list* of members", with the chairman then to be chosen by the elected members. This was the Commission's preferred option. If this could not be agreed, a second option was suggested. This provided that at least the District Board chairman be elected by all proprietors meeting together; the respective upper and lower proprietors then going on to their own separate meetings to elect their own (equal number) of representatives—normally three upper and three lower—to serve on the Board.

As noted earlier, both options were rejected at the time. Further efforts—most notably the 1971 Government White Paper proposals for creation of more widely representative Area Boards—have suffered a similar fate.[14] What then of the *1986 Act*? Was any progress achieved?

The Elgin Commission's preferred (first) option proved to be as unacceptable to Government in the 1980s, as it had been to Government in the early 1900s. Ministers gave similar short shrift to the reform proposals of 1971. But rejection was not total. The *1986 Act* did incorporate a variation of the Elgin Commission's second option. While voting distinctions and privileges were retained, Board chairmen were to be elected by all proprietors [Section 14 & Schedule 2(3)]. And the limited democratisation of local administration proposed in the 1971 White Paper was not totally dis-regarded. Non-proprietorial cooptees were to be appointed by Board members [Section 16 & Schedule 2(5)&(6)]. Certainly, the first steps, albeit few, limited and fragile, had been taken towards re-construction of local fishery management in Scotland. The question was: were these steps leading forward or backward? More important, would they work?

It was unlikely that this new system applicable to District Board membership would lead to greater unity and harmony. While a commonly elected proprietor—in place of the proprietor with the highest rateable value, usually a netsman—would now take the chair, retention of the system of "privileges and distinctions" in relation to voting and Board membership [Section 14 & Schedule 2(3),(4)&(6)] seemed likely to ensure that common interest in the welfare of the fishery would still take second place to faction—and particularly in the case of major fisheries. Whether the addition of co-opted members, an apparent token recognition of the 1971 White Paper "democratisation" proposals, would perform any useful function, only time would tell.

Certainly, where major needed improvements were proposed, substantial new (private) funding could now be made available. New provisions in the Act enabled Boards to raise loans to the sum of twice their total annual assessment, and a higher sum—given approval by proprietors representing four-fifths of the total District valuation [Section 15(8)]. It was possible this even might open the costly (financial) route to long-needed "Amalgamated Boards" in several areas [Section 2 & Schedule 1]. Where there was a "progressive will", there was now at least a "way".

And while many Peers made clear during Lords Debates on the Salmon Bill that they had a "will" for much greater powers over a wide variety of matters affecting local fisheries—ranging from water abstraction, fish farms, stocking and ova planting, to obstructions and board amalgamation—the fact that Government firmly resisted these demands was not surprising. The *1986 Act* clarified the legal position of the Boards. Under the 1860s legislation there was uncertainty whether District Boards were "public statutory", or "private" bodies. The new Act spelled it out. They were now purely *private* bodies [Section 14(1),(6)&(8)].

It was an extraordinary move by Government. Management provision had actually moved *backward* from the 1860s legislation! The last vestiges of public interest in the management of the Scottish salmon resource were now erased. The Act made express provision for the District Boards to be re-constituted and henceforward to operate as private "voluntary associations". No longer therefore could there be any question of their being "public bodies" and hence publicly accountable.

But there was a price to be paid: no further statutory powers (over and above those provided in the Act) would be granted; and as exclusively private bodies, funding for various costly improvement undertakings must come solely from private sources. As Lord Gray warned on those occasions during the Bill when Peers' zeal on these matters became excessive: 'Did they wish the Boards to be re-constituted as *public* bodies'? The response of their Lordships was always the same. They retreated.

Backward-looking, or timorously forward-looking, the adequacy of the *1986 Act's* new local management provisions would only be discovered when they were put into practice. The possibility of new leadership, new (private) Board-raised funding, and new co-optee representation, offered at least hopes of modest and perhaps improved variations on the old and dis-credited system.

Supplementary Provisions: Conservation Promise

So much then for these principal sections in the new Act. What of other provisions? What hope did they provide?

First, there were the Act's "Illegal Possession" provisions [Sections 22 & 32]. These, backed up by strengthened powers to bailiffs and police seemed likely to ensure that Dennis Canavan's "wee crofter widow-woman"—a person many times brought to the attention of Members during Canavan's lively presentations in the Salmon Bill Committee—would see to it that no more "gift salmon" were left on her door-step. If not, she might well find herself in court facing up to 2 years imprisonment! Second, there was "Dealer-Licencing" [Sections 20 & 31]. Though seriously weakened by the absence of "Salmon Tagging"—which would greatly facilitate identification of caught salmon—this provision too seemed likely to cause the prudent small illegal operator to think carefully before acting. Finally, there were the new (Government amendment) provisions which required that "licensees" be on board at all times—except when able to provide a certified sick-note—when salmon fishing is being conducted [Section 36]. These provisions were specifically designed to restrain the alleged excesses of North-East English drift-netsmen and their registered "consignees".

Other provisions which were the source of modest conservation hopes included: the "East Coast Salmon Net Fishery Review" [Section 39] which would examine the adequacy of salmon stocks and management in both the English and Scottish fisheries of the North-East; new "bait and lure" restrictions [Section 8] which local District Boards could introduce on local angling waters—given the consent of the Scottish Secretary; and new controls on sea-netting "in waters frequented by migratory fish" round the English and Welsh coasts [Section 37] which, given the "consent" of the regional Water Authority, could be introduced by the area Sea Fisheries Committee.

Collectively, these could well lead to better protection, enforcement and regulation; with the attendant possibility that more salmon would be enabled to return to Scottish, English and Welsh foreshores and estuaries, and even a few escape into—or more remain in—upstream waters.

There was also the Salmon Advisory Committee. Though not part of the Act, it could have a significant impact on a range of important matters, including tagging, Low-Water netting restraints, and acquisition of better catch-data and other information vital to improved management. The Advisory Committee could recommend action on any or all of these and other matters. And while the responsible fisheries ministers were neither required to act, nor provided with relevant enabling powers, nevertheless if convinced, they could seek appropriate legislation.

Future Prospects

This then was the new Salmon Act which had been produced. It failed to meet established century-old requirements. It set out local management provisions which were regressive even in 1860s terms. It did, however, provide modest hopes of improved protection. And despite its alarmingly antiquated provisions relating to exploitation, it was nevertheless possible that improvements to meet modern conservation, economic and equity aims might at least partially be attained. All was dependent on the initiative of reformers and proprietors, and on the response of their "representative" bodies, fisheries officials, politicians and the courts.

Beyond the provisions of the Act, and in the longer term, many positive developments seemed within the bounds of possibility. Farmed salmon might yet render "wild" netting un-economic. The ASCT might succeed in removing many more nets by voluntary means. The Crown Estate Commissioners might finally agree to curtail, even terminate, their net-leasing policies. The food-producing ministries (MAFF and DAFS) might yet be prised loose from control of the salmon resource, and their powers transferred to the Department of the Environment or an appropriate environmental/recreation protection and promotion agency.

Indeed, another Government with different political leanings might view all salmon matters very differently. Under such circumstances the (1965) Hunter Committee's proposed "Area Boards", its concept of a "Scottish Anglers' Trust"; these together with established provisions to meet modern conservation and low-exploitation requirements might all be raised to new priority. And then there were the Scottish Nationalists and the Labour Party. Should either, on its own, or both acting together make progress with devolutionary demands, the Act's "privatised" provisions might experience a sudden and dramatic reverse. One extreme does tend to provoke its opposite. Nationalisation—though perhaps in this envisaged modern instance with an enhanced conservation and participant emphasis, linked to substantial state funding and resource support[15]—is something which has worried Scottish landed and "watered" proprietors for the last fifty years. Angling, with more than 4 million UK participants, is Scotland's most popular sport.

In the shorter term, the future path seemed well marked. Prospects for change would depend on proprietors and reformers making use of statutory opportunities now available; taking private improvement initiatives; and pressing the Advisory Committee and ministers for action on important issues.

One thing was clear. If the Scottish salmon suddenly plummeted into terminal decline, taking with it the enormously valuable rod-tourism economy, proprietors would have only themselves to blame. Many complained bitterly about the Act. It was a "Netsman's Charter", a "wee tim'rous beastie", the "Body of the 1868 Act in New Clothes".[16] But outside the minority of active riparian owners, what efforts had they made? The view of most was that 'salmon politics should be left to the full-time professionals'. And who were they? Commercial fishermen; many titled and influential. Was it therefore so surprising that a re-written "Netsmen's Charter" had been produced?

References

1. *House of Lords: Parliamentary Debates*, Vol.469, No.26, 14 January, 1986, col.1048.
2. For details of the Elgin Commission, its recommendations and proposals for the Scottish salmon fishery, see Chapter 1 above.
3. For details of Calderwood's contributions see Chapters 1 and 2 above.
4. See Chapter 6 above, p.124.
5. See Chapter 10 above, p.211.
6. For details see Chapter 2 above.
7. See Chapter 9 above, p.183.
8. See Chapter 10 above, p.213.
9. See Chapter 8 above, p.158.
10. In fact, it was netsmen who were the first—and so far the only—to seek (and successfully) deployment of Section 21. See Chapter 13 below, pp.285-86.
11. It is important to recognise that increase of a Fishery District Annual Close Time, or alteration in its starting and ending dates, will not automatically have a direct effect on the size of net catches taken. Where netting time or opportunity is reduced, increased effort may ensure catch levels are maintained or increased. Conversely, where netting time or opportunity is increased,

stock scarcity or any number of other factors may mean that lower rather than higher catches are taken, even given greatly increased effort.

12. See Chapter 10 above, p.203.

13. See Chapter 1 above, pp.18-19

14. See Chapter 2 above, p.32.

15. See *Appendix C* below, p.316 Dennis Canavan here made clear that modern Scottish Labour Party thinking on increased public involvement in Scottish salmon fisheries included "improved access" for anglers, "wider representation and control" in relation to management, and "greatly strengthened restraints on such netting interests as those which annually rape the Tay and most other Scottish rivers of their salmon resource". It was further pointed out that Canavan's "overall concept for restoring and maintaining the salmon resource varies little from reform proposals advanced by such eminent Scottish salmon authorities as Lord Elgin (1902), W.L. Calderwood (1909), Jock Menzies (1930), and more recently, Lord Hunter's Committee (1965)".

16. See *Appendix B* below, p. 309.

Chapter 13

THE SALMON ACT IN PERSPECTIVE

"The wild salmon resource should be treated *not* as a food-resource, but as a liesure resource".

John Gummer [1]

"[Government] does not have any statutory guidance on the *sharing* of the [salmon] resource. [This is] a *political* matter, and [will] require a *political* decision".[2]

"I urge [Members] to view the [weekly netting slap increase] regulations as a *precautionary measure* to *reduce* the *exploitation of salmon in home waters*. Neither the rodsman, nor the netsman will have a future if salmon stocks are allowed to decline. ...[It should be recognised] that the salmon caught on the rod, in effect, provides greater opportunity for constituents of Opposition Members, and indeed, for those of my hon. Friends".

Michael Forsyth[3]

"The regulations are part of a systematic campaign to destroy the salmon netting industry".

Brian Wilson [4]

In the immediate aftermath of the Salmon Bill, there were bitter recriminations. Nobody was happy with the new Act. Salmon proprietors, netsmen, anglers, conservationists, tourism interests, all freely expressed their distress and disappointment. Government had turned its back on the requirements of modernity. Indeed, the new Act, antiquated even before it became law, was seen by some as a direct "incitement to immediate [perhaps extreme radical] future reform".[5]

Eight years have now elapsed since passage of the Act. There has been no immediate, nor even mildly radical reform of this re-written "Netsmen's Charter". This however, does not mean that there has been no activity—quite the contrary.

New provisions in the *1986 Salmon Act* have been implemented, others tested. A number of minor legislative changes have been sought. These undertakings have required energetic and determined efforts. Salmon fishery proprietors have been fully engaged: rod fishery owners with lobbying and a wide range of privately-financed "improvement" activities; netsmen with fiercely defending their re-trenched "monopolistic rights" of exploitation.

Perhaps most significantly, there has been much activity by Government, its MAFF and DAFS officials, and their salmon scientists. There are signs that these officials and agencies have finally been persuaded that the future of the United Kingdom's remaining salmon resource, much reduced in the last century, lies in effective conservation and enhancement.[6] Indeed, there is a growing public recognition that in an era of declining stocks (a 60 per cent drop in world catches over the past 20 years) the wild stock is being greatly over-fished, while farmed salmon can fully supply the commercial market. Rod-tourism has risen to overwhelming economic dominance.

PRIZE-WINNING FLY-TYER, Oliver Edwards celebrates first salmon with host Lord Thurso.

It is seen as merely commonsense to strengthen low-exploitation rod-fishing, while reducing the high-exploitation activity of net-fishing. It is also perhaps significant that the balance of "salmon science" research has swung from down-stream (nets-orientated) subjects, to up-stream (angling/conservation-orientated) subjects. This domestic activity has been complemented and reinforced by several international initiatives aimed at reducing exploitation in the North Atlantic and within separate national jurisdictions. Progress has also been made in improving high seas regulation and curbing illegal fishing/piracy.

Salmon Act Activity

Government said that the Salmon Act had three principal objectives. These were "administrative modernisation", "flexible salmon fishery regulation", and "poaching reduction". The measures proposed to achieve these somewhat misleading objectives were modest at best.* How have they progressed?

Modernisation and Regulatory Achievements

"Administrative modernisation", in terms of installing elected (Scottish) District Board chairmen [Section 14 & Schedule 2(3)], and then co-opting suitable tenant representatives [Section 16 & Schedule 2(5)&(6)], was completed by 1988—at least in relation to the 50-plus Districts (of 108) where Boards actually exist. It might be noted that angling proprietors succeeded netsmen in the chair of at least two important Boards, including the Aberdeenshire Dee and the Deveron—and came very close to a third on the Tay.

Four Amalgamated Boards [Section 2 & Schedule 1] have been brought into existence. This has reduced the total number of Salmon Fishery Districts to 100. Joint (Amalgamated) Boards now exist for: 1. the North Esk, South Esk and Bervie, three rivers near Montrose which had operated informally under a Joint Board for many years; 2. the Forss, Dunbeath, Berriedale, Wick and Thurso Fishery Districts have been amalgamated to become the Caithness District Salmon Fishery Board; 3. two Fishery Districts in the Isle of Lewis (Hebrides) have amalgamated to become the East Lewis District Fishery Board; and 4. two Fishery Districts on the Isle of Skye. But what of the "Wild West" (coast) of Scotland (from Ardnamurchan to Cape Wrath) where Amalgamated Boards remain most urgently needed? Sadly, from these districts, no initiative has been forthcoming. Modified "salmon anarchy" continues to rule. [7]

* For brief descriptions of these and other important Sections in the Act, see Chapter 12 above, *Figure I, The 1986 (UK) Salmon Act: Summary List of Key Provisions*, pp.261-63.

The 1986 Act's "flexible regulatory" powers [Section 3], were quickly put to the test. Proprietors and lobbyists persuaded the Scottish Secretary to use his new enabling powers to increase the Scottish Weekly Close Time for nets from 42 to 60 hours in May, 1988. This important achievement provoked an hysterical reaction amongst netsmen, of which more will be said later. The Scottish Secretary also approved "baits and lures" restrictions [Section 8] in a number of Fishery Districts. Finally, initial soundings were taken to secure an alteration to the Annual Close Time [Section 6] of the River South Esk in Angus.

The expressed object of the application was to achieve a one-month extension, from 31 October to 30 November, in the rod-fishing season. This application was not supported by all the relevant South Esk angling proprietors. It was felt that many "red" (spawning) fish would be taken. There were also suspicions that if a such an application succeeded, a follow-up to extend the South and North Esks netting season might not be far behind.[8] Organiser of the application was one of the Stansfeld clan, the family which holds a substantial interest in the Montrose giant netting firm, *Joseph Johnston's*. The initiative lapsed.

In England and Wales, Water Authorities (since July 1989 the Regional Administrations of the National Rivers Authority [NRA]) for Wales, the South-West, Yorkshire, Anglia and Northumberland, making use of the "enabling provisions" afforded by Sections 33 (Placing and Use of Fixed Engines) and 37 (Byelaws Under Sea Fisheries Regulation Act, 1966), have sought specific important objectives. In North and South Wales, and in the South-West (Devon/Cornwall), Section 37 is proving useful in securing reductions in estuary/shore netting, and restriction of sea-fishing in certain coastal areas "frequented by migratory fish".

In the North-East of England, Sections 33 and 37 have been used for a rather different purpose: to try to introduce fixed-nets. To this end, a 1987 Northumbrian Water Authority (NWA) initiative was launched in the vicinity of the River Wear. There was a storm of protest. Ultimately, following a Public Inquiry and other actions by rods/conservationist and tourism objectors, the initiative was defeated—for the time being.[9] In 1991, Government, joined by a formidable alliance of Regional NRA's (Anglian, Yorkshire and Northumbrian) mounted another North-East fixed-net intitiative.[10] This fared better. In 1993 bye-laws were confirmed enabling more fixed nets to be introduced into the Northern Area of the Northumbrian fishery—it was the NRA's attempt to introduce them into the already heavily exploited *Southern* Area which had provoked such strong opposition in 1987. Implementation, however, has been deferred. This time, fishermen in the *Northern* Area, where many fixed-nets already are sited, have vigorously objected. They contend there are no more suitable berths. Currently, only one new fixed-net has been introduced, and this is in the *Southern* Area, where it is being used for "scientific experimental" purposes only.

Anti-Poaching Half-Measures

What then of the Act's principal "anti-poaching" measures: Dealer-Licensing [Sections 20 & 31] and Illegal Possession [Sections 22 & 32]? During the debates on the Bill, Minister Gummer and Government's supporters repeatedly stressed the importance of Dealer-Licensing. "Without Dealer-Licensing, ...all else will fail", contended Gummer.[11]

By February 1990, after two rounds of consultations, Dealer-Licensing was dead. It was alleged that opposition from fish farmers and dealer registration complexities rendered the scheme unviable. Failure of Dealer-Licensing meant that any hope of securing a "chain of prosecution", as Lord Denning termed it, "from the man at the top, to the poacher at the bottom" had been shattered. Those fishermen throughout the United Kingdom who allegedly dabble in illegal operations could breathe a sigh of relief. Opportunities to continue the lucrative side-line of "laundering" poached fish and other allied illicit activities would remain.

Government's Illegal Possession provisions have fared better. It seems that tightened sanctions provided by Sections 22 and 32 have enabled more prosecutions to succeed. Tweed and a number of East Coast fisheries authorities maintain that poaching incidence is much reduced. In other areas positive attainments are not so clear. There also is still the problem of penalties meted out to offenders. While stronger sanctions are available to the courts, there is a wide variation in how they are applied. In Borders and Highland areas, penalties tend to be applied at the upper end of the scale, while in certain districts of the Welsh Principality fines levied have been derisory, and costs awarded even in serious poaching incidents represent but a fraction of NRA prosecution costs.[12] Consideration has been given by the Welsh Regional NRA to an "offender licensing" scheme. Under this scheme, a convicted poacher, instead of being fined and/or imprisoned, would be released on "licence". If, however, during the period of this licence he should be found within a given distance of a particular river(s), he would be brought before the courts again. Under these circumstances the penalty could be severe.

NE Review: Protection for 'Endangered' Netsmen

Of greatest concern to legislators at the time of the Salmon Bill, and to national and international salmon interests since, has been Section 39, the North-East (English/Scottish) Salmon Net Fishery Review. The *Review Report* was due in November 1989. It finally appeared in October 1991, a voluminous document.[13] A separate statement of *Joint Recommendations* by the MAFF and DAFS fisheries ministers included: unspecified statutory re-definition (under Section 21) of certain modes of net fishing in Scotland; and in North-East England, a gradual phase-out of the drift-net fishery by natural attrition as licensees leave the fishery, and by making available increased opportunities for shore-based fixed-net operations.[14]

The Report and ministerial recommendations caused much concern amongst both rod and net interests. The North-East English netsmen denounced the recommendations as "draconian and unacceptable". Rods/conservationists and up-stream interests, equally outraged, contended that the recommendations did not go nearly far enough, quickly enough. Nor was this the end. In an apparent effort to "pass the buck", a July 1992 MAFF-initiated "Project" undertaken this time by the NRA considered, amongst other things, how management of the North-East salmon fishery could be improved by making available new fixed-net opportunities "giving priority to those surrendering their drift-net licences". The NRA duly decided there was opportunity to introduce (more) fixed-nets into the Northern Area of the Northumbrian fishery—though, as noted above (p.274), implementation has been deferred.

Perhaps the most notable feature of the *NE Review Report* is that emphasis is given *not* to reducing catches, but merely to gradually *shifting* North-East (English) netting from sea-based, to land-based (fixed-net) operations.

It is also to be noted that the Report does *not* seek to establish the significance of the North-East (English) rod fishery in relation to the net fishery, in terms of exploitation and economic contribution.

In fact, rods take between 1-5 per cent; nets 95-99 per cent of the total reported North-East (English) *salmon and sea-trout* catch. The 1988 season was one of the best for rods; of a reported catch of 110,200 fish, nets took 105,000, rods 5200 (4.7 per cent). Up-stream salmon and sea-trout fishings with enormous productive potential exist on Tyne, Wear, Coquet, Tees and other North-East rivers and their tributaries. It is worth noting that in 1870 the Tyne alone produced a catch of 130,000 salmon and probably at least an equal number of sea-trout—though records of this species were not maintained, many salmon fishery operators and owners regarding the sea-trout as an unwelcome competitor and pest. Other rivers and streams, ravaged, neglected or ignored in the past, today provide promising prospects for restoration and development from Humberside in the south to Middlesbrough in the north.

Official figures suggest that salmon (and sea-trout) rod-tourism in the Region generates revenue of about £1m. annually. [15] However, a recent independent North-East salmon economy survey (the *1992 NE Region Survey*) estimates that within ten years this figure could increase to £102m. and provide support for more than 16,000 tourism-linked jobs.[16] Full attainment of these goals for this tourism-dependent Region, it is pointed out, depends on many more fish being enabled to enter rivers during the May-September in-season period (thus extending the productive rod-fishing season from the current back-end six weeks, after the nets come off, to a full 35-plus weeks) and a four-fold increase in the rod-catch to 20,000. Alternatively, it has been estimated elsewhere that termination of domestic netting in the North-East of England would bring a four-fold increase in the numbers of fish entering rivers—and being available to anglers.[17]

Currently, even rods' 1-5 per cent catch is at risk. In Northumbria, the threat posed by the prospect of fixed-net introductions—possibly into estuary "conservation box" sanctuaries—is clear enough. In Yorkshire, the situation has descended from grave to diabolical. In 1989, the total rod catch was 11 salmon/grilse, and 97 sea-trout—the worst ever since catch records began. For the same period, Yorkshire nets took 6280 salmon/grilse, and 22,740 sea-trout—that is, 99.3 per cent of the total Yorkshire Regional catch, and the second highest per/net licence (379.1) sea-trout catch on record.[18]

The opportunity to take even ten per cent (2400) of this catch by rods could have a significant impact on the local Yorkshire economy. Restoration of the ravaged Yorkshire Esk, which in the mid-1960s produced up to 900 salmon to rods; revival of the once-prolific migratory fisheries of the Trent, the Ouse and its many fine but obstructed tributaries; development of the many free-flowing becks and streams along the coast giving access to the sea; all such activity could help restore an important and highly productive community economic resource.

Given the need to move more swiftly on North-East interceptory-nets if UK credibility and international net-reduction initiatives are not to suffer, "external aid" has been rendered. Icelander, Orri Vigfusson, Chairman of the 14-nation *International Committee for*

Purchase of Open Seas Salmon Quotas has explored possibilities of a compensated phase-out, aiming for permanent removal of North-East drift and fixed-nets. However, after initial positive negotiations with North-East fishermen in 1991, the situation regressed. MAFF and the NRA took a dim view of "foreign meddling"; neither was there full initial support from the UK salmon fishery and conservation community.

In early 1993, however, the *North Atlantic Salmon Fund (UK)*, under the guidance of the AST, S&TA, the Association of Scottish District Fishery Boards (ASDFB) and the Fishmongers' Company was finally established. It now operates under the chairmanship of AST Chairman, Sir David Nickson. A number of prominent netsmen serve on its committee.[19] The Fund aims to raise £180,000 annually—the bulk to come, it is hoped, largely from anglers and riparian owners *via* Scottish District Boards—to meet UK commitments on lease-outs, or net-purchases (currently Faroes and Greenland) secured by the International Committee. Provision to remove North-East nets is *not* within the *Fund*'s formal remit; this, despite the fact that most Scottish fishery interests remain reluctant fully to commit themselves to costly Open-Seas reductions until first the North-East drift-nets have been removed. Many rod interests also feel understandably unhappy that of any "saved" fish which do make it back to Scottish shores—fish for which they will have paid a high price—the netsmen, as usual, will extract the bulk of any surplus bounty produced.*

Certainly, the pressure on North-East drift-nets continues. Most recently a (December 1993) 100,000-signature Petition was presented to the Prime Minister, and two vigorous, comprehensive parliamentary initiatives have been spearheaded by the Earl of Kimberley.[20] Though Lord Kimberley's assaults clearly shook NRA Chairman Lord Crickhowell, there has, as yet, been no *direct* sign of a remedial response by the NRA or MAFF.[21]

Haaf-Nets: Split-Decision

On the West coast too there have been problems. The Solway haaf-nets have been a major source of discontent for more than a century. They are thought to take a heavy toll on in-running fish, particularly

* See below *Figure 2, A Layman's Guide to Scottish Salmon Law Reform: Alternative "Packages"*, p.282. Implementation of "Package 1" would go far towards ensuring full, un-reserved, long-term financial commitment of Scottish interests to the NASF(UK) and Vigfusson's International Committee.

in the top-pocket estuarial sector from shoals heading up murky, narrow, low-water (tidal) channels towards the Rivers Eden and Border Esk. Since passage of the 1986 Salmon Act, haaf-nets have been subjected to important legal challenges.

On the Solway South (English) shore, the number of haaf-nets (operative within the North-West Water Authority jurisdiction—now

A LINE OF HAAF-NETTERS on the Solway.

the NW Regional NRA) was reduced from 235 to 165 in 1988. This reduction later withstood a vigourous (London) High Court challenge, and several submissions to the Ombudsman by English haaf-netsmen.

On the Scottish Solway (North) shore, haaf-nets were subjected to two lengthy and complex legal challenges in 1988 and during 1991/92.[22] The basic objective of both actions was to establish that the haaf-net is an illegal instrument. Reference was made to Section 25 (Fixed Engines in the Solway) of the 1986 Act, and provisions in other relevant legislation. These actions, however, failed. "Traditional usage" dating from Viking times, it seems, supersedes commonsense and modern interpretation of the law. Haaf-netting was not included in the (August 1992) *NE Review* Statutory Orders defining legal netting methods under Section 21 (Permitted Methods of Fishing). Other approaches to reducing haaf-netting are being considered.

Advisory Committee: 'Poodle' or 'Rottweiler'?

Finally, there has been the activity of the Salmon Advisory Committee. Although not included in the 1986 Act, ministers promised that the Advisory Committee would investigate and monitor important salmon issues both within and outside the remit of the 1986 Act. Four Reports have so far been published. They include: 1. on the status and information on salmon stocks; 2. on net-fishing during low-water; 3. on natural smolt production; 4. on artificial stocking as a management policy.

The first Report calls for new legislation to secure "essential information" on fishing effort, and stresses the need for substantial and long-needed improvements, particularly in the quality of catch records. The Advisory Committee agreed that such information was vital to effective management of local fisheries and improving understanding of broader fishery conditions and trends. No legislation has followed, nor have steps been taken to improve the quality of catch records. The Second Report concludes, that there is no consistent evidence of over-fishing during low-water, and hence that there is no need for low-water netting restraints. The Third Report concludes that the supply of wild river-bred smolts could be greatly improved by ensuring maximum habitat improvement. The Fourth Report maintains that artificial stocking is to be avoided, and indeed is a waste of time, effort and money, except under very special, supportive circumstances—a finding in sharp contrast with the experience of such countries as Norway, Sweden, Russia and Iceland.

Some have been critical of the Advisory Committee. They maintain that it has been the "departmental poodle" many feared; that it has produced no ministerial (or other) legislation intitatives; and that the key issues, including tagging—which is all the more vital following the demise of Dealer-Licensing—have not been addressed. Others contend that its Reports have provided useful guidance on important issues; that legislation may well follow; and that many private fishery improvement initiatives have been encouraged. While the latter observations are probably fair comment, it can only be said that so long as the Committee remains seemingly impotent—as initially feared—in its attempts to persuade ministers to consider, let alone take legislative action sought (which, after all, was its principal envisaged role) its utility must remain open to question.

Proprietorial Activity

Angling 'Improvers'

In addition to involvement in many of the above activities, angling proprietors have been busy with initiatives of their own. Substantial privately-funded nets buy-outs have been achieved. The Atlantic Salmon Conservation Trust (ASCT) has been a primary agency in securing these reductions. The acquisition of most fixed-netting rights in the Moray Firth in 1986-'87, was followed by nets buy-outs on the Aberdeenshire Dee and Don, the Tweed, the Solway Annan, the Tay, the Spey and lesser purchases elsewhere round the Scottish coast.*

The effect of these developments, together with voluntary netting restraints long-operative on several rivers in the far North-East (including the Kyle of Sutherland system, the Brora and Helmsdale) and the North coast (notably the Rivers Halladale and Forss) is that domestic netting has been substantially reduced in Scotland's premier fishery. These reductions may partly account for the almost 50 per cent decline (from 640 tonnes in 1987, to 330 tonnes in 1990) in reported Scottish net catches.

In the Borders/Tweed area, an organisation named AGAINST (Action Group Against Interceptory Netting for Salmon and Sea-Trout) has lobbied to secure termination of drift-netting in the North-East (English) coastal fishery. Although not fully satisfied with the ministerial *North-East Review* recommendations for a gradual phase-out, its leaders hope to ensure the "process commences immediately and is completed in a reasonable time".[23]

New salmon Trusts and Foundations have been created to carry out various privately funded improvements on Scottish rivers. One fishery/ engineering consultancy is currently advising on plans for substantial improvements on 17 Scottish rivers. In England and Wales, private initiatives have encouraged NRA fishery improvement activities and formulation of a large number of proposed NRA "action plans". Perhaps the two organisations which currently lead in fishery improvement work are the Tweed Foundation[24] and West Galloway Fisheries Trust—a body concerned with the Rivers Luce, Bladnoch, Cree and Water of Fleet in the Solway Firth[25]. Both have adopted the "integrated catchment management" approach to improvement and maintenance of salmon fisheries. Much attention is given to a number of up-stream management issues; issues to which little concerted and consistent professional attention has been given in the past.

* It is important to note that of those nets "acquired"; some have been "bought out"; others "leased out" for a period. It also is important to note that *not all* nets in these districts have been removed. In the Dee District, some coastal nets remain; on Tweed, the principal estuary nets at Tweed-mouth remain in operation; the Annan still has Solway "certificated (stake) nets", haaf-nets and certain ancient Royal Burgh of Annan devices with which to contend; many lower Tay estuary nets remain in operation; on Spey, the Crown Estate owns and reserves its rights in relation to coastal nets in the District.

While these ambitious programmes are welcome and much-needed, there is a problem: money. Will there be sufficient funds to carry them out? * Improvement undertakings often involve a sizeable financial commitment over a number of years—indeed sizeable pledged Board contributions to the NASF(UK) for the foreseeable future fall into this category. And what of the need for strengthened high-cost protection in estuary and coastal sectors from which nets have been removed? Salmon trusts and foundations, together with District Boards, and whatever other private and public sources may be tapped, can in some instances supply substantial funds. But can what is essentially private funding be expected to carry the full burden of "improvement finance" in even the large and relatively affluent Fishery Districts like Tay, Tweed and Dee? And what of the vast majority of small Boards and Districts where hopes of adequate private funding are slim or nil?[26]

In those Districts where net reductions have opened the door to greatly improved rod fisheries, with all the potential for development of local rod-tourism this means, is there not a strong case for assistance from the Scottish Development Agency (SDA) and other Scottish Office agencies? And in the Regions of England and Wales, the same question can be asked: Is not a sizeable Exchequer commitment requisite if promising local programmes and "action plans" are to be converted into "practical actions"?[27]

* For improved funding possibilities, see below p.283, *Figure 2*, "Package 1", 2(b) "Re-Construction of District Boards.

FIGURE 2

A LAYMAN'S GUIDE TO SCOTTISH SALMON LAW REFORM: ALTERNATIVE "PACKAGES"

In order that the threatened Scottish wild Atlantic salmon may be assured future survival as a "heritage" symbol, and economic (natural) resource of great community value, it is vital that high-exploitation (netting) give way to low-exploitation (angling) practice.

Furthermore, in order that there may be a healthy river stock, adequate in numbers to support a sustained and profitable fishery, there are two paramount requirements. These are: good management, and good protection. Of even greater importance, if these are to be achieved, they must be based upon: good laws and good finance.

Outlined below are alternative "packages" which incorporate basic elements relevant to legislative reform of existing Scottish salmon fishery law. The first envisages termination of net fishing; the second, its continuation within a modified and modernised management system, together with a "Supplementary Package".

PACKAGE 1: Termination (with Compensation) of Net Fishing

This option provides a clear and simple programme. Adoption is dependent on continued pressure to achieve salmon laws to meet modern conservation, economic and low-exploitation requirements. Most important, adoption is dependent on Government conviction of benefits to be secured—*political*, economic and conservation.

1. "Nets Retirement" Compensation Programme

Following modified lines laid down by Elgin Commission, a small Commission armed with executive powers will meet individually with all owners of net fishings—coastal, estuary and river—round the Scottish coast.

a) Compensation subject to negotiation, the amount agreed based on private dealings of Commissioners with proprietors;

b) If no agreement, then Commissioners, using standard market procedures, calculate the amount, and pay the proprietor;

c) If proprietor still objects, then he may take the matter to arbitration/tribunal within 30 days.

All monies to be paid from a "Nets Retirement Fund" established by Government/Central Fisheries Authority for this purpose.

2. Statutory Reform: 1986 Act and Supporting Legislation

Substantial revision of existing salmon laws required. Key provisions in new laws to include:

a) *Provisions to improve regulation and increase restraint on upstream (angling) waters*:

—consideration to be given to catch quotas, prohibition on sale of (rod-caught) fish, and catch-and-release;

b) *Re-construction of District Boards*:

—number of Boards to be reduced, with possible introduction of Area Boards (similar to those recommended by the Hunter Committee and proposed in the 1971 White Paper);

—elected members to include salmon proprietors, with minority (collective) representation from Regional Purification Board, local Planning Authority, Tourism interests, Scottish Natural Heritage and independents;

—Boards no longer "private voluntary associations", but "mixed" (private/public) bodies. Boards now eligible for public funding.

c) *Introduction of Area Inspectors*, appointed and accountable to the Central Authority, to deal mainly with protection and enforcement, with appropriate powers and sanctions. Pump-priming by Central Authority to get Area Inspectorates in place. Area Boards thereafter to provide 50 per cent of funding to cover annual expenditure on Area Inspectorates.

d) *Finance* for Boards to come from private proprietorial (fishery assessment) and voluntary sources, and from public agencies and commercial interest groups (indicated above) on basis of established levy formula.

e) *Nets Proviso*: Where it may be established that incoming runs provide stocks surplus to conservation and angling requirements, or where fish may be required for experimental purposes, the Scottish Secretary to be provided with enabling powers which he may use to introduce appropriate regulations, on application from the concerned Board(s).

PACKAGE 2: Modernised Management

In the mid-1980s the *Salmon Conservancy* formulated a comprehensive plan as the basis to ensure long-term conservation. It provides a useful model for modernised management. *

The central feature is a "5-Point Plan". It aims "to share the salmon resource fairly among many diverse groups and individuals involved, whether commercial fishermen, sporting fishers, tourists or trade. But above all, it seeks to ensure that the over-riding needs of conservation are met, and that the wild Atlantic salmon remains a living part of our natural heritage".

5-Point Plan

1. *The Setting of Realistic Net Catch Quotas* Quotas would be based on the average net catches for individual fishery districts. They could involve a reduction in the number of days each week when the nets may be set.

2. *The Introduction of Area Inspectors* The Area Inspectors would be responsible for administering net catch quotas and for ensuring that the dealer-licensing system is properly observed. They would be accountable to a new Central Salmon Authority.

3. *Dealer Licensing* The introduction of dealer licences similar to those which work so well for sales of game would greatly restrict the illegal sale of salmon.

4. *Net Fishing Licences* These would be implemented by the new Central Authority, working in close consultation with the District Salmon Fishery Boards.

5. *Drift Net Controls* Strengthened controls would be introduced to ensure effective regulation of the North East English Drift Net Fishery.

In conclusion, the Salmon Conservancy states that "Together with steps taken [further] to improve fishery management, control exploitation of the North Atlantic fishery and encourage anglers to be more conservation-conscious, this approach offers the best hope for success in the future." Perhaps the greatest advantage of this approach is that it would involve minimal revision of existing legislation.

* See, *Saving the Salmon—It's a Matter of Common Sense* (brochure), "The 5-Point Plan", (London and Glasgow: Salmon Conservancy 1984). Quotations which follow are taken from the brochure. Founded in 1984, the Salmon Conservancy was dissolved in 1992. It performed a particularly useful behind-the-scenes function during the period of the Salmon Bill. For further details see above Chapter 4, p.86 and n.34; also Chapter 7, pp.129-30.

SUPPLEMENTARY PACKAGE: "Mutual Exchange"

This package is short, simple, has been used in modified form before, and *involves no changes in legislation*. It can provide for direct, if only partial, improvement in up-stream conservation and angling stocks. Arrangements secured would be solely on the basis of private agreement between the contracting parties. It works this way:

Netting Proprietors in a Fishery District agree to: remove "X" bag (stake) nets, reduce river netting by "Y" stations, and limit netting effort by "Z" amount;

This in return for agreement by

Angling Proprietors in that District to: make "W" cash payment, provide "X" share in up-stream "Angling Development Enterprise", and possibly provide for transfer of "Y" angling fishery(ies) to netsmen, along with "Z" netting rights at certain times on certain up-stream (angling) waters. Any or all of these elements may be involved in a Mutual Exchange.

Netsmen: Seige Mentality

For all their clamour and commotion, netsmen in fact have been subjected to only one new statutory restraint: the 1988 increase of the Weekly Slap from 42 to 60 hours—an action long-sought and desperately needed, particularly on heavily netted rivers with long estuaries. The fury of netsmen over what they regard as this Government betrayal remains great.[28] In other respects, netsmen's archaic rights are fully intact: they may fish for 24 hours a day, as intensively as they like, and take as many fish as they can catch; all this under conditions where there is little or no effective regulation, and no independent monitoring of catches and catch records. In fisheries where nets remain in full operation—as on the North Esk, and in many districts on the North and West coasts—these nets continue to take their customary 97 per cent of the total peak-season catch. All this is in keeping with maintenance of the traditional lop-sided "imbalance" between nets and rods re-written into the *1986 Salmon Act*. Indeed, due to a 1992 DAFS "re-definition" of certain netting methods under Section 21—an action vigorously opposed by no less a person than former DAFS Minister Lord Sanderson of Bowden during debate in the House of Lords[29]—it is possible that some Scottish estuary netsmen may be enabled to extend their activities and increase catches.

Altogether, salmon proprietors have been fully occupied. Rod fishery owners have concentrated on up-stream improvements and securing, where possible, reductions in netting. Netsmen, on the other hand, have developed a seige mentality. With increasing desperation, they have sought to fight off nets-reductions and any real or imagined statutory encroachments on their hereditable (or, in England/Wales, licensed) monopolistic control of the salmon resource.

Ministerial, Official and 'Salmon Scientific' Activity

Ministers and Government have certainly been kept busy by the lobbying and demands of salmon fishery interests in relation to changes sought under the *1986 Act* provisions. But they have also been equally busy with initiatives of their own.

On the one hand, they have been busy in their traditional role of providing support for the food-producing interests. Of the "visible means of support" they have supplied, two massive "salmon economy" Surveys are of particular interest. They concern Government's apparent determined efforts to put in place officially sanctioned "absolute minimum" values on what in fact are the very large contributions made by the salmon rod-fisheries of Scotland, and (potentially) England/Wales, to local and regional tourism-dependent economies.

Visible Supports

During the course of the Salmon Bill proceedings, Government was constantly embarrassed by figures which showed the enormous and disproportionate contribution which salmon angler/tourism makes to the economy of Scotland. With up to £210m. in generated revenue, and support for 30,000 jobs, this contribution dwarfed that of commercial netting—up to £5m. and 800 jobs.[30] How was Government to reconcile this massive imbalance with its stout defence of the netsmen's continued legal right to take the bulk of the catch?

The answer was simple. Government generated its own figures. In October 1989, a Report on *The Economic Importance of Salmon Fishing [sic] and Netting in Scotland* (hereafter called the *1989 Scottish Survey*) was published jointly by the Scottish Tourist Board (STB) and Highlands and Islands Development Board (HIDB)—both agencies under the control of the DAFS Minister. The *1989 Scottish Survey* estimated that anglers produced only £50m. p.a., and provided

TOURISM TREASURE. ... Fresh from the sea, a 12-pound summer salmon from the Spey.

support for a mere 3360 "Full-Time Job-Equivalents"—an abstract concept that was not defined. Netting, it was estimated, produced £3m., and support for 390 Full-Time (FT) Job-Equivalents. While these figures showed a wide discrepancy between rod and net contributions, they were a fraction of the gross figures produced by the *1983 Scottish Survey*. Indeed, with netsmen's jobs apparently so few, Government and DAFS could now argue, "Why worry"? Were not *they* the "endangered species"?

A separate *1989 Review and Briefing Report* on the consultants' data provided a ready explanation for discrepancies. [31] The *1989 Scottish Survey* referred only to *anglers'* contribution; it *excluded* the contribution of "accompanying groups". Similarly it did *not* include "real jobs"—be they full-time, part-time or seasonal. These adjustments, once made, produced interesting results. The *1989 Scottish Survey* data produced totals that now conformed closely to those of the *1983 Scottish Survey*—£150m. p.a. and 28,100 "real jobs".

The complementary *MAFF Salmon Economy Study* for England and Wales was done by different consultants, and published in September 1991.[32] It took a different approach by estimating the total *capital* value of English and Welsh salmon fisheries—£75m. rod fisheries, £3m. net fisheries. It also estimated £16.4 annual expenditure by salmon anglers.

These estimates too bemused informed fishery interests. The *1992 NE Survey* dismissed them out of hand. It reckoned a minimum (England/Wales) rod-fishery capital value at £190m. As for "angler expenditure" values: adjustments to incorporate the contribution of "accompanying groups", and in terms of base-figures evolved in the *1983 Scottish Survey* and the *Review and Briefing Report*, brought annual expenditure totals into a range between £148m. and £250m.[33] No employment support figures were produced.

The purpose of these Government Surveys appears to have been to diminish substantially the *gross* economic importance of the United Kingdom salmon fishery. Through construction of "absolute minimum" values, they served to minimise the importance of salmon angling, in terms of the revenue generated and the range and number of local jobs supported. They stressed what is officially termed, the "valuable contribution" of salmon netting. The irony is that despite these enormous Government efforts, even these "absolute minimum" figures show just the reverse: the lop-sided economic importance of the recreational fishery.

The other main "visible supports" which Government and its salmon scientists have provided the food-producing interests have already been mentioned. These relate mainly to the North-East fishery and include the *NE Review Report*, the *1992 NRA "Project"* on the North-East fishery, and the *1987 Wear Inquiry*. They represent the determined efforts of Government and MAFF to construct a "positive response" to the unrelenting pressure from Tweed, Scottish and international fishery and conservation interests. It is a response which appears to encompass actions to reduce North-East "interceptory" netting, but which in fact could result in actions which will only increase it. Even a schedule for a rapid reduction in the *number* of drift-nets could produce little or no reduction in the *size* of the drift-net *catch*, while additional fixed-netting will clearly increase the overall catch total.

Enabling Information

While ministry officials have been supplying traditional support to the food-producers, they have at the same time started issuing information of great value to rod and conservation interests. These data show the continuing high catches by Scottish nets in many districts where net reductions have not taken place. [34] In relation to England/Wales improved data since the mid-1980s confirm—massively—that net-fishing, according to reported catches, is predominantly a loss-making activity, while still it accounts for over 95 per cent of the combined (net and rod) catch.[35]

The point is that this information is more than adequate to bring *all* net-fishing in the United Kingdom to a virtual halt: in the (English) North-East through Section 4 enabling provisions under the *1967 Sea Fish (Conservation) Act*; in England/Wales generally through repeal of Section 26 of the *1975 Salmon Fisheries Act* (concerning net licensing, and Net Limitation Orders); in Scotland, through the various *1986 Salmon Act* enabling provisions earlier noted.

The responsibility for informed and decisive action devolves upon Scottish and English Ministers. They must be convinced of the merits of the reforms sought.

An Historic Precedent

In 1988, important salmon fishery reform action was taken. It concerned Government's decision, following extensive consultations with concerned interests, to increase the Scottish Weekly Close Time.[36] This decision challenged successfully the "conservation imperative" as defined by officials and salmon scientists. Issues of "sharing" and "management" of the salmon resource, acquired legitimacy. It set an important precedent.

The Scottish Fisheries Minister, Michael Forsyth, tackled the issue of "conservation" directly. Government, he said, "reached the conclusion that our priority is the need to assist conservation of stocks in Scottish rivers generally".[37] This position, he admitted, had led to conflict with DAFS scientists who maintained that an increase in the Weekly Slap was not needed, because "most, if not all, rivers in Scotland are fully stocked".

Government, said Forsyth, was not convinced. All that the scientific evidence had shown was that "young salmon can be found in all Scottish rivers where access and water quality are adequate". This did not mean that "all rivers are fully stocked". Increasing the Weekly Slap would lead to a "larger number of eggs being deposited", and in some areas that might "well result in increased production of smolts".

Under heavy pressure from MPs opposing the measure, Forsyth turned from issues of conservation, to those of "sharing" and "management". He acknowledged that to increase the Weekly Slap would likely mean that the share taken by nets would be smaller, and by anglers somewhat larger. This was not to say that "all fish presently taken by netsmen" would fall to anglers. The "conservation balance", a minimum of 75 per cent of the total passing the nets, would be available to "increase the spawning".

How could he justify this encroachment on property rights and netsmen's traditional 80-plus per cent share of the catch? While recognising the existence of the heritable property right of netting proprietors, Forsyth made an historic—in terms of Scottish salmon law—observation. "There is no reason why netsmen should continue to take some 75 to 80 per cent of the fish landed. Their heritable rights give them no entitlement to that or any proportion of the reported catch".

Who, then, would benefit from this initiative to increase upstream stocks? "Hoteliers and the many small businesses in rural Scotland" would get much of the money, he said. "We are talking about a [absolute] minimum value to the Scottish economy of £50m. for angling and £5m. for nets". Members, he suggested should consider the impact on their constituencies of "the benefits that come from rod fishing".

Forsyth observed that salmon farms were continuing to produce "growing numbers of salmon for the table and for export". This was another reason for "encouraging the tourist industry by a shift in emphasis from netting to angling". Altogether, he concluded, in the face of spirited resistance from netsmen's supporters, "It makes sense to encourage the tourist industry".

MORE TREASURE. . . . Two late-June Deveron Sea-Trout (3lbs. and 4lbs.).

Forsyth provided a brilliant precedent for reformers. Change need not be justified solely on the grounds of "conservation", as defined by ministerial salmon scientists, nor the Minister's understanding of the "conservation" issue. Change equally could be justified on the grounds that "management" of the fishery to effect an alteration in existing "shares" to nets and rods, was desirable for reasons of substantial and demonstrable public and economic benefit. *

Briefly, then, salmon reformers owe ministerial officials and their salmon scientists a large debt of gratitude. They have made substantial amounts of valuable new information available. By inference more than by direction, they have indicated how best this information can be used to achieve reform targets. Perhaps most significant, being now mainly involved in up-stream (angling fishery) research, they are developing greater understanding and sympathy with up-stream problems. Traditional scientific vested interest in down-stream fisheries is being replaced by rapidly strengthening scientific vested interest in up-stream fisheries.

At an April 1992 S&TA (Scotland) conference on "The Salmon and the Scientist", Richard Shelton, Director of DAFS' Pitlochry Salmon and Freshwater Research Laboratory made a telling observation. He conceded that productive river angling depends on management to secure more fish in a river than the minimum "conservation stock" required for spawning. This passing remark, albeit extracted under considerable pressure from Scottish S&TA members led by their Chairman Lord Marnoch, spoke volumes to salmon law reformers present.

Since 1986, therefore, the "rules" of the "new game" of salmon law reform have been set. A guiding precedent has been achieved. New parameters of strategy, tactics and support have evolved. All this provides promising opportunities for achieving a better balance between the netting and angling interests.

International Activity

The 1986 *International Atlantic Salmon Symposium* in Biarritz, as noted in Chapter 11, produced a number of strong, unanimously endorsed resolutions. What has been the response of the United Kingdom authorities?

* Forsyth's statement here is indicative of increasing support of ministers and Government for the conservation and economic logic of the rods/conservation case. Indeed this provides the basic rationale for *A Layman's Guide to Scottish Salmon Reform*. See *Figure 2* above, p.282, para. 1.

First, "salmon tagging" remains an initiative about which much has been promised but little delivered. Both France and Ireland were set to introduce tagging but failed to implement it. Here in the United Kingdom, following the demise of Dealer-Licensing, Government authorities supported by most salmon bodies have once again expressed interest in tagging. No action, however, has followed.

Second, drift-netting has been eliminated by all NASCO countries, with two exceptions: Ireland and the UK. Currently the UK is under heavy pressure to follow suit. MAFF and the NRA have been left in no doubt about the strength of international feeling and that emanating from fellow NASCO members. At the June 1992 *Fourth International Salmon Symposium*, Atlantic Salmon Trust Chairman, Sir David Nickson, led in condemning the UK Government's failure to act. Urgent messages of deep concern from then-President George Bush and Secretary of State James Baker were communicated to Prime Minister John Major and Minister Gummer. Indeed, one of Bush's last acts as President was to sign a measure in November 1992 "imposing trade sanctions on any nation that allows its vessels to fish with drift-nets in the North Atlantic starting in 1994". Shortly after, European Community Commissioner for Fisheries, Manuel Marin, stated that the North-East (English) salmon fishery must be developed in terms of the "socio-economic prosperity" it can generate, particularly sport-fishing. Iceland's Orri Vigfusson, as noted above, has not only been active in securing open-seas nets reductions, he also has initiated talks with North-East netsmen about compensated reductions.

Third, there have been encouraging developments in relation to "improving and co-ordinating national salmon fisheries inspectorates". Experiments in satellite surveillance on the high seas have shown great promise. Ship movements and their fishing activities can be closely monitored. Orri Vigfusson and his *International Committee for the Purchase of Open Seas Salmon Quotas* have recently produced impressive evidence of the potential for successful use of this system in tracking down and curbing "salmon pirates"—activity which, equally importantly, has served to strengthen bonds between the fisheries authorities of the NASCO treaty nations concerned. Inspection in UK waters also has been much-improved by extension of aerial (aircraft) surveillance. This has proved of particular value in monitoring Scottish coastal waters during summer peak-period salmon runs.

In other respects, however, there has been little sign of forward movement. Failure of Dealer-Licensing, and a continuing dilatory approach to salmon tagging, have severely undermined hoped-for strengthening of the inspectorial function. In Scotland the inspectorate remains severely under-staffed, and lacks effective powers of supervision, enforcement and sanction; all this due mainly to the still near-total absence of appropriate provisions in the Salmon laws. * In England and Wales, in the face of wide-spread poaching at sea, Government has sought to improve the inspectorate through strengthened "self-regulation". As in Scotland, with limited funds and personnel, insufficient powers and ineffective sanctions, and too little support from the courts, the NRA inspectorial function remains limited. The *1986 Biarritz Symposium* proposed that European Community funds be sought to assist in improving inspectorates. So far as the UK is concerned, EC funds have neither been secured nor—according to NRA and Departmental fisheries officials with whom I have spoken—sought.

Fourth, a start has been made on "rods conservation" measures. In several Scottish, and a few English and Welsh fishery districts, "baits and lures" bye-law restrictions are now in place. In some English and Welsh (NRA) districts, voluntary rod-catch limits have been set by some fishery operators—although even the daily quotas are often more than most anglers may hope to catch in many seasons. There is also increasing emphasis on voluntary catch-and-release. Most back-end hen fish taken on Tweed, Tay, Dee and Deveron are now returned as a matter of course. Many fishery operators in England, Wales and Scotland retain rules banning sale of rod-caught salmon. Only on Tweed (after 15 September) is there any statutory ban in place.

What does all this mean, and how does it relate to the principal *1986 Symposium* commitment made by the UK Government and its fisheries authorities to reducing netting, and giving "priority to development and maintenance of recreational fisheries"? There has been much talk and some action. Perhaps most importantly, nets in the North-East, and elsewhere in England and Wales, have been subjected to at least minor new legal restraints and, in some instances, reductions. In Scotland, nets have been privately purchased and removed from many premier fisheries. New statutory restraint, however, has been restricted to the 1988 18-hours increase in the Weekly Close Time.

What of future positive action? Will the United Kingdom follow major international nets-reduction achievements in the Faroes, Greenland, Iceland, Norway and Canada? The answer is 'yes'. What is not so clear is 'when'. There are signs of significant accommoda-

* See *Figure 2*, "Package 1", 2(c), and "Package 2", "5-Point Plan", 2. Introduction of Area Inspectors would greatly strengthen local control and regulation of fisheries.

tions. Attitudes are changing and international pressure continues. Here too official facts and figures are becoming available which enable concerned interests to press the United Kingdom Government for the needed reforms.

The Politics of Salmon

In the eight years since passage of the *Salmon Act*, a start has been made on translating recognised principle into practice. It has not been easy. The Act's fundamental flaws and damaging weaknesses remain. Nevertheless reform prospects are slowly ticking along. The Act's principal Sections already have been deployed, many enabling provisions explored and tested. Riparian owners in many areas have, as was hoped, stepped boldly forward and are pressing on with important improvements. Netsmen combine fierce rear-guard resistance with apparent acceptance of the inevitable. Within domestic and international salmon arenas, within ministerial and salmon science contexts, there have been important developments. All appear to accept that the long-term interests of conservation, economy and heritage can best be ensured by consolidating the low-exploitation activity of rod-fishing while reducing or removing the high-exploitation activity of net-fishing.

In North America, the Atlantic Salmon Federation (ASF) and Restoration of Atlantic Salmon In America (RASA) have long acted on this principle. In the United Kingdom the AST and S&TA now are pressing *nearly* similar demands—though the AST remains self-shackled by its "science only" remit and charitable status, and (in the minds of many) handicapped by its founding links with the commercial fishing establishment, while S&TA (FM Hall) policy still falls short of full commitment to statutory reduction of the nets-dominant *status quo*. S&TA (Scotland) harbours no doubts. All nets must go. It is "economic luncacy", declares former Scottish Council Chairman, Lord Hunter, that they still remain.[38] How these bodies, and particularly S&TA (Scotland), will fare against the weight of the ASDFB, which still remains the officially recognised representative body of Scottish salmon proprietors, and which staunchly defends the nets-dominant *status quo*, remains to be seen.[39] Also, should it come to new major (Scottish) statutory initiatives at Westminster, it will be interesting to discover whether S&TA (Scotland) will take the lead, or (as during the Salmon Bill) be confined to a subordinate role behind the S&TA (FM Hall). One might note that as of October 1993, S&TA (FM Hall) Director, Christopher Poupard, now doubles as administrator of both S&TA's London and Edinburgh offices.

Clearly there are many obstacles still to surmount. But the point to be recognised is that there *has* been a change in attitude and in will. There is ever greater and more relevant information available; key issues have been identified; awareness within all sectors of the fishery community and well beyond has been generated. But most importantly, there is a clear and increasing *will* to achieve those changes needed to bring the UK and Scottish fisheries into conformity with the requirements of this modern age. * It is these developments that generate hope that tragedy may yet be averted.

Political Action and 'Demonstration Effect'

The principal legislative steps to achieve required changes are clear enough and have been oft-discussed in this and preceding chapters. What now is needed is political action. And as those who have been engaged in salmon politics over the past two decades—and in some instances much longer—will know, this poses the most difficult challenge.

At the mouth of most salmon rivers is a town or other urban settlement. Whether merely the size of Berwick, Annan or Perth, or cities like Newcastle, Newport or Aberdeen, it is in these conurbations that most salmon area voters reside. In the past, salmon netting has provided local jobs, returns for thriving businesses, and occupied an established place in the local economy. The up-stream fishery, on the other hand, has been regarded as a minority interest, concerned with leisure and recreation, not "work". Those principally involved are not only few, but seen by town dwellers as wealthy and privileged, often outsiders. In other words, salmon rod-fishing has not been regarded as serious commercial enterprise capable of producing substantial economic benefits. Given this background it is hardly surprising that politicians have tended to support the traditional commercial interest, the netsmen.

It is this "town and gown" obstacle which must be addressed in salmon areas throughout Scotland, England and Wales. Local residents must be made aware that the commercial tables have turned, that it is the rod-fishing industry which now promises major benefits. Jobs in the valleys, income for families, many new business ventures—not to say new rating and tax revenues for local Authority and national

* For general guides to modern change in the Scottish salmon fishery, see *Figure 2* above p.282.

Exchequer coffers—these are the important benefits to be secured. A persuasive grass-roots "demonstration effect" is needed.* But to achieve it, yet more resources—time, money, expertise—supplied mainly by private rod-fishery interests will be required. Given the extent of financial commitment of private fishery owners already indicated, will there be adequate funds? Should this take priority over other fishery funding commitments?

Many Scottish District Boards and salmon proprietors concede they can see no end to relentlessly growing fishery management expense. Protecting the rivers against poachers often absorbs more than 80 per cent of Boards' annual budgets. The situation is serious, and will grow worse. It has long been apparent that Area Inspectors, with extensive powers, appointed, paid and accountable to the Central Authority (DAFS or an independent body thereof) could perform this most vital function.[40] Properly protected coastal waters and well-stocked rivers supporting burgeoning rod-tourism businesses would quickly repay Government funding outlays, and in time provide impressive savings as substantial new revenue for the Exchequer. Furthermore, Boards would thus be enabled to use their existing sparse resources for local management purposes and "demonstration effects" as needed. But for Government to agree this support it is likely that proprietorial (statutory) concessions would be needed. Public access to salmon angling could be improved. And might not this be supplemented by direct public representation on Boards?**

These are thoughts to consider. Indeed, in Scotland, given this modern era of democratic, and increasingly volatile "home rule" populist sentiment, this could well be the politically prudent path to follow. It is well to remember that the *1986 Salmon Act*, in the view of many of its critics, remains an insult to the vast majority of people in Scotland.[41] There also is a growing body of opinion which contends that needed changes may more readily be facilitated by ministries with primary commitment to "environment, recreation and tourism"—the Department of the Environment (and its principal new agency, the NRA) and the new Ministry for Heritage—than the food-producing ministries of MAFF and DAFS.[42] It is here worth

* The importance of a persuasive "demonstration effect" cannot be over-stated. See *Figure 2*, "Package 1" above p.282. Acceptance of, and support for needed change is fundamentally dependent on "*political* benefits" which politicians involved may gain.

** See *Figure 2*, "Package 1", 2 (b), (c) and (d).

repeating that there are some in these ministries who accept this position and are working quietly to provide support.[43] Continued pressure lends encouragement.*

A Tale of Two Newcastles

In the Spring of 1990 I visited a salmon restoration project on the shores of Lake Ontario, not far from my native roots near Toronto in Canada. My Ministry (Ontario Ministry of Natural Resources) guide, fisheries biologist Les Stanfield, pointed to where Wilmot's Creek, of historic salmon-culture fame, finally running clear of estuary reed beds, enters the Lake.[44]

Was there not a river-mouth settlement, I asked? Stanfield confirmed that there was—and still is. Its name, I inquired? "Newcastle", he replied.

It was a reflex reaction. I swiftly scanned the estuary banks and distant foreshore sections for the customary coble berths, the ranks of fixed engines, the net-drying racks and bothies. But all in vain. "Alright", I conceded, "I give up. Where do the netsmen operate"?

Stanfield expressed surprise. "No commercial fishing here or anywhere else in Lake Ontario", he declared. "There used to be during the early years of colonisation. Nets in this Newcastle area took up to 50,000 fish a year until the early 19th century. Slaughter on the fishing grounds did 'em in".

"But when the fishery is restored (already runs of planted steelhead and Pacifics, I knew, had recently been established) commercial fishing will re-commence"?

Stanfield eyed me for a moment. "What's the point?" he replied. "No money or employment in net fishing. Wasteful use of a valuable resource. Besides, the locals wouldn't have it. Loads of money in outfitting, tackle, accommodation and so on. Tourism, the angler, rod fishing, that's what the modern salmon fishery here is all about. And with the low rate of rod exploitation, we're guaranteed bumper propogation".

As we drove back to Toronto, I reflected on another Newcastle I knew, a Newcastle facing out onto the North Sea. "Wasteful use of a valuable resource", Stanfield had said. I thought of the drift nets, the "self-policing" fishermen, the coastal fixed nets, the intensity of commercial fishing, with—unbelievably—the prospect of worse to come. "What's the point?", Stanfield had queried. What indeed! He could have been speaking not just of the North-East, but of the entire UK

* See *Figure 2*, "Package 1", above p.282, para. 1; "...adoption is dependent on continued pressure".

salmon fishery.

Life has taught me there is no such thing as "identical experience". Each is singular and individual, and it is a foolish person who suggests otherwise. Yet a similar or parallel experience may provide symbols, structures, guides, possibly inspiration, support, encouragement.

In its way, this is what this chance 1990 Canadian experience did for me. Nets destroyed the Ontario salmon resource at Newcastle. Now stocks are gradually being restored. Rod-tourism is burgeoning. The nets are gone and the locals, politicians, officials and fishery scientists wouldn't have it any other way. It all provided a powerful metaphor for where our UK salmon fisheries have been, are now, and in the not too distant future—given continued effort and the blessing of Dame Fortuna—are destined to be going.

References

1. *Press Briefing*, (Statement by Fisheries Minister, John Gummer), Whitehall, London, 23 October, 1986.
2. *Minutes of a Meeting of the Migratory Fish Committee*, Salmon and Trout Association, Fishmongers' Hall, London, 17 March, 1992, p.3. (Italics added).
3. "Salmon (Weekly Close Time) (Scotland) Regulations, 1988", Second Standing Committee on Statutory Instruments, etc., *Parliamentary Debates: House of Commons*, 4 May, 1988, col.26. (Italics added). Hereafter referred to as *Weekly Slap Debate*.
4. Ibid., col.24.
5. See *Appendix C*, below, p. 316.
6. One who remains staunchly un-persuaded is DAFS' Inspector of Salmon and Freshwater Fisheries, Robert B. Williamson. While prepared to accept that where "there is a lot of netting, then angling may suffer—and in some places and at some times it has—", he goes on to state, "Equally, the *local netsmen know that their operations do not destroy the stocks*". (See Robert Williamson, *Salmon Fisheries in Scotland*, (Pitlochry: Atlantic Salmon Trust, for Tay Salmon Fisheries, 1991), p.19. ...By contrast, it is interesting to note the observations made by a previous incumbent of Williamson's office nearly 90 years ago. In his *Annual Report [for the year 1906] to the Fishery Board for Scotland*, W.L. Calderwood stresses that "the salmon which enter our rivers are the somewhat limited company upon which we are entirely dependent for the upkeep of the stock. If, then, we persistently remove, season after season, those breeding fish, we are, in spite of close-times, following a most dangerous policy". *Netting, and estuary and river netting in particular, said Calderwood "has been responsible for the decline of the stock of fish"*. If netting was responsible for decline in the early 1900s; and since the intervening years have seen only an intensification of effort and increase of efficiency as new methods, materials and opportunities have been exploited; one wonders how, in this modern era of salmon scarcity, it can be contended that netsmen "do not destroy the stocks"?

7. See David Shaw, "The Pillagers", *Trout and Salmon*, (January 1985), pp.62-66
8. See David Shaw, "Montrose Monkey-Business?", *Trout and Salmon*, (January 1988), p.55.
9. See two-part series on the "Wear Inquiry" by David Shaw, in *Trout and Salmon*: "Battle for the Wear", (December 1987), pp.52-3; and "A Step in the Dark", (January 1988), pp.64-5.
10. See David Shaw, "Fixed Net Fears", *Trout and Salmon*, (April 1992), p.68.
11. See David Shaw, "Tagging Talk", *Trout and Salmon*, (April 1990), p.99.
12. See, "The 1000 Catch", *The Kingfisher* (Newsletter of the Welsh Regional NRA), Issue 13, Winter 1991/92, p.3. A poacher was convicted of "being in possession" of 36 salmon "in suspicious circumstances". The poacher was fined £50. The Welsh Regional NRA sought £2000 costs, but was awarded only £150 by the court.
13. MAFF and DAFS (Joint Publication), *Salmon Net Fisheries: Report of a Review of Salmon Net Fishing in the Areas of the Yorkshire and Northumbrian Regions of the NRA, and the [Scottish] Salmon Fishery Districts from the River Tweed to the River Ugie [in NE Aberdeenshire]*, (HMSO: London, 1991). Hereafter this study is referred to as the *NE Review Report*.
14. See, Joint Announcement by MAFF and DAFS, "Government Publishes Results of North-East Coast Salmon Netting Review", *MAFF News Release*, 17 October, 1991, pp.6.
15. See, MAFF, *An Economic Evaluation of Salmon Fisheries in Great Britain: Summary Report*, (prepared for MAFF, by Centre for Marine Resource Economics, Portsmouth Polytechnic), July, 1991, Table 9. (Hereafter referred to as the *MAFF Salmon Economy Survey*). Also, for multiplier adjustment, see D. Shaw, *Salmon and Sea-Trout Angling and the North-East Tourism Economy: Revenue Input and Employment Support Projections*, June 1992. (Hereafter, *1992 NE Region Survey*).
16. See, *1992 NE Region Survey*, op. cit.
17. Letter from W.T.W. Potts, to MAFF Fisheries Minister, D. Curry, dated 27 September, 1991.
18. See, *NE Review Report*, op.cit., Tables 19-23; and NRA, *Salmonid and Freshwater Fisheries Statistics for England and Wales, 1990*, (MAFF Directorate of Fisheries Research, 1992), Tables 9 to 12. (Hereafter, *MAFF Salmonid Statistics*).
19. These include Noel Smart of Joseph Johnston's (North Esk), Ian Mitchell, Managing Director of Tay Salmon Fisheries Company, and Robert Clerk, agent for the Crown Estate Commission, and manager of the CEC estuary and foreshore fishings on the Spey. (*Note*: Following an August 1993 agreement, the Spey estuary nets have been removed. It is understood the CEC agreed to lift them for a 30-year period; that no cash was involved; but that certain weeks on the Gordon Castle (former estuary netting) water are to be allocated to the CEC for letting as rod fishings. The Crown is now concentrating on developing the potential of its Spey rod fishings. The CEC continues to lease out a large number of coastal netting stations round the Scottish coast).
20. See, *House of Lords: Parliamentary Debates*, Vol.539, (No.54), 5 November, 1992, cols.1572-1596; and Vol.550, (No.13), 9 December, 1993, cols.1088-1112

21. This is not to say there have been no *indirect* signs. See, for instance, "Enabling Information", below, pp.289 and 292; "...By inference more than by direction [salmon scientists and fisheries officials] have indicated how best this [new] information can be used to achieve reform targets" (p.292).

22. See articles by David Shaw in *Trout and Salmon*, "Solway Salmon Hopes", (June 1988), p.70; "Haaf Nets Illegal?", (October 1988), p.27; "Haaf-Net Sense", (January 1989), p.29; "Haaf-Nets Challenge", (August 1990), p.67; "Haaf Nets in Court", (March 1991), p.37; "Haaf-Baked Decision", (March 1992), p.111.

23. AGAINST, *Project Report: October 1991*, (circular).

24. See Derek Mills (ed.), *Tweed Towards 2000: A Symposium on the Future Management of the Tweed Fisheries*, (Aberystwyth: Cambrian News, 1989), *infra*.

25. See Alastair Stephen, *West Galloway Fisheries Trust: Annual Report, 1989-90*, (mimeo.).

26. See, for instance, *Forth District Salmon Fishery Board: Annual Report, 1991*. Chairman Alastair Dickson observes that "neither individual proprietors nor landowners can on their own protect this [fishery] environment from all problems". (Para.2.0) The Forth District catchment is well in excess of 1500 square miles. The Board has but one employee/bailiff. The Forth Board must finance its staggering number of duties from £69,000 raised by assessment on (private) proprietors. Failure of several proprietors to pay up the past two years (1990 and 1991) has put terrible strain on the Board in its "management, protection and improvement" role. Resource provision already thread-bare, has had to be further cut. (See paras.6.2 and 7.0). Rather than exceptional, the plight of the Forth Board—sadly—merely provides a classic and common instance of the ludicrous (self-imposed) situation faced by the majority of Scottish District Boards over the past 130 years.

27. See, W.H. Atkins (Consultants), *Review of the River Teifi: Offer of Services: Technical and Financial Proposals*, (April 1992). It is interesting that here, the Teifi rod fishery interests, are being required to meet not only the cost of the "improvements", when eventually these are sorted; but also of the "assessment" itself, upon which, presumably, the projected "improvements" will be decided. Pleading constant and chronic shortage of funds, the Welsh Regional NRA is seemingly self-restricted to a near-exclusively "advisory" role. The NRA has a statutory duty to "maintain, improve and protect" game-fisheries. This is merely yet another sector in which the NRA clearly is failing spectacularly to fulfil these duties. It is a devastating failure, generating grave concern, in nearly every NRA Region.

28. See, *The Salmon Net* (The Magazine of the Salmon Net Fishing Association of Scotland), issues (produced annually) for the years 1985-1991. While perhaps of greatest interest to students of Abnormal Psychology, the Magazine does provide lively entertainment and often contains much useful information.

29. See *House of Lords: Parliamentary Debates*, Vol.541, (No.86), 28 January, 1993, cols.1403-1404.

30. See D. Shaw and Colleagues, *A Survey of Salmon Angling and the Scottish Tourism Economy: Revenue Input and Employment Support*, March 1983, (hereafter referred to as the *1983 Scottish Survey*).

31. See, David Shaw, *Review and Briefing Report on Salmon Angler / Tourism and the Scottish Economy: Overall Expenditure and "Real Jobs"*, December 1989, (hereafter referred to as the *1989 Review and Briefing Report*). The latter document is a detailed critique of the *1989 Scottish Survey*.

32. See, *MAFF Salmon Economy Survey*, op.cit.

33. See *1992 NE Survey*, op.cit., p.3, and n.4.

34. In fact Scottish catch data, from the early 1980s, has been available in far greater and more revealing detail since rods/conservation pressure in the late 1970s helped to secure both qualitative and quantitative improvements in presentation. Indeed, the current (1992) Scottish Office, *Scottish Salmon and Sea-Trout Catches, 1990: Statistical Bulletin*, provides an excellent example of further useful refinements to data presentation that has taken place—albeit that the more figures and graphs used; the more open to query and interpretation they are.

35. Perhaps most useful and informative are the official *Salmonid and Freshwater Fisheries Statistics for England and Wales*, or "Salmonid Statistics" reports which have been produced by MAFF (1989), and MAFF for the NRA (1992). These data provide truly massive confirmation for conclusions reached more thirty years ago by the renowned (1961) *Bledisloe Committee*, by the (1974) *Report on the Salmon Fisheries of England and Wales*, published by the Water Authorities Association, (entitled, *Taking Stock*), and the (1985) Welsh Water Authority *Report on the Status of Welsh Salmon and Sea-Trout Fisheries*, to name but three important and relevant official studies.

36. These consultations exposed the historic raw nerve at the root of rod-net relations. While rod and net bodies assumed predictable stances, the position taken by the ASDFB (Association of Scottish District Salmon Fishery Boards), the body which purports to represent Scottish salmon proprietors, and indeed which is recognised by Government as such, showed clearly the extent to which netting proprietors still retained dominance—though now not without spirited challenge—in the late 1980s. See particularly, David Shaw, "Salmon Close Time Shock", *Trout and Salmon*, (April, 1987), p.54.

37. See, *Weekly Slap Debate*, op. cit., cols.3-26.

38. Hon. Lord Hunter, "A Policy that is 'All at Sea'", *Salmon and Trout Association Yearbook*, (1994), p.15.

39. There have been indications of a weakening in ASDFB resolve. ASDFB President Lord Thurso, himself a prominent netsman as well as rod proprietor, drew much recent criticism for his spirited defence of Scottish coastal "interceptory" nets. [For details see *The Scotsman*, Letters Columns, over the period 10 January-31 January, 1994. Amongst Thurso's critics were the Scottish S&TA Chairman, Lord Marnoch, Lord Hunter, T.A.F. Barnes, the S&TA (FM Hall) Chairman, and the NASF's Orri Vigfusson.] The extent of displeasure with Lord Thurso's stance was further manifest at the ASDFB 1994 AGM. Lord Thurso did succeed in securing re-election as President—a post he has held for more than 20 years—but by only one vote.

40. This was one of the five principal points in the *Salmon Conservancy's* policy for Scottish salmon fishery reform. "Introduction of Area Inspectors: The Area Inspectors would be responsible for administering net catch quotas and ensuring that the dealer-licensing system is properly observed. They would

be accountable to a new Central Authority". [See, *Saving the Salmon—It's a Matter of Common Sense* (brochure), "The Five-Point Plan", (London and Glasgow: 1984)].

41. See, for instance, Brian Wilson, "The Real Priorities Ignored in Salmon Bill", *Glasgow Herald*, 21 January, 1986.

42. See, *House of Lords: Parliamentary Debates*, 5 November, 1992, cols.1572-76. During a debate on "North-East Drift Net Fishing", the Earl of Kimberley argued forcefully for a shift of MAFF's salmon responsibilities to the NRA's parent ministry the DOE, and the Ministry for Heritage.

43. See n.21 above.

44. See David Shaw, "Salar Resored?: Ontario Saga", *Trout and Salmon*, (November 1991), p.62.

APPENDIX A

Scots netsmen to blame for decline of salmon?*

The BBC2 programme, The World About Us, tonight asks who or what is to blame for the salmon's decline? DAVID SHAW, whose articles in *Trout and Salmon* Magazine have made him a thorn in the side of the Scottish salmon fisheries establishment, says it is long past time for the blame to be laid squarely where it belongs—on Scotland's entrenched netting interests.

WE HEAR much about the increasingly desperate plight of the salmon within the full range of his North Atlantic home waters. It is a very sad story and yet another searing indictment of the seemingly unlimited capacity of our own species for greed, devastation, and sheer brute rapacity.

We all know something of the distressing record of his decline and disappearance over a century ago from many once salmon prolific waters in France, Spain, Germany, and Poland. Today, we hear regularly about the huge assaults carried out in distant waters: on the feeding grounds off Greenland and the Faroes; on the ocean migration routes; in offshore and inshore waters—particularly off the Northern Irish coast and in the heavily drift-netted waters of Northumbria. What is to happen if the current three-mile offshore limit is abolished, as proposed by the Government?

Incredible as it may seem, the last hurdle which salmon must surmount is by far the greatest. The commercial interests lying in wait on Scottish coasts and river estuaries extract an astonishing and largely unknown quantity of these "survivor" in-running stocks. The effect of these final wholesale slaughters is that on many premier and secondary rivers, during the seven month (February to August) netting season, precious few salmon manage to pass these nets and enter the fresh waters of their home rivers.

How did this situation come about? Very largely it is the product of the archaic 1860s Scottish Salmon Fishery Acts which have remained in force, virtually intact, to the present day. Efforts have regularly been made over the past 100 years to change them. But on every occasion the commercial netsmen, the vested interests who by virtue of provisions in the 1860 Acts control nearly all Scottish District Salmon Fisheries Boards have easily defeated each challenge.

* David Shaw *Glasgow Herald* 3 May 1985

What this means is that these commercial interests have been able to retain virtual "local monopolistic control" of the Scottish "wild" salmon resource. Furthermore, in the face of sharply decreased in-running stocks, equally sharply declining catches (a 50% decline in the past 20 years from 2000 to 1000 tonnes and a sharper 25% drop in the five-year period from 1977-1981) and pressure from rapidly increasing quantities of "farmed salmon" reaching the market, these "wild" netsmen now even more fiercely defend this privileged position and even seek to extend it.

As the law stands, a commercial netsman on, for example, the Tay, Tweed, or the North Esk (for its size almost certainly the world's most productive salmon river for the nets) may ply his trade 24 hours a day. There is no limit to the number of nets he may shoot. The object is to catch as many fish as possible. No consideration is given to escapement. Most netting operators still reward their crews with bonuses for surplus catches.

Furthermore, the netsman is subject to no effective supervision from an external authority. His catches are not monitored. The figures that he is required to submit to the DAFS may not correlate with the numbers of fish actually caught.

The 1860s laws were designed for the fishery conditions which then existed. But today, can there be any comparison?

The use of power winches, motor propelled cobles, and light, flexible and in murky estuary conditions nearly invisible multifilament nets accord an awesome efficiency never dreamed of in the 1860s.

As for restrictions: there is a weekly 42-hour mandatory close time (from Saturday noon till Monday 6 a.m.) for the nets. In principle, this is an important provision. But in practice, how effective is it? In most rivers any incoming fish must run a lengthy stretch during this period if it is to clear the highest netting stations. How many do? How many salmon are seen let alone caught by rods on many upstream beats during the April-September in-season period?

Beyond the estuaries there are the foreshore and coastal fixed nets. In 1861, Alexander Russel observed: "A sail along almost any portion of the coast of Scotland . . . will show the shore is draped in salmon nets." Things have changed very little. Officially, reported catches indicate that coastal nets take about the same number of fish as the estuary nets. But do they?

In many districts, particularly along the West coast where District Salmon Fishery Boards have not been created, netsmen operate free from any effective supervision. How effective are the close times here? How often do stormy seas prevent the weekend removal of nets? Why is it that Aberdeen Monday morning auctions in mid-summer are often packed with heavy consignments of salmon from distant Northern coastal districts?

The recent decision of the Crown Estate Commissioners (CEC), which holds extensive netting rights round the entire coast of Scotland, to lease out many stations long non-operative has caused much concern. Given the wild-fire spread of highly sophisticated modern-day poaching, is it any wonder that many well informed persons—including many *legal* netsmen—hotly contend that a number of these stations, often in isolated locations, are simply fronts for "laundering" salmon illegally caught by drift-netters and others?

It is as obvious now as it was 100 years ago that a few simple reforms would quickly serve to put things right. Net-licensing, flexible net quotas, dealer-licensing and with a new system of area inspectors would, together with some form of tagging of dead fish, serve to get more fish back into Scottish rivers, ensuring the survival of a now endangered species.

Given time such provisions would not only serve to boost and then to stabilise dwindling net catches at equitable levels, but the welfare of upstream fishery interests, of salmon-dependent communities and tourism interests would also be secured.

The commercial netting industry contributes about £5m and supports about 800 full-time jobs while taking 80% to 85% of the annual reported catch. The visiting salmon angler currently supports more than 30,000 jobs and generates more than £140m for the Scottish economy.

But the deeply-entrenched obstacle to reaching these goals remains. As America's leading salmon conservationist, Richard A. Buck, said: "The basic salmon problem is socio-political, not scientific".

The dominant netsmen, although perhaps a little shaken by the recent outcome of the Deveron Inquiry when Mr George Younger rejected an application for an extension of the netting season, remain as determined and influential as ever. The lineup reads like a print out from Burke's Peerage. Lords Lovat, Thurso, Lansdowne, Mansfield, Granville, Strathconnor; the Dukes of Norfolk, Argyll, Wellington; the Duchess of Westminster, to name a few, are names which surface regularly when Scottish salmon fishery matters arise.

DAFS, the controlling ministry with which the netsmen have long and closely-retained links continues steadfastly to defend the *status quo*. And from those satellite departments—the HIDB, the Scottish Tourist Board, the Scottish Development Agency—which come under the umbrella of the current DAFS Minister Lord Gray, and which are most vitally linked with salmon economy and tourism issues, there is profound silence.

Clearly, attainment of commonsense controls and effective management reforms of the Scottish salmon fishery cannot be secured overnight. This, Lord Thurso, who is currently sponsoring a Private Member's salmon Bill at Westminster, is discovering for himself. It will take time. At least in recent years the mythical shroud of "all's well" has been lifted. Many influential and concerned people are now aware of the *real* problems.

Indeed, the recent formation of the *Salmon Conservancy* under the initiative and guidance of the prominent Glasgow industrialist Douglas Hume, vice chairman of the Howden Group of companies, offers real hope for the first time.

Mr Hume has ensured that the conservancy's primary efforts are directed at surmounting the hard core of coastal and estuary obstacles.

In the interim, one wonders: would not an extension of the weekly close-time to 72 hours and a reduction of the netting season by two months at the start and three weeks at the end serve at least to ease the current crisis.

Is it not possible that our increasingly powerful amenity, recreational, trade and conservation lobbies may be prodded with a very big stick and that they in turn may be able to cause our fisheries administrators and MPs to secure the necessary emergency legislation—and not next year, but right now?

APPENDIX B

Salmon Bill: new clothes but same archaic body*

A NEW Scottish Salmon Fishery Bill has been awaited for over 100 years. The Bill is now in Commons Committee and is expected to become law soon. Will it meet now urgently needed conservation, angler/tourism-dominant and modern management requirements? *Trout and Salmon's* DAVID SHAW, who has been following the Bill, suggests that conservationists and anglers are in for a very big disappointment.

THE world's leading authority on salmon, Anthony Netboy, recently made a critical observation. "In the face of sharply declining stocks and recent alarmingly increased exploitation by many Scottish netsmen, strong conservation provisions in the new Salmon Bill are not merely necessary, they are imperative!"

Professor Netboy maintains that measures advocated by the Glasgow-and-London-based Salmon Conservancy could go far towards meeting at least minimum interim requirements. The Conservancy has called for an increase in the weekly close-time for nets to 72 hours; an increase in the annual close-time for nets to 212 days; and the phasing out of Scottish coastal and North-East English fixed nets which take so high, indiscriminate and largely unknown a toll on returning stocks.

In the longer term, Professor Netboy stresses that only the Conservancy's stronger provisions calling for the introduction of net licensing and net quotas, together with much-improved control and enforcement by the central authority, can assure the future of "survivor" stocks and meet international fishery requirements.

Tayside's Michael C. Smith, Scotland's leading angling spokesman, points not only to poor rod catches but to the current grave threat to salmon-dependent local economies posed by rivers "empty of fish" during the March to September netting period. "A few weeks at the end of the season —after the nets have come off —and a few at the beginning cannot for much longer hope to sustain an economy which provides employment for over 30,000 and pumps up to £210m annually into tourism-linked Highland enterprises."

* David Shaw *Glasgow Herald* 21 May, 1986

Can it make any sense at all, he asks, for the "wild" salmon netsman to continue to extract 85%—and during peak, summer months up to 97%—of the total catch while supporting a mere 600 full-time jobs and generating £5m annually, most of this money going into the pockets of a very few? "Why must wild-salmon be netted at all when farmed salmon can now fully supply the food market? Surely the time has come for the wild fish to be preserved as principally a recreational resource?"

So does the new Salmon Bill meet these basic requirements called for by Professor Netboy and Mr Smith? Does it meet even the Conservancy's minimum demands?

Briefly, the answer is no. The Bill is virtually empty both of conservation and angler/tourism provision.

What then is in the Bill? The Bill provides for a Scottish salmon dealer-licensing scheme. It provides also for new measures aimed at tightening up the existing law in relation to persons in Scotland, and also Wales and England, found to be in possession of illegally-caught salmon. And what do these measures mean?

They mean that a few more river fish may be expected to survive to spawn. Rather more significantly, however, they mean that perhaps a great many more salmon and sea-trout may survive illegal depredations in UK coastal waters duly to return to fill Scottish legal coastal and estuary nets. Given the abnormal event of summer high waters it is even possible that a few of these surplus fish may escape upstream to enhance rod and spawning prospects.

For the rest, the Bill seeks merely to modify slightly and even extend the long-archaic Scottish salmon fishery management structure, and to prop up the authority of the dominant netting elements, by affording them a few new avenues for defending and perhaps enhancing their interests.

New flexible weekly and annual close-time provisions seem perhaps the most vulnerable to future initiatives of dominant netting interests intent on altering local netting times to allow them to catch more salmon. The Bill also contains provisions whereby amalgamation of existing salmon fishery districts into larger area boards—whether or not the majority of districts approve —may be achieved.

And for angling proprietors, the repeal of the key provision that the chairman of a district salmon fishery board must be the proprietor with the "highest rateable value" —nearly always a netsman —affords some promise that in a very few secondary districts a rod proprietor could emerge as board chairman

Since envisaged future boards will retain a 50:50 balance between net and rod interests, it will be appreciated that control of the chair will continue to mean majority control of the board.

So what went wrong? Why this "wee tim'rous beastie" of a Bill? Why have urgently needed conservation and angler-tourism requirements been virtually ignored?

A recent Tory Monday Club field sports study group report put it very simply: "What else was one to expect from 'food-producing' ministries?" —that is, MAFF (Ministry of Agriculture and Fisheries for England and Wales) and DAFS (Department of Agriculture and Fisheries for Scotland). The responsible Ministers—Lord Gray of DAFS and Selwyn Gummer of MAFF—the report states, have once again been "sold a pup". Provided with out-dated, irrelevant and wrong information these Ministers, it is contended, have been persuaded by their civil servants, including such leading Scottish Office officials as DAFS Under-Secretary Boyd Gordon, to endorse continued emphasis on antiquated "food-producing" requirements.

But why, one might ask, have these civil servants advised such a course? Again the answer is relatively simple.

Bureaucratic Inertia, departmental "Imperialism" and long-standing mutually beneficial relations with the netting interests. are felt to be key factors. After all, just as in the TV series *Yes Minister*, no entrenched bureaucratic authority willingly submits to change. And is it not natural that any department will all the more vigorously resist change when it can recognise that a sizable sector of its domain might be lost—and in this instance most likely transferred to the DOE (Department of the Environment)?

As for the established link with the netting interests: in return for DAFS access to coastal, estuary, and often up-stream fisheries in salmon fishery districts over which netting interests exercise control (and hence the opportunity to conduct "scientific experiments" concerned principally with providing support for DAFS "food producing" policies), the netsmen secure up-to-date research and resource support for specific problems with which they are principally concerned.

The fact that the British taxpayer continues to support these very private interests and in sums amounting to several million pounds over the past few years —with such fisheries as the North Esk and its netting proprietors Joseph Johnstons being principal beneficiaries—is a point never raised.

But there is another explanation for why modernisation has been so fiercely and successfully resisted. This cuts to the very core of Highlands life, culture, and particularly politics.

Few would dispute that the Highlands Region is perhaps the leading anachronistic social curiosity of the modern Western world. It is a region where a residual aristocracy has managed through its hold on often vast properties to retain an extraordinary level of influence and often community authority.

The practical result is that what these eminent persons wish to be legislated will often be legislated. More to the point, what they do not wish to be legislated, won't. As many of these persons retain important, and not so important netting rights they are steadfastly opposed to any change in the salmon laws which might result in the smallest encroachment on these rights.

One can work right round the coast of Scotland from interests of the Duke of

Norfolk on Nith, the Duke of Wellington on Stinchar, the Duke of Argyll and Duchess of Westminster on the West Coast, Lords Kimball and Thurso in the North, Lords Lovat, Burton, and Leven in the Moray Firth area; down to, for instance, Tay and the interests of Lords Lansdowne, Mansfield, and Ronaldshay, to name but a few.

Basically, as perhaps most clearly demonstrated by Lords Lansdowne and Thurso in the Lords Debates, these elements are determined to retain the privilege of exercising their rights in almost exactly the form they have for the past 100 years. Given this position is it then so strange that the current Bill has been described as the "archaic body of the 1862 Salmon Fishery Acts in new clothes"?

As for such foreign national bodies as S&TA and AST: since each has closely-retained links with aristocratic and fishmongering interests, is it so surprising that they should adopt a very restrained approach? Indeed still S&TA, a body which claims to be the national representative body of salmon anglers, fights shy of any clear policy commitment to reduction of netting.

At its recent AGM it was prepared finally to accept "reduction of netting" as but one of many "strategies" to get more fish into rivers. Nothing more.

But what about MPs? And what about the STB (Scottish Tourist Board), HIDB (Highlands and Islands Development Board) and SDA (Scottish Development Agency)? Why do they not press hard the reform requirements?

The near-total absence of Highland salmon-area MPs from the Commons March debate and from the 18 Member Commons Standing Committee currently considering the Bill was, and is, a startling revelation. Where are they? Have they been warned off?

As for the profound silence from the STB, HIDB, and SDA, one might perhaps observe only: is this any wonder? Given that DAFS' Lord Gray is also the Minister responsible for each of these agencies, should we have expected anything different? A recently created "Fishing for Tourists" STB working party may help. Yet is this not too little and far too late?

So much for why the Salmon Bill has been fitted out with its existing form and content.

But what about the current committee stage? Is there any chance that needed conservation and/or angler-tourism provisions may yet be worked into the Bill?

The short answer is no. Due to some quite superlative parliamentary and preparatory departmental engineering, the Bill's structure and principal provisions will remain. The dead hand—or in the view of some, the extraordinary vital presence—of the dominant interests will not be lifted.

It is to be hoped, however, that a few important amendments may be secured. Principally, altered provisions which would place upon the Scottish Secretary the statutory requirement to consult with specified interests —rather than leaving him yet again with virtual license to act as he sees fit—may ensure the operation of a few important safeguards.

These requirements would seem to be of particular importance in relation to the formation of future "amalgamated boards," and even more vitally to future applications by district boards, (in effect, the netsmen in most instances) to alter or extend existing weekly and/or annual close-time periods.

To this end, the efforts of Opposition spokesmen including John Hume Robertson (Opposition Leader on the Bill), Tam Dalyell, Dennis Canavan—and to the everlasting shame of absent Opposition Highland MPs including Robert Maclennan, Charles Kennedy, Sir Russell Johnston, Malcolm Bruce and Robert Hughes—the North-East English MPs Alan Beith and Stuart Randall, are to be strongly commended.

It is interesting to note that of the 18 committee members only, seven are Scots (three of these with very marginal constituency concern with salmon); 10 are English (seven of these with no constituency salmon interests); one only is Welsh; and this on a Bill concerned almost totally—32 of 37 provisions with Scottish salmon!

It is likely that the committee stage, with more than 160 amendments to be considered, will not be completed before the end of May. DAFS is confident the Bill will become law before the summer recess.

This then is the sorry saga of the Salmon Bill. Netsmen and most establishment interests can now safely breathe a long sigh of relief.

For conservationists and angler tourism elements the Bill and all the activity surrounding it have provided the sternest lessons yet in the *real-politik* of Scottish salmon. It is to be hoped these lessons have been absorbed.

One might observe only that it is bitterly distressing that such an enormous amount of effort, parliamentary time and taxpayers' money have been expended to achieve what in the end amounts to a comprehensive consolidation of the totally antiquated, and potentially terminally destructive salmon fishery *status quo*.

It has served also to make a mockery both of poor *Salmo salar* and of all those who have worked so long and hard for his survival. This is something which our international salmon fishery partners will be quick to see.

And at what cost to already rock-bottom UK credibility and influence in these vital forums? Tayside's Michael Smith nicely sums up what seems the inevitable conservation effect of the Bill when he states, "Not one more fish will be put into Scottish rivers." It is a pity and a criminal waste.

APPENDIX C

Salmon tide on turn with an unlikely champion*

Has the Scottish Establishment this time gone too far? DAVID SHAW suggests that by ignoring modern conservation, fishery, and economic requirements, they have served merely to bring very close the forces of change, and a surprising new champion.

IN the fading hours of next Thursday the fate of the United Kingdom's wild salmon is to be decided by our "salmon politicians" at Westminster.

Enough has been written since the Salmon Bill first made its parliamentary appearance 10 months ago for most to realise that this "UK Salmon Bill" is not "UK" at all. It is a Scottish Bill with one or two UK-wide provisions to meet specific requirements which bear closely on Scottish interests. Furthermore it Is not about dominant modern conservation, angler-tourism, and local economy requirements. Rather, the Bill is carefully designed to bolster protection of that most endangered of species, "the wild salmon netsman."

For netsmen, therefore, the Bill is good news. It is, in essence, a rewritten "Netsman's Charter". Scottish rod proprietors, too, can take some measure of satisfaction from the Bill. Its provisions should mean that despite yearly decreasing catches on most rivers they can look forward with some confidence to the capital values of their fisheries continuing to appreciate. Among today's fashionable purchasers, the status of owning a beat has clearly become more important than its capacity to produce fish!

As for the visiting angler, the indigenous Scottish tenant, and the "client" local angling association, these expendable elements have been treated with customary contemptuous disregard. Indeed, it is possible that certain amendments to the Bill restricting "angling methods" —spinning, prawn, worm, and bait fishing to be banned by local District Fishery Board enabling bye-laws—could mean that rods will get even less for their money.

And then there is great *Salmo* himself. All that can be said is that for those fish still so foolish as to try to run most Scottish rivers during the seven-month netting season, only the 3-10% of "160-IQ-equivalent champion" salmon can hope to survive. And these are the fish which rods must continue to *try* to catch!

* David Shaw *Glasgow Herald* 16 October, 1986

So given this framework, these interests and objectives, what positive provisions do we have in the Bill?

First, there are the Bill's "Illegal Possession" provisions. These, backed by strengthened powers to bailiffs and police should discourage much small-scale illegal activity. Second, there is "Dealer-Licensing." This provision too should cause the prudent small illegal operator to think carefully before he acts. Finally, the new (Government amendment) provisions which require that "licensees" be on board at all times when salmon fishing is being conducted should act to reduce alleged excesses of North-East English drift-netsmen.

But will these provisions cause the illegal fisherman engaged in large-scale operations to terminate his activity? The short answer is: not likely. Still, if one adds to these provisions, the new legislative controls on Scottish Inshore Fisheries, the ban on carriage of monofilament nets in Scottish waters, envisaged additional Northumbrian Water Authority bye-law restraints on drift-netting, enforcement support from the DAFS Sea Fishery Protection Service, aerial surveillance during peak-run periods, all this backed by some severe penalties handed out to inshore fisheries transgressors the past few years—and *almost all* paid for by the long-suffering British taxpayer—it could be said that cumulative protection of salmon returning duly to be caught in Scottish coastal and estuary river nets will be much improved.

In terms of local salmon fishery management improvements, new "Board Amalgamation" provisions could ensure that some measure of order may soon be brought to the "Wild West" fisheries of the North and West coasts. And if the long-enshrined requirement that the chairman of a District Salmon Fishery Board (DSFB) must be the "proprietor with the highest rateable value" is actually repealed, then it is possible rod proprietors could displace netsmen-chairmen on a few boards, and a few long-sought local reforms be duly effected.

There is one late initiative which should bring a certain vitality to the proceedings of next week. To their immense credit, Welsh "Cinderella" interests have baulked at being closeted in a virtual legislative cul-de-sac. Illegal Possession and Dealer-Licensing provisions will apply to the Principality as much as to Scotland and other areas of the UK. Welsh interests are well-informed about the imperative requirement to ensure these provisions are more than merely marginally effective. And this is "Salmon Tagging."

Under the initiative of Welsh Salmon and Trout Angling Association's veteran salmon activist D.A.M. (Artie) Jones, a "Public Petition" with up to 150,000 UK-wide signatories is to be presented to Parliament. The petition seeks incorporation of Salmon Tagging in the Bill. It seeks also to ensure the Government is held to its promise to implement a "Standing Advisory Committee on the Atlantic Salmon" with statutory powers.

So much for the Salmon Bill. But where do we go from here?

So long as the current Government remains in power, the short answer seems, very sadly, clear: nowhere!

The Act in itself, as one commentator has put it, will serve merely as "a direct incitement to immediate future reform!"

Dennis Canavan, MP for West Falkirk, has emerged from the Salmon Bill proceedings, to the surprise of many, as arguably the UK's leading "salmon politician." Indeed, the contributions of Mr Canavan and Tam Dalyell in particular have been crucial in exposing weaknesses and rallying repeated all-party attacks on the Bill and its hapless Government leaders (John MacKay of DAFS, and Selwyn Gummer of MAFF). Should a Labour government take office after the next General Election it is rumoured that Mr Canavan will assume the office of DAFS Minister.

Now, Mr Canavan has long sought statutory provision for a Scottish Anglers' Trust. Many persons however, fear what "democratisation" could mean if ever his concept of a SAT were brought to fruition. Yet so far as Scotland's salmon fishery is concerned, Mr Canavan has made it clear he recognises that a "public fishery free-for-all" is not the answer.

He is aware that the jobs of over 30,000 people in the Highlands and elsewhere are dependent on "salmon in rivers." Mr Canavan, therefore, speaks principally of "improved access;" of "wider representation and control." He speaks also of greatly strengthened restraints on such netting interests as those which annually rape the Tay and most other Scottish rivers of their salmon resource. Indeed, Mr Canavan's overall concept for restoring and maintaining the salmon resource varies little from reform proposals advanced by such eminent Scottish salmon authorities as Lord Elgin (1902), W. L. Calderwood (1909), Jock Menzies (1930), and, more recently, Lord Hunter's Committee (1965).

While the final act of the current Salmon Bill charade is being played out, these are thoughts not to be forgotten. It is entirely possible that the Scottish Salmon Establishment, by slamming hard the door on obvious and urgently-needed modernisation requirements, has done us all, and great *Salmo,* a very large favour.

Slightly altered private ownership rights—this is all that's needed! —within the general framework of State supported and much-strengthened local administration may thus have been brought several steps closer, and in double-quick time!

APPENDIX D

Legal aid along the salmon ladder*

SALMON politics is about the power and influence of a few titled Scottish lairds. It is about the ability of this minority to tame MPs and ministers, and to ensure that the relevant civil servants dance to their tune. It is about their determination to re-secure their feudal property rights, no matter the cost to the salmon or to the many Highland communities dependent on the fish in their rivers.

Fresh legislation has been sought almost since the Salmon Acts were first passed in the 1860s. Very quickly, informed and eminent people saw that changes were needed. They realised that if salmon were to get up their home rivers in adequate numbers, a few restraints—nothing too radical—would have to be placed on commercial netting in Scottish rivers and estuaries. The reasoning was obvious: to maintain adequate stocks, a proportion of each salmon run entering the river would have to be allowed to pass the top-most nets. To secure this, and a number of other common sense requirements, the extension of central government's supervisory powers over fishing was seen to be essential.

But this was without reckoning on the influence of Scottish landed and "watered" interests. These have shown repeatedly that they can do with their salmon fisheries almost exactly as they please. Attempts at reform have been bludgeoned into submission. (The most recent victim was the Hunter Report of 1965.)

The result is that a few very wealthy and often titled people still exercise what amounts to "local-monopolistic" control over virtually the whole of Scotland's wild salmon resource.

The situation has now reached the point that on such rivers as the Tay, few fish get past the river nets and into the up-stream waters during the 7 month netting season. On the Tweed and most other Scottish salmon rivers (and indeed the Welsh and English too) it is much the same.

There is certainly a grave conservation problem. But there is more. In the past 20 years angler-tourism has grown to become a vital sector in Scotland's rural economy. It supports over 30,000 jobs and generates up to £210 million annually for salmon-dependent river communities. Collectively, salmon anglers comprise less than 2 per cent of the 13 million annual visitors to Scotland, yet

* David Shaw *The Guardian* 4 May, 1987

they generate more than 20 per cent of the Scottish Tourism Industry's annual earnings. Commercial netting, on the other hand, provides full-time employment for less than 600, and generates only £5 million—most of this money going into the pockets of a very few—while still removing up to 97 per cent of the recorded catch during summer months.

On most rivers, despite great increases in the numbers of rods fishing, anglers' catches have dropped dramatically. On the once-legendary Tay, reported rod catches have fallen by nearly 70 per cent, from over 14,000 in 1973 to less than 5,000 in 1986. As one Tay hotel owner recently put it: "We need fish in the river. No fish, no anglers. No anglers, we are finished." For tourism interests throughout the Highlands their plight has got steadily worse.

The principal needs of Scotland's salmon fisheries are clear enough. So has the recently passed Salmon Act succeeded in meeting them?

There was a little tinkering with the archaic acts of the last century. But principally this has served to re-trench the wide-reaching private rights of the same old feudal minority. The Act will tighten up considerably on illegal fishers in coastal waters, and it will strengthen catch-restraints on the in-shore commercial competitors of north-east England. It has also stepped up legal and criminal sanctions against fresh-water/river poachers. A new UK-wide salmon dealer licensing scheme should serve further to tighten these new restraints.

But what of Scottish estuary and coastal netsmen, the salmon's most devastating enemy? Their local monopolistic rights have been preserved virtually intact. Hence, this season on the Tay, the commercial fishermen remain fully entitled to work their nets 24 hours a day, taking as many sweeps and as many fish as they can. Where nets are worked by competing companies on opposite banks below Perth, the river is once again effectively blocked. The still intact 42-hour weekly close-time should mean that at least a few lucky summer fish will continue to pass the Tay's top-most Scone Estate stations (owned by the Trustees for Viscount Stormont, son of the chairman of the Crown Estate Commissioners, Lord Mansfield), before netting again starts at 6am on Mondays.

One or two loopholes have been opened by the Act in Scotland this could mean, in time, that weekly and perhaps annual close-times may be increased—and hence that more fish may clear river nets. It is possible, too, that a new Salmon Advisory Committee may prod ministers into action on reforms in Welsh and English (as well as Scottish) salmon fishery districts. These are the rod-tourism industry's best hope.

A unanimously-backed resolution endorsed at the October Biarritz Third International Salmon Symposium may also help. The resolution called for national governments of salmon-producing countries to reduce netting and to give priority to development and maintenance of recreational fisheries. A new body, the Atlantic Salmon Conservation Trust (ASCT), is now busy buying up netting rights. (In Scotland all are owned privately, or by the Crown Estate Commissioners.) But whether this will serve to get more salmon into rivers, or merely increase the catches of the principal stations remaining, is not yet clear.

Certainly, if the UK wild salmon fishery were to be prised away from the authority of the food-producing ministries (Ministry of Ag and Fish, Department of Ag and Fish in Scotland), and transferred perhaps to the Department of the Environment, then gradual progress may follow. There is also the chance that market dominance of farmed salmon, currently at 8 : 1, may eventually render wild salmon netting no longer economic. Such developments, given luck and political will, may in time come to pass.

BIBLIOGRAPHY

This is a select bibliography of principal books, articles and documents used in this study.

Annual Report of the Fishery Board for Scotland. Edinburgh: HMSO, 1932.

Association of River Authorities. *Taking Stock*. London: March 1974.

Association of Scottish District Fishery Boards. *Report of the Proceedings of the First Annual General Meeting of the ASDFB*. (mimeo.) 2 December, 1931.

Association of Scottish District Fishery Boards. *Salmon Fisheries of Scotland*. Farnham: Fishing News Books, 1977.

Association of Scottish District Fishery Boards. (mimeo.) *Circular*, dated 23 July, 1982. [NB: Netsmen's plight].

Association of Scottish District Fishery Boards. *Minutes of a Meeting of Council, held on 23 January, 1987: Amendment to Item 5(a)*. (mimeo.) [NB: ASDFB rejection of proposed Weekly Close Time increase].

Atkins, W.H. (Consultants). *Review of the River Teifi: Offer of Services: Technical and Financial Proposals*. (mimeo.) London: April 1992.

Atlantic Salmon Trust. *Memorandum of Association of the Atlantic Salmon Research Trust Limited*. 10 April, 1967.

Atlantic Salmon Trust. *Annual Acounts*, (Income and Expenditure Accounts), for the years 1982-1986.

Atlantic Salmon Trust. "Fish Farming Statistics, 1985". *Progress Report*. May 1986.

The Bledisloe Report. [being the *Report of the Committee on Salmon and Freshwater Fisheries*. Cmnd. 1350. London: HMSO, 1961].

British Field Sports Society. *Record of Meeting Organised by the British Field Sports Society (BFSS) to Discuss the Salmon Bill Now Before the House of Lords*. (mimeo.) Edinburgh: 17 January, 1986.

Buck, Richard A. "Stewards of the Salmon: Closing Address". *Third International Salmon Symposium*. (mimeo.) Biarritz, France: 21-23 October, 1986.

Calderwood, W.L. *The Salmon Rivers and Lochs of Scotland*. Second Edition (revised). London: Edward Arnold, 1921.

Calderwood, W.L. *Salmon and Sea-Trout*. London: Edward Arnold, 1930.

Catlow, Laurence. "A Question of Sport". *Trout and Salmon*, (December, 1986), 58-59.

Civic Government (Scotland) Act, 1982. [NB: Legislation to be used to introduce Dealer-Licensing in Scotland].

DAFS (1979) Discussion Document. [Department of Agriculture and Fisheries for Scotland. *Salmon and Freshwater Fisheries: Review of the Present Law and Administration.* (mimeo.) Edinburgh: DAFS, 28 December, 1979.]

Department of Agriculture and Fisheries for Scotland. *Salmon and Freshwater Fisheries: Review of the Present Law and Administration.* (mimeo.) Edinburgh: DAFS, 28 December, 1979. (The *1979 DAFS Discussion Document*)

Department of Agriculture and Fisheries for Scotland. *Scottish Salmon and Sea-Trout Catches, 1990: Statistical Bulletins*, (1982-94).

"Deveron's Day of Judgement", *Trout and Salmon*, (June 1983), 13.

The Deveron Report. [*Report of An Inquiry into Representations on the Petition of The Deveron Salmon Fishery Board for a Change in the Annual Close Time in the District*, mimeo., File No. FRC/1/38/2, (Edinburgh: DAFS, Chesser House, December 1984), pp.68.]

Drury, Esmond. *S&TA Memorandum*, (mimeo.), 1972.

Editorial. *The Salmon Net*, No.XV, (1982). [NB: The netsmens's plight].

The Elgin Report. [being the *Report of the Royal Commission Appointed to Inquire into the Salmon Fisheries of England, Wales and Scotland.* Cmnd. 1188. London: HMSO, 1902].

The Field. "Letters Column", in issues from 27 September, to 19 December, 1973; and leaders, articles and letters in issues from 9 January to 3 April, 1975. [NB: nets vs rods].

Fisheries Bill (1980), Part V (Miscellaneous) Clause 32. [NB: This Clause, provides that Section 5(3) of the *Fishery Board (Scotland) Act of 1882*, (duty of the Secretary of State to make an Annual Report regarding fisheries) shall cease to have effect].

Fishery Board for Scotland: Report for 1906. Edinburgh: 1907.

Forth District Salmon Fishery Board. *Annual Report, 1991*. (mimeo.).

Game Fair [S&TA] Petition to the Secretary of State for Scotland. (mimeo.). 1983.

Glenbeg. "The Salmon Debate", *Flyfishers' Journal*, (Winter 1976).

Hawkins, A.D., Urquart C.G., and W.M. Shearer. *The Coastal Movements of Returning Atlantic Salmon*. Department of Agriculture and Fisheries for Scotland, Scottish Fisheries Research Report Number 15, (1979).

Hodgson, W. Earl. *Salmon Fishing*. London: A&C Black, 1927 (2nd reprint). [NB: The first edition of Hodgson's book was published in 1906].

Hume, Douglas. "Chairmans Letter". *Safe Passage: The Newsletter of the Salmon Conservancy*, (Spring, 1986).

The (First) Hunter Report. (*Scottish Salmon and Trout Fisheries: First Report By the Committee Appointed by the Secretary of State for Scotland*. Cmnd. 2096. Edinburgh: HMSO, July 1963).

The Hunter Report. (*Scottish Salmon and Trout Fisheries: Second Report By the Committee Appointed by the Secretary of State for Scotland*. Cmnd. 2691. Edinburgh: HMSO, August 1965).

Hunter, Hon. Lord. "A Policy that is 'All at Sea'", *Salmon and Trout Association Yearbook*, (1994), 14-15.

Inshore Fisheries (Scotland) Act, 1984. [NB: Enabled the Scottish Secretary, by Statutory Order, to declare certain areas extending six miles from the coast, as "static net reserves" and "fish nursery areas". Also, see below, Scottish Office News Release, *Proposals for Static Gear Reserves*).

"Landings of Salmon, Grilse and Sea Trout in Scotland". *The Salmon Net*, No.XV, (1982).

Lawrence, D.W. *The Solway: Memorandum to Lord Hunter's Committee*. (mimeo.). (Supplement to the Memorandum from the Nith Fishings Improvement Association, dated 24 October, 1962.)

Licensing Act (Scotland) 1976. [NB: Concerned issue of penalties against hoteliers convicted of Illegal Possession of salmon; raised during Salmon Bill debates.]

MAFF and DAFS. *Joint Announcement by the Fisheries Departments in Great Britain: Membership of Salmon Advisory Committee Announced*. MAFF Press Release, 10 February, 1987.

MAFF and DAFS. *Salmon Net Fisheries: Report of a Review of Salmon Net Fishing in the Areas of the Yorkshire and Northumbrian Regions of the NRA, and the [Scottish] Salmon Fishery Districts from the River Tweed to the River Ugie [in NE Aberdeenshire]*. HMSO: London, 1991. [NB: In the text, this study is referred to as the *NE Review Report*].

MAFF. *An Economic Evaluation of Salmon Fisheries in Great Britain: Summary Report*. (Prepared for MAFF, by Centre for Marine Resource Economics, Portsmouth Polytechnic), July, 1991. [NB: In the text, this survey is referred to as the *MAFF Salmon Economy Survey*].

MAFF News Release. *Joint Announcement by MAFF and DAFS: Government Publishes Results of North-East Coast Salmon Netting Review*. 17 October, 1991.

Mills, Derek (ed.). *Tweed Towards 2000: A Symposium on the Future Management of the Tweed Fisheries*. Aberystwyth: Cambrian News, 1989.

Misuse of Drugs Act, 1971. [NB: Concerned issue of "Onus of proof" during Salmon Bill debate on Illegal Possession of salmon].

National Rivers Authority (NRA). *Salmonid and Freshwater Fisheries Statistics for England and Wales, 1990*. MAFF Directorate of Fisheries Research, 1992. [NB: In the text, this document is referred to as, *MAFF Salmonid Statistics*].

Netboy, Anthony. *The Atlantic Salmon: A Vanishing Species?*. London: Faber, 1968.

Netboy, Anthony. *Salmon: The World's Most Harrassed Fish*. London: Andre Deutsch, 1980.

Netboy, Anthony and David Shaw. "The Plight of the Scottish Salmon", *Atlantic Salmon Journal*, (Spring, 1986), 15-18.

"The Nets on the Deveron: Trout and Salmon's Observer [David Shaw] Reports on the Banff Hearing". *Trout and Salmon*, (August, 1983), 41-2.

Parliamentary Debates: House of Lords. Vol.469,(No.26), 14 January, 1986, cols.990-1055.

Parliamentary Debates: House of Lords. Vol.470,(No.34), 28 January, 1986, cols.545-614.

Parliamentary Debates: House of Lords. Vol.470,(No.35), 29 January, 1986, cols.627-661.

Parliamentary Debates: House of Lords. Vol.470,(No.36), 30 January, 1986, cols.799-882.

Parliamentary Debates: House of Lords. Vol.470,(No.42), 13 February, 1986, cols.295-397.

Parliamentary Debates: House of Lords. Vol.470,(No.50), 25 February, 1986, cols.974-1035.

Parliamentary Debates: House of Lords. Vol.481,(No.160), 30 October, 1986, cols.866-886.

Parliamentary Debates: House of Commons. Vol.93,(No.70), 4 March, 1986, cols.232-258.

Parliamentary Debates: House of Commons. Vol.93,(No.71), 5 March, 1986, cols.259-286.

Parliamentary Debates: House of Commons. Vol.102,(No.161), 23 October, 1986, cols.1340-1388.

Parliamentary Debates: House of Commons. Vol.102,(No.162), 24 October, 1986, cols.1389-1427.

Parliamentary Debates: House of Commons. Standing Committee D, (Salmon Bill [Lords]), April-June, 1986. [The Committee held fifteen Sittings; starting 22 April and ending 12 June.]

Potter, E.C.E. and Swain, A. "Effects of the English North-East Coast Salmon Fisheries on Scottish Salmon Catches". *Fisheries Research Technical Report, No.67.* Lowestoft: MAFF Publications, 1982.

Report of the Committee on Salmon and Freshwater Fisheries, Cmnd. 1350. London: HMSO, 1961. (*The Bledisloe Report*).

Report of An Inquiry into Representations on the Petition of The Deveron Salmon Fishery Board for a Change in the Annual Close Time in the District. (mimeo.). File No.FRC/1/38/2. Edinburgh: DAFS, Chesser House, December 1984, pp.68. (*The Deveron Report*).

Report of the Royal Commission Appointed to Inquire into the Salmon Fisheries of England, Wales and Scotland. Cmnd. 1188. London: HMSO, 1902. (*The Elgin Report*).

Salmon Conservancy. *A Future for Scottish Salmon,* (being the text of a Policy Briefing Paper presented by Michael Vickers at the First AGM of the Salmon Conservancy, held 3 December, 1984 at Edinburgh), (mimeo.).

Salmon Conservancy. *Saving the Salmon—It's a Matter of Common Sense,* (brochure). 1985.

Salmon Conservancy. *Minutes of a Meeting of the Steering Committee of the Salmon Conservancy, held on Wednesday, 26 February, 1986, at Glasgow Chamber of Commerce.* (mimeo.).

Salmon Fisheries (Protection) (Scotland) Bill, 1982. (The *Strathcona Bill*).

Salmon and Freshwater Fisheries (Protection) (Scotland) Act, 1951.

Salmon and Freshwater Fisheries in Scotland: Proposals for Action Arising from the Hunter Report. Cmnd. 4821. Edinburgh: HMSO, November 1971. (The *1971 White Paper*).

"Salmon (Weekly Close Time) (Scotland) Regulations, 1988". Second Standing

Committee on Statutory Instruments. *Parliamentary Debates: House of Commons*, 4 May, 1988, cols.1-26. [NB: Debate on proposed 18-hours increase to the Weekly Close Time for nets; hereafter referred to as the *Weekly Slap Debate*.]

Salmon and Trout Association. *[Briefing Paper for] Salmon Bill (H.L.), Second Reading—House of Commons, 4 March, 1986*. (mimeo.). 28 February, 1986.

Salmon and Trout Association (Scot). *Parliamentary Brief by the Scottish Committee of S&TA: The Salmon Bill*. (Copy), dated 2 March, 1986.

Salmon and Trout Association (Scot). *Parliamentary Brief by the Scottish Committee of S&TA: The Salmon Bill*. (Amended Draft), Aberdeen, 3 March, 1986.

"Scots Ban on Gill-Nets?". *Trout and Salmon*, (April, 1982), 19.

Scottish Salmon and Trout Fisheries: Second Report By the Committee Appointed by the Secretary of State for Scotland. Cmnd. 2691. Edinburgh: HMSO, August 1965. (The *Hunter Report*).

Scottish Salmon and Trout Fisheries: First Report By the Committee Appointed by the Secretary of State for Scotland. Cmnd. 2096. Edinburgh: HMSO, July 1963. [The (First) *Hunter Report*].

Scottish Information Office. *Salmon (Amendment) Bill: Non-Attributable Background*. (mimeo.). 6 November, 1985.

Scottish Office News Release. *Proposals for Static Gear Reserves*, (5 February, 1985), with appended Annex A, and Map showing areas of proposed prohibitions.

Scottish Office News Release. *No Change in Deveron Salmon Arrangements*, Item No.1487/84, 27 December, 1984.

Scottish Tourist Board/Highlands and Islands Development Board. *The Economic Importance of Salmon Fishing [sic] and Netting in Scotland*. October 1989. (NB: Also referred to as the *1989 Scottish Survey*)

Sea Fish Industry (UK) Acts, 1959 and 1962. [NB: Legislation under which the 1962 ban—by Statutory Order—on drift-netting in Scottish waters was effected].

Shaw, David. *Net Realities: A Four-Part Series*. *Trout and Salmon*, (January-May 1980).

"Part 1—The Most Severe Threat to the Salmon's Survival Exists Not on the High Seas, But in its Home Waters", (January 1980), 37-40.

"Part 2—The Solway: A Coast Where Salmon Are Harrassed Relentlessly", (February 1980), 56-60.

"Part 3—The North Esk: A Netsman's Dream Come True", (April 1980), 74-78.

"Part 4—The Nets Resist Legislative Reform: A Luxury They Can No Longer Afford", (May 1980), 51-54.

Shaw, David. *Forthcoming Salmon Legislation: But What About the Angler and Salmo Salar?*. (mimeo.). February, 1980.

Shaw, David. *Future Scottish Salmon Fisheries Legislation and Angler / Conservationist Provisions*. (mimeo.). June 1980.

Shaw, David. *Scottish Salmon Legislation: Domestic Conservation Requirements*. (A Brief Prepared for the Council for Environmental Conservation (CoEnCo)). (mimeo.). London: August 1981.

Shaw, David. *The Disappearing Scottish Salmon: Economic Effects and Conservation Requirements*, (A Brief for Scottish MPs and other interested parties). (mimeo.). London: October 1982.

Shaw, David and Colleagues. *A Survey of Salmon Angling and the Scottish Tourism Economy: Revenue Input and Employment Support*. (mimeo.). March 1983.

Shaw, David. "The Pillagers". *Trout and Salmon*, (January, 1985), 64-66.

Shaw, David. *More Protection for the Netsmen?*. (mimeo.). January, 1985.

Shaw, David. "Scots Netsmen to Blame for Decline of the Salmon?" *Glasgow Herald*, 3 May, 1985.

Shaw, David. "The Salmon Bill: Salmon Salvation or a Sell-Out?". *Trout and Salmon*, (February, 1986), 50-51.

Shaw, David. "Les Saumons d'Ecosse Survivront-Ils?" *Saumons* (Journal de l'-Association de Defense du Saumon Atlantique [AIDSA]), No.56, (Spring 1986), 3-5.

Shaw, David. "Salmon Bill: New Clothes, But Same Archaic Body". *Glasgow Herald*, 21 May, 1986.

Shaw, David. "Salmon Tide on Turn With An Unlikely Champion". *Glasgow Herald*, 16 October, 1986.

Shaw, David. "Salmon Bill: Moment of Truth". *Trout and Salmon*, (October, 1986), 62.

Shaw, David. "Lines From Abroad: UK Legislators Awaken to the Plight of the Atlantic Salmon". *Atlantic Salmon Journal*, (Autumn, 1986), 8-9 and 42.

Shaw, David. "Waterloo at Westminster". *Trout and Salmon*, (December 1986), 54-56.

Shaw, David. "Legal Aid Along the Salmon Ladder". *The Guardian*, London, 4 May, 1987.

Shaw, David. "Lines From Abroad: Sorry UK Contrast". *Atlantic Salmon Journal*, (Spring, 1987), 26-27.

Shaw, David. *The Wear Inquiry: A Two-Part Series*. *Trout and Salmon*, (December 1987, and January 1988).

"Part 1: Battle for the Wear". (December 1987), 52-3.

"Part 2: A Step in the Dark". (January 1988), 64-5.

Shaw, David. *Review and Briefing Report on Salmon Angler/Tourism and the Scottish Economy: Overall Expenditure and "Real Jobs"*. (December 1989). (mimeo.). [NB: In the text, this document is referred to as the *1989 Review and Briefing Report*. It is a detailed critique of the official (Scottish Office) *1989 Scottish Survey*].

Shaw, David. "Salar Restored?: Ontario Saga". *Trout and Salmon*, (November, 1991), 62.

Shaw, David. *Salmon and Sea-Trout Angling and the North-East Tourism Economy: Revenue Input and Employment Support Projections*. (June 1992). (mimeo.). [NB: In the text, this study is referred to as the *1992 NE Region Survey*).

Stansfeld, J.R.W. *A Paper on Scottish Salmon Fisheries*. (mimeo.). 31 October, 1983.

Stephen, Alastair. *West Galloway Fisheries Trust: Annual Report, 1989-90*. (mimeo.)

The Strathcona Bill. [*Salmon Fisheries (Protection) (Scotland) Bill, 1982*].

Vickers, Michael. "Salmo: Know Thine Enemy". *Countrysport*, (June, 1985), 40-42.

Vickers, Michael. "Salmon Reform". *Countrysport*, (July, 1985), 6.

Vickers, Michael. *The Salmon Conservancy: A Future for Scottish Salmon*, (being the text of a Policy Briefing Paper presented at the First AGM of the Salmon Conservancy, held 3 December, 1984 at Edinburgh). (mimeo.).

Welsh Water Authority. *Working Group Report on the Status of Welsh Salmon and Sea-Trout Fisheries*. Brecon: October,1985.

Welsh Water Authority. *Salmon Bill: Briefing Note*. 2 October, 1986.

The (1971) White Paper. (*Salmon and Freshwater Fisheries in Scotland: Proposals for Action Arising from the Hunter Report*. Cmnd. 4821. Edinburgh: HMSO, November 1971).

Williamson, Robert. *Salmon Fisheries in Scotland*. (Pitlochry: Atlantic Salmon Trust, for Tay Salmon Fisheries, 1991).

Wilson, Brian. "The Real Priorities Ignored in Salmon Bill". *Glasgow Herald*, 21 January, 1986.

Wolfram, Gerry. "Won't You Come Back Home?". *Atlantic Salmon Journal*, (Winter, 1991), 18-19.

INDEX